Policing Rio de Janeiro

A POLICEMAN.

(Permanente.)

Thomas H. Holloway

POLICING
Rio de Janeiro

Repression and Resistance

in a 19th-Century

City

Stanford University Press
Stanford, California
1993

Stanford University Press
Stanford, California
© 1993 by the Board of Trustees of the
Leland Stanford Junior University
Printed in the United States of America

CIP data appear at the end of the book

FRONTISPIECE: Lithograph from a collection by the
Ludwig and Briggs studio in Rio de Janeiro, 1846–49.
From Briggs, *The Brasilian Souvenir*.

Published with the assistance of the
Hull Memorial Publication Fund
of Cornell University

To the people of Rio de Janeiro, who have resisted.

Preface

This book began, as many others have, by accident. While spending 1980–81 as a Fulbright Senior Lecturer at the Federal University of Santa Catarina, I began to explore local archives in Florianópolis. Having completed a major project on the social history of European immigration to São Paulo, and knowing that Santa Catarina had also been a center of immigration in the nineteenth and early twentieth centuries, I intended to research the comparative aspects of the immigration experience in those two regions of Brazil. In the state archive of Santa Catarina, I found that one of the largest documentary collections was that produced by the local police system. Beginning in the 1840's and running to the end of the empire in 1889, the chief of police of the province submitted frequent reports to the provincial governor, including information on personnel matters, the daily activity of police patrols, the results of investigations and judicial proceedings, and the jail population. This diverse and detailed record formed a fascinating image of certain aspects of life in the city and surrounding region, including several small communities that shared the island of Santa Catarina with the capital city of Florianópolis (known until 1893 as Desterro), and on the adjacent mainland.

I have long been interested in the possibility of recovering as much as possible about those people often left out of official history or relegated to marginal stereotypes. Rather than providing a window on the lives of people in the lower levels of Santa Catarina society, however, the police view was more like that seen through a lens or a prism. By selectively focusing on specific types of behavior in circumscribed locations by certain categories of people, police records revealed bits and pieces of everyday life refracted by their physical presence and institutional mandate and their informal relationship to the rest of society. The police system, in turn, was shaped by the legal and political system, the class structure, and the ideological and cultural context in which it was created and put to work. As is the case with many other types of historical documents, what the records revealed about the society that produced them was far beyond their ostensible purpose.

I became immersed in the world of the police on the streets of Florianópolis in ways that local historians best appreciate, but then faced a problem. Florianópolis had the institutional apparatus due its status as a provincial capital, but as an isolated, marginal, and stagnant town of some twelve thousand inhabitants in the nineteenth century it could not be taken as typical of major urban centers. Furthermore, its institutions were established by the national government in Rio de Janeiro, and hardly ever with the specific concerns of Florianópolis in mind. To study the police system, the people the police affected, and their relationship, it was clear that I would need to broaden the inquiry.

I thought I would compare Florianópolis (a provincial backwater) with Rio de Janeiro (the national capital) and São Paulo (an expanding commercial and administrative center). Background reading and exploratory research in the archives of the latter two led me to the conclusion that Rio was a case study in itself because of its relevance as a focus for political and social issues, as something of a laboratory for institutional and procedural experimentation, and as a major population center. In Florianópolis the police chief reported the activities of street patrols to the governor. In the national capital his counterpart reported them directly to the minister of justice of the empire, and they were eventually transferred to the National Archive in Rio de Janeiro, established in 1838 as a dependency of the ministry of justice. Those records, complemented by material from other Rio archives and library collections and placed in a comparative, conceptual, and interpretive context, became the basis for this book.

I have generally resisted the temptation to link repression and resistance in the nineteenth century explicitly to more recent events, particularly the military regime of 1964–85 and the continuing phenomena of urban riots, gang activity, street crime, and police violence in Rio de Janeiro. Such matters were never far from my consciousness as I researched and wrote this book, but to do justice to them would require another study, filling the gap from 1889 to more recent times. For those interested in the contemporary scene, however, this book might serve as something of a benchmark and starting point, relevant in two ways. First, the political role of both the military and civilian police in the 1964–85 regime has much deeper historical roots. And second, regarding social war and the institutional response, as well as rivalries among branches of the police system, and the general relationship between police and urban society, the continuities from more than a century ago are striking.

I thank Cornell University and the Brazilian Fulbright Commission for enabling me to dedicate an extended period to archival research during mid-1986 and the 1987–88 academic year; Carlos Hasenbalg of the Centro de Estudos Afro-Asiáticos, Conjunto Universitário Cândido Mendes, for providing a point of contact for research in Rio de Janeiro; Peter Fry for facilitating that connection and for sporadic advice and assistance beginning twenty years ago; José Murilo de Carvalho, Marcos Bretas, and Eduardo Silva of the Fundação Casa de Rui Barbosa for useful discussions on various aspects of the social history of Rio de Janeiro; and Maria Yedda Linhares, Luis Carlos Soares, Nancy Naro, Ilmar Rohloff de Mattos, Gloria La Cava, Joel Rufino dos Santos, Yvonne Maggie, Rosa Maria Araújo, Rachel and Paulo Carvalho, Michael Conniff, and Liz and the late Tony Leeds for Carioca hospitality, both personal and professional.

In the Arquivo Nacional, the assistance of Eliseu de Araújo Lima and Elizabeth Abib Vasconcelos Dias was essential in orienting me to the collection. I also thank Fernando, Edson, Adilson, and Rogério for finding and transporting untold bundles of documents to the reading room. Judy Holloway provided essential help in coding some of the information and in recording other archival material. In her imaginary encounters with Pedestre Braga on the streets of Rio in 1850 she got a sense of the time travel that keeps many historians going back to the documentary record. Colonel Erasto, historian of the Military Police of Rio de Janeiro, and Major Pita and Corporal Bello, custodians of the Military Police Archive, graciously accommodated my request to explore the internal workings of that institution in past time. I also thank the staffs of the Biblioteca Nacional, the Arquivo da Cidade do Rio de Janeiro, the Instituto Histórico e Geográfico Brasileiro, and Olin Library of Cornell University.

I am grateful to Richard Graham, Sandra Lauderdale Graham, Robert Levine, Reid Andrews, David Hess, Patricia Walker, Gary Okihiro, Richard Gist, Ann Blum, Janet Bridgers, and Kevin Days for careful reading and valuable comments on all or parts of earlier drafts. I did not adopt all of their suggestions, but they helped me see where I needed to be more explicit and where I needed to be less insistent. And their encouraging words came at important moments.

These institutions and individuals have been helpful, but I alone am responsible for the contents of this volume.

T. H. H.

Contents

Tables, Figures, and Maps   xiii

A Note on Place Names, Currency, and Orthography   xv

ONE ▲ Introduction   1

TWO ▲ Foundations, 1808–30   28

THREE ▲ Crisis, 1831–32   64

FOUR ▲ Transition, 1833–41   107

FIVE ▲ Maturity, 1842–65   166

SIX ▲ Continuity, 1866–89   229

SEVEN ▲ Conclusion   272

Appendixes   295
Notes   305
Bibliography   339
Index   363

Tables, Figures, and Maps

Tables

1. Arrests in Rio de Janeiro, 30 May–17 June 1831 78
2. Arrests in Rio Police Jail, 1850: Selected Categories of Detainee, as Percentage of a Total 1,676 Arrests 196
3. Arrests in Rio Police Jail, 1850: Selected Public Order Offenses by Selected Categories of Arrestees 198
4. Arrests in Rio Police Jail, 1850: Offenses Against Property 200
5. Arrests in Rio Police Jail, 1850: Type of Offense by Legal Status of Detainee 202
6. Arrests in Rio Police Jail, 1850: Type of Offense by Selected Groups of Detainees 202
7. Slaves in Rio Calabouço, 1857–58 207
8. Slaves in Rio Calabouço, 1857–58: Type of Offense 208
9. Arrests in Rio Police Jail, 1862 and 1865: Category of Detainee 210
10. Arrests in Rio Police Jail, 1862 and 1865: Public Order Offenses 211
11. Arrests in Rio Police Jail, 1862 and 1865: Offenses Against Person, Property, and "Neutral" 212
12. Arrests in Rio Police Jail, 1862 and 1865: Types of Offense 212
13. Reported Crime in Rio, 1862 and 1865 214

14. Prisoners in Rio de Janeiro House of Detention, 1875:
    Type of Detainee 253
15. Population of Rio de Janeiro, Urban Parishes, 1872:
    Slave or Free 254
16. Arrests in Rio Police Jail, 1875: Slave or Free 255
17. Arrests in Rio Police Jail, 1875: Type of Offense 256
18. Arrests in Rio Police Jail, 1875: Destination upon Exit ... 258
19. Crimes Reported in Rio de Janeiro, 1875 259

Figures

1. Coffee Exports from Rio de Janeiro, 1817 to 1851–52 ... 20
2. Population of Rio de Janeiro, 1799–1890 by Legal
   Status 26
3. Population of Rio de Janeiro, 1838–72 27
4. Arrests in Rio Police Jail, 1850, by Month 194
5. Arrests in Rio Police Jail, 1850, by Day of the Week 195
6. Going to the House of Correction (lithograph) 206
7. Persons Detained in Rio de Janeiro Police Jail,
   1868–88 250

Maps

1. Central Section of Rio de Janeiro, ca. 1850 19
2. Administrative Districts of Rio de Janeiro, ca. 1870 25

A Note on Place Names, Currency, and Orthography

Some confusion may result from the toponym Rio de Janeiro in this study, because in common and formal usage it has referred to a variety of geographical and administrative units. Unless otherwise specified, Rio and the city of Rio interchangeably designate the administrative area formally separated from the surrounding province of Rio de Janeiro in 1834. Since that time the area, the boundaries of which have changed little, has been variously designated the Corte (seat of the Royal Court), the Município Neutro (Neutral Municipality), the Federal District (after the establishment of the Republic in 1889), the state of Guanabara (from 1960 to 1975), and since 1975 the municipality of Rio de Janeiro within the state of the same name. When statistics, administrative jurisdiction, or narration of events refers to the urbanized downtown portion of the city (roughly bounded for much of the nineteenth century by four hills: Castelo, São Bento, Livramento, and Santo Antonio) or some other specific location, the area under discussion will be further specified. From 1834 to 1975 the capital of the surrounding province of Rio de Janeiro was the city of Niterói on the east side of Guanabara Bay, and Rio province was administratively distinct from the city of the same name. Any references to the province or locations in it are specifically designated as such in the text.

Until 1942 the unit of Brazilian currency was the *mil-réis*, composed of one thousand *réis* and written 1$000. (In 1942 the mil-réis became the *cruzeiro*, comprising one hundred centavos and written Cr$1,00.) In numerical notation, eight hundred réis (the daily wage of a military police soldier in 1860) was written $800. At the average exchange rate for 1860 of 52 U.S. cents to the mil-réis, the soldier's wage was roughly equal to 42 U.S. cents per day. Exchange rates with British pounds or U.S. dollars provide only an approximation of the local purchasing power of the wages and other monetary sums mentioned in this book, but the following series (from Duncan, *Public*, p. 183) provides a rough guide:

Year	Average value of one mil-réis in U.S. cents
1830	46
1840	63
1850	58
1860	52
1870	45
1880	45
1890	46

One thousand mil-réis, in turn, was called a *conto* or *conto de réis*, written 1:000$000. As an example, for the fiscal year 1868–69 the total budget of the civil police system of Rio de Janeiro was 358 contos, 660 mil-réis, and 750 réis, written 358:660$750. At the 1870 exchange rate of 45 cents to the mil-réis, that sum was roughly equivalent to US$161,397.34. There is no meaningful cost of living series available to which these data might be compared, but whenever possible I have given a comparative context for the mil-réis figures mentioned in the text.

In an effort to reduce inevitable variation, and following editorial practice standard in Brazil, I have modernized the orthography and diacritical marks of most titles of sources, terms that for lack of an adequate English equivalent have been retained in the original Portuguese, and of proper names (except where the former spelling has been retained in Brazilian usage, e.g., Gilberto Freyre, rather than the technically correct modernization Freire).

Researchers in pre-twentieth century materials quickly adapt to the evolution from, for example, Nictheroy to Niterói, Castello to Castelo, Commercio to Comércio, Motta to Mota, Brazil to Brasil, and to the many other orthographic variations in the Portuguese language.

Policing Rio de Janeiro

Vidigal: "Yes, I know, but what about the law?"
D. Maria: "Oh well, the law . . . just what is the law, major, if you please?"
The major smiled with frank modesty.
—Manuel Antônio de Almeida,
Memórias de um sargento de milícias, 1853

The police were the great terror of those people, because whenever they entered a tenement house great damage was done. With the excuse of preventing or punishing gambling and drinking, the urban guards invaded rooms, broke everything, put everything in shambles. It was a matter of long-standing hatred. —Aluízio Azevedo, *O cortiço*, 1890

[Ayres] speculated that the shouts of the protesting crowd stemmed from an ancient instinct for resistance to authority. He remembered that man, upon being created, immediately disobeyed the Creator, who had, after all, given him a paradise to live in. But there is no paradise that can match the pleasure of opposition. Man gets used to laws, sure; he will bend his neck to power and whim, fine. That's what a plant does when the wind blows. But to bless power and obey the law always, always, always, is a violation of primitive freedom, a freedom as old as Adam. —Machado de Assis, *Esaú e Jacó*, 1904

ONE

Introduction

This is a history of one of the fundamental institutions of the
modern world through which the power of the state intruded
into public space to control and direct behavior. It is also a study of
the way people reacted to that intrusion, and the subsequent interaction between the repressive arm of the state and the people it
most directly affected. The historical development of the police of
Rio de Janeiro, through a dialectic of repression and resistance,
was part of a more general transition from the traditional application of control through private hierarchies to the modern exercise
of power through public institutions. The process of dynamic interaction is explored here as it emerged through time, focusing on
the point at which repression and resistance rubbed against one
another on the squares, streets, and back alleys of Brazil's capital
city. The heat from that friction was the catalyst for the formation
of institutions and procedures that sealed a glaze of modernity over
traditional attitudes and relationships, protecting and strengthening them.

Generalizations about the emergence of the state need to be
grounded in a specific reality, a time, place, and area of activity that
constitutes a manageable unit—a stone in the immense mosaic of
the transition to the modern world. As in a mosaic, each stone is
unique and complex, with its own shape, color, and internal structure. This book explores that general process in a specific place—
Rio de Janeiro, Brazil—through the political independence, state

formation, and nation building that took place between the end of the first and the beginning of the last decade of the nineteenth century. Some parts of this study are unique to Rio de Janeiro, some are generalizations that apply to Brazil as a whole, or at least to other cities, and some might have parallels in other neocolonial areas on the periphery of the modern world. As a case study it is relevant for understanding the more general transition, and for exploring the relationship between the individual, society, and the state in the history of Brazil—itself a large mosaic from which many stones are still missing or only vaguely perceived.

From the perspective of those who make and enforce the rules, the behavior that police and courts try to prevent or punish ranges from unwanted to unacceptable to threatening to dangerous to injurious. Because these strong terms involve order and disorder, right and wrong, good and bad, it is difficult to write about them without being judgmental. This study examines sensitive themes involving deeply ingrained values and assumptions. It explores alternatives to official police concepts of criminality and law enforcement. It counterposes a dialectic of repression and resistance that is secondary to the conflict arising from classes in contradictory relationships to the means of production. This dialectical analysis, rather, sees historical change emerging from the clash of opposing forces that are on one side political, institutional, structured, and well documented, and on the other side social or socio-cultural, diffuse, and accessible now only through fragments of information and indirect inference. Because of such peculiarities, it is necessary to provide here some guidelines as to the methodological assumptions and conceptual concerns that inform it and also to characterize the physical, social, and economic development of the city of Rio de Janeiro from 1808 to 1889.

This chapter introduces the interpretive framework and the physical setting for the chronology that follows. Chapter 2 discusses the foundations of the police system of Rio de Janeiro in late colonial times, when the Portuguese royal family brought to Brazil the institutions of enlightened despotism, through political independence and the reign of Pedro I. Chapter 3 more closely examines a sequence of political and social crises in Rio de Janeiro from Pedro's abdication in April 1831 to late 1832, when new institutions that arose from the crises began to take hold. Chapter 4 studies the development and operation of those new instruments of control and the response of the people they most directly affected during the interregnum of the 1830's. Chapter 5 explores the recentralized police and judicial system from the 1840's through the mid-1860's, when Rio's police were delegated broad authority to keep the behavior of the city's population within acceptable bounds and to punish those who stepped over the line. Chapter 6 looks at the continuity and expansion of the structures of control, which were marked by further institutional experimentation, during the late empire. The conclusion will hark back to some of the notions introduced here, and consider themes that emerge in the intervening chapters.

The middle chapters deliberately follow a chronological progression familiar to students of Brazil's political elite because it was closely concerned with policing the nation's capital city, and its representatives and agents were directly involved in developing an institutional response to the threat posed by the nonelites. The social origins and nature of that threat, as the elite defined it, are difficult to recover with any completeness. Myriad small challenges came mostly from illiterate and powerless people who had little direct way of recording what they did and why, in a medium available now. The evidence of their resistance is available primarily through the record of their actions found in documents left by the institutions created to repress such behavior. Though the chronological chapters are organized according to the development of those institutions and their operation, the patterns of resistance—more diffuse, atomized, and variable—underlie and inform this entire book. The sources give a hint at the relationship between those who held power and those subject to it. The ability to record, transmit, and act on information through the written word was one of the instruments through which power was maintained in the hands of the few and exercised against the many. The resulting record reveals how the two sides in this social war have been bound together in unequal struggle. It also provides glimpses of the world of the nonelites that historians understand poorly and seldom have the opportunity to examine.[1]

Themes

Police institutions of the modern type, in western Europe and such historically related areas as Brazil, emerged during the multifaceted transition from the eighteenth to the nineteenth century, which coincided roughly with the spread of liberal ideology among the powerful few and the application of impersonal mechanisms of coercion to the powerless many. State institutions assumed authority previously exercised primarily through personalistic hierarchies. Related changes included the transition from the arbitrary will of the sovereign to judicial procedures based broadly on the rights of man and citizen, and from public torture to disciplinary incarceration as the focus of punishment, and the development of bureaucratic institutions, such as the police, to fill public space. Michel Foucault, in a major interpretive essay on this process, saw the result as a "carceral" or disciplined society, in which the modern prison becomes a metaphor for the condition of modern humankind.[2]

Extending the metaphor beyond the literal prison to those people not locked behind bars and watched by guards, the forces guiding behavior become internal and psychological, enforcing the self-control and self-discipline that makes most people in the modern world self-regulating. To seek to understand the ways in which such a collective mental state is inculcated and maintained would lead to the broadest consideration of the human condition, far beyond the material at hand.[3] This study is a more restricted examination of another mechanism—institutional and physical, if not as impenetrable and all-encompassing as prison walls—by which behavior is kept within certain limits. Using the police, the state assumed the task of protecting property that had been largely left to private individuals in traditional society and began to exercise control over public behavior that had not been a focus of attention in the premodern state.[4] In Foucault's vision of interlocking modern institutions, the courts and prisons that provide pervasive regulation at the top of the pyramid of control were extended into the public realm "by an organ of surveillance that would work side by side" with courts and prisons, "which would make it possible either to prevent crimes, or, if committed, to arrest their authors; police and courts must work together as two complementary actions of the same process."[5]

Brazil, on the periphery of world capitalism, went through a halting and incomplete process of modernization that was contemporaneous with one in the western European countries that have so often been the source of ideological inspiration and institutional patterns for Latin American political elites.[6] Rejecting the colonial past, but with few established models to combat what they saw as a serious problem of disorder in the streets, the Brazilian elite developed sui generis police institutions for their capital city. Structures and operating principles in the history of Rio's police that are analogous in function to those of other countries were built up through trial and error from local resources and traditions. Institutions initially copied from Europe—notably the justice of the peace (from England), the national guard (from France), and the uniformed but civilian policeman patrolling a familiar beat (from cities in England and the United States)—were eventually rejected in favor of homegrown organizations and procedures. Thus, nineteenth-century Rio de Janeiro offers a case study in the transition from traditional to modern institutions not as one more misguided transfer from the core countries to the periphery but as a process to be understood on its own terms, in the interplay among the repressive purpose of the newly consolidating state, the resources available from which to build instruments of power, and the resistance of many people in urban society to the control thus imposed.

Comparative studies of policing often comment on the historical relationship between the London Metropolitan Police, the famous bobbies created in 1829, and the sociocultural environment in which they have operated. The bobbies normally have carried no firearms and have been legendary for their impartial courtesy and firm restraint in dealing with both crowds and criminals. This is seen as made possible by a general consensus in England regarding the legitimacy of a police presence in social relations and of the law itself, even among antisocial or criminal elements. In the historiography of the United States there is much discussion of a degree of consensus and public support for the upholders of the law who defend the democratic rights of a democratic majority in a democratic society.[7] In Rio de Janeiro regular policing began in 1808 and improved administration of police patrols by armed and uniformed men began in 1831, contemporary with similar institutional developments in western Europe and earlier than in the United States.[8] But no Brazilian of any social class or ideological position would think of interpreting the historical role of the urban police in terms of consensus and legitimacy. Proponents see police forces as necessary agents of order and discipline, while critics see them as the authoritarian state in repressive action. The two positions are not incompatible, and what is common to them is the absence of legitimacy and consensus in Brazilian society and political culture.[9]

The hostility between the forces of repression and the sources of resistance in Brazil is related to the imposition of apparently modern bureaucratic institutions of control on a society that was lacking in other fundamental attributes of modernism. Equality before the law, for example, one of the essential bases of the modern liberal project, has never been more than a slogan intended, in that characteristically Brazilian expression, *para inglês ver*, for the Englishman (i.e., the outsider we are seeking to impress) to see. Equality before the law, most saliently, was included in the constitution of 1824, which formally governed Brazil's institutions through the fall of the empire in 1889, and has been formally confirmed in similar documents since that time. But more than a century and a half after the promulgation of the principle, a perceptive interpreter of Brazilian culture observed that "the citizen in Brazil is the subject of impersonal laws, as well as of the brutal power of the police, which serves to differentiate him systematically and to exploit him ruthlessly, making him into an 'equal but inferior' (*igual para baixo*), in a clear perversion of liberal concepts."[10] This study examines the process by which modern police institutions buttressed and ensured the continuity of traditional hierarchical social relations, extending them into impersonal public space. The apparent contradiction is one example of the incomplete or discontinuous historical processes that help account for many of the characteristics of contemporary Brazil, including the divergence between formal law and the institutions ostensibly charged with enforcing it and socio-cultural norms guiding individual behavior.[11]

In the historiography of Brazil, police power and judicial institutions have been examined in the context of the politics of independence and nation building as a major grievance Brazilians of some social and economic standing had against the colonial regime, and as important instruments by which those in power could reward friends and punish political enemies, thus protecting their status. The terms of this discourse often revolve around competition among rival factions for control of the state apparatus, restrictions on business and political activity and voluntary association, as well as the vague realm of policing ideas and their communication through the public forum and the press.[12] Those are important aspects of political and intellectual history because access to the instruments of power and the authority of the state to regulate such matters are at the heart of the political process. The numerous regional revolts of the first half of the nineteenth century have been the subject of much commentary and some serious study.[13] But such approaches often take for granted the social context of police action, and little has been done to examine the historical development of resistance and repression that forms the persistent, everyday environment of Brazil's cities.[14]

In contrast to these discussions of institution building and the exercise of power from above, there is an approach to social history from below that in large measure takes the regulating institutions of the state for granted and makes use of the documentation they left to reveal the conditions suffered by the disenfranchised masses. Since Gilberto Freyre established the dichotomy half a century ago, the master-slave framework has figured prominently in studies of Brazilian social history, and appropriately so. Despite major changes since slavery was declared illegal in 1888, Brazil still lives with the legacy of the social relations, institutions, and attitudes built up over the previous 350 years when it was a society of slaves and masters. With the expansion of scholarly interest in these issues since the 1960's, Brazilian history from below has often focused on slaves.[15]

One result of this focus, important though such studies have been in expanding our understanding of slavery as an institution and of the slave experience, has been to leave largely unexamined the historical role and experience of another social category that by the first half of the nineteenth century, before slavery's decline in Rio de Janeiro, was similar in size to the urban slave population. This category might be generally labeled the free poor, or the nonslave lower classes, including the "patronless poor,"[16] and was subdivided into more specific groups: marginal drifters, domestic servants, many people involved in the lower levels of artisan and eventually industrial production, retail trade and provisioning, and such services as construction, transportation, public accommodations—and the rank and file of the police system. A few such people descended in part from the natives who were in Brazil when the Europeans first arrived. Some were former slaves, and many more, the majority, were the descendants of slaves, with whom they continued to interact in many ways. Many of those same people, it needs to be recognized, were also the descendants of slave owners, rejected by their paternal ancestors of Portuguese origin because of the degraded status of their maternal ancestors of African origin—the literal rape of Africans that was an essential element of the figurative rape of Africa. Another significant sector of the nonslave urban underclass, increasing proportionally during the nineteenth century, was of more recent European origin, and the Portuguese predominated among the immigrant groups.

The master-slave dichotomy becomes less and less adequate in the course of the nineteenth century for understanding the workings of Brazilian society in general and urban Rio de Janeiro in particular. This is so not only because slavery was outlawed in 1888 but because that legal event was the culmination of social, economic, and ideological processes that extended in various complex ways through the previous half-century.[17] The nonslave urban lower class grew both in absolute terms and in proportion to the decline of slavery after mid-century. Nonslaves were internally diverse and ethnically complex, and while most were black or brown, an increasing proportion were Portuguese immigrants. What they shared in the eyes of the elite were negative attributes: they had neither wealth, nor status, nor power.[18] When any of these people, slave or free, broke the rules of acceptable public behavior, they could expect to bump up against the institutions of repression the elite instituted to keep them within certain limits. The records those institutions left—selective, distorted, and filtered—reveal most directly the nature and location of the boundary the elite drew around acceptable public behavior and how that behavioral code was enforced. But they also reveal that many people in Rio de Janeiro, both slave and free, conducted their lives according to a different and contradictory code.

At the risk of narrowing comparative possibilities, let us be clear that this is not a study of what is called, in the Anglo-American euphemism, law enforcement.[19] There were many laws that the police system used to justify its actions, and there were occasional discussions within the system of the legal basis for one or another policy or practice. But the police also took repeated and acknowledged action for which there was no legal basis. Engaging in *capoeira*, for example, was not made illegal until the promulgation of the penal code of the republic in 1890. In the century preceding, the police of Rio imprisoned thousands of people for capoeira and applied hundreds of thousands of strokes of the lash to their bodies during the nineteenth century, both before and after the enactment of the 1830 criminal code that clearly defined the boundaries of criminal behavior but did not mention capoeira. At the other extreme, the transatlantic slave trade was against Brazilian law after 1831, yet hundreds of thousands of Africans were illegally imported and enslaved during the ensuing twenty years, with the knowledge, acquiescence, and often the connivance of the authorities. The same hierarchy of political, judicial, and police institutions that arrested and punished capoeiras, with no pretense of legal grounds, abetted the violation of laws prohibiting the transatlantic slave traffic.[20] So rather than focusing on law enforcement, this study explores the changing definition of what was permissible behavior and what was not, and on the selective application of laws. Understanding the distance between universal form and relativistic function and how modern institutions intruded into premodern attitudes and behavior are central to understanding the historical development of Brazilian society.

Capoeira was one of a range of "offenses against public order" that in themselves injured no person or property, but which those who set the rules and established the police found unacceptable. As will become clear in the chapters that follow, the vast majority of the time and energies of the police system was directed at the repression of such behavior, which included vagrancy, begging, curfew violation, disrespect to authority, verbal insult, unspecified disorderly conduct, and public drunkenness. There was, of course, real crime in Rio de Janeiro—theft, assault, property damage, personal injury, murder, and related offenses. The same police force handled them all, from curfew violation and disrespect to robbery and killing, although the degree of involvement of the judicial hierarchy and techniques of punishment varied with the severity of the offense and the status of the offender. The seamless association of behavior that is nearly universally condemned (theft or murder) with the victimless violation of arbitrary rules (curfew violation) or symbolic defiance of authority (disrespect) is one of the slickest examples in the history of class society of imposing guilt by association and evil by extension. Most people who might have frequented taverns late at night or who might have gathered around a policeman making an arrest and shouted insults at him did not steal or kill. Yet they were beaten with the same club and thrown in the same jails.

In order to pull away from that judgmental trap, I feel the need to state explicitly that this is not a study of criminality, just as it is not a study of law enforcement. One reason for this caveat is methodological: police records reflect many aspects of institutional activity that are related to but quite distinct from all the legally proscribed acts committed against other people or property. If the latter is criminality, then even the standardized and technologically sophisticated procedures of today's police forces provide only a partial record. In other words, many illegal acts go unrecorded. Crime existed before there were police bureaucracies to keep records, and it is well known that an apparent increase in crime rates may as logically result from increased zeal and efficiency on the part of the police and bureaucratic reporting procedures, or in the willingness of victims to report transgressions, as from an actual increase in criminal or illegal activity.

More generally, I avoid the term *criminality* because of the implicit bias it introduces into an analysis already fraught with the potential for projecting our values as students of history onto the people we study. There is a tendency, promoted especially by those who make and benefit from laws, to associate law-abiding behavior with goodness and illegal acts with immorality. But the degree of overlap between legal and good and between criminal and bad shifts in place and time and varies with the point of view.[21] More contrasting examples might help clarify this issue: Stealing food to nourish a starving child was (and is) illegal. Was it therefore immoral? Enslavement and whipping was legal. Was it therefore moral? Raising a hand against being beaten by a police sword during an arrest was illegal resistance. Was it also an immoral act? In this study I do not try to draw some arbitrary line between justifiable resistance to repression on the one hand and criminal behavior on the other.[22] It is possible to examine the relationship between officially approved norms of police behavior and unacceptable brutality, but not to draw a clear line separating good police from bad police. People who lived in the past, in another place, owe us nothing, and we should not expect anything of them. If we choose to recreate a memory of historical actors from what we find in documents, artifacts, and images, their former existence becomes intermingled with our own, and not vice versa. The subjects of this study, those who repressed and those who resisted, exist now only in the mind of the reader. The reader will also decide who among them was good and who was bad.

When I define the violation of externally imposed rules of behavior as resistance, then, I am not saying that police breaking up a fight in a tavern was a bad thing, that shouting an epithet at a policeman was a good thing, that the arrest or beating of a name caller was a bad thing, or that the imprisonment of small groups of slaves quietly chatting on a street corner was a bad thing. I am saying that people with the resources and authority to create police forces came to consider fights, epithets shouted at agents of authority, and slave gatherings unacceptable, and they created and directed the police to repress such behavior. But "power is exercised rather than possessed," as Foucault points out, "not exercised simply as an obligation or a prohibition on those who do not have it; it invests them, is transmitted by them and through them; it exerts pressure on them, just as they themselves, in their struggle against it, resist the grip it has on them."[23] By continuing to resolve their differences by fisticuffs (or razors and daggers), by refusing to humble themselves in the presence of brutal and arbitrary agents of the state, by continuing to meet and drink and socialize in public and semipublic places the people resisted. To the extent that the institutions of the state reflect and defend the interests of a specific class or classes at the expense of the interests of others, coercion will be not only threatened but applied. That the others should resent and resist such coercion is not surprising, nor is it a measure of their "barbarity." Rather it is a reflection of their humanity.

An exploration of such issues finds elucidation in the ideas of Max Weber, despite his tendency to focus on stability and rationality rather than on the unpredictability of conflict and its disruptive effects. Behind quite different modes of discourse, Weber and Foucault have more in common than might appear at first glance. In discussing "the bases of legitimacy of an order" (a set of rules of behavior, in his terminology), Weber examines the relationship between a small group in power and the many who eventually submit to its will: "It is very common for minorities, by force or by the use of more ruthless and far-sighted methods, to impose an order which in the course of time comes to be regarded as legitimate by those who originally resisted it." He then qualifies that explanation of how authority thus imposed becomes an unchallenged expectation, referring to reasons other than force of habit that might explain submission: "*So far as it is not derived merely from fear or from motives of expediency*, a willingness to submit to an order imposed by one man or a small group, always in some sense implies a belief in the legitimate authority of the source imposing it."[24] In other words a person might submit to authority either because he or she believes it is legitimate, or because it is expedient to do so, or out of fear. Foucault, less calmly and more specifically, suggests that during the old regime brutal punishment was "a policy of terror: To make everyone aware, through the body of the criminal, of the unrestrained presence of the sovereign."[25] The police of Rio de Janeiro, established in the new era of increasing bureaucratic rationality, explicitly recognized terror as one of several weapons at their disposal in their ongoing effort to force submission from people who by their actions declared the structures of power to be illegitimate.

Despite allusions to social warfare and to a dialectic of repression and resistance that led to the historical development of police institutions and practices, I do not refer here to class struggle in the classical sense. For one thing police authorities and the objects of police repression were not bound in struggle by contradictory relationships to the means of production. Any analysis of the dominant mode of production in nineteenth-century Brazil must look to the centers of export agriculture and to Brazil's position on the periphery of the capitalist world economy. Realizing that the urban realm explored here was complementary to export agriculture helps explain the social configuration of the city (for example, the economic focus on the waterfront and the salient presence of dock workers and sailors). That in turn tells us something about the specific patterns of repression and resistance in Rio de Janeiro, but it is secondary to the plantation base of the larger social formation.[26] Furthermore, I think that class struggle presumes some degree of collective consciousness and generalized forms of goal-oriented action on both sides. The creation and deployment of police institutions might be thought of as a weapon in a one-sided version of class struggle, in which a shared awareness of collective interests, a perception of the potential for conflict, and the political and institutional means to maintain the existing class structure all were monopolized by the dominant class.[27] Despite myriad examples of resistance to the control thus imposed, the historical outcome in Rio de Janeiro was likewise one-sided, reflecting in one city, albeit an important one, the essential continuity of power relations in Brazil from colonial times to the modern era.[28]

Approaches

A guiding principle of this study is that forces created in the mind of the historian do not cause anything in history. People may have been motivated by forces that they perceive and act upon, but not those that the historian perceives and projects back on the historical actors. People cause things to happen, sometimes by deliberate decision and action, sometimes unknowingly by their behavior, and sometimes despite their intentions. It is incumbent on the historian to try to see what those forces were and what effect they had on people's actions, but to make the forces the cause literally dehumanizes the past. It implies that individuals do not count and that people, alone or in groups, cannot do anything about their situation—they are at the mercy of forces. I do not think that is true, and my position is based not so much on ideological stance or theoretical principle as on a reading of history. The dynamic of history, I believe, lies not in the inexorable working of theoretical forces created in our minds now but in action taken by people then.[29] Organizing and interpreting the historical record is not to reduce historical actors to the whim of a structure imposed after the fact. Rather it is to aid in our efforts to decide what information in the record is relevant to our purpose and how those relevant elements are related through cause and effect, precedent and consequence.[30]

One way to formulate my approach to the policing of Rio de Janeiro is to conceive of a dialectical process involving, for purposes of analysis, four stages: ideas, institutions, actions, results. Ideas and institutions are the stuff of so much historical study because they are often well documented and are dear to the hearts of the literate elite. But institutions do not just happen. They are created and maintained to lead toward some objective, solve a perceived problem, or meet a felt need. Since the advent of bureaucratic structures and reporting requirements, the actions of the police are relatively well documented, so historical research of the sort reported in this book becomes possible. The record keeping and reporting was itself a result of the development of a modern state apparatus. It was intended to provide those in power with enough information ("knowledge" in Foucault's terms) so that they could regulate the institutions they established to achieve their various objectives. In the area of social control that institution—or set of interrelated institutions in Brazil's case—was the police, acting in conjunction with related political, legal, judicial, and penal institutions.[31]

I am interested in the connections between ideas held by the elite and represented by the institutions they created and the members of society at large who did not share the ideas and had nothing to do with creating those institutions except in the negative sense. In the case at hand, members of the political elite measured the behavior of urban society against their ideal, found much of that behavior unacceptable, and developed police institutions in response. The connection thus comes through actions—the creation of institutions, their operation as they faced challenges large and small through time, as well as the reactions of those affected by the system. The result of those interactions then comes back to the decision makers, it is integrated into their ideas—mind-set, ideology, perceptions, objectives—and future decisions regarding the institutions and their operation are based on the conclusions thus reached.

Put another way, ideologies envision ideal states toward which action is directed. One type of action is to use authority and material and human resources to create institutions, the purpose of which is to aid in achieving the goals of those who hold power. When people take action through institutions, the results are monitored through observation, record keeping, and reporting, and assessed by those in a position to maintain or alter the institutions and their activity. It is important to recognize that this cycle does not take place in self-contained isolation, nor does it aim toward, much less achieve, some absolute and unchanging standard of behavior. As measured by the objectives of those who created and supervised the system established to police Rio de Janeiro, it often did not work very well. It was not characterized by functional equilibrium but by friction and dysfunction, despite recurring claims by police officials that, for example, just "one more crackdown" would rid the city of street gangs, or that an adequate asylum and a final police sweep would definitively end the problem of beggars.

It would be mechanistic and limiting to block out formal sections of each of the chapters that follow along the lines of ideas–institutions–actions–results, but it is an approach that I have used as an informal set of guideposts while sifting through the material.

An underlying concern for such interaction leads to a mode of presenting the material that brings together two areas of historical analysis that are too often considered discrete. It is possible to trace the historical trajectory of politics and institutions without much exploration of the broader social context for the events described. And histories of social groups sometimes convey the impression that the political and institutional context was static and more or less irrelevant to the daily lives of the people being studied. But as Emília Viotti da Costa has observed, "It is impossible to understand the history of the powerless without understanding the history of the powerful. (And, of course, the reverse is also true.) History from the bottom up can be as meaningless as history from the top down."[32] I deliberately intermix the discussion of pertinent political events and institutional developments, in chronological order, with a consideration of the effects they had on the people on the streets. An individual incident or statistic may seem inconsequential in isolation, but accumulated they formed an awareness in the minds of the policy makers of the effect of their actions, and they took new action in that knowledge. As Foucault says in discussing the exercise of power, "none of its localized episodes may be inscribed in history except by the effects that it induces on the entire network in which it is caught up."[33] As I recover these episodes from the documentary sources in which they were inscribed, the dialectic of repression and resistance dictates such a mode of presentation. A variety of pressures, changing through time, have pushed the cycle forward. In the case of police activity, an important determinant of the perception of a problem and the institutional response to it is the nature of the behavior that the police activity is intended to control. This is why unacceptable behavior and the institutions created to contain it are analyzed here through time as two poles of one dialectical process.

Another reason not to force the discussion into boxes in a cyclical model of causality is that I intend this book to be more than a methodological exercise. Revealed in the reams of police reports and memoranda and statistical compilations are myriad personal dramas, large and small. I want to recover what I can of what the relationship between the state and individuals was like—how the institutions affected the lives of ordinary people and how those people responded. That is why, in describing specific incidents in some detail, I name names—to give historical actors and agents a personal presence on these pages. This is not an eccentric attempt to identify each of the inhabitants of Rio de Janeiro (which grew in population from 50,000 to 400,000 in the period examined) but rather a small effort to make good on the hope that each person who ever lived is deserving of being recalled for who he or she was.

People, their behavior, and their interactions with others are also aggregated and manipulated here into totals, percentages, quantitative comparisons, columns on charts. The use of the existing statistical record and the creation of new categories are simply techniques for making generalizations across society and through time that individual cases illustrate and personalize. Quantification helps us understand individuals by providing context for their experience. It does not lead to mathematical proof or truth or accuracy nor does it dehumanize history. The real depersonalization of the historical record lies in the fact that the vast majority of people are utterly forgotten, and their memory unrecoverable.

Another image that might help illustrate my approach and indicate where this study fits among more holistic analyses of the transition to the modern world is that of a clutch in a motor vehicle. A driver's verbal command to a horse, backed up by an occasional flick of the whip kept a carriage moving. A modern vehicle moves by the impersonal application of pressure and friction. In a figurative sense, this is not a study of the entire vehicle of Brazilian society but of how power was transmitted and control maintained in urban Rio de Janeiro. It examines the transition from the personal hierarchy of driver and horse connected by harness and whip to the institutionalized and impersonal application of pressure through friction at the clutch. It looks closely at the way people on the other side resisted the application of such pressure and the response of those in power to tighten control and make the pressure more efficient.

Though I do not allow such a literally mechanistic approach to dominate my presentation and analysis, it nevertheless illustrates something of the relationship I see between repression and resistance in nineteenth-century Rio de Janeiro. The introduction of modern bureaucratic institutions gave traditional elites new mechanisms for coping with the pressures from below that were the social consequence of peripheral capitalism and the legacy of slavery. The main and general objective of those few in control who benefited from this figurative journey was to keep the vehicle moving and to stay in command. Most of the people in Brazil had no control over the vehicle, and its movement yielded little benefit to them. For the few to maintain status, power, and derive material benefit, many had to be subordinated to their will or excluded. The many for their part accommodated themselves to such control, exploitation, or marginalization as best they could (through expediency or fear, as Weber suggested), knowing full well the cost of active resistance.

Some people considered marginal and irrelevant by the elite found refuge in isolated agricultural subsistence, tucked out of sight and out of mind in the vast interior of the country until the few in power encroached upon their isolation. The powerful could ignore the isolated peasantry or exert the loose control of patron-client ties. Others of the free poor resisted control in myriad quiet and passive ways, sought escape through the relative anonymity of urban life, or simply found themselves on the streets as part of a growing population that had never known any other existence. In the city these people struggled for survival and social space alongside slaves under more direct subjugation. Their behavior and that of the slaves with whom they closely interacted often violated rules established by the powerful few, and by their incessant though small acts of resistance the many elicited a repressive response from the state. Their resistance to control and exploitation caused friction, drag, and the inefficient operation of the vehicle, so those in power redesigned and strengthened the clutch assembly. Friction was never eliminated; indeed it was inherent in the way power was (and is) applied. This study focuses on the origin, evolution, and interaction of the parts of Brazilian society where repression and resistance scraped against one another. I hope the results will be relevant for an understanding of the vehicle, the road, and Brazil's historical journey.

Places

Physical geography strictly constrained the historical development of Rio de Janeiro.[34] The safe harbor created by the huge and nearly enclosed Guanabara Bay made the general location attractive for European maritime activities in the south Atlantic. The first precarious outposts of the French and Portuguese were established on the spit of land projecting from Sugarloaf rock toward the entrance to the bay, and on Castelo hill—promontories that could be protected from the indigenous population as well as from seaborne intruders. The latter location became permanent, and from the definitive establishment of the Portuguese base in 1564 to the mid-1700's the fortified town huddled along the beach area connecting the hills of Castelo and São Bento (see Map 1). Artillery batteries shielded the shore and the bay, and a now-forgotten defensive wall protected the land side, which projected no farther than the space between the hills of Santo Antonio and Conceição. Habitation clustered among granite outcrops and low stretches of sandy flatland, interrupted by small lakes and swamps fed by runoff from the frequent rainstorms of a semitropical climate.[35]

A spurt of growth came with the transfer of the colonial capital from Salvador, Bahia, in 1763, primarily in response to the gold and diamond boom in the interior province of Minas Gerais. Rio's role as administrative capital of Brazil for nearly two centuries (until the inauguration of Brasília in 1960) had a profound effect on the social development of the city. The institutional presence of the colonial then national governmental apparatus was everywhere, in palaces, administrative offices, and eventually the two houses of parliament. Direct support services like the military and ecclesiastical establishments, located in fortresses and barracks, churches and monasteries, occupied important locations and employed a significant segment of the population. Indirect support activities, such as provisioning the city with fuel, water, and food, transportation and communication, as well as artisan activities and retail trade, busied much of the rest of the economically active population for most of the nineteenth century. Only from the 1870's did small-scale industrial activity begin to supply the clothing, household items, and processed foods previously imported or produced in artisan shops or kitchens.[36]

Activity on the docks expanded along with the administrative importance of the city, as ocean shipping was connected with mule trains to serve the landlocked mining centers of the interior. Not until the nineteenth century did the export of coffee from the hinterland in the province of Rio de Janeiro bring new life to com-

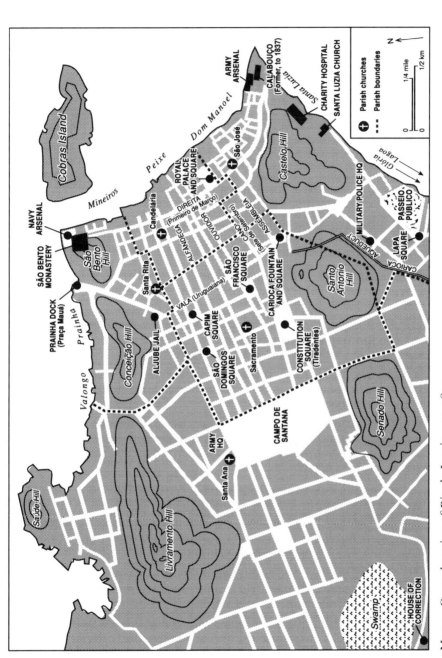

Map 1. Central section of Rio de Janeiro, ca. 1850.

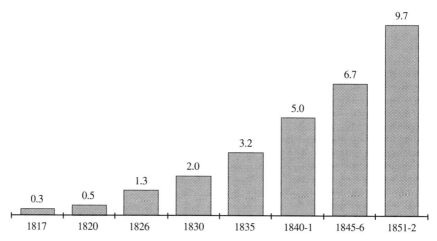

Fig. 1. Coffee exports from Rio de Janeiro, 1817 to 1851–52, in millions of arrobas (1 arroba = 15 kg.). From Stein, *Vassouras*, p. 53.

mercial, financial, and transport services as mining declined. When coffee did emerge it amounted to another boom. As shown in Figure 1, coffee exports through Rio in 1835 were ten times the figure for 1817, and by mid-century exports had tripled over the fifteen years previous. Coffee exports from Rio grew more slowly after mid-century, reaching a high of some 15 million arrobas per year in the early 1880's, then tapering off as São Paulo replaced the hinterland of Rio as the center of the industry.[37] Most other economic activities of the nineteenth century, including the important slave market, rested directly or indirectly on public administration and the coffee trade.

Because the city lacked deep water piers until late in the nineteenth century, ship loading and unloading was done by small lighters that could land at many docks along the extensive waterfront from Saco do Alferes and Gamboa along Valongo, site of the slave market, and Prainha (site of the present passenger pier at Praça Mauá) around São Bento hill to the beaches of Peixe, site of the naval arsenal, customs house, and the city produce and fish market, and Dom Manoel, fronting on the royal palace and the army arsenal, where most passengers landed and from which ferries connected Rio to Niterói across the bay. Further around Calabouço point was Santa Luzia beach, site of the charity hospital, the city slaughterhouse (until 1853), and the beggars' shelter from

1854 to 1879. Work along the waterfront was labor-intensive, with oarsmen, stevedores, porters, and ship's crews intermingling in their respective tasks, supervised by a variety of slave drivers, foremen, supercargos, city market inspectors, clerks, and merchants. Complementary to such activity were public accommodations—places to eat, drink, sleep, and satisfy other physical and social needs. As the economic heart of the city, the focus of hectic activity, and center of social life for various categories of unattached and semi-attached people, the waterfront fringe required special vigilance by police.

Beyond the waterfront the points of reference most relevant for the history of policing the city include public gathering points—parks, squares, and main thoroughfares—as well as police barracks, offices, jails, and prisons. The Passeio Público (public promenade), the city's oldest park, dates from the 1780's when a small lagoon was filled and landscaped to provide a pleasant place for those with leisure to stroll and view the bay. Just behind it, on the site of a colonial monastery on Borbonos Street (now Evaristo da Veiga), the military police headquarters has been located since 1832. On around Santo Antonio hill was the most important public fountain, in Carioca Square, fed by the eighteenth-century aqueduct of the same name bringing water from the Carioca River on the slopes of Corcovado. Runoff from the fountain was channeled down what became known as the street of the ditch (da Vala, now Uruguaiana), eventually entering the bay at the Prainha dock. Part of the aqueduct water was taken farther along what became known as the street of the pipe (do Cano, now Sete de Setembro) to another fountain in the square at the side of the viceroy's palace, which became the downtown imperial palace after independence.

To one side of Palace Square was the army arsenal, a main base for training, administration, and supply, where the police delivered detainees for military conscription. A little further on near the rocky point of the same name was the Calabouço, the jail for slaves held for disciplinary punishment or recaptured after escape. In the other direction from the Palace Square, Straight Street (Direita, now Primeiro de Março) curved toward the navy arsenal, with the island of Cobras (snakes) just offshore dominated by a massive fortress and shore battery. Many conscripts were also delivered to the naval arsenal for ships' crews and to work in the manufacture and handling of naval stores. Adjacent to São Bento hill, topped by its seventeenth-century monastery, was Conceição hill, topped by a fortress overlooking the slave market on one side and the bishop's residence on the other. Further down from the bishop's palace, near the junction of Prainha (now Acre) and Vala streets, was the Aljube jail, the old ecclesiastical prison that the government leased from the Church in 1808, which served as the main detention center until the mid-1850's. Nearby were the squares of Santa Rita, Capim, and São Domingos and further inland the main barracks of the city's army garrison, fronting on the large open field known as Campo de Santana (and a series of other names, most recently the Praça da República).

The Campo was long a parade ground for the army, a grazing and loading area for mule trains to and from the interior, a gathering site for washerwomen and watercarriers around another large public fountain, and a dumping ground for much of the city's waste. It was also a battleground in several political clashes in the years after independence and a favorite venue of Gypsies, vendors, sneak thieves, and assorted hangers-on, before it was fenced and landscaped in the early 1870's. Inland from the Campo de Santana along Nova do Conde Street (now Frei Caneca), a prison complex was built beginning in 1834. The slave Calabouço was moved to the site in 1837, and sections of the prison had been in partial use for some years before its formal inauguration as a penitentiary and detention center in 1850. Farther out Mataporcos Street, next to Espírito Santo Church, was the military police cavalry barracks. From the other side of the Campo de Santana back toward the downtown area was Rocio Square (known as Constitution after 1821 and now Tiradentes), where the central station and secretariat of the civilian police was located for much of the nineteenth century.[38] The city's main house of dramatic and musical entertainment (now site of the João Caetano Theater) was on one corner of the Rocio on the way to São Francisco Square, site of the large church of the same name and the military academy (now housing part of the Federal University of Rio de Janeiro).

A dense network of streets connected these points, skirting hills, running into blind alleys, and opening onto squares and waterfront installations. Regular lighting with whale oil streetlamps, "except when there was a full moon," began in the downtown area soon after 1808, and during the 1850's streetlights were converted to piped gas made from coal imported from England. Most streets were so narrow that two carriages could barely pass, but most traffic was pedestrian in any case—burdens from water kegs to bags of coffee moved through the city atop the heads of slaves. To an English visitor in the 1830's, the normal hubbub of activity on the streets of Rio de Janeiro, "narrow, very dirty, and full of abominable odors," seemed to be a chaotic violation of order and tranquility. There the constant comings and goings of individuals or groups of slaves carrying goods or water, "the incessant chatter of the population, the rumble of carts on irregular paving stones, the horrible whine of oxcart axles, barking of numerous dogs, ringing of church bells, and frequent explosions of fireworks," made the daily clamor "worse than the busiest and most crowded parts of London." That characterization of daytime bustle contrasts with an account of the quiet that descended on the city as church bells tolled curfew, when "every slave 'heels it;' and woe be to him that is caught" by police on the street after 10 P.M. "Nothing could be more surprising to a stranger from the north . . . than to find the streets and the beautiful suburbs of the city almost as tenantless and silent as the ruins of Thebes or Palmyra." The same visitors commented that they "found few cities more orderly than Rio de Janeiro; and the police are so generally on the alert that, in comparison with New York and Philadelphia, burglaries rarely occur." Writing in the mid-1850's, they said they "felt greater personal security at a late hour of the night in Rio than in New York."[39]

The churches scattered over the skyline loomed above two- and some three-story buildings, in which the standard pattern was for public facilities to occupy the ground floor with living quarters directly upstairs. With only a degree of specialization by neighborhood, taverns and the range of retail businesses were interspersed with coffee brokerage firms and governmental offices. Lesser accommodations for slaves and dependents ringed interior patios where many such people labored. This arrangement and the compact layout of the old downtown area mingled all classes and social types constantly in their residential and occupational activities.

After mid-century as Botafogo, Tijuca, and other more commodious outlying areas began to be accessible as middle class residential enclaves, many old downtown buildings were converted into tenements known formally as *estalagens* and informally as *cortiços* (beehives). By police count, as of 1875 some 33,000 people, more than 10 percent of the downtown population, lived in cortiços, and many more lived in rooming houses known as *cabeças de porco* (pig's heads, recalling the maze of cavities left after boiling down the skull of a pig for headcheese).[40] The decline of slavery after mid-century facilitated this transition because the gradual change to free labor relieved people of status from the burden of controlling the working population—their own property—by night as well as by day. Nonslave working people who could afford neither suburban housing nor the attendant transportation costs became concentrated in the downtown area, and the state-sponsored apparatus of repression moved in to replace functionally the control that members of the former slave-owning class increasingly abdicated as they moved with their house servants to the suburbs.

Four of the administrative parishes which from the 1830's were also police districts—Santa Ana, Santa Rita, Candelária, and São José—bordered on parts of the waterfront. Only the central parish of Sacramento was landlocked. In the early part of the century much of Santa Ana parish, whose dominant feature was the Campo of the same name, was vacant hills and swamp land; Engenho Velho was still classified as a rural parish in the 1821 census. Glória, separated from São José in 1834, included the areas now known as Catete, Larangeiras, and Flamengo. Lagoa, named for the Rodrigo de Freitas lagoon, included all of Botafogo, as well as the rural area eventually occupied by Copacabana, Ipanema, Leblon, and Gávea. The geographic and demographic expansion of the city was reflected in the creation of new administrative subdivisions: Santo Antonio in 1854, São Cristóvão in 1856, and Espírito Santo in 1865 (see Map 2). In the absence of adequate roads or public land transportation, through the first half of the nineteenth century ferry boats provided regular service from the downtown docks to Botafogo Bay to the south and São Cristóvão in the north. By the late 1860's mule-drawn trollies connected the downtown via Flamengo and Botafogo to the botanical garden on Rodrigo de Freitas lagoon, spurring development of what is now known as the south zone of the city. The opening in 1858 of the Pedro II railroad station, at the corner of the Campo de Santana formerly occupied by Santa Ana Church, eventually provided access by train to suburbs now known collectively as the north zone.

The population of Rio de Janeiro grew by a factor of ten from the late eighteenth to the late nineteenth century, as shown in Figure 2. The near doubling of the population from 1799 to 1821 is attributable to the transfer of the Portuguese court to the colonial

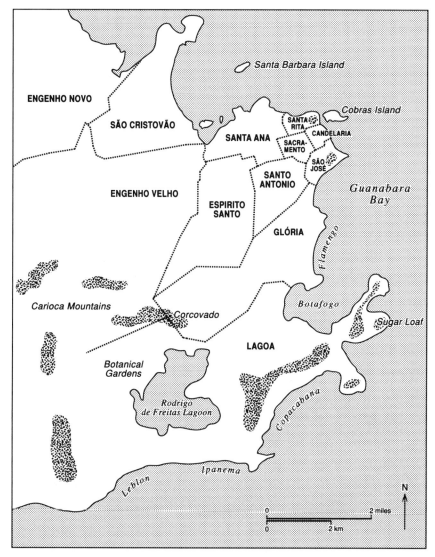

Map 2. Administrative districts of Rio de Janeiro, ca. 1870.

capital in 1808 and the subsequent establishment of royal government in Rio de Janeiro. Some 10,000 to 15,000 people were in the
entourage, and the increased demand for services and provisions
led indirectly to the city's further expansion.[41] Another doubling in
the brief period between 1838 and 1849 is due primarily to expan-

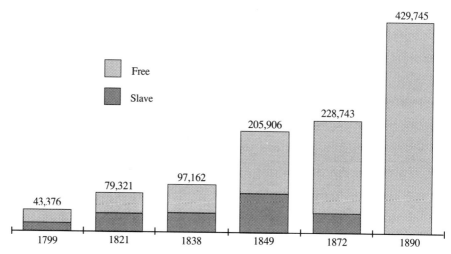

Fig. 2. Population of Rio de Janeiro, 1799–1890, by legal status. Based on Appendix 1.

sion of commerce and services attending the coffee boom in Rio's hinterland. The similar proportional growth from 1872 to 1890 reflects not only further expansion of administrative activities, but the incipient industrialization of Rio, which by the end of the century was the site of considerably more manufacturing than São Paulo or any other city in Brazil. Although the proportion of slaves in the population was highest in 1821 at 46 percent, the slave population grew along with the city itself until mid-century, when the influx from Africa was ended at the same time that labor demand in the interior coffee zones drew slaves out of Rio.

Data on the composition of the population by slave, free Brazilian, and free foreigners for the middle of the century are shown in Figure 3. Along with the decline of slavery after mid-century, these data illustrate the increasing importance of European immigration. In addition to the increasing and always proportionally dominant flow of Portuguese, significant numbers of immigrants began to arrive from Italy and Spain in the last years of the century. Division by gender also reflects a population of immigrants—the forced transfer of Africans in the first half of the century and the "voluntary" flow of Europeans desperate to make a living in the second half. In 1838 men were 56 percent of the population. By mid-century they were 59 percent until 1872. In 1849 of a slave population of 78,855 there were 52,341 (66 percent) born in Africa.

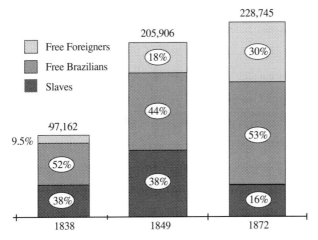

Fig. 3. Population of Rio de Janeiro, 1838–72. Based on Appendix 2.

Among those 66 percent were men (34,362 to 17,938). At the same time there were 36,320 Europeans in Rio, 80 percent of whom were men (28,936 to 7,384).[42] This was just the sort of population—in flux, predominantly male, and predominantly outsiders or in statuses that might resent the social order and have little stake in its preservation—that could be expected to engage in behavior police authorities found disturbing, dangerous, or threatening.

When in 1808 members of the Portuguese royal entourage arrived in Rio de Janeiro, the capital of a colony most had previously known only through administrative reports and balance sheets, they encountered a hostile and dangerous population, the public space of the city dominated by Africans in bondage in a way the courtiers had never known at home. One of the institutions they brought from Lisbon was the General Intendancy of Police, which had been created in 1762 as one of the reforms of enlightened absolutism. The office of intendant in Rio de Janeiro, established in 1808 and complemented the following year by a militarized police corps, was the foundation on which the city's police institutions were built. The government met the challenge of bringing the inhabitants of Rio de Janeiro under control with a repressive apparatus that grew along with the problem it was created to resolve.

T W O

Foundations, 1808–30

The police force as it is known today is an artifact of the modern
state, dating only from the late eighteenth or early nineteenth
century in western European countries.[1] In colonial Brazil there
was no institutional structure of professional, uniformed police
separate from the judicial system and military units. Central to
Brazil's step-by-step transition from colony to nation was the establishment of a police force in a modern mold, first and most effectively in Rio de Janeiro and eventually in the capital cities of major
provinces. Judicial control over lesser crime was also concentrated
in the hands of the new police officials. Despite the rhetoric of a
change from colonial domination to autonomy and liberty, the new
officials were functionally similar to the lesser magistrates of the
old regime, with the authority to judge and punish people whose
relatively minor offenses fell within their jurisdiction. A major difference that developed in the evolution from the colonial to the
national institutions was that the new organization had the beginnings of an administrative bureaucracy that made the exercise of
police power more standardized and efficient. In yet another example of a recurring process, the introduction of progressive
reforms and institutions based on the latest models from what
Brazilians considered advanced countries prevented a rapid and
fundamental break with the past and reinforced the control in the
hands of the existing elite.

The Colonial Legacy

Such institutions during the colonial age had been established under the Afonsine Code of the mid-fifteenth century, the Manueline Code of the early sixteenth century and the Philipine Code of the early seventeenth century. These were attempts to give some order to the accretion over centuries of laws, decrees, customary practices, and precedents from ancient Rome and the Visigothic kingdoms that followed Roman rule in Iberia as well as in the judicial practices of the Iberian inquisition.[2] In addition a significant but largely unacknowledged influence from the Moslem kingdoms of medieval Iberia lingered linguistically in the *alferes* (junior military officer), *alcaíde* (constable), *almotacél* (petty judge), *aljube* (ecclesiastical jail), and *meirinho* (bailiff).

As Brazil had become in the eighteenth century the economic lifeblood of Portugal, a series of reforms inspired by European enlightened despotism made Portuguese colonial control more pervasive and efficient and more oppressive to the emerging Brazilian nativists. Portugal established an elaborate judicial system in its colonies that was essential to the maintenance of the empire, and judges were among the principal representatives of the monarchical authority Brazilians grew to resent. Criminal law was governed by Book V of the Philipine Code, which specified the mechanisms of absolutism. Only agents of the crown, not private individuals, could initiate proceedings. Only royal judges could collect and evaluate evidence, deciding what was relevant and what was to be excluded, and judicial torture was an important instrument for extracting confessions. Trials pitted the judge together with the prosecutor against the defendant, who had no rights; proceedings could be held in secret if the judge saw fit. And legal punishments included physical mutilation, branding, drawing and quartering, and whipping.[3]

In colonial times rudimentary vigilance was carried out by an unarmed civilian watchman (*guarda*), hired by the town council to make the rounds and keep an eye out for suspicious activity, and the neighborhood inspector (*quadrilheiro*), appointed by local judges.[4] These functionaries, who would not even merit the label "officer," had no more powers of arrest than any ordinary citizen. Their role in society was qualitatively different from the police forces developed during the early nineteenth century. The power

theoretically embodied in the monarch was delegated to his administrative, military, and judicial representatives but not further entrusted to the guard, who had no authority to take action on his
own initiative. The watchmen had instructions to apprehend any
wrongdoer caught red-handed, and in practice they might affect
behavior simply by their presence, but authority remained with
those higher up in the system.

In times of civil disturbance or when an armed force was required for crowd control or an arrest, a judge or other official
might call for a detachment of army troops from a local garrison,
militia units, or reserves called *ordenanças*. Only the army was professional, and the officer corps formed a semiclosed corporate
group by the eighteenth century. The militias were made up of
local residents who wore uniforms when on duty and were armed
and given some training by regular army officers, but aside from
sporadic exercises and ceremonial functions they were called up
only in emergencies. The third-line ordenanças consisted of most
other members of the free, able-bodied, male members of the community. Few had uniforms or weapons other than those they could
supply themselves, and little effort was made to train them in military skills. The militias and particularly the ordenanças were not
much as fighting forces, but by their membership in these organizations most free male citizens of good standing (i.e., not criminals,
vagabonds, or other marginal social types) identified themselves
with the regime and with the forces of order. The paramilitary
units became important as the agents of local administration and
gave Brazilians a place in the lower orders of a "false, but functioning, colonial aristocracy."[5] This system of patronage and social control functioned with some regularity only in and around provincial
capitals and other major towns. In the rural zones of the immense
and sparsely settled colony, the will of the local landlord or regional
boss held sway, backed by armed retainers in private service.

The Brazilian elites that supported the moves toward independence from Portugal had a clear interest in maintaining stability
and social calm. They were aided in these objectives by the process
of independence itself, which progressed in stages from 1808, with
the transferral of the Portuguese royal family to Rio de Janeiro, to
1831 with the abdication of Pedro I. With nearly half the population enslaved, with all economic activity beyond peasant subsistence
based on slave labor, and the slave uprising in St. Domingue fresh

in the thinking of the dominant class, it was important to avoid a political breakdown in the process of breaking from Portugal. Independence amounted to a conservative political transition involving piecemeal institutional changes, sparing the country the destruction, animosities, and chaos a major civil war might have entailed.[6]

A general problem following formal independence was how to replace the institutions by which the colony functioned in the interests of the Portuguese commercial elite with mechanisms by which the new nation would operate in the interest of the Brazilian commercial elite and their essential partners engaged in export agriculture and extractive activities. The partners, British commercial and financial interests, were generally content to leave the internal reordering of Brazil to the Brazilians as long as the results did not clash too directly with British objectives.[7]

Among the principal areas of pressure for a clear break with the colonial past during the first decades of independence were basic attributes of the state the Brazilians hoped to create: criminal legislation, judicial institutions and procedures, and the exercise of police power. In a broad sense Brazil belatedly participated in the reform movement that swept the Atlantic world in the age of enlightenment and revolution in the last half of the eighteenth and first half of the nineteenth centuries, a movement generally identified with liberal ideology. Brazilian liberals, and even conservative nationalists of the independence period, saw the extant police and judicial procedures both as antiquated relics of a bygone era and as a legacy of colonial oppression. A dilemma emerged reflecting the contradictions of a liberal ideology within a highly stratified society held together by political patronage, economic exploitation, and physical coercion. The political leaders recognized that any fundamental break in the domination on which Brazil's society and economy rested could be dangerously disruptive to their own status and control. At the same time they wanted to move out from under colonial despotism and monarchical absolutism.[8]

The Police Intendancy

The police as a separate institution had its beginnings before formal independence, as the transferral of the Portuguese Court to Brazil brought the establishment of the General Intendant of

Police of the Court and the State of Brazil on 10 May 1808. This police intendancy was based on the French model introduced into Portugal in 1760. It had responsibility for public works and ensuring the provisioning of the city in addition to personal and collective security.[9] These responsibilities included public order, surveillance of the population, the investigation of crimes, and apprehension of criminals. Like the judges of Rio's high court of appeals, the intendant held the rank of *desembargador* and was also considered a minister of state. He had the power to decide what behavior was to be declared criminal, establish punishment he thought appropriate, and then to arrest, prosecute, pass judgment, and supervise the sentence of perpetrators. He thus represented the authority of the absolute monarch, and consistent with colonial administrative practice his office combined legislative, executive (police), and judicial powers. The royal decree establishing the intendancy confirmed the concept of granting judicial authority over minor offenses to the police in the following terms: "As there are crimes that require no punishment other than some correction, the Intendant may in such cases arrest such persons as deserve correction, keeping them imprisoned for a time judged by the Intendant as proportional to the disorder committed, and as seems necessary for correction."[10]

In order to assist the intendant in correcting unacceptable behavior, on 27 June 1808 the prince regent divided the city into two judicial districts and established the new position of criminal judge (*juiz do crime*) for each. The criminal judges were subordinated to the intendant and had the same combination of judicial and police functions in their districts as he had over the city as a whole.[11] Thus the concept of combining judicial and police functions at the local level, building on the principles that oriented the colonial system, dated from the founding of police institutions in Rio de Janeiro.

The first intendant of police, Paulo Fernandes Viana, held the post for nearly thirteen years until 26 February 1821, when his removal was a principal demand of a military and civilian crowd urging João VI to adopt the liberal constitution that the Lisbon Cortes had yet to promulgate. Viana, a native of Rio de Janeiro, was a decisive administrator with broad authority over city services whose public works projects did much to make the colonial capital into a livable city by the standards of the courtiers and officials accompanying the royal family in exile. Particularly important were the paving of the main streets and access roads to connect the various parts of the city, the construction of aqueducts and public fountains to improve the water supply, and the first regular and widespread installation of whale oil streetlamps.[12] Long after other public works and city services became the responsibility of specialized agencies during the nineteenth century, the police remained in charge of public lighting. Viana also carried out policies that exacerbated tensions between the native inhabitants of Rio and the several thousand functionaries and their families who accompanied the prince regent in the flight from Portugal. One important source of resentment, for example, was the confiscation of private dwellings for the members of the royal entourage, which Viana ordered by simple fiat to which there was no appeal.[13]

John Luccock, an Englishman who lived in Brazil from 1808 to 1818, left an impression of police investigative techniques under Intendant Viana. A desk containing important business papers was stolen from Luccock's office, and he and an associate called on the intendant personally once they had identified a suspect, a mulatto in their service. They suggested that an arrest warrant, promptly served, might yield evidence of the crime, but instead Viana told them to return in a week to check on the progress of the case. When they returned to the police offices they were surprised to learn that the suspect had been arrested soon after their first visit, and "thumbscrews had been applied," but no confession was forthcoming. After another week had passed they went back and heard from Viana that after more interrogation assisted by thumbscrews, a "tacit" confession had been obtained. The return of the papers would have given Luccock independent confirmation of the guilt of his former servant, but Viana asserted that the culprit had destroyed the evidence. Luccock never saw the papers or the mulatto again and decided the prudent course was not to ask about his fate.[14]

The Guarda Real de Polícia

Another innovation following the transfer of the royal family to Brazil was the creation of a full-time police force organized along military lines and given broad authority to maintain order and pursue criminals. This was the Guarda Real de Polícia, established in May 1809. Like the intendancy of police to which it was subordinate, the Guarda Real was intended to replicate in Rio de Janeiro an institution in Lisbon. The first commander, Colonel José Maria Rabelo, had served in the Portuguese counterpart and gone to Brazil with the royal family. Intendant Viana paid for the salaries and uniforms of the new police corps by using his broad authority to borrow funds and solicit contributions from those in a position to pay. Within a few years funds to support both the office of the intendant and the Guarda Real were gathered primarily from charges for services and from license fees collected from businesses or the promoters of public events.[15] This method of financing the police force reflected the political ambiguities of the moment. The Portuguese monarchy at this juncture operated on old-regime principles of royal absolutism through institutions developed in the preceding half-century of enlightened despotism—developments generally known in Portugal and its empire as the Pombaline reforms.[16] Authority in principle still emanated only from the monarch, but funding for the new police came from fees, private loans, and grants from local merchants and property owners. This reciprocity between the source of state authority and the economic elite is a specific example of the more general relationship that explains much of the conservative evolution toward political independence in Brazil and the concurrent development of state institutions.

Regular army troops could be called from garrison duty in forts and barracks during public emergencies, but they might be ordered away on campaigns for extended periods and unavailable for police duty. The permanent mission of the new Guarda Real, in contrast, was to "maintain public tranquility . . . and many other obligations relating to civil order."[17] It was stationed at several locations in or near the downtown area to facilitate patrolling and quick response to disturbances. Originally authorized at a strength of 218 officers and men, the Guarda Real never reached half that total. Although it remained small, numbering 75 men in 1818 and about 90 by the late 1820's, its full-time police mission made it more effective than the old system of sporadic vigilance by civilian watchmen. Its officers and men were transferred from the ranks of the regular army, and like army troops they were paid only a token stipend beyond their room and board in the barracks and uniforms.[18]

Members of the Guarda Real became notorious as Viana's ruthless agents. The most famous among them, celebrated or reviled by contemporaries and later historians on both sides of these issues, was Miguel Nunes Vidigal, who transferred to the new unit from the colonial militia, which he had entered as a cadet in 1770. He held the rank of major in 1809 and served first as adjutant and then second in command of the new police force. Vidigal became the terror of the vagrants and idlers who might meet him coming around a corner at night or see him suddenly appear at the *batuques* that frequently took place in the outskirts of the city. These were gatherings of common people, mostly slaves, who socialized, drank sugarcane brandy, and danced to Afro-Brazilian drum music late into the night. Without even pro forma deference to legal procedures, Vidigal and his soldiers, hand-picked for their size and strength, proceeded to beat any participant, miscreant, or vagrant they could capture. These brutal attacks became known in the folklore of the city as "shrimp dinners" (*ceias de camarão*), recalling the flaying necessary to get at the pink flesh of those crustaceans. Instead of the usual military sword, the normal equipment of Vidigal and his grenadiers was a whip with a long heavy shaft tipped by rawhide strips, used as both club and lash. Following the beating viciously and indiscriminately administered to slave and free alike at the time of arrest, slaves were returned to their owner's custody or submitted to the intendant or his assistants, the criminal judges, for judgment. Nonslave detainees were kept in the short-term lockup, the *casa de guarda* on the Palace Square (now XV de Novembro), from where some of the able-bodied were selected as conscripts for the army or navy without further legal formalities and others went to a longer term in the city jail.

Vidigal also personally led assaults on *quilombos*, the encampments of escaped slaves that formed in the wooded hillsides surrounding Rio. These hideouts were close enough to the urban center that *quilombolas* could sneak into the city at night to forage for supplies, and their twinkling campfires and throbbing drums left the downtown residents jittery. One of the better publicized of Vidigal's exploits came on 19 September 1823, when he led a force of police and regular army troops against a quilombo on Santa Teresa hill. The next morning he triumphantly entered the city on a prancing stallion at the head of a column of more than two hundred half-naked men, women, and children, many wearing seashell necklaces and feather decorations suggesting African cultural elements, who had been captured in the raid.[19]

Luccock's impressions of the Guarda Real confirm the folkloric legacy of Vidigal's tenure in that institution. With tactful word play he suggested that the members of the corps were chosen "rather from their personal knowledge of bad characters than their own claim to a good one," and that "the powers entrusted to this body are, perhaps, too great for the habits and the mental culture of men who had been selected for it." After recurring disciplinary problems, when Luccock left Rio in 1818 each police patrol consisted of two men of the Guarda Real and one from the militia or the regular army, "the latter being considered a check on the former."[20] From what is known of the conscript army and the ragtag militia, one wonders what sort of check they might have exercised on the police soldiers. Robert Walsh, an Englishman resident in Brazil in 1828 and 1829, left both a physical description and a similarly circumspect assessment: "The police are a large body dressed like soldiers, with blue jackets and crossbelts of buff leather, and resemble exactly the gendarmes of France. They are not distinguished either for temperance or proper conduct."[21]

The Guarda Real established patterns characteristic of Rio's front-line police force through later periods of shifting ideological winds and institutional experimentation. The rank and file members were drawn from the free lower classes who were important targets of police repression. They had wide leeway in carrying out their mission, following guidelines laid down by the civilian administrators and judges who maintained overall control. And their methods mirrored the violence and brutality of life on the streets and slave society generally. In another similarity to later patterns, the police were organized from the first as a military institution so that the coercive force they exercised could be controlled by discipline, channeled through hierarchy, and directed at specific targets. The underlying rationale of a military organization is to concentrate, regulate, and direct force against an enemy. The enemy for Rio de Janeiro's police was society itself—not society as a whole, but those who broke the rules of behavior established by the same political elite that created the police and directed its action. This exercise of concentrated force can be seen as defensive, protecting the people who made the rules, owned property, and controlled public institutions that needed defending. The police force can also be seen as offensive, aimed at establishing control over territory both social and geographical—the public space of the city—by subjugating slaves and restraining the free lower classes through in-timidation, exclusion, or subordination as circumstances required.

Invoking military terminology and concepts to understand Rio's police is not a figurative analogy for illustrative purposes but a de-scription of the way the institution was conceived and the way it operated. The police were like a standing army fighting a social war against adversaries all around them. Contact with the enemy came with the guerrilla actions of capoeira gangs, acts as subversive as absenting oneself from the control of one's owner and refusing to work, and myriad small individual violations from petty theft to insolence to being on the streets after curfew. Also like a standing army, the police force was conceived as the coercive instrument of those who created, maintained, and controlled it. Unlike warfare against an external enemy on the battlefield, however, the objective was not to exterminate or eliminate the adversary. The goal was repression and subjugation, the maintenance of an acceptable level of order and calm, enabling the city to function in the interest of the class that made rules and created the police to enforce them. From the standpoint of that class, Vidigal and the Guarda Real were a success, despite the occasional need to impose discipline and rein in the excesses of police practices. Striking terror in the hearts of idlers, vagrants, and recalcitrant slaves was just what they wanted to accomplish.

What his employers and superiors thought of Vidigal's perfor-mance might be inferred from his career; not so with Paulo Fer-nandes Viana. The first intendant was identified with royal abso-lutism and made enemies among the factions of the political elite through his exercise of the intendant's broad authority over many aspects of life in the city, from expropriating residences for mem-bers of the royal entourage, to granting business concessions to favored merchants, to awarding lucrative contracts for city services. While Viana was forced from office in the liberal coup of Febru-ary 1821, his military factotum Vidigal was kept on through the political changes from that time until 1824. He was promoted to general in March 1822, at which time his commission was trans-ferred from the militia to the more prestigious regular army, and he became the commander of the Guarda Real de Polícia. Among the various commendations and decorations Vidigal received the most distinguished was that of Cavalier of the Imperial Order of the Southern Cross, awarded him by Emperor Pedro I in December 1822. He retired with honors and the rank of field marshal in November 1824.[22] To Vidigal's enemies he and his whip-wielding grenadiers were the ruthless and brutal agents of arbitrary state authority. To his admirers they were the embodiment of the steadfast forces of order and public tranquility. The middle ground is not that they were neither but that they were both.

Patterns of Arrest

The procedures Vidigal became famous for—administering corporal punishment during street patrols—had no legal basis beyond the informally delegated authority of the intendant. One problem with summary punishment, of course, was the absence of a reliable method of determining guilt or innocence beyond what a police soldier might quickly conclude from the scene before him. If the more general purpose of the action was to intimidate slaves and street people into submission, however, the specific guilt or innocence of those whipped was not so relevant. Records of arrests during his tenure suggest that one of the criteria Vidigal used for deciding whether to go after a person, in addition to observation in flagrante delicto, was whether that person was black.

The British merchant Luccock observed that in Rio during the period Viana and Vidigal were in office, "the laws were so imperfect, or so imperfectly executed, that white people seemed to have been gradually confirmed in the persuasion that they were above their influence. Few of that class had, I believe, been recently apprehended for crimes, except those committed against the state; and mulattoes enjoyed like exemptions in proportions as their color approached the dingy or fair."[23] Recent research confirms that from 1810 to 1821 very few white people, and few nonslaves for that matter, were arrested by Rio police. Leila Algranti has studied the 5,078 cases that fell under the intendant's jurisdiction from June 1810 to May 1821. For the years for which the series is complete, 1811–15 and 1818–20, the intendant handled an average of 526 cases per year.[24] (A fuller discussion of these data is with Appendix 3.) In a descriptive sense these were misdemeanor crimes or petty offenses—those the intendant, acting in his capacity as a judge, was authorized to dispose of, from apprehension of the offender, judgment of guilt or innocence, through sentencing and supervising punishment. No prosecuting or defending attorneys, nor any judicial authority outside the office of the intendant, were involved at any stage. The 1810–21 data in Appendix 3 are suggestive of what authorities considered the range of problems the intendancy of police was directed to resolve during Paulo Fernandes Viana's term as intendant.

At a time when nearly half the population of Rio was enslaved and the transatlantic slave traffic was unrestricted, it is no surprise that 80 percent of all those judged were slaves and that 95 percent of those had been born in Africa. Another 19 percent of the total were former slaves (*forro*, a label sometimes informally applied to any nonslave black whether free by birth or manumission, but that would not be applied to a white person). Only about 1 percent were free persons who had never been slaves (60 of the 4,776 cases for which the status of the defendant could be determined), and most of them were probably foreign sailors whose shore-leave flings had landed them in the hands of the Guarda Real. It seems probable that during the ten years these arrest data cover, more than 60 free persons committed the sort of offenses that were within the intendant's jurisdiction. Some nonslaves may have been conscripted directly into the army, and others may have been remanded to higher courts in deference to their racial status. Either of these destinations would have spared the culprit a hearing before the intendant for sentencing. Whatever the questions raised by missing data, very few white people were brought before the intendant for petty crimes, even though few of the offenses he handled pertained exclusively to slave status. Recent arrivals from Africa constituted the primary threat or were the object of closer surveillance compared to Brazilian-born slaves.

Of the offenses only slaves could be charged with by virtue of their condition, the most important was escape, which accounted for 751 cases, 16.4 percent of the total, the most of any single reason for arrest. Fugitive slaves were usually held to be reclaimed by their owner with no further punishment other than the use of their labor in public works. The next largest category was arrest for capoeira at 438 (9.6 percent). Although it was related to the gymnastic martial art/dance associated with capoeira in Brazil today, in the nineteenth century the term was applied to a range of activities involving primarily slaves, though as the century progressed increasing numbers of free people as well. Perpetrators were often arrested singly, but capoeira was usually a group activity. Organized gangs with designated leaders, internal hierarchy, and recognized neighborhood "turf," competed among themselves, engaged in territorial battles, and committed acts of violence (but seldom theft). They were the scourge of the police and the terror of the white upper classes, and much police energy, from the establishment of the intendancy in 1808 through the 1890's, went into repressing capoeira.[25] Most capoeiras were armed with razors, clubs, or daggers at the time of arrest, and it is probable that many of those arrested for "group disorders" as well as weapons possession and stone throwing were engaged in the range of activity generically labeled capoeira. A few men were even arrested for "whistling like capoeira"—making the sound by which members of the gangs communicated when out of one another's sight.

Taken together, the offenses that fall under the general heading of crimes against public order, which did not in themselves result in property loss or personal injury, accounted for over 40 percent of the total. If offenses relating to slave escapes are added, some 60 percent of arrests are accounted for. About 12 percent of all arrests were for offenses that directly involved physical assault or injury to another person, mostly from confrontations between or among people of a similar social category rather than attacks by slaves on free people. Nearly a quarter of the arrests were for petty crimes against property, mostly involving theft. Of the 750 cases in which the nature of the object stolen can be determined, 223 (30 percent) were for stealing articles of clothing, and 113 (15 percent) were for stealing food. Some slaves who stole food might have intended to resell it elsewhere in the city for cash, but many were trying to increase or enrich their meager diets or provide food for their children or other people close to them.

The following examples from 1820 provide a fuller impression of these cases than cold statistics can. The ethnic or geographic term following the single name for slaves designates the person's nation of origin in Africa (*crioulo* refers to native, or Brazilian origin).[26] This standard usage was to help distinguish among the many slaves who shared common Portuguese names and to keep track of which ethnic groups were engaging in what sorts of proscribed behavior. From the terse shorthand phrasing of the police clerk emerge tantalizing hints at the individual skirmishes in the social war between the forces of repression and resistance. Tijuca listed as part of some sentences refers to forced labor on the road then under construction through the region of that name, over the hills separating the downtown area from the isolated western part of the municipality of Rio. The intendant of police in his capacity as supervisor of public works had in these arrestees a steady stream of man power, which he could transfer from jail cell or whipping post to road crew—all within his administrative purview. In these as in thousands of similar skirmishes the loser was forced to supply labor to the victor:

1 March:
Bonifácio, mulatto slave of Colonel João Pedro de Carvalho, for making three wounds on the person of the black Sebastião, slave of Dona Luiza So-and-So [*de tal*], with a knife that was not found on him at the time of arrest. None of the wounds is serious. Three hundred lashes and three months in prison.

15 March:
João Benguela, slave of Joaquim de Souza, for capoeira, armed with a pointed blade. Three hundred lashes and three months Tijuca.

Francisco Antônio, pardo freedman, for disorder in the house of a woman, with a knife, which was taken from him. Three months in prison.

José Cabinda, black freedman, for capoeira. He was armed with a knife, which was taken from him. Three months Tijuca.

22 March:
Malaquias, crioulo freedman, because "stop, thief!" was shouted after him as he ran with a knife in his hand, which he dropped before being arrested. Three months Tijuca.

23 March:
Manoel Cabinda, slave of Joaquim José Siqueira, found with a stick in his hand. One hundred lashes.

2 April:
João Benguela, slave of Constâncio So-and-So, for directing insulting and slanderous words at Teresa Maria de Jesus, and trying to butt her with his head. Two hundred lashes.

Manoel Moçambique, slave of José Gomes, for stealing some sausages and pork, which were returned to their owner. Two hundred lashes.

10 November:
Francisco Cabinda, slave of João Gomes Barros, for playing *batuque* at a large gathering of blacks. The drum was confiscated. Three hundred lashes, Tijuca.[27]

Such incidents and the quantitative context shown in Appendix 3 provide an operational definition of what was involved in maintaining "public tranquility and civil order"—the general charge of the intendant of police, the Guarda Real, and the various police institutions and forces after them. One conclusion to be drawn from these 1810–21 records is that the intendant, his staff, and the Guarda Real that patrolled the streets in his name spent most of their time keeping slaves in line. Some police action was to apprehend thieves and break up fights, but most of it was to capture fugitive slaves, prevent groups of slaves and free blacks from gathering in the streets or acting in a way the police patrol considered suspicious, disorderly, or disrespectful, and to deprive the same category of people of any instrument that might be used as a weapon. The restrictions on weapons possession are especially indicative of how the threat was perceived. A police edict of December 1816 specified that any slave "found with a fixed blade or folding knife, or any instrument of iron or even a sharpened stick with which he might injure or kill, even without having committed such injuries, will be whipped with three hundred strokes of the lash and sentenced to three months' labor on public works." If such an instrument was found or if it was determined that the culprit had thrown away a weapon to prevent its discovery in the search following arrest, the penalty was to be administered "without any further formality or legal procedure." This was no sumptuary law to prevent commoners from wearing swords as a badge of rank to which they had no right but a draconian measure to deprive slaves of the instruments of aggression and self-defense. In addition to the 213 slaves who came before the intendant for weapons possession, 631 arrested for other crimes had weapons possession added to the original offense. Free people were to serve three months at labor on public works for weapons possession, but very few whites were brought before the intendant for that or any other offense.[28]

Punishments were brutally severe for the smallest infraction even by the standards of a few decades later and in comparison with urban slavery elsewhere. In contrast to the standard applications of 100 to 300 lashes for petty offenses in Rio de Janeiro, often followed by several months of chain gang labor, from the southern United States comes the following report of crimes and punishments of slaves in Richmond, Virginia in 1825: "Stealing three dollars, twenty lashes; three blankets, fifteen; four dollars, twenty-five; a calico dress, fifteen lashes; a pair of boots, thirty-nine; one featherbed, ten."[29] If slavery in patrimonial, Catholic Brazil was milder than in the capitalistic, Protestant United States, that difference hardly extended to the punishment of urban slaves for petty crimes.[30]

Authoritarian Liberal Reforms

In April 1821 following the public demonstrations that forced Viana out of office in February, King João VI returned to Portugal, leaving his son Pedro as prince regent. Pedro was more decisive and authoritarian than his father, but he fancied himself a promoter of liberal political principles through measures he presumed to impose by royal fiat. The incongruity of such a combination was most prominently exhibited when he sent troops to dissolve the constituent assembly and then unilaterally decreed the "liberal" constitution of the empire in March 1824. Similar cross pressures contributed eventually to his abdication of the Brazilian throne in April 1831 when he said he would "do everything for the people, and nothing by the people."[31] Pedro had the virtue of being consistent in his contradictions, first displayed when at age 22 he was left to exercise authority in Brazil as regent.

In May 1821, less than a month after assuming the regency, Pedro took the first of several steps to introduce due process into police and judicial practices. He decreed that no one could be arrested except by a judicial warrant or in flagrante, that formal charges had to be brought against all detainees within 48 hours of arrest, that no one could be imprisoned without being convicted through due process in open court, and that shackles, chains, and torture could not be used as punishment. Two weeks later he decreed that a similar list of protections from the liberal Portuguese constitution would be enforced in Brazil.[32] These were included as items in a detailed list of the "civil and political rights of Brazilian citizens" guaranteed by Article 179 of the 1824 Constitution, which included the general declaration that "the law will be the same for all, whether in protecting or in punishing." That document defined citizens as "those who were born in Brazil, whether born free or freedmen" (*quer sejam ingênuos ou libertos*). Other than a provision excluding freedmen from the electoral college and high office, this was the only hint in the constitution of the empire that slavery existed.[33]

The new intendant of police, João Ignácio da Cunha, continued in the policy direction Pedro established in 1821 by ordering that slaves arrested for capoeira, weapons possession, or disturbing the peace were to be freed without further punishment unless formal charges were brought. In November of that year the military committee in charge of security in the capital, invoking the "dangerous consequences one may expect from treating such individuals leniently," urged the minister of war to do what he could to reinstate the former policy of allowing the Guarda Real patrols to whip such offenders on the spot, then release them to their owners. Whipping, the committee pointed out, was the only punishment "that intimidates and instills terror in those committing these physical attacks and murders." The committee recognized the interests of the slave owners in this problem, noting that if the slave was arrested and later released, his owner was liable for the costs of his subsistence while in jail. If the detainee were immediately whipped and delivered to his owner, the latter suffered no expense or lost labor of the slave.[34] In a sharply worded reply the new intendant protested that under the old orders to whip capoeiras at the moment of arrest and ask questions later, many free blacks, who could not legally be subjected to the corporal punishment reserved for slaves, had been summarily beaten. He made ironic reference to the futility of physical punishment intended as a deterrent, saying that if whipping could resolve the problem there would not be one capoeira in Rio de Janeiro.[35] Thus with Paulo Fernandes Viana replaced by an advocate of an early version of civil rights and João VI replaced by his authoritarian liberal son, Vidigal's "shrimp dinners" were no longer officially condoned.

Part of the transition from absolutism to the rule of law was, in Antônio Candido's apt assessment, "to disguise the arbitrary will of those in charge under a pretense of legality. . . . The police of an absolute sovereign are ostensive and brutal, because an absolute sovereign is not concerned with justifying his acts. But the police of a constitutional state must be more refined," because they represent the will of a group held together by delicate consensus.[36] The consensus among elite factions was tested during the decade between the promulgation of these reforms and the aftermath of Pedro's abdication, but the slaves and free rabble whom the military committee wanted to continue to terrorize were marginal to the political process. Their opinions on the matter of whipping did not count except insofar as the risk of a brutal beating served to deter their resistance to their condition. The constitutional state, the anti-reformers argued, need not concern itself with justifying its arbitrary acts to the people who were necessarily the objects of repression. The need for control of the many superseded the liberal principles espoused by a few. Faced with no obvious alternative method for keeping slaves under subjugation in an urban environment in which many were outside the control of their owners, those in charge began a process of regulating the scale and form of brutal punishment that made the new state complicit in terrorizing the population. The carceral society Foucault envisioned, in which the citizens of the modern state internalized the mechanisms for their own control, had little basis in a society made up of masters and slaves.

Reducing the degree and frequency of indiscriminate police attacks on slaves and the free lower classes did not mean that whipping was quickly eliminated. It remained as the formally sanctioned coercive basis of both private and public subjugation of slaves, and the state increasingly assumed the role in the urban environment of the whip-wielding overseer on the rural estate. An edict of December 1823 confirmed the authority of the police to whip slaves in the act of arrest, and in March 1826 the intendant ordered that any slave arrested for capoeira be summarily given one hundred lashes and detention in the Calabouço slave jail, where owners could retrieve them after paying the cost of their subsistence since arrest.[37] The approach after 1821, in slave whipping and other aspects of police activity, was increasingly to refine and standardize procedures, making the instruments of repression more precise and efficient. This trend toward specificity, exerting just the force necessary to maintain an acceptable level of "order and public tranquility," was not a rejection of the authoritarian methods of Viana and Vidigal. Rather the period from 1808 to 1821 was a period of institution building and experimentation, and the problem eventually became that of regulating a police force that had been delegated wide authority at the time of its establishment in 1808–9. Military discipline, standing orders, and specific instructions were one set of techniques for directing and controlling police activity. Requiring the police to submit to civilian judicial authority through warrants, hearings, and court orders was another. Turning Vidigal and his grenadiers loose on the streets of the city to bludgeon "idlers and vagrants" and subjecting slaves to three hundred strokes of the lash for playing a drum or carrying a stick officially gave way to arrest and jail on a judicial order for free people and one hundred strokes and detention in the Calabouço for slaves.

Control, of course, was far from perfect in 1823, and recurrent institutional experimentation to keep up with the growth and change of Rio de Janeiro preoccupied those in charge of the police in the succeeding decades. But by the 1820's patterns were established that informed later efforts. With independence Brazilian authorities had the autonomy to do what they thought best, given their perception of the problem and the resources they had available. They self-consciously manipulated the instruments of state power to extend their authority into the public space of the capital city. The 1824 Constitution set forth the structure of government and included a variety of statements of general principle, but it left many of the fine points to subsequent ordinary legislation. It mentioned in passing that an elective system of local justices of the peace should be established and anticipated that a criminal code would provide for detailed guidelines and procedures in that area. Several institutional experiments were tried before and after the promulgation of the constitution with varying degrees of success. Some of these measures became notorious and some were never fully implemented, but together they illustrate how the authorities of the 1820's perceived the problem of unacceptable public behavior and what they tried to do about it.

The Curfew of Aragão

In the aftermath of intendant João Ignácio da Cunha's restrictions on whipping and similar arbitrary police action at the time of independence, thefts, assaults, and general disruption of life in the city seemed to increase. Even the 1823 formal reintroduction of whipping at the point of arrest did not have the desired effect, and in January 1825 a new police intendant, Francisco Alberto Teixeira de Aragão, issued a set of police regulations that became known in Rio as Aragão's curfew (*o toque do* Aragão). This edict authorized police patrols to make inquiries of anyone they felt disposed to stop. Any person, slave or free, who failed to submit to questioning was considered to be resisting authority and would be subject to "whatever violent methods the circumstances require." As an incentive for police diligence, rewards were authorized of 4$000 for the arrest of a thief (*ladrão*) and 20$000 for a robber who attacked his victims (*salteador*), to be paid to members of the police force or any private citizen. The rewards were to be paid out of the property of the person arrested, if he had any. (The regular salary of a soldier in the Guarda Real was 2$400 per month at this time, so the arrest of a thief could bring considerable bonus pay.)

A curfew was established of 10 P.M. in the summer and 9 P.M. in winter after which patrols were authorized to stop and search anyone for illegal weapons or instruments that might be used in a crime. To signal the curfew the bells of São Francisco Church and São Bento monastery were to ring for a solid half hour so that no one could claim ignorance of the time of day. The order for enforcement carried the restriction that it not be abused "nor be applied to well known persons of integrity (*nem se adote para com as pessoas notoriamente conhecidas e de probidade*)." Slaves could be searched at any time of the day or night and were to be whipped for possession of any weapon including wooden sticks. After curfew, whistling in the streets or passing any similar signal was prohibited, and this prohibition was extended "to blacks and men of color any time after dark, even if prior to the curfew." Any slave found after curfew "in any store, tavern, bar, or gambling house" was to be sent to the Calabouço and whipped; any free person was to pay a fine of 4$800 for the first such offense (more than a week's wages for a free artisan) and double that for the second. The owner or cashier of the offending establishment was also to pay a fine of 9$600, double that for the second infraction, triple that and loss of his operating license for a third offense. The same penalty was to apply to businesses that permitted gatherings on their premises, "especially blacks, after their business was completed." Any store or tavern that bought stolen goods from slaves was to pay a fine of 40$000 and be closed permanently. The edict imposed heavy fines on property owners who rented rooms to vagrants, persons of bad conduct (*mal procedidos*), professional gamblers, those with no visible means of support or who had "scandalous customs," an antique euphemism for promoting prostitution. Any fines collected in the enforcement of these regulations were to be divided with half going to the arresting officers or citizens and half to the intendancy of police. As part of the new incentives, Aragão increased the size of the Guarda Real de Polícia and ordered that its officers be paid a monthly bonus from the coffers of the intendancy of police in addition to their army salaries.[38]

Aragão's instructions, centering on the curfew and on the sites of public entertainment and social interaction for both slaves and the nonslave lower classes, put the civil rights provisions of the constitution in a more realistic context. "The law will be the same for all" turned out to be a high-minded statement of principle that had little to do with life on the streets. Slaves could expect to encounter special barriers because they were property, not citizens. But these regulations explicitly discriminated against free blacks and men of color as well. On the other end of the scale, persons of "integrity" were spared the restrictions of the curfew and the indignity of being searched for weapons. More broadly, these regulations discriminated against activities that the white elite for the most part did not engage in, but which were central to the social life of poor people and slaves in Rio.

Among the measures never put into full operation was a royal edict of November 1825 ordering the establishment of assistants for the intendant of police to be called *comissários*. The regulations that were to govern this new position illustrate the public order concerns of this transitional period, reflecting the particular attention the highest authorities of the imperial government gave to activity they found threatening. Among the nineteen detailed articles, many of which duplicated the regulations Aragão had issued in January, was the following: "Because the most important duty of the police is to repress and prevent crimes," comissários were to impede any assemblage, day or night, that might result in disorders, "especially gatherings of blacks, slave or free."[39] There was special concern for the free rabble, the social detritus that fell in the margins of this society of masters and slaves. Comissários were not to allow in their jurisdictions "vagrants, deserters, or individuals who have no profession or means of subsistence, nor persons of scandalous customs, those who live from gambling or other illicit activity, those who engage in ostentatious display or have objects of great value" without adequate explanation. Similarly, they were to "proceed against beggars, those faking illness, hermits, people requesting alms etc. without a permit from the police or beyond the limits the police establish." Comissários would keep close vigilance over strangers arriving in their jurisdictions to find out if they were suspected of crimes or if they had the necessary "titles, permits, or passports." Among the varied duties of the intendant was to control people's movements by issuing permits to both foreigners and Brazilian citizens for travel both within the country and to and from other countries. Any stranger without such a passport was automatically suspect.[40]

As one might expect, there were special provisions regulating slavery and the activities of slaves. Comissários were to eradicate quilombos by all means at their disposal and turn over to the intendant for reward all quilombolas and other escaped slaves as well as thieves and bandits. They were to register all professional slave hunters, the *capitães do mato*, and supervise them closely, demanding to be informed of all slaves they captured "to prevent extortion from owners, and so that such slaves are not held for long periods in stocks or private jails." Any slave arrested for disorderly conduct, illegal weapons possession, or committing any crime was to be "immediately whipped in the most public place of the district." Such whippings were to be independent of any further criminal prosecution the offense might call for and were not to exceed one hundred lashes at a time.

Aragão's regulations and the comissário proposal, although they came after the constitution and other statements of liberal principle restricting police action in favor of individual rights, were a reversion to the spirit of absolutism.[41] Their basis lay in the ancient law codes and the decrees and regulations accumulated during the period of criminal legislation by fiat of the king or his delegated agents. With that general background and precedent to draw upon, these measures were also pragmatic and specific responses to the perceived social problems in the urban environment. While Aragão's curfew was remembered for years—everyone in the city was subjected to the half hour of incessant church bells every evening—the comissário structure was not fully executed even in the city of Rio de Janeiro and was soon left aside in favor of a quite different initiative—the justice of the peace.

The Justice of the Peace

The locally elected lay judge was a project envisioned in the 1824 Constitution and was dear to the hearts of the liberal reformers of the first empire, as the reign of Pedro I is known. As the first clear break with the concept of judicial authority emanating from the monarch, the justice of the peace had the potential to be a major turning point in the way power was exercised and society regulated.[42] The proposal to institute the justice of the peace was debated from 1824 on, and the law authorizing the institution was approved in October 1827. From the start the main proponents of the institution saw the police function of the local judge as central to their purpose. Bernardo Pereira de Vasconcelos, a central figure in the liberal reform group in parliament and an advocate of the new judicial position, said in parliament in June 1827 that "we want to establish a judge that I will call 'of police' (*policial*). Even though the name does not strike me as very appropriate, I'll leave it at that." Vasconcelos went on to criticize the traditional approach to policing in Brazil, which focused on punishment after a crime was committed. The justice of the peace, he said, would correct that "error of our predecessors" by "assuming the duty of preventing infractions."[43]

The law of 15 October 1827 did give the local elective judge broad powers to exercise vigilance over his jurisdiction, break up illegal gatherings, gather evidence of crimes, and arrest and judge violators. Whatever foreign models might have inspired the initiative (the British, French, and United States prototypes were invoked at the time), the mandate of the justice of the peace as both a police agent and local judge followed the Portuguese colonial tradition of combining such functions in the hands of local officials. The difference was the source of the authority and legitimacy of the justice of the peace, which would come from the people who elected him rather than from the monarch. Also like the colonial pattern, in which deliberately overlapping jurisdictions served as a sort of inefficient check on the arbitrary whims of individual office holders, the mandate of the justice of the peace overlapped in Rio with those of the intendant of police and his subordinate criminal judges.

The anomaly of an elected judge at the local level with no clear relationship to the appointed judicial hierarchy bothered some involved in the discussion of the proposal. Diogo Antônio Feijó, a member of the moderate liberal faction in parliament who later became minister of justice and regent, expressed such reservations during the 1827 debates and advocated a mechanism by which an appointed district judge (*Juiz de Direito*) would have the authority to review the decisions of the justices of the peace. He intended this power of oversight to make the justices more cautious in their deliberations and to spare the common people, who would have little other recourse, from arbitrary lower court rulings.[44] No such clause was included in the law creating the office, but in 1831 Feijó used his authority as minister of justice to bring the justices of the peace in Rio into the authority structure of the central government, stripping them of autonomous jurisdiction.

No one seemed quite sure in 1827 how these contradictions would be worked out in practice, and it was easier for the liberal ideologues in parliament to create a local police magistrate in principle than to establish the functioning system of repression that Vasconcelos wanted to see in place. What there was of the latter in Rio was left in the hands of the intendant and the Guarda Real, which were not affected by the law creating the justice of the peace. Like his appointed predecessors, the justice of the peace was authorized to call up the militia in times of crisis. He was also authorized to appoint civilian ward inspectors (*inspetores de quarteirão*) in his jurisdiction, the unpaid part-time volunteers who were to assist in local surveillance. But without control over a functioning police force the justice of the peace had no instrument by which to carry out his police mandate. It was like hiring a carpenter and providing him with a nail and a board; what was missing was the hammer. In any case the first holders of the office in Rio de Janeiro were not elected until 1830. The initiative was not put to the test in the capital until the eve of the fundamental political crisis following the abdication of Pedro I in April 1831, an experience that changed the institution in practice from the theoretical ideals the reformers envisioned in 1827.

State Control of Slaves

There are several other developments of the 1820's that predated the establishment of the justice of the peace as a functioning institution and thus are part of the context in which the elected judges eventually operated. One important example of the widening state authority during the 1820's was the elimination in Rio de Janeiro of the capitães do mato (bush captains), the private bounty hunters who at least as far back as the seventeenth century had been an important part of the system of maintaining control over slaves in Brazil. In many areas they became a proto-police force with their own armed assistants who were granted concessions by local governments to hunt down fugitive slaves.[45] In a prestate administrative system, semiprivate institutions like the capitão do mato, tax farming, and the granting of permits to build private toll roads, helped the government achieve objectives considered of public utility with a minimum of direct expense or administrative burden. For the state builders of the early nineteenth century, such mechanisms confused the private interests of the contractors with the public objectives of the state.

Slave owners wanted to minimize escapes but had to balance the burdens of the constant imprisonment or armed surveillance of their workers against the fees paid to the capitão do mato. Both were elements of the administrative overhead costs of forced labor. In contrast, because he was a private operator paid a fee for each successful operation, the capitão do mato had an interest in maximizing the number of runaways available for capture. Without them he would be out of a job. He also had the option of choosing for himself whether or not to exercise his profession, how diligent he was to be, and how to negotiate the terms by which he would return the slaves he brought in. For example, no official could force a capitão do mato to attack a quilombo if the bounty hunter considered the risks higher than the potential profit. Calling in army troops was a cumbersome alternative not adaptable to the small-scale or individual operations the bush captains specialized in. The dedication a capitão do mato and several armed assistants brought to hunting runaways came from the shared expectation of a monetary reward. To a similarly small squad of army conscripts being assigned to head for the hills in pursuit of an escaped slave would be tantamount to an invitation to desert. As frustrating as government officials and the slave-holding class might have found such shortcomings, they had no practical way of replacing the private bounty hunters with a more manageable and efficient system until the institutional expansion of the late colonial and early independence period.

The police institutions established in Rio after 1808 eventually took over the task that bush captains had formerly handled, as the apprehension of escaped slaves became the most important specific category of police activity (as reflected in the 1810–21 data in Appendix 3). At that point the capitão do mato became not only superfluous but a threat to the very system he was supposed to assist

in maintaining. The intendant received a series of reports of capitães do mato accused of kidnapping slaves and holding them for
ransom or illegal sale. (Separate from the 751 cases of capture of
escaped slaves shown in Appendix 3, for example, under crimes
against property there are two cases of theft of slaves for delivery
to a capitão do mato.) Reportedly this was sometimes done with the
connivance of the slave, who would later secretly get a share in the
booty thus extorted from the owner as the price for getting his
slave back. Guarda Real squads raided camps of bounty hunters
who were illegally holding slaves on the outskirts of the city or were
violating the recently imposed restrictions on weapons possession
by private individuals. In a police action of December 1822, six "soldiers of a capitão do mato" were arrested along with the six slaves
they were holding for ransom and one slave who was not a fugitive;
in early February 1823 a bush captain named Apolinário da Costa
Gonçalves was arrested in the company of Isabel Maria, a mulatta
former slave, and seven slaves they were planning to sell illegally
"in other parts" (fora da terra).[46] The campaign was eventually successful, and after the 1820's the private slave hunters no longer
figured importantly in the network of repression in and around
the city either as auxiliary force or as criminal element.

This modernization of the system for hunting down escaped
slaves made the resolution of this problem more efficient and put
it under state control. Making police responsible for slave hunting
also prevented the private interests of the capitão do mato from
becoming a source of disruption and eliminated an autonomous
armed authority that violated the principle of monopoly on the
exercise of force that is characteristic of the modern state. The
same armed gangs that engaged in the formerly legitimate task of
capturing escaped slaves could too easily slip into highway robbery
or attacks on rural residents. Monetary rewards for capturing
slaves were still offered to police soldiers as an incentive to diligence, but the Guarda Real was always available on call, and military discipline required its members to go after fugitives when so
ordered. Nevertheless, the problem of slave hunters making illegal
and excessive demands on the owners was not necessarily resolved
by eliminating private operators in favor of the police, if Luccock's
observations serve. In the English merchant's blunt assessment, the
Guarda Real soldiers "soon became corrupt, abused their authority, and not only individually engaged in practices inconsistent

with their office, but adopted a general system of violence and extortion."[47]

With the elimination of the capitão do mato during the 1820's, controlling the urban slave population became increasingly shared by the owners and the state. Another area of such collaboration in the mutual interest of subjugating the slave population was in the direct task of disciplinary punishment. Through the 1820's police authorities continued to administer correctional whippings at the slave owners' request, charging a minimal fee of 160 réis per hundred strokes plus 40 réis per day for subsistence and asking no questions about the supposed offense. One relic of the slave era that should still shock the modern reader is the ledger recording receipt of payment for this service for the year 1826. A total of 1,786 slaves, among them 262 women, were whipped in the Calabouço at their masters' request during the year, an average of nearly five per day. Most were subjected to 200 strokes of the lash, while a few got by with 50 and another few suffered 400 strokes.[48] At such a rate the jail staff had to spend several hours of every working day whipping slaves. It is necessary to see this system not simply as a case of the state providing a paid disciplinary service for the private interests of slave owners. In a larger context with slavery so pervasive in early nineteenth-century Rio, so central to the economic relations and class structure of Brazilian society, the whipping service was system maintenance. It puts in stark relief the state as an instrument of the dominant class, serving the need of that class to control through physical violence those who provided the muscle power on which this commercial economy depended. (These 1826 data also provide a contrast to the whipping services cities in the southern United States provided to slave owners. An 1807 ordinance in Charleston, South Carolina, set a fee of 25 cents for the correctional whipping of slaves in the city's workhouse, limited to a maximum of 20 strokes. In New Orleans the maximum was 25 lashes, and the service cost 12.5 cents.)[49]

Prisons

The police institutions established in 1808 represented clear steps toward more comprehensive and standardized means of controlling behavior, but the fate of those punished beyond a summary beating on the street or a judicially ordered flogging changed little from the previous century. Police reform preceded penal reform by several decades, and the city's jails were no more than dungeons and holding tanks where people were locked up together for the terms meted out by a variety of authorities. In the 1830's the construction of a House of Correction on a modern mold got under way, eventually ameliorating the conditions of incarceration, but in the period of João VI and Pedro I being jailed meant being confined in miserable squalor.

The Calabouço, where slave whippings took place, was located on the side of Castelo hill facing Guanabara Bay, near the Santa Casa de Misericórdia hospital. (The word *calabouço* takes its meaning from the bilge deck of a ship, connoting a dark and humid dungeon.) It was the only jail in the city designated exclusively for slaves, but not the only one in which slaves found themselves. Perhaps two hundred slaves were crammed together in its several large rooms at any one time. Most were sent there by their owners for correctional whipping, but captured runaways were also held there until claimed by their owners, as were slaves "on deposit" who might be property of the estate of a deceased owner awaiting disposition of the inheritance or slaves sold but awaiting transfer to a new owner. Sanitary conditions were horrible, as were the heat and stench in the unventilated bays, and the scant food that jailors were supposed to supply from fees charged the slave owners. A recurring problem in the Calabouço was that when the fees due for holding or whipping a slave accumulated to an amount exceeding what the owner thought the person being punished was worth, the owner might simply abandon his property. Procedures called for such forfeited slaves to be sold at auction so the government might recover what it could of the cost of running the institution, make space in the jail, and get the slaves back into the hands of someone who might use them. When the new minister of justice of the provisional regency looked into the situation in the Calabouço in May 1831, he ordered the sale of the many slaves "whose owners have not appeared for years."[50]

The Calabouço was only one of several prisons existing in Rio in 1808 that made use of former military facilities. Forts had been built on the hills of the city and the islands in Rio Bay since the Portuguese first permanently occupied the site in the 1560's to expel French interlopers. During the eighteenth century several massive fortifications were built over the old sites. Paid for with the mineral wealth of the gold boom, they were made necessary by the recurring colonial wars of the period. By the early nineteenth century they had become militarily superfluous for the most part, but with thick walls, sentry posts and guardhouses, and solidly constructed powder magazines they were easily converted to hold prisoners in instead of enemies out. At various times the forts on the islands of Cobras, Santa Barbara, Lage, and Villegaignon, as well as the São João and Santa Cruz forts on opposite sides of the entrance to the bay, were used as prisons. At times of civil disturbance excess prisoners were sometimes held on ships anchored in the harbor, and short-term detainees were often kept at temporary facilities adjacent to police stations and guardhouses scattered around the city.

As unpleasant as a term in one of these facilities was, none of them could rival the Aljube jail. According to several detailed firsthand reports, both the Calabouço and the Aljube were execrable, but the Aljube, where most people imprisoned for common crimes and minor offenses served their sentences from 1808 to 1856, usually came off worse. From 1747 until the arrival of the Portuguese court in 1808, the main jail for common criminals had been located in the courthouse next to the viceroy's palace, which became the royal palace. To convert the courthouse into temporary lodging for members of the royal entourage, the government needed another site to lock up criminals. They requested the use of an ecclesiastical jail the church had built in 1732 at the base of Conceição hill. (*Aljube* is the Arabic word for ecclesiastical jail. By the perquisites of their estate, priests in colonial times could be tried only by church tribunals, whether for violating church regulations or for criminal offenses, and were detained only in ecclesiastical jails.) The Aljube by 1808 far exceeded the church's needs, so the bishop agreed to the request, provided one cell be set aside for the disciplinary detention of priests as needed.[51]

The Aljube had nine rooms of varying sizes on the ground floor that could be used as prisons, plus a series of smaller rooms above that would serve as a reception area, infirmary, and jailor's offices. Police officials calculated that allotting each prisoner a floor area of 7 by 12 spans (about 4.7 by 8 feet), the Aljube had space for 192 people. It became the destination of most people, whether slave or free, being held for trial or sentenced for petty offenses and common crime, and the most violent and hardened bandit was tossed in the same room with a boy accused of filching a piece of fruit in the market. It was poorly ventilated and poorly drained; the rear of the building was cut into the solid rock of the hill behind and groundwater constantly dripped into the rooms holding prisoners. In 1828 an inspection committee sent to the Aljube by the municipal council of Rio reported their revulsion at entering this "bilge containing all vices, this infernal cave. . . . The appearance of the prisoners made us tremble in horror. Poorly covered with filthy rags, they approach on all sides complaining against whoever sent them to such torture (*suplício*), without convicting them of any crime." The ground-floor dungeons were entered through a hatch in the ceiling, and in the largest they counted 85 men, slave and free, sleeping on the damp stone floor. The accompanying jailors told them that in the two rooms with the worst conditions "many prisoners die of suffocation, especially in the summer." The inspectors counted a total of 390 prisoners. Recalculating the floor space, each person confined to the Aljube in 1828 had an area of about two feet by four feet. By early 1831 the prisoner population of the Aljube was reported to be "more than 500."[52]

What the inspectors heard from some of the wretched creatures in the dungeons of the Aljube about being locked up without being convicted of a crime may well have been the case. One of the main criticisms liberal reformers made of the old legal and judicial system was that it was arbitrary. In practice this meant that charging a person with a crime, the basis for conviction, and the sentence were largely left to the whim of the presiding magistrate. If the judge were the intendant of police or one of the criminal judges who assisted him, the case was disposed of by the same authority under which the arrest was made. There was no public or officially neutral presence at the judicial proceeding and at the lower level for minor crime there was often no record of the case. A petty thief or a man who had beat up another in a brawl or insulted a police officer was brought before the presiding authority, the arresting officer or a bailiff stated the charge and described the event, and the judge pronounced sentence. The culprit was immediately taken to the Aljube and dropped down a hatch into a stinking pit. When another inspection was carried out in 1833 the chief of police found 340 prisoners in the Aljube, for 43 of whom there were no records. No one could say why they were there, what their sentence was, or how much of it they had served.[53]

The Criminal Code

This situation moved reformers to advocate a code defining criminal activity clearly and prescribing the punishment for each type of offense. A separate code of criminal procedure would then specify the way a person accused of a crime would be treated after arrest. The procedural code appeared in 1832, but in December 1830, before Pedro I abandoned the throne and precipitated an institutional crisis at the highest level, parliament had approved a criminal code that specified principles set forth in the 1824 Constitution, fulfilling a major objective of the liberal reformers. It became the legal basis for police action for nearly sixty years until it was replaced by the similar but updated penal code of the republic in 1890.[54]

The code definitively replaced the arbitrary and inconsistent accretion of laws and regulations Viana and Vidigal worked under, which were still reflected in Aragão's 1825 regulations and because of which people were left to rot in the Aljube jail. Under the old regime the intendant of police and a variety of other judicial and administrative authorities could declare an activity illegal simply by issuing a regulation. Those orders often specified a penalty, but punishment might also be determined by the circumstances. Deciding whether specific activity fell under a law or regulation was left to lower-level police and judicial authorities. Later legal scholars criticized the 1830 code for some ambiguity and mild punishments, but it was a major improvement over the previous era. The code defined what behavior was considered criminal, the degrees of culpability and complicity, the mitigating and aggravating circumstances. It prohibited punishment under ex post facto laws as well as any punishment not established by law, established degrees of punishment to fit specific crimes, and generally satisfied the liberal urge to bring Brazil into the modern era. Although a few offenses were added to the original list, and some penalties were altered in later legislation, the 1830 code was remarkably comprehensive and consistent for the time. Several of its general provisions deserve comment as reflections of the political and ideological environment in which the code was written and as background for understanding its eventual application by police and judicial authorities.

The most severe punishment was death by hanging, to be imposed only on the leaders of slave insurrections involving twenty or more persons, murder under aggravating circumstances or committed during a robbery. The first major alteration of the code, following the suppression of a planned slave rebellion in Salvador, Bahia, in 1835, also made it a capital crime for a slave to murder or inflict serious injury on his owner, a member of the owner's family or household, or his overseer. Next in severity was *galés* (literally, "galleys," recalling the time when such a sentence was served chained to a bench while rowing a ship). This meant labor on public works, and those serving galés were to wear leg irons and chains, either alone or in groups, at all times. "Prison with labor," in contrast to galés, referred to daily labor inside a prison establishment, not involving chains and shackles. "Simple prison" was confinement with no requirement that the inmate work.[55] Fines were assessed like a form of progressive taxation, with heavier fines for those with more ability to pay. They were determined "by what the condemned could earn per day from his property, employment, or industry." The crime of "light physical injury," for example, was to be punished by "one month to one year in prison, and a fine corresponding to half the time" of the sentence. If the judge sentenced a person to six months in prison and a fine of half the time, the monetary amount of the fine was calculated according to what the normal income of the condemned person would have been for three months. A convict unable to pay a fine was to have it commuted to sufficient time in prison with labor to earn wages equivalent to the fine.

Although the criminal code necessarily made more explicit references to slaves than did the 1824 Constitution, there was never a special body of legislation, or *code noire*, specific to slaves in Brazil. Slaves were often referred to in legal documents as "slave persons" (*pessoas escravas*), responsible for their actions and subject to punishment for the same crimes as free people (with the exception of the crime of "insurrection," which only slaves could commit). The major difference was in the form of punishment. Capital punishment and galés were to apply in the same way to slave or free. Lesser penalties for slaves were to be converted to whipping, the number to be set in the sentence. Article 60 of the criminal code did not go on to specify how many strokes of the lash were to replace a given term in prison, but it did specify that no more than 50 lashes were to be administered in any given day, and after the punishment the slave was to be returned to his or her owner. Although tempered somewhat by the limitation, the lash continued to serve its triple purpose. It remained the degrading and brutal symbol of slave status, it ensured that the owners would be deprived of as little of the slave's labor time as possible, and it was considered to hurt the slave to a degree similar to a prison term for a nonslave. Only those who felt the cut of rawhide on their bare flesh could evaluate such an equivalency. Free people, including former slaves, were not to suffer whipping or any other corporal punishment or torture. Reducing a free person to slavery was a crime punishable by three to nine years in prison, "but never less than the time of the illegal captivity of the victim, plus one-third," in addition to a fine equal to one-third the time of the sentence. The code made no explicit mention, however, of the relationship between master and slave or any rights or restrictions regarding either party.

Women received more special attention in the code than slaves. A woman pregnant at the time of conviction for a capital crime was not to be executed until 40 days after giving birth. Women convicted of a crime for which the normal sentence was galés would serve the term in prison with labor instead. In the definitions of specific crimes, there were some hints of the attitudes of the writers of the code toward women and of the status of women in this patriarchal society. "Deflowering a virgin" less than seventeen years old was a separate crime from seducing an "honest woman" of the same age, but for either the penalty was exile for one to three years from the district where the victim lived. Rape was considered of two types. "Carnal copulation with any honest woman through violence or threats" was punishable by three to twelve years in prison, but if the victim were a prostitute, the penalty was to be one month to two years in prison. Kidnapping (*rapto*) only applied to the taking of women "for libidinous purposes," by violence if the victim were over seventeen and by violence or seduction if she were under that age. There were to be no penalties for any of these "crimes against the security of honor" if marriage between perpetrator and victim followed the event in question. And for all of these offenses an additional penalty was that the offender was to provide a dowry for the victim, unless he raped a prostitute.

Whatever such legal artifacts might suggest about the society that produced the criminal code, police and the courts were hardly burdened with many cases relating to "the security of honor." The dominant concern of the police was with the "common" crimes of theft (*furto*, taking property without the knowledge or permission of its owner) and robbery (*roubo*, involving threat or injury to the property owner during the act of theft); threats, insults, resisting arrest; physical injury both light (causing pain but not permanent damage) and serious (causing permanent physical damage to the victim); and vagrancy, begging, and possession of illegal weapons. These crimes were defined and regulated by the criminal code, but there were many other minor violations that preoccupied the police but which were not mentioned in the 1830 document. These included the public order offenses of disorderly conduct, public drunkenness, and curfew violation, as well as activities on the margin of legality such as gambling and prostitution. Many of these and similarly undesirable activities were regulated by city ordinances, and others continued to be proscribed by police regulations and unspecified tradition in the interest of "order and public tranquility." But the criminal code set the standards and the framework within which such lower-level regulations and police procedures developed.

Conclusion

The standardization of the criminal code, like modernizing the police, expanding state control over hunting runaway slaves, and providing a correctional whipping service for slave owners, had the general objective of making institutions more responsive to the needs of the members of the Brazilian elite who took over the colonial regime and began to create from it a state that would function in their interest. From the standpoint of the social class that made the rules and created the police to enforce them, part of what needed establishing and protecting—less tangible than person, property, or public building—was an urban environment of order, calm, and stability. For the people who ran Rio de Janeiro, the purpose of the city was to provide port facilities, commercial and financial services, and administrative and regulatory activity in support of international and regional commerce and export agriculture. Another important set of activities in the national capital involved the institutions of government, from the royal household to parliament to the ministries of state and the army and navy. None of these and other related support activities, including the routine of daily life, could operate smoothly in an atmosphere of uncertainty, disruption, and fear.

Nor could the city function if the slaves who labored in the lower reaches of nearly every institution and activity stopped working or turned on their captors. A given individual act of recalcitrance, flight, disruption, or counterattack from a person in bondage or relegated to the margins of society might not in itself threaten the relations of domination and subjugation by which Rio de Janeiro society was bound together, but such an act could not go unanswered. Impunity would set a bad example and could lead to a more serious breach in the invisible wall of the prison of enslavement and the invisible barriers by which the nonslave rabble were kept at bay. The recurring refrain of "order and public tranquility" was not invoked for some abstract moral reason, but because without an adequate level of such conditions the city would not work.

Whatever else we might conclude about the slaves and free lower classes of the city, we must recognize that they had little immediate, positive interest in following the rules of behavior written by the elite or in maintaining an environment in which the public and private business of Rio de Janeiro could be efficiently transacted. They did have an interest in avoiding Vidigal's cudgel, sparing themselves from being chained to a post and whipped mercilessly, breaking rock on a road gang, or spending time in the dank and fetid dungeons of the Calabouço or Aljube jails. Coercion and subjugation were required in order to reach the level of order and calm that the people who issued the laws and created the police wanted to achieve. The resistance of slaves and the nonslave lower classes was met by a new apparatus of police and legal codes that had not existed in colonial times and that had been established with the explicit intent of repressing behavior unacceptable to those in charge.

From the establishment of the police intendancy in 1808 to the promulgation of the criminal code in 1830, Brazil went a long way toward autonomy—not when Prince Pedro drew his sword on the banks of the Ipiranga and shouted "independence or death" on 7 September 1822, but when the Brazilian elite began to take charge of its own internal affairs and to build the institutions and procedures of independent nationhood. The intendancy and the Guarda Real de Polícia remained in Rio de Janeiro as important legacies of the last years of the colonial regime, but those two related agencies had been adapted piecemeal to the demands of the new era. By 1830 the office of justice of the peace seemed to its advocates to hold the potential for reordering the relationship between the population and the authority of the state, and the criminal code was widely hailed as providing the basis for curbing the arbitrary exercise of state power, making life predictable and creating an environment that was amenable for conducting the public and private business of the capital of the empire. With Pedro I on the throne, however, political independence was not yet complete. Nor had the institutional transition run its course. Several crises in 1831–32 hurried the process along portentously.

THREE

Crisis, 1831-32

Dramatic events in 1831 and 1832 brought the liberal reforms of the first empire and hopes for an orderly transition to full nationhood fundamentally into question. Out of that traumatic period came institutions and procedures of repression that from the street looked remarkably like the old days of absolutism. The period from the late 1820's to the late 1830's is often viewed as the "liberal decade" or the "liberal interlude" in the political history of Brazil.[1] For the people in the lower reaches of urban society, however, such a periodization is inappropriate. If there was a liberal interlude for people affected by the police system in Rio de Janeiro, it was a brief time in 1821 and 1822 when João Ignácio da Cunha replaced Paulo Fernandes Viana as police intendant and issued orders restricting the beating of people at the moment of arrest. The effects of that reaction to absolutist policy lingered, but the trend from then on was back toward tightening control. By late 1832 that system was in place and in operation, ready to be turned to repression that focused on social rather than political opponents.

The streets and squares of the national capital were quite literally the stage on which major events were played out in times of political crisis, and never more so than in the tumultuous period from April 1831 to April 1832. As politics moved from the chambers of parliament and palace corridors into public space, it involved a threat to public tranquility, the maintenance of which was always a first priority of government. The institutions and policies that emerged from that series of crises—the subordination of local police and judicial processes to the minister of justice, the formation of a new militarized police force also under the minister of justice—became the basis for the police system of the rest of the empire. The institutional legacy of that turbulent time remains to this day in Rio de Janeiro and in major urban centers throughout Brazil, in ways unforeseen by the politicians whose immediate task was to save their government from assault from several quarters and keep the slaves under submission and the lower classes under control.

The civil and military police of the empire had their precedents in the intendancy established in 1808 and the Guarda Real de Polícia of the following year, and those institutions in some ways represented the formalization of practices through the colonial era. Thus there was considerable continuity in the function of the new structures emerging from the cauldron of 1831–32. At the same time that cauldron was hot enough to melt the old molds, and the clear break with the past completed the process of political independence and institutional innovation begun with the arrival of the Portuguese court in 1808. As at other times in Brazil's history, the crisis was political, involving power struggles among factions of the elite and their supporters, but the resolution had broad social results. Out of the 1831–32 watershed came mechanisms of repression persisting far beyond the power vacuum that followed the first emperor's decision to abandon his throne.

Abdication of Pedro I

In the late 1820's many signs pointed to the impossibility of Pedro I retaining his position. There were forces pulling him to more direct involvement in European dynastic politics but even stronger pressures to push him out of Brazil. The authority of the intendant of police and the Guarda Real waned along with that of the monarch, and in March 1831 gangs of radical nativists began to wage sporadic battles with pro-Portuguese toughs in the streets of Rio. Minister of Justice Manoel José de Souza França, who was sympathetic to the nativist cause (and served in the same post through the first few weeks of the regency), took the lead by calling the recently elected justices of peace in the city together and instructing them to patrol their districts as police. In their support the minister ordered loyal infantry and cavalry troops to be stationed at strategic points, at the disposal of the justices of the peace. Such an unprecedented expedient was necessary, the minister recalled, because the police intendancy "was so discredited in public opinion that it would have been idle to expect it to achieve any results in the pacification of the animated spirits" abroad in the streets.[2] Thus the first major initiative to put into operation the police powers vested in the elected judges came from the ministry of justice, as did the troops to back up the judges' authority.

By the time a crowd of several thousand soldiers and citizens converged on the Campo de Santana on 6 April, the justices of the peace, who were among the few holders of public office not beholden to the emperor, had emerged as popular leaders. A delegation of the justices presented Pedro with the crowd's demands that he appoint a Brazilian ministry to replace his pro-Portuguese advisors. His refusal precipitated the abdication in the early hours of the following morning.[3] That act left the legitimacy of the ensuing regency in question, and the military units that had joined the civilian nativist crowds and forced the fall of the emperor remained in various degrees of insubordination during the ensuing weeks. In November 1830, before the abdication, parliament had passed a law reducing the size of the army, which had swollen during the Cisplatine War of 1825–28 to some 30,000 men, to a modest 12,000. Such a direct attack on the military may have led some officers to support or acquiesce in Pedro's abdication, but the provisional regency treated them no better. Among its first actions was a decree of 4 May 1831, confirming a total authorized troop strength of 12,000 nationwide. Under the May decree, the Rio de Janeiro garrison would consist of four infantry battalions of 572 men each, and one battalion of fixed artillery of 492 men, for a total of 2,780 army troops in the city.[4] Many rank-and-file soldiers were summarily dismissed from service in the process of reducing the size of the army. But cutting the army by more than half deprived many officers of the basis for their status and influence: the presence of troops under arms. A duly commissioned member of the officer corps belonged to a corporate entity which was strongly defensive of its prerogatives, protective of its members, and in some families close to hereditary. While the decree of 4 May was intended to pressure surplus officers to resign, it probably pushed many of them into resuming the seditious position that had been so important on 7 April.

The common soldiers for their part were unruly elements forcibly conscripted from the free lower classes who had no recourse to the exemption from "recruitment" enjoyed by sons of the civilian elite.[5] They lived under the strict routine of the garrison isolated in their daily regimen from surrounding society and were kept in line by rigid discipline and the most brutal and arbitrary forms of punishment, including forced marching with a heavy pack, whipping (the only social category other than slaves and chain gang prisoners so treated), and disciplinary confinement in the dungeons of several forts around the city and the bay. These soldiers could be counted on to take any possible advantage of slackened discipline, and the events in the streets of the capital during 1831 provided a series of such opportunities.

The Law of 6 June 1831

No group should have been more keenly aware of the power of an armed crowd to affect political events than the leaders of the provisional regency. Just such an assembly, stubbornly massed in the Campo de Santana, had been instrumental in forcing Pedro's abdication in April. The political leaders of the regency had nearly two months from the abdication until the general assembly convened to set their legislative agenda. The very first law the assembly approved, on 6 June 1831, gave the central government broad powers to define and maintain "public order." This law marked the beginning of conservative centralization at least in the exercise of police power. It clearly subjected the justices of the peace to central authority in addition to challenging the political leverage of the military units. It was an explicitly transitory measure, but it set a tone and direction as well as several important institutional precedents.[6]

First, the new law increased the penalty for the crime of illegal assembly, which in the criminal code had included only monetary fines, to a three- to nine-month prison term. (Illegal assembly was defined in the code as any meeting of three or more persons with the collective intent to commit a crime or prevent another person from exercising rights or carrying out duties.) It then prohibited unauthorized nighttime gatherings of five or more persons, providing a jail term of one to three months for violators. No evidence of criminal intent was necessary to invoke that measure. Any suspicious person could be stopped by police patrols, and if they found illegal weapons the culprit would be arrested and delivered to the competent authority for prosecution. Any person arrested while committing crimes against public order would henceforth be held without bail. Several provisions had the appearance of strengthening the power of the justice of the peace, who was given authority over public order crimes (such as illegal assembly, weapons possession, disturbing the peace) and the power to deputize a delegate (*delegado*) and appoint up to six officers to form a proto-police staff in each of the sixteen judicial districts in the city. An apparently minor gesture, which nonetheless established an important symbol for civilian police authority, provided for a distinctive badge for these officers "so that they may be recognized, respected, and obeyed." Anyone using such a badge to falsely impersonate a police officer was to spend three months in prison. (A decree of 14 June specified that the justice of the peace would wear a shoulder-to-waist sash one span [*palmo*, about eight inches] wide, of one yellow band bordered by two green bands. His delegate would wear a similar sash of one yellow and one green band.)[7]

Following this expansion of the police personnel directly under the justice of the peace, however, the intendant of police and the existing criminal judges plus two additional criminal judges created by this law for Rio de Janeiro—all agents of the central government—were given the same authority over public order offenses as was given to the justices of the peace. These intentionally overlapping jurisdictions gave the government the right to step in and take over from the justices of the peace when it deemed necessary. More directly, the central government could by this law suspend any justice of the peace found guilty of malfeasance (an offense elaborately defined in article 129 of the criminal code) or negligence, and any judge who failed to proceed "with the necessary diligence" in the prosecution of public order crimes was to be held as an accomplice.

The Municipal Guard

In addition to thus bringing the justices of the peace into the authority structure of the central government, the law of 6 June moved to replace soldiers with civilian municipal guards as the mainstay of the police force in each local judicial district. This short-lived institutional experiment reflects the assumptions of its creators regarding the nature of the public order problem, and their attitudes as to which social categories were arrayed along the battle lines of the social war.

In several ways this organization anticipated the paramilitary national guard authorized in August 1831, particularly in the criteria for membership. In order to ensure that only members of the upper sectors of the socioeconomic hierarchy served as municipal guards, members were to have the qualifications required for electors (i.e., a minimum income of 200$000 per year, excluding former slaves and anyone who had been convicted of a crime). They were not to be paid for their services but would be provided arms and ammunition at government expense and required to serve when called up by the justices of the peace or their delegates. Recognizing that such an armed force was a political risk, the law provided that any of these guards who misused their weapons or failed honorably to carry out their duties, in addition to answering for any crimes thus committed, would be ineligible to serve as guards for one to three years. Establishing this municipal guard was explicitly a temporary expedient "until such time as the national guard is organized." The idea of creating a paramilitary national guard had been under discussion for some months, beginning at least as early as November 1830. A parliamentary committee had in early May presented a draft proposal for establishing the national guard, and it was being discussed and refined even as the law of 6 June was promulgated.[8]

On 14 June the regency issued the regulations organizing the municipal guard that parliament had authorized a week earlier.[9] In each justice-of-the-peace district, the guards were to be formed into squads of 25 to 50 men each. They were to be organized by and under the operational command of the justices of the peace, who would in turn operate under instructions from the government or "other criminal or police authorities." Until such time as the government could arrange to furnish arms and ammunition, members would be required to report for duty with whatever weapons of their own they might have, and if they had no firearms they were to bring for duty at least a lance on a staff ten spans long. As a last resort the civilian militia would be armed with spears.

Surveillance of the population was among the important tasks of the guards, and they were to report to the justice of the peace in their district "any occurrence about which they obtain information by whatever means, relating to public security or regarding private individuals, observing all prudence and secrecy that such information, by its nature, might require." Their general mission was to "maintain public security and arrest malefactors." Included in the oath each member was to swear, in addition to strict obedience to the constituted authorities, was the promise to do everything possible to "suppress disturbances, stop fights, and arrest criminals in the act, reporting immediately any information (they) might receive regarding any criminal act or plans for perpetrating crimes." The municipal guard is best known for its role in the political disturbances during the few months of its existence, but in its founding charge and its day-to-day operation it was a police force intended to repress common crime and violations of public order.

In the fragile institutional environment of 1831, the age-old risk of creating an armed force that might take action on its own or even turn on its creators was in the minds of the regency authorities. One safeguard was the restriction of membership to the propertied or salaried classes, but the government was still concerned about the potential political risk of arming large numbers of civilians. To further specify the hierarchy of authority, the regulations of 14 June stipulated that the municipal guard could take up arms only on the orders of its commanders, who in turn were to give such orders only "when requisitioned by police authorities," which could include the justices of the peace, the intendant of police, or the minister of justice. The guard corps in each district was to have no communication with guards in other districts "under any pretext," nor were guards allowed to "deliberate or make representations" to the government. Any such political meeting would be declared an illegal assembly, and those present would be punished under the provisions of the law of 6 June, the same law authorizing the creation of the municipal guard itself.

A few weeks later on 5 July, the regency government appointed a minister of justice ready and able to put these laws into effect: Diogo Antônio Feijó. He quickly became the strongest figure at a weak moment in the political history of Brazil. Feijó's actions in resolving a series of crises during the year he was minister of justice put a lasting imprint on the police system of Rio de Janeiro.[10]

Police Riot and Popular Rebellion

Concern about the loyalty of military units was justified by an open rebellion just a week after Feijó took office. On 12 July the 26th infantry battalion of the regular army, one of the units scheduled for dissolution under the order of 4 May, declared itself in revolt. Feijó quickly put the newly authorized municipal guard to its first test, bringing together 600 of these armed civilians to surround the rebel barracks near the São Bento monastery. Faced with this response from the government and a promise of no reprisals if they accepted the transfer of their unit out of the capital, the troops agreed to stand down. Still the situation was delicate. A battalion at full strength comprised 572 men, and the government did not have sufficient force or the effective authority to compel the submission of a well-armed unit of such size acting in concert.[11] In order to separate the rebellious soldiers into smaller units while transport ships were made ready, the government decided to use them for guard duty at points around the city on the night of 13 July, the eve of their departure for Bahia. Thus on the night of 13 July the troops of the Guarda Real de Polícia, who provided normal police patrols, had ample opportunity to discuss the situation with their army colleagues who had rebelled at São Bento. Out of these circumstances developed the most serious crisis since the abdication of Pedro I on 7 April.

On 14 July, as ships carried the former rebels of the 26th infantry away from Rio de Janeiro, most of the troops of the Guarda Real de Polícia left their barracks against orders and stormed through the city, looting businesses, attacking passersby, by some reports killing several people, and generally "spreading panic and terror."[12] Following this rampage the police units proceeded to the Campo de Santana in rebellion, accompanied by a growing crowd of civilians, demanding the return of the 26th infantry and an end to corporal punishment in the military.[13] The next morning General José Joaquim de Lima e Silva, military commander of the capital, ordered regular army units to form in Constitution Square (now Praça Tiradentes) just three blocks from the Campo de Santana. Instead of serving to intimidate the rebellious soldiers of the Guarda Real, however, most of the army troops joined their police colleagues in opposing the government. The majority of the military units in Rio, including its police force, joined by civilian advocates of radical liberalism and anti-Portuguese nativism, as well as many sympathetic onlookers, made up a crowd of some four thousand challenging the constituted authorities. The rebels, lubricated by sugarcane brandy, well armed and controlling an area including Constitution Square and the Campo de Santana, engaged in sporadic disputes among themselves, which were punctuated by gunshots and bloodshed. Civilian residents of the area fled toward the waterfront section of the city to find safe haven and remove themselves from cross fire, and some managed to put their families on ships in the harbor to escape the confusion and danger.

Feijó called upon the two houses of the legislature, the cabinet, and the council of state to meet together in the downtown imperial palace, where the child emperor and his tutors were also lodged for the duration of the crisis. The entire hierarchy of the national government was thus collected in one building, virtually besieged. The General Assembly was in continuous session for the next six days, from 9 A.M. on 15 July to 2:30 P.M. on 20 July. To stall for time the government asked the rebels to put their demands in writing for due consideration by the extraordinary session of Parliament. The petition, presented with more than 500 signatures attached, demanded the resignation of the cabinet; the convocation of a constituent assembly to revise the constitution; the deportation of 89 named individuals, including seven senators, members of the council of state, high army officers, judges, and well-known merchants; the dismissal of high government functionaries who were Portuguese by birth; and a prohibition on immigration from Portugal for ten years.[14] Several changes in the cabinet on 17 July resulted from political realignments in the ruling clique, but there was no response to the rebels' petition. One of the changes was the replacement of Minister of War José Manuel de Moraes by General Manuel da Fonseca Lima e Silva, who as commander of the emperor's personal guard had played a decisive role in the abdication of Pedro I three months before. He was the brother of regent General José Francisco Lima e Silva and also brother of the military commander of the capital, General José Joaquim Lima e Silva.

With most of the capital's military units including its police force in open rebellion the city was "submerged in terror." Outlaw elements had reportedly committed murders and robberies at various points in the city. Groups of rebels surrounded the imperial palace itself at one point, chanting slogans, waving weapons in the air, and threatening to set fire to the nearby customshouse. The recently organized municipal guards in Feijó's own words, "withdrew in fear, and because they are poorly armed and without discipline, cannot reestablish order."[15] In an effort to remedy that situation, on 17 July Parliament attempted to reorganize the municipal guard by appointing a general commander, taking operational control out of the hands of the justices of the peace in each district.

The same law expanded eligibility for service to include many young men who could not vote but who were of the same social category as members. The constitutional provisions regarding voting requirements, used to determine eligibility for municipal guard service, set the minimum age at 25 then lowered it to 21 for those married and thus presumed independent of their fathers, or for commissioned military officers, graduates of law school, or ordained priests. Men who, regardless of their age, remained unmarried and dependent on their fathers could not vote unless they held public office. The lower age limit of 25 and the formal recognition of patriarchy not only disenfranchised a significant number of these *filhos-família*, but it also deprived the elite civilian security force of the service of many able-bodied young men well prepared physically for the sort of police duty the guard was called to perform. Furthermore, by their continued dependence on their fathers, such men were often less tied to professional or family obligations than those married and earning their own way in the world and thus could take time for guard duty with less disruption of the family business or their own source of livelihood. The law of 17 July expanded eligibility for the municipal guard to include dependent sons as young as 16 of those citizens who met the income and other requirements for voting. This opened the ranks of the municipal guard to include a sizable group of men age 16 through 24, and for some older but still in their father's household who had the same stake in the maintenance of order as had their fathers.[16]

As another emergency measure to provide some semblance of a police force during the July crisis, Feijó agreed to the creation of an ad hoc unit made up of "trusted officers" who would patrol the capital. This led to the quick formation of what became known variously as the Battalion of Officer-Soldiers, the Volunteers of the Fatherland, the Sacred Battalion, and the Warriors of the Fatherland. The proposal that loyal officers dispense with seniority and status and assume the functions of common soldiers was the idea of Colonel João Paulo dos Santos Barreto and Major Luis Alves de Lima e Silva, who were elected commander and subcommander respectively. (Luis Alves de Lima e Silva, future Duque de Caxias, was the son of regent José Francisco Lima e Silva, and both the military commander of the capital and the newly appointed minister of war were his uncles.) This force grew in a few days to include more than four hundred members of the professional officer corps who, as Feijó approvingly noted, "strapped cartridge belts over their badges of rank." Ironically, many members of this volunteer group of loyal officers were available to patrol like common soldiers because their own troops were part of the rebellious crowd in the Campo de Santana or because the recent reductions in troop strengths had left them without a command position.[17] Their first priority was to establish control over the strip of public buildings along Rio's main waterfront area, stretching from Calabouço point and the army arsenal to the navy arsenal at the base of São Bento hill—both of which contained crucial supplies of arms and ammunition—and including the imperial palace, chamber of deputies, and the customshouse with its adjacent port and warehouse facilities.

With a cordon of protection reestablished, the extraordinary session of Parliament played a waiting game. Over the next several days many of the civilian bystanders, tired of the show, went home; some of the mutinous troops left the rebel ranks as well. Other soldiers, receiving promises there would be no reprisals, agreed to rejoin their officers and submit to authority. Loyal officers patrolled the city, now joined by reorganized and reassured civilians of the municipal guard. Thus the threat posed by those rebels who remained in arms, leaderless and increasingly isolated, lessened considerably. By 19 July Parliament felt confident enough to pass a resolution rejecting the rebel demands as "absurd and unconstitutional," and the following day the government had enough of a force gathered to move in and arrest those who remained in the Campo de Santana. After the dungeons of the forts around Rio were filled with former rebels, military and civilian, the government disbanded several army units and transferred others to distant provinces. Many soldiers and some officers were dismissed from service, and by a law of 30 August the size of the army was reduced even further, to ten thousand soldiers nationwide. Conscription was suspended, as were promotions for most remaining officers.[18] According to the most liberal Rio press, the rebels of July 1831 were doing little more than exercising the right of the citizen to petition the government to free the country of its enemies. To the victorious forces of established order, whose physical control of the city had been briefly but seriously threatened, the rebels were the worst class of demagogues, anarchists, and mutineers.[19]

In the middle of these traumatic events, on 17 July, the general assembly approved a law abolishing the Guarda Real de Polícia, whose collective insubordination had fueled the crisis. Its officers were reassigned to regular army units; the rank and file were dismissed from service and offered free transportation to "retire to their provinces."[20] Since 1809 the Guarda Real had supplied a militarized force for patrolling the city, protecting public buildings, and for quelling civil disturbance. Although Feijó had little choice but to disband the unit, the problem that immediately ensued was how to replace the policing function the Guarda Real had fulfilled for more than twenty years, while the city had grown and changed. Gone were the days when Vidigal and his squad of whip-bearing grenadiers could maintain a semblance of order in the streets through a reign of official terror. Even though the Guarda Real had lost its cutting edge during the late 1820's, it was a base that might have been rebuilt if its members had not gone beyond the pale on 14 July 1831.

Restoration of Control

Feijó understood that controlling the capital meant more than keeping seditious gangs of republican agitators from embarrassing or threatening the government. Immediately after the events of July 1831 he took several interim measures—all without precedent in the untried authority of the regency and all intended to centralize power in the hands of the government and reestablish control over the streets of the city. On 20 July Feijó declared that any justice of the peace who declined to bring charges against those involved in the vanquished rebellion would himself be held accountable as an accomplice under the law of 6 June. He further ordered the justices of the peace of the city of Rio to attend weekly meetings presided over by the intendant of police to exchange information on the possibility of revolutionary plots and coordinate their response to threats to public tranquility.[21] This was one of several measures of the early regency that brought the justices of the peace in Rio under the direct control of the central government. On 27 July he authorized the intendant of police to distribute weapons to owners of businesses located on unpatrolled streets and on the outskirts of the city. Local squad leaders of the civilian municipal guard were to see that these weapons were not misused. At the same time he issued instructions for reorganizing the newly expanded municipal guards to provide regular street patrols. For his actions Feijó received praise from Evaristo da Veiga, a newspaper publisher, member of the chamber of deputies, and intellectual leader of the moderate liberal faction that emerged victorious in these power struggles in the streets and in parliament. Veiga proclaimed that the decisive measures of the minister of justice kept "society from the threat of being invaded by hordes of barbarians" and that if "those citizens with an interest in order were asked, they would say that they have anchored their hopes on Sr. Feijó and his civic courage."[22]

The threat the municipal guard was intended to address was more fundamental than the rallies and machinations of the political opponents of the regime. What made political conflicts so threatening was not just that they had the potential of bringing down the regime. While the government was preoccupied with political insurrection, the latent threat of social insurrection could manifest itself. The specter of anarchy so insistently raised in political debate and the press was more than a rhetorical device, and it did not refer narrowly to political protests and military mutinies. Those sorts of disturbances, which have been stressed in traditional historiography as the backdrop for the sequence of political events of this period, were probably easier to deal with than the endemic danger posed by what Evaristo da Veiga called the "hordes of barbarians" below.

Looking back on the last years of the first empire, when judges were notoriously corrupt and the police ineffective, Feijó's predecessor as justice minister, José de Souza França, lamented in May 1831 that "the elimination of the severe laws of the old police, by which many crimes were prevented, also has led to the increase in crimes." When order had broken down in March before the abdication, "criminal activity mixed with the demonstrations." França said he did what he could to bring the perpetrators to justice, and although "some were arrested, others escaped, and are in hiding."

Advocating a more efficient criminal court system and better ostensive patrolling and surveillance than the Guarda Real had been supplying, he stated his case thus: "Especially in large societies, public security is better served by preventing crimes than by punishing them."[23]

The chronic problem of common crime—theft, robbery, assault, and murder—as well as the ongoing challenge of controlling the slave population of the city and the poor lower classes generally had grown to alarming proportions in the political distractions leading up to and following the abdication, which culminated in the virtual absence of state authority in many parts of the city during the July crisis. When he took over the ministry in mid-1831, Feijó reported to parliament that "the capital was living in horror and alarm. Robberies and murders were taking place in the daylight, on the streets, in view of the authorities." He blamed much of the problem on the laxity of the police in preceding years and attributed the progress during the year he was minister to the "untiring zeal, vigilance and patriotism of the justices of the peace." He claimed that there were as many as five hundred arrests a month of "vagrants, troublemakers, and those who carry illegal weapons." He clearly differentiated such public order offenses from political agitation, but the political paralysis of the capital had created an environment in which the vagrants and troublemakers thrived.[24]

Looking back several years later, one Rio newspaper claimed that from 7 April through July 1831 there were three hundred victims of murder or physical injury in the capital as a result of actions by gangs of thieves who robbed at knife point, "indiscriminately sacrificing native and foreigner alike in their brute ferocity."[25] That was probably little more than an exaggerated guess, but it reflected some people's sense that such activity increased in the period of institutional uncertainty. A listing of arrests and reported crimes in Rio for the nineteen days from Monday 30 May through Friday 17 June 1831 provides a more detailed picture of the situation, as shown in Table 1. Police clerks recorded eight other crimes during the same period for which no arrests were made, including two murders, three cases of bodies found with wounds indicating foul play, one robbery in which the victim was injured, and one case each of light and serious physical injury.

Several aspects of the data in Table 1 require comment. First, this is not a sample, but a report of all arrests and reported crimes

TABLE 1

Arrests in Rio de Janeiro, 30 May–17 June 1831

Offense	No.	%
Disorder and insult		
Free	29	12.9
Slave	34	15.2
(Subtotal)	(63)	(28.1)
Weapons possession		
Free	24	10.7
Slave	14	6.3
(Subtotal)	(38)	(17.0)
Curfew violation		
Sailors	20	8.9
Slaves	14	6.3
(Subtotal)	(34)	(15.2)
Vagrancy	35	15.6
Ordinance violations (unspecified)	11	4.9
Subtotal	181	80.8
Theft (*furto*)	25	11.2
Light physical injuries	5	2.2
Serious physical injuries	4	1.8
Attempted theft	4	1.8
Attempted murder	4	1.8
Enticing slaves	1	0.4
Subtotal	43	19.2
Total	224	100.0

SOURCE: Arquivo Nacional do Rio de Janeiro IJ6 165 (Ofícios do Chefe de Polícia da Corte [do Rio de Janeiro]), 20 June 1831.

in the city during these nineteen days. That is not to say it reflects the true level of criminality or, in more descriptive terms, the immoral or illegal things that some people did to other people or their property in Rio in that period. It is a fundamental methodological fallacy to assume that records of arrests and reported events reflect the incidence of crime. What these data measure is the functioning of the police system. If crimes of violence against person and property were as prevalent as tradition has it during the "anarchy" of 1831, then these data suggest that the police system was not working very well because only 13 arrests out of 224 were for such offenses.

The efficacy of another type of police action—patrolling the streets to prevent illegal activity—is also not measured by arrests.[26] On the contrary, to the extent that ostensive patrolling has the desired repressive effect, as Minister of Justice França had pointed out, it should cause a reduction in criminal activity and subsequent arrests for such violations. The Guarda Real de Polícia had acquired a reputation for laxity by 1831, but the rates of arrest shown in Table 1 suggest that they were still on the job. These data for nineteen days just before Feijó took over the ministry of justice show total arrests at a monthly rate of about 350. If he and the justices of the peace under his direction were as zealous as he asserted, backed up as they were by municipal guards and the merchant class armed and organized by the government, his claim of arrests reaching 500 in some months is entirely possible.

As for what *is* revealed in Table 1, those arrests involving an offense to people or property (including one case of persuading a slave to run away) make up just one-fifth of the total. The rest are for victimless or public order offenses. Most of the people the police arrested were violating their condition of subjugation or marginalization, either in fact or in potential, and the categories and subdivisions reveal information relevant to the needs of controlling their activities. More slaves than free people were brought in for disturbing the peace or insulting another person, and although the order is reversed in the case of weapons possession, a significant number of slaves were arrested for that offense, which was made more serious and urgent by the law of 6 June. Intendant Aragão's orders of 1825 had established a general curfew of 10 P.M. in summer and 9 P.M. in winter, but the curfew specified in this 1831 report was sunset (which would be around 6:30 P.M. in the month of June), and the two categories subject to it were slaves and sailors, not other free persons. Minister of Justice França had ordered this change in response to the breakdown of order in March 1831. The problem of ship crews on shore-leave sprees was endemic in Rio, and when the sunset curfew for sailors was reconfirmed in November 1832, it was praised as "a police order that contributes considerably to public tranquility."[27]

Table 1 reflects the purpose of the Rio police system that was apparent at its inception and remained the general pattern through the rest of the empire. That purpose was to arrest people who committed physical assault, murder, theft, and similar crimes against a person and property. But most police activity was directed toward maintaining the hierarchy of subordination and domination. Slaves were a special object of police attention, but their offenses fell into the same categories as those of free people. The categories of transgressions themselves hint at what the social order meant in practice. Status was not merely an abstract scale of prestige and respect, but even those symbolic forms of behavior were enforced by law by making insult a punishable offense. It was important to discipline those who engaged in disorderly conduct or insult to authority because such behavior was the first step toward breakdown of the social order. Vagrancy, like disorderly conduct and disrespect, was defined in practice by the assessment of the arresting officer. And a selectively applied curfew is an explicit statement that certain categories of people were denied behavior allowed to others. Possession of an instrument that could be used as a weapon, usually some sort of blade, dagger, or club, was assumed prima facie to be evidence that the possessor intended to use the tool aggressively. Yet it should be pointed out that by the definition of the criminal code, theft (furto) did not involve physically confronting and coercing the victim to yield the stolen object. What is known today as being held up or mugged was called roubo (and will be referred to as robbery in this study, to distinguish from furto). Although the 25 cases of theft in Table 1 represent a significant category of arrest, there was only one case of robbery reported during these three weeks—and the perpetrator escaped.

The municipal guard was not formally segregated from the rest of society by race, but its members were distinguished by an income requirement, and eligibility was screened by the local justice of the peace. There could hardly be a clearer way of showing who was interested in increased repression than to establish an income requirement for members of a part-time police force of civilians organized by the state. To join the municipal guard it was not enough to want to help in the fight against disorder. It was necessary to be of a specifically defined upper segment of the economic hierarchy. Service in the guard was also not paid, so each member's income had to come from elsewhere. A clear way for the slave, black, brown, and poor people to express the resentment of have-nots against haves, then, was to engage in street battles with municipal guard patrols.

A series of daily reports of activities by municipal guards in the days immediately following the July crisis illustrates the range of situations these patrols faced. From the justice of the peace of São

José parish on 27 July 1831, just a week after the rebellious crowd in the Campo de Santana had been dispersed, came the following report:

Last night a patrol of municipal guards brought before me two blacks and one mulatto. The guards reported that the prisoners belonged to the two groups into which the blacks and mulattos divided themselves, numbering more than 200, to attack the civilian guards by throwing stones, which in fact they did, wounding the chief of the patrol on the head. This took place about seven in the evening, and the action showed coordination and pre-meditation, because one of the groups divided, the two parts going in opposite directions.

The following day the commander of the municipal guards reported to Feijó that two slaves, Adriano and João, both carpenters by trade, had been arrested in a group of 25 or 30 who were insulting and throwing stones at a patrol of municipal guards. In this incident also the leader of the patrol was injured. The commander assured Feijó that he had given strict orders that if such an incident were to recur, "not one was to escape." There were other routine incidents, less immediately threatening than rock-throwing gangs but indicative of the challenge of keeping the lower classes in line. On 25 July a patrol arrested Jeremias and João, both slaves, and Brazilian-born former slave Thomé José for disorderly conduct. The freedman had injured two men with an iron bar, which was taken from him. Also arrested were Domingos, a slave, for disorderly conduct and possession of a dagger; and Joaquim, a slave, for carrying a knife. Black freedman Cezario Mariano was arrested on 26 July, for "insulting a white man with words and gestures." There was also the case of slaves Manoel and Salvador, arrested for capoeira on 26 July, and on the same day the arrest of free mulatto João de Souza Nunes, accused by José Joaquim da Costa of injuring him and robbing him of the considerable sum of 1:600$000. Costa was also brought in for investigation.[28]

These were the sorts of incidents the municipal guards faced as they patrolled, involving slaves, former slaves, capoeira gangs, artisans both slave and free, mostly black or brown people, some interpersonal violence, and occasionally a serious theft or assault. Insults a free black publicly directed at a white man were a clearly articulated threat to the hierarchy of domination. The message attached to the stones municipal guards saw coming at them in the night from groups of black men may have been less articulate, but it was just as threatening to the hierarchy and more threatening to life and limb. As one chronicler assessed the development of what he called the "repressive apparatus" in Rio de Janeiro in this period, loss of political control "must, by the natural course of ideas, raise the subversive instincts of the lowest rabble, always ready for anarchic attacks and bloody mutinies."[29] The elite expected dangerous and threatening resistance from the lowest rabble, slave and free—the majority of the city's population. Those expectations were realized when institutions broke down in mid-1831, clearly showing those in charge the need for a repressive response that would be regularly and effectively implemented. The repressive apparatus can be described in institutional and political terms, but the underlying rationale for the development of such institutions must be understood as a dynamic process of interaction connecting repression from above and resistance from below in an inexorable dialectic.

Founding the National Guard

Evidence that the civilian municipal guard was not very effective during and immediately following the crisis of July 1831 made the formation of a paramilitary national guard all the more imperative. The criteria for membership would be similar, but the national guard would be organized along military lines and better armed. Although it had been talked about in political circles for some months, its creation came as a direct response to specific events in the city of Rio de Janeiro in the first half of 1831. As with many other measures instituted in the process of state building, the guard was intended to be a national organization, and units were eventually formed throughout the country. Also similar to the experience of some other institutions, it was formed first and most effectively in the capital of the empire. On 18 August 1831 Parliament authorized the establishment of the national guard, replacing the civilians who had helped keep order in the city since early July. Its function in policing the city was related to its national role as the armed force of the propertied class, but it was also specific to the circumstances of the national capital. Here as elsewhere in the political and social history of Rio de Janeiro, local and national events occupied the same stage. There is ample reason to examine the guard in the national context.[30] But its effectiveness as an instrument of repression is most fruitfully examined at the local level—the way it worked on the streets day-to-day as one part of the complex police system built up during the first decades of the nineteenth century.

The guard was to replace the paramilitary militias and *ordenanças* inherited from the colonial regime as well as the civilian guards authorized in June 1831. The charge enunciated in the law illustrates the multifaceted role the moderate liberals saw for the guard, only some aspects of which it eventually fulfilled. Beyond the generic duty of defending the constitution and the freedom, independence, and integrity of the nation, the guard was to assist the army in the defense of the nation's borders. As an internal police force, the guard was to "maintain obedience to the law, and preserve or reestablish order and public tranquility." Furthermore, the same introductory statement included a preemptive warning against a political role for the guard, declaring that any independent action it might take "with regard to public affairs is an attack on liberty and a crime against the constitution."[31] It was to be an instrument, not an agent of authority, formally subordinated to the civilian minister of justice at the national level (and directly in Rio, as capital of the empire) and put under the control of regional and local political and judicial appointees of the central government and the justices of the peace. In a clear break with the past, when militias and ordenanças were in form and function a reserve force of the army, the guard was to have no institutional connection with the professional military or the ministry of war, except that instructors could be assigned from the army to train the guard in military skills, and weaponry could be acquired through army procurement channels.

Two other aspects of the guard are important for understanding the expectations of its founders and its eventual role in practice: criteria for membership and internal organization. In principle all able-bodied free male citizens between the ages of 18 and 60 and not otherwise exempt who met the income qualifications for voting (100$000 per year) were required to become members of the guard, except that in the four largest cities of the country—Rio, Bahia, Recife, and São Luiz de Maranhão—minimum eligibility was qualification to be an elector, or 200$000 per year. Service in the guard was thus made one of the obligations of citizenship, as was voting. In Rio the minimum required income of 200$000 was far enough down the economic hierarchy to include most independent artisans, merchants, and salaried employees but exclude many members of the urban lower classes without enough independent money income to qualify. It also excluded the urban underclass, which had little access to legitimate sources of livelihood—the vagrants, drifters, beggars, and thieves who accumulated in Rio and other large port cities and who became principal targets of police repression. The dregs of society were left to supply the conscripts necessary to fill the rank and file of the much-reduced regular army, further distinguishing the military institution from its paramilitary counterpart. Guard membership in the four cities where the minimum criteria of elector status excluded former slaves (and those who had been convicted of crimes) was not formally segregated by race as the colonial militias had been. It did, of course, exclude another 40 percent or so of the male population: those who were slaves.[32]

Guard service was not compensated, and although the government was supposed to provide weapons and necessary equipment, members were expected to supply their own uniforms. Legally exempt from guard service were active duty military personnel, the clergy, holders of political or judicial office, jailors, officers of the law, and members of the police. Because eligibility lists and requests for exemption on professional or personal grounds were decided by local boards headed by the justices of the peace, there was ample opportunity for the wealthy and powerful to relieve themselves or their sons and clients from the obligation to serve in the rank and file. Rather than duplicating or merely reinforcing the existing authority structure, guard service was intended to extend the responsibility for defending property and the social order to those members of society who had a stake in the status quo. In practice many of those with the most to defend found a way to avoid active duty service. In Rio that burden fell disproportionally to the retail merchants, artisans, clerks, and similar members of the petty bourgeoisie who were economically privileged in the relative context of society but who lacked the power, directly or through a patron, to obtain an exemption.[33]

The other principle envisioned in the law creating the guard that was to distinguish it from the regular military was internal democracy. Members of the noncommissioned and officer corps, with the exception of the highest positions of legion and provincial commanders, were to be elected by members of the corps. This provision reflected the hopes of the moderate liberal advocates of the guard that those men eligible for service would embody the virtues of responsible citizenship. Experience soon showed that too many of those elected to officer positions were the candidates most lenient in matters of internal discipline or those who could be counted on to minimize the burdens of guard service for the subordinates who elected them.[34] Internal democracy eventually yielded to the requirements of internal discipline, first through administrative fiat at the provincial level and then through changes in regulations by 1850 for the entire corps, making offices appointive after that date.

Although some of the first national guard members participated in the suppression of a seditious uprising in October 1831, the details of its uniform were not issued until late December still during the process of organization.[35] By February 1832 the guard was first presented to the public of the capital with a parade of two thousand infantry and four hundred cavalry. By May of that year the force had been built to three cavalry squadrons and five infantry battalions, totaling four thousand men. They were called upon to patrol the city on a regular basis, a duty Feijó considered an intolerable burden that such part-time volunteers should not have to bear indefinitely.[36] Unlike many of the guard units in Rio Province and other outlying areas, those in the city were reasonably well armed and equipped if not well trained. Many of the officers and men had been members of the extinct militia and ordenança units, which the government was attempting to subordinate to the centralized authority then developing; in Rio many had been members of the short-lived municipal guards.[37]

The national guard became for a time an important part of the apparatus of repression available to police the city of Rio, although not always as its advocates envisioned or later commentators on that institution have supposed, considering its historical reputation as the paramilitary instrument of the landowners in the clientelistic politics of rural areas. In order to understand the limited role of the guard in Rio in practice, we need to go back to the crisis of authority that followed the rebellion of July 1831, to the establishment of institutions that shared and eventually took over its police function.

Breakout at Snake Island

Toward the end of September some of those arrested in the July rebellion were being released from detention, and tensions mounted as they joined their comrades on the streets, where a major demonstration of their discontent took place on 25 September at a public meeting.[38] On the night of 28 September 1831 a large group of civilian municipal guardsmen fired on a crowd of political demonstrators assembled in the city's main theater, killing three and wounding many others.[39] Tensions remained high as another armed rebellion erupted just a week after the theater massacre, this time involving political prisoners and the military garrison on the Ilha das Cobras. This island adjacent to the São Bento hill was the main base of the coast artillery, one of only two military units in Rio that had remained loyal to the government in mid-July. Parts of the imposing fortress on the island had been used as a prison from time to time, and an unused powder magazine had been converted for such use in May 1831.[40] Other political detainees were being held in a prison ship (called a *presiganga*, an adaptation of the English "press gang") anchored nearby. One of those held in the fort was Cipriano Barata, who had been one of the Brazilian delegates to the Lisbon Cortes (along with Feijó) during the period just before independence a decade before. In 1831 he was editor of the radical liberal newspaper *Sentinela da Liberdade* and an advocate of republicanism. Barata and other militants convinced their guards in the coast artillery unit and the presiganga to release the prisoners and join them in revolt.

The government had considerable forewarning that such an attempt might be made, and on the night of 6 October municipal guards were called out to protect streets and installations on the adjacent mainland. The following morning the rebels directed musket fire at the city and insisted on safe passage away from Rio. The government reacted with force. Involved in the retaking of the Ilha das Cobras were the officer-soldier battalion that had been formed during the July crisis, a force of about 400 municipal guards, and some 200 members of the national guard then still being organized. One municipal guardsman, Estêvão de Almeida Chaves, was killed by a musket ball. This martyr to the cause of constituted authority, the only municipal guard killed in the line of duty in the short existence of that institution, was a Portuguese bookkeeper. His funeral the next day became a major state occasion. The national guardsmen acquitted themselves well in their baptism by fire, and the officer most recognized for his decisive action in defending established authority was Major Luis Alves de Lima e Silva of the Officer-Soldier battalion. The 200 prisoners taken in the assault were locked up on the restaffed prison ship, and the Officer-Soldiers were left to garrison the main fortress. Barata and several others were subsequently exiled to Bahia to remove them physically from the political hothouse of Rio de Janeiro.[41]

On the day of the conflict Feijó sent a message to Parliament recognizing the fundamental importance of maintaining government control of Rio de Janeiro. He also made explicit the relationship between the propertied class and the forces of order in the following terms:

The chamber of deputies must know that six thousand armed citizens, not the sort that on 15 July spread panic in the capital, but six thousand industrious property owners, each of whom represents family and fortune, who constitute the mass of the richest and most populous city of the empire, have declared that they can no longer suffer the disturbance and fear, the inconvenience and damage, caused by the anarchists. The indifference of the general assembly, regarding the calamities passing before their very eyes, is very deeply felt and disagreeable. . . . At this moment the municipal guard is in arms to defend itself from its enemies, without sleep or sustenance. Only strong and prompt remedies can save the capital, and with it the nation.[42]

With dissolution of the Guarda Real de Polícia in July there had been a breakdown of the institutional basis of repression. Even the regular military forces could not be counted on in the emergency, and in the view of the minister of justice the central political institution—the chamber of deputies—was indifferent and paralyzed. That vacuum sucked away the rhetorical cover for law and order, as those representatives of "family and fortune" with a direct material stake in keeping the "anarchists" at bay took up arms to defend their interests.

Feijó's typically blunt criticism of the inactivity of the deputies made him no friends, and when he asked Parliament to declare a state of emergency and temporarily suspend the constitutional guarantees of citizenship, he narrowly survived a vote of censure.[43] Furthermore, his characterization of the municipal guard as a de-

termined and united force six thousand strong was either deliberate exaggeration for effect or wishful thinking. In a less sanguine
assessment those in immediate charge of the municipal guard complained that "a great number of citizens refuse to serve on street
patrols" and that the justices of the peace were forced to take legal
measures against recalcitrant guards to force compliance. Even the
patrols guarding the imperial palace in the suburb of São Cristóvão
were shorthanded because "there is no one who will do this on a
volunteer basis."[44] Service was required for all those eligible, but it
was not compensated nor was any provision made for replacing in
their regular profession or activities those who served as guards.
Many citizens quickly found routine guard duty a burden once the
political crisis was dissipated. Clearly this "volunteer" civilian organization was inadequate to intimidate and instill fear in the city's
lower classes, nor did its members have the training, discipline,
time, or inclination to serve as a permanent police force for a city
of the size, social complexity, and political importance of Rio de
Janeiro.

The Military Police

Before the October incident on Cobras Island, on 30 August,
Feijó had taken the initiative to establish a militarized, permanent,
professional replacement for the civilian municipal guards. The
legislature had authorized the national guard only twelve days earlier, but Feijó anticipated that while a police force was indispensable, "it is not possible that the patriotism of the national guard will
grow to the point that they can permanently assume the duty of
policing the city." Instead, he suggested "the citizens can entrust
the security of their persons and patrimony to a professional corps,
well chosen and well paid." The institution approved by law on
10 October 1831 started its existence as the Corpo de Guardas Mu-
nicipais Permanentes or permanent municipal guard corps.[45] (Until
1858 *permanente* was part of its formal title, and its soldiers were
informally referred to as *permanentes*. By 1866 it was designated the
Corpo Militar de Polícia da Corte, and since 1920 it has been formally designated the Polícia Militar. For the sake of consistency it
will be referred to in this study as the military police.)
It was the functional replacement for the Guarda Real abolished
in the crisis of the previous July with several key differences. First,

like the national guard it was subordinated to the civilian minister of justice, not the minister of war or the intendant of police. Second, its rank-and-file soldiers were not army conscripts but recruits who volunteered specifically for this unit and had better pay and living conditions than most army troops. In the Guarda Real a soldier's salary had been a token 2$400 per month, and at the time of its founding a soldier in the military police was paid 18$000 per month. That rate, supplemented by room and board in the barracks, gave the military police rank and file an income similar to what a free wage earner might make as a store clerk or artisan. Feijó wanted the military police to be well paid, but knew that only men in the lower strata of free society would consider 18$000 a livable income. Third, police soldiers were not subject to corporal punishment. Discipline was reinforced by an array of psychological techniques to ensure obedience and a commitment to duty and was backed by harsh prison sentences for violators. Whipping, however, a major grievance of the common soldiers in the regular military (and which remained so in the navy until 1910), was not an authorized form of punishment. Its absence in the regulations of the military police set that unit apart.[46]

Feijó himself issued the instructions for the new police, which were entered into the order of the day on 29 November 1831 along with instructions to begin patrol duty immediately. The previous day a mutiny of prisoners in the notorious Aljube jail had brought out some four hundred municipal guards. Although the outbreak was successfully subdued, it again revealed the deficiencies of the civilian volunteers and made deployment of the military police more urgent.[47] The operating instructions specifying the original mandate of the military police show what Feijó had in mind when he established this force. They also provide a standard against which the performance of the corps and later changes in procedures can be measured. Patrols were to circulate day and night with infantry in the city and cavalry in the suburbs. In the downtown area where reinforcement from a nearby patrol was to be within the sound of a whistle, patrolmen might go out alone or in pairs with larger groups patrolling isolated areas. Patrols were to arrest anyone who was committing a crime, had recently committed a crime, or was about to commit a crime, those in any gathering of three or more persons with criminal intent (a reiteration of the criminal code definition of an illegal assembly), or those in any unauthorized nighttime gathering of five or more persons (as specified in the law of 6 June 1831). They were to maintain crowd control at authorized public events and arrest anyone engaged in mutiny or riot, committing acts offensive to public morals, or carrying weapons. Patrols were permitted to search any suspicious person for weapons and enter private residences during the daytime hours to effect an arrest. At night they were supposed to enter residences only if there were calls for help from within. They could enter taverns, stores, and other public buildings at any time to make an arrest or break up meetings of slaves.

Those detained were to be taken before the justice of the peace one day, the criminal judge the next day, and the intendant of police on the third day. This provision was intended to relieve any one of these authorities from the need to be on duty constantly, but it also revealed the way justices of the peace in Rio had been incorporated into the lower reaches of the centrally controlled judicial system by this early date, which made them indistinguishable in this lower criminal court function from the intendant and criminal judge. Furthermore, it reflected the transitory nature of the institutional structure in 1831, with three judicial officials of different origins and mandates given overlapping and interchangeable functions. Within a year the code of criminal procedure would abolish the post of intendant of police, and the justices of the peace were stripped of their authority over police and criminal matters less than a decade later. In the meantime the important thing for Feijó was to get a functioning police force onto the streets of the city.

For all his firm resolve in the face of political assault on constituted authority and the threat of social disruption, Feijó was not the arbitrary authoritarian his enemies in the radical press made him out to be. By the instructions of November 1831 military police patrols were to give no special treatment to any person, and with everyone they were to be "prudent and circumspect, maintaining the civility and respect due the citizen by right." They were, however, authorized to "apply the force necessary to carry out their mission" against anyone who resisted being "arrested, searched, or observed." Feijó did not intend such a clear statement in defense of what are now called human rights as hollow rhetoric. This taciturn priest was not given to verbal posturing. Furthermore, there was little in the climate of public opinion that would have caused him to make such a statement in internal police operating instructions as a pro forma gesture to liberal ideological abstractions. He included these provisions in the instructions to counter the previous policy of unregulated and arbitrary brutality, from the intendant's authority to punish people for minor infractions as he saw fit to Vidigal's "shrimp dinners" and similar vicious treatment of the city's common people in the previous two decades.

Feijó understood that the goal was to achieve a manageable balance between resistance and repression. The Guarda Real had shown that the unchecked and brutal exercise of arbitrary authority on the part of the institutions created to maintain order could become disruptive and add to the problem it was supposed to help resolve. The experience of the last years of the first empire, and particularly the anarchy of the early regency, showed the dangers of laxity. The more recent experiment with municipal guards, giving propertied civilians the responsibility to police the city on a part-time, voluntary basis, showed how important the hierarchy and discipline of a professional military organization was. It was necessary to repress the individual and collective acts of resistance that in the aggregate defined the problem of public order in the concentrated social environment of the city. But it was prudent to keep that repression within manageable bounds. The criminal code provided the framework in which the limits of permissible behavior were systematized, specified, and focused. Feijó hoped the new military police could provide the instrument of repression that he and his successors could wield with the precision necessary to establish and maintain an acceptable level of order.

Evidence that the minister of justice meant what he said—and why he said it—came a few weeks after the military police went on duty, not in press or parliament, but in an internal memo to the commander of the permanentes. It deserves extensive quotation for what it reveals about Feijó, the subordination of military to civilian authority, and the role of the military police in Brazilian history.

Several times I have personally witnessed beatings of blacks by military police. Whereas no article of the instructions regulating patrols gives them such authority, you must inform them that they will be severely punished, with all the rigor of the law, if they offend any person in any way, be that person free or slave. The action of the patrols is limited only to arresting those persons falling within the instructions, using against them only the force necessary to overcome resistance. Patrols should also be informed that in addition to the punishment they will suffer, I will find it very disagreeable to hear that chosen citizens, who must be the first to provide the example of respect for the law and the rights of others, might be looked upon as the enemies of their fellow citizens.[48]

Whether or not he found such conduct disagreeable, Feijó was instrumental in creating an institution destined to be caught in the contradictions of what might be called authoritarian liberalism—itself an inconsistent label, but appropriate for the likes of Pedro I, Feijó, and a series of other figures in Brazilian history caught in a similar contradiction. Beginning in 1831 the military police were assigned to carry out the distasteful and burdensome task, alternately boring and dangerous, of urban repression. They were the coercive instrument of state authority in a slave society held together by the threat and reality of physical domination of the many by the few. Yet when their methods of carrying out that general assignment became so direct and public as to intrude on the sensibilities of the social and political class that created and maintained them, the military police were taken to task and given a lecture about respecting the rights of citizens. Feijó represented a liberalism that sought to eliminate the exercise of power by the absolute monarchs of the previous era so that members of his class could pursue their interests free of arbitrarily imposed restrictions and exactions. But his awareness of the social threat from below, sharpened by the political events in the streets of Rio de Janeiro during 1831, led him to be the implacable architect of a police structure shaped by the needs of the group that assumed power in Brazil in the aftermath of absolutism.

Other aspects of the behavior of some military police also bothered Feijó, as similar incidents recurring through the following decades concerned his successors in the political elite. In May 1832 the minister of justice warned the commander of the military police that three soldiers of the corps who were drunk while on patrol in downtown Rio must be identified, reprimanded before the assembled corps, and expelled from the service. Such behavior, said Feijó, "brings discredit and shame on the entire corps" which otherwise "deserves the esteem and praise of the capital."[49] Even as he ordered the expulsion of the three men who were drunk on duty, he attributed the difficulty the new unit had in reaching its authorized strength of four hundred to the "repugnance Brazilians have for the military profession, always so poorly and inequitably paid."[50] While they were volunteers who received better pay and treatment than army conscripts, soldiers of the military police from the beginning were drawn from the underemployed lower classes of the city's nonslave population—those who overcame whatever repugnance they had for military service and were willing to subject themselves to rigid military discipline in return for the low pay Feijó referred to. When some of them occasionally conducted themselves in ways characteristic of some other members of their class, they injured the sensibilities of the class that had created the military police to do its bidding. When they were found drunk on duty, the offense was compounded. Not only did they bring shame on the corps and foster the disrespect of the civilian population for the first-line representatives of state authority, but drunk soldiers could not contribute much to the task at hand.

The propertied classes needed protection and wanted order, as was clearly set forth in the statement by the regency closing the first session of the General Assembly after the abdication on 1 November 1831: "When peaceful means are fruitlessly exhausted, it is necessary to draw the sword of justice to contain the seditious persons whose incessant attacks on order and public tranquility begin to hinder the sources of national wealth, as if to eliminate peace, personal security, and security of property from this hospitable land."[51] Such a general statement, unobjectionable on its face to the liberal mind-set, must be placed in the context of the place and time. Some 40 percent of the people of Rio de Janeiro were themselves property. They had no personal security. On the contrary, an increase in the ability of the state to maintain order reduced the personal safety and the small opportunities urban life could provide for some slaves. Another indeterminate but significant proportion of the city's population had no property to protect other than the scant clothes on their backs, and for some the tools of a trade or the stock of a retail business that could fit in a basket carried on their head or a folding table on the street. An increase in the state's ability to control people's actions hurt these members of the nonslave lower class, at least to the extent their preferred behavior violated norms set by the state. And the "sword of justice" did little to defend the meager property of these people or make life safer for them. National wealth was a concept relevant only to those few who could hope to acquire wealth of any kind, and its increase required the maintenance of order and public tranquility.

In the plantations, mines, cattle ranches, and rubber-collecting trails—the sources of Brazil's national wealth—the workers had to be kept working by the lash or by desperation. In a commercial and administrative center such as Rio de Janeiro, seditious persons had to be contained and the streets kept safe so that property could be moved and sold and the business of state conducted.

The brief experience of the civilian municipal guard showed that the propertied classes were unwilling or unable to provide protection and order for themselves at the level of consistency and professional competence required by the Rio de Janeiro of the 1830's. One way to ensure that the men in the force established to provide security would do what was expected of them was to subject them to military discipline. Militarization of Rio's police was partly a result of tradition, following the pattern established by the Guarda Real from 1809 to July 1831, and it seemed particularly appropriate in the tumultuous environment of 1831–32 when units of the regular army were an important and recurring part of the public order problem. But it was also a mechanism to ensure a certain level of efficiency and discipline in dealing with the unruly lower strata of society, who were both the objects of repression and the source of the rank and file of police troops.

Although the military police has always been under the minister of justice or his successors and from the beginning it has been institutionally distinct from the army, in the nineteenth century it was common for regular army officers to serve a tour of duty in the police. Uniforms were different from those of the army, but the ranks, titles, statuses, and sense of corporate identity have been very similar to those of the regular professional military. *Polícia* eventually became part of the formal designation of the corps, but there have never been any policemen in the organization. There have been soldiers, corporals, sergeants, lieutenants, captains, majors, and colonels.[52] The military police rank and file have always been volunteers, who were paid more than army conscripts and who had a sense of ongoing mission that few of the army soldiers captured by force and virtually imprisoned in military posts must have felt. It would be an exaggeration to label the military police an elite corps, but it is important to keep in mind what distinguished them from the regular army and civilian society since 1831.

At the time of its inception the military police shared its mission with several complementary or overlapping organizations that reflected the prestate institutional environment of the early regency. Those groups, including the ad hoc Battalion of Officer-Soldiers (which was formally dissolved in 1833), the interim civilian municipal guards, the justices of the peace, and the national guard, eventually left the task to the new organization whose very name—the permanent municipal guard—reflects its historical role. The soldiers Feijó saw beating blacks on the streets of Rio in February 1832, the ones he praised for bravery and efficiency in putting down an armed rebellion in early April, and the three soldiers he ordered expelled for being drunk on duty in May of that year were the direct, lineal predecessors of the military police of today.

Caxias's Baptism by Fire

During its organization the military police corps was headed on an interim basis by army Colonel Theobaldo Sanches Brandão, and the second in command was Major Luis Alves de Lima e Silva. The latter became commander of the corps in October 1832 and held that position during its formative years until December 1839. The professional trajectory of the Duke of Caxias, as Luis Alves de Lima e Silva is known in history, illustrates fundamental continuities from colony to independent state, bridging the institutional hiatus and ideological experimentation of the regency. His career also helps to clarify the nature of the military police in relation to the broader society as well as to other military and civilian institutions established during this formative period.

Born in Rio Province in 1803 into a family of officers serving the colonial regime, he followed the practice of military families of the time by becoming a cadet at five years of age in 1808. Commissioned by João VI in 1818, he first saw action in the independence movement in 1822, joined Pedro I's personal guard, the Batalhão do Imperador, and participated in the disastrous 1825–28 campaign to retain Uruguay as part of Brazil. Later he commanded Brazilian forces and then all allied forces in the Paraguayan War (1865–71), served three times as minister of war as well as in a variety of other high government posts, died in 1880, and subsequently became the patron symbol (*patrono*) of the Brazilian Army. His success in suppressing several regional revolts in the name of national unity from 1839 to 1852 along with his steadfast loyalty to the regime have been used by Brazilian nationalists to illustrate what the role of the army was ideally to be and how the exemplary officer was to conduct himself.[53]

In the early days of April 1831 Caxias, 27 years old and already a major, was serving as second in command of the emperor's personal guard under his uncle, Colonel Manuel da Fonseca Lima e Silva. Caxias offered to defend the emperor from the demands of the "anarchists," but he reluctantly marched with his unit when it joined the other proabdication forces and the civilian crowds in the Campo de Santana on 6 April. The emperor's guard was one of the units disbanded in the aftermath, and Caxias was one of many officers left without a command position. During the crisis of July 1831 he was one of the organizers of the officer-soldier battalion, whose members elected him second in command. As a leader of the group that filled the gap in public security in the first months of the regency and commander of one of the units that successfully subdued the Ilha das Cobras rebellion on 7 October, Caxias built a reputation as a decisive officer respected by his peers and loyal to the regime. He thus became a likely choice for a top position in the newly created military police. The fact that one of Caxias's uncles was military commander of the capital, another was minister of war, and his father a regent of the empire doubtlessly improved the young major's chances for the post.

In most accounts of his life Caxias's service in the military police is considered an early and minor part of a long and illustrious army career. Though less obviously the raw material for commemorative biographies, the administrative and procedural precedents he established during his tenure as commander of Rio's military police left a lasting imprint. The first major test of the police, five months after it was formed, involved not bureaucratic infighting but the defeat of an armed and hostile adversary—the stuff of which martial reputations are made. Feijó personally ordered the future Duke of Caxias to assume field command of the police troops on the day of this incident and quell yet another military revolt on the streets of the capital "with fire and steel."

As the first anniversary of the departure of Pedro I approached in April 1832, there were persistent rumors that the events that began with the abdication had yet to run their course. Beyond the ideological basis for the continuing political disputes, there was now honor to be recovered and scores to settle. The cost of political instability became clear, according to one chronicler who examined these developments closely, as "families became frightened, many left the city, the bond market fell, and commerce was paralyzed."⁵⁴ The Abrilada, as this incident is known, was a direct outgrowth of the rebellion of mid-July 1831, and its roots can be traced to the abdication of Pedro I a year earlier. The individual connecting the events was Major Miguel de Frias. While serving as an aide to General Francisco Alves de Lima (Caxias's father), Frias had announced the abdication to the assembled crowd on 7 April 1831. He had been imprisoned in Villegaignon fort in Rio Bay for his insubordination during the theater incident of 28 October. Subsequently, following the lead of the prisoners on the Ilha das Cobras in early October, Frias convinced his guards to join him in rebellion. On the night of 2 April the conspirators—an unlikely coalition of radical republicans and monarchical restorationists—issued a broadside calling for the dissolution of the regency government and the convocation of a constituent assembly.

Early the following day escapees from the forts of Villegaignon and Santa Cruz landed in Botafogo Bay, at that time still considered the isolated outskirts of the city. During the morning of 3 April the armed party, some two hundred strong and dragging an artillery piece, managed to march unobstructed from Botafogo to the Campo de Santana. There Major Frias, in the company of civilian supporters and military colleagues, declared Brazil a republic. They were quickly attacked by both cavalry and infantry of the military police, first with musket fire and then in a charge with fixed bayonets. When the smoke cleared there were eight rebels dead and several more wounded, while ninety others had surrendered. Three soldiers of the military police were wounded and one was killed. His funeral the next day, like that of the municipal guard who died on the Ilha das Cobras the previous October, provided the regime with an opportunity to commemorate and sanctify this supreme sacrifice to the cause of order and legality. Major Frias managed to escape on horseback, pursued by Caxias himself. Caxias reached the house where Frias was hiding, confronted him, then left without making an arrest. Frias escaped to the United States a few days later, returned to Brazil when a general amnesty was declared in October 1833, and went on to serve with distinction in several military and administrative positions, retiring as a brigadier general. Caxias's refusal to arrest the fugitive he had run to ground, who had led a rebellion in which one of Caxias's own men was killed, is often cited as the magnanimous gesture of a comrade in arms. It also illustrates the bonds of corporate solidarity in the Brazilian officer corps.[55]

National Guard vs. Military Police

With the Abrilada put down and another conspiracy by the Restorationist party later in the month easily dispensed with, Caxias turned his attention to consolidating the military police and coordinating its activities with the national guard. The two organizations began to function simultaneously in the last months of 1831, and Caxias had been temporarily assigned as an instructor to give some semblance of military order to the guard before his reassignment to the newly formed police unit. It was not long before recurring disputes began to arise between these institutions. Military police developed the impression that the national guards were "fair-weather warriors" more concerned with their official position and elegant uniforms than with the daily routine of keeping order on the streets. National guardsmen, by their very eligibility for membership, already had a certain level of economic standing and the social status that went with it—above that of most soldiers of the military police. Membership in the guard conferred official confirmation of that status and the authority of an officer of the law.

Compounding these questions of relative status was the bureaucratic issue of the parallel operation of two forces, one military and one paramilitary, with overlapping jurisdictions and an uncertain chain of command. Feijó contributed to this problem in June 1832, just before resigning as minister of justice, when he tried to clarify the relationship between the guard and the military police. Feijó ordered that when the national guard went into action against the "enemies of order and public tranquility," that is, in a riot or rebellion that would justify such mobilization, the entire military police corps would be placed under the orders of the commander of the guard. At the same time, he ordered a military police soldier be put on duty as a permanent orderly for the national guard commander.[56] The soldier could act as a messenger between the guard and his parent unit, but this also had the symbolic effect of putting a member of the military police always at the beck and call of the high command of the national guard.

In September 1832 the minister of justice who replaced Feijó in late July reiterated the June instructions, saying the military police would be under the direct command of the national guard "whenever the guard needs to meet to take action against those who disturb order and public tranquility." At all other times the military police would take orders directly from the minister of justice.[57] For Caxias and his subordinates the rub was that they were burdened with the everyday tasks of patrol and vigilance—tracking down runaway slaves, hauling in drunks and vagrants, standing guard at public fountains to maintain order and in theaters to prevent the rowdy sons of the upper class from being excessively disrespectful, and similar unedifying assignments. When something happened that might break their monotonous routine and provide the opportunity for concerted, large-scale military action, they would be put under the orders of the part-timers of the more prestigious national guard. There was also the suggestion that police soldiers, drawn primarily from the lower orders of society, could not be trusted to fight for the interests that national guardsmen, because of their class origins, could be expected to want to defend when a major battle in the social war broke out.

Disagreement at the highest levels over what the proper role of each unit should be was reflected in the sharply worded memoranda passed between unit commanders. The minister of justice, who had direct authority over both the armed corps, was occasionally called upon to resolve intractable disputes. On the streets the conflicts ranged from verbal insults to simply working at cross purposes and ended in armed confrontation and reciprocal arrests. These altercations suggest some of the reasons why the national guard was eventually relegated to an auxiliary and then a vestigial role in policing the city, while the military police moved in to fulfill that task on a fuller and more consistent basis. The cases provide information on the more general activities of the police organizations and their relationship to society.

In early July 1832 a police soldier was in a store on Saco Street when a slave entered carrying a stick that might be used as a weapon. Following his standing orders, the police soldier took the stick away, and when the slave asked to have it back, the soldier hit him. Fearing a more thorough beating, the slave left in a hurry. From the doorway of the store the permanente shouted the all-purpose call for assistance, "Stop, thief!" (*Pega, ladrão*). A national guard patrol heard the cry, approached, and asked what the problem was. The soldier thereupon began to insult and provoke the guardsmen, by their account, to the point of drawing his sword in a threatening way. More national guards came on the scene, and they put the military policeman under arrest. When they took away his sword to take him into custody, the police soldier protested in one of the few ways left to him, outnumbered as he was. He took off his uniform jacket and threw it on the ground, along with his cap and sword belt, declaring that if they were going to take his sword they might as well take everything. The national guard battalion commander who received the report sent it on to a justice of the peace for disposition of the case, along with the jacket, cap, and belt as evidence.

There is some irony in the way the levels of this incident paralleled the social hierarchy. First the police soldier deprived the slave of his stick, then the guardsmen deprived the permanente of his sword. Apparently the slave who was struck for the temerity of asking the police soldier to return his stick was forgotten as the dispute escalated to involve the injured dignity of the guardsmen, their rebuke and arrest of the police soldier, and his singular reaction. The sword was both the symbol and instrument of authority, just as a stick in the hands of a slave represented the threat of violence from below. A few days later the military police managed a turnabout. After a national guard patrol had arrested another police soldier, a military police cavalry detachment confronted the guardsmen and liberated their comrade. Feijó himself instructed Caxias to identify those under his command who were involved and discipline them if circumstances warranted. Feijó's blunt order did not indicate why the guardsmen had detained the police soldier in the first place, but the more serious breach of discipline was the subsequent action of the police cavalry.[58]

The Code of Criminal Procedure

Such confrontations did not bode well for coordination between the professional military police and the paramilitary guard, but before long there were other institutional developments that made more complex coordination necessary. The military police soon began to serve as a multipurpose force permanently on call to serve the needs of a variety of masters, who sometimes worked at parallel rather than unified purposes. The clearly organized criminal code of 1830 had superseded the jumble of codes, laws, and regulations inherited from the colony, but the unsettled environment of 1831–32 was hardly conducive to making much progress toward the next step in replacing the colonial judicial system—establishing the institutions and processes by which the criminal code could be applied. In the interim the old police force in Rio had been dissolved, two new ones established, and in police matters the justices of the peace had been brought under the effective control of the minister of justice. The institutional transition would not be complete, however, without a new code of criminal procedure.

That law, approved in November 1832, swept aside the overlapping and vaguely defined judicial positions inherited from the old regime. It set up a new hierarchy of judges with circumscribed jurisdictions; laid out the procedure for gathering evidence, lodging complaints, effecting arrests and bringing charges; and specified how trials were to be conducted and the steps to appeal. The rights of those suspected or accused were protected through provisions for search only on a judicial warrant, arrest was allowed only on a warrant or in flagrante, the writ of habeas corpus was confirmed, trial guaranteed in open court with cross examination of witnesses. Provisions for Brazil's first jury system for serious crimes fulfilled another liberal promise of the 1824 Constitution. Certainly by comparison to the old regime in Brazil but also to the range of analogous systems then extant in Europe and the relative state of judicial anarchy reigning through much of Spanish America in 1832, the code of criminal procedure together with the earlier criminal code gave Brazil a set of modern and liberal guidelines regarding criminality and judicial procedures.[59]

The central figure in the structure the procedural code established was the justice of the peace. The law prescribed new methods of electing the local judges and specified their authority to exercise local police functions and judge minor offenses. These were defined as violations of municipal ordinances and crimes punishable by a fine up to 100$000 or a prison term of up to six months with a fine of half that time. Each justice was to be assisted by a legal clerk (escrivão) who was to draw up all necessary documents for the exercise of the judge's authority, and as an officer of the court serve legal papers. The local judge was also assisted by ward inspectors (inspetores de quarteirão). The office of ward inspector had been authorized in the 1827 law creating the justices of the peace, abolished by the law of 6 June 1831, and then reintroduced with qualifications and duties newly specified in the procedural code. The local judge was to divide his district into subsections of at least 25 residences (each a contiguous area but related only figuratively to a physical city block bounded by four streets) and nominate an inspector for each ward from among the "well-regarded" residents over 21 years of age for confirmation by the municipal council. They were to keep an eye out for illegal or suspicious activity in their ward, warn beggars, vagrants, drunks, and prostitutes to change their ways or suffer further legal action, arrest in flagrante, and carry out the orders of the justice of the peace. The position of delegado, the assistant to the justice of the peace authorized on 6 June 1831, was abolished.

Also eliminated at this time was the office of police intendant, one of the last vestiges of the pre-independence police system. The staff he administered in the secretariat of police along with its records were turned over to a new official created by the procedural code, the chief of police. By all accounts the framers of the code did not think through the implications of replacing the intendant with a chief of police, but it turned out to be a momentous precedent. Rio's police chief emerged as an important figure in the decade following promulgation of the code, and police chiefs in each province acquired great power and importance throughout Brazil by the judicial reform of 1841. The origin of the police chief's eventual authority was the procedural code of 1832, which provided that district judges (Juizes de Direito) would be appointed from among men who were at least 22 years old, were graduates of law school, and had at least one year of experience practicing law. They were given several important responsibilities, including that of overseeing and instructing the justices of the peace. Elsewhere in the code was the provision that "in populous cities there can be up to three district judges, with cumulative [i.e., overlapping] jurisdiction, and one of them will be the chief of police." It is indicative of the little concern the writers of the procedural code gave the office of police chief that they did not specify the rights and responsibilities of the office nor its relationship to other police and judicial authorities. That omission soon became glaringly apparent as the new structure was put into operation in succeeding months.

Before appointing a permanent official to the position, the min-

ister of justice tried to fill the gap with a regulatory decree specifying that the police chief was to serve as a liaison between the
government and the justices of the peace, but the wording of the
procedural code did not allow for much more than that. In frustration the minister said in May 1833 that "a better-organized police
is indispensable. The justices of the peace cannot carry out the task
satisfactorily, and one cannot put the military police at the disposition of so many judges without the loss of the necessary unity." As
minimally outlined in the procedural code, "'police chief' is a
meaningless title that only serves to burden the judge who holds
it." He anticipated that the public would expect the office to function like that of the former intendant, though that would be an
illusion because the police chief "does not have the authority to
issue a single search warrant, nor even one arrest warrant."[60] What
he did have, however, was the power and authority of the district
judge, for holding that office was a prerequisite for appointment
as chief of police. The man appointed as Rio's first permanent police chief, an untested but well-connected twenty-year-old lawyer,
applied disparate provisions of the procedural code in ways its writers had not envisioned and made much more of the office than
more senior political figures, at the time they drafted the code,
imagined it would be.

Eusébio de Queiroz, Chief of Police

The background and career of Eusébio de Queiroz, one of the
formative figures in the development of the city's police institutions
and procedures, well illustrate the continuity of personnel, ideology, and administrative practices through the long transition to
independence. He provides an apt parallel to Luis Alves de Lima e
Silva, the commander of the military police. Eusébio de Queiroz
Coutinho Matoso Câmara was born in 1812 in Luanda, capital of
Angola, where his father served on the high court of the Portuguese colony. Eusébio's father was a career colonial judicial officer
who had also been born in Angola, where his father had also served
as a judge. He transferred to the kingdom of Brazil in 1816, where
he served in various judicial positions in Minas Gerais, Pernambuco, Bahia, and the capital through the tumultuous era of independence, the regency, and the beginning of the second empire.
From 1829 until his death in August 1842, Eusébio's father served

on the nation's highest court, the Supremo Tribunal de Justiça, in Rio de Janeiro.

The younger Queiroz was tutored by his father and private teachers and became a member of the first class of the law school newly authorized in 1827 to be established in Recife, Pernambuco. He was the first candidate examined for entrance, receiving his law degree in September 1832. By October of that year he was back in Rio where on 7 November he was appointed criminal judge of Sacramento parish. That office was formally abolished by the code of criminal procedure just three weeks later, but Queiroz, like others holding positions in the old hierarchy, stayed on until the new measures were put into practice. In March 1833 he was promoted to district judge, and on 27 March of that year, three months to the day after his twentieth birthday, Queiroz took office as the city's police chief.[61] With a six-month hiatus in 1840-41 occasioned by his political disagreements with the liberal group promoting the premature declaration of the majority of Pedro II, Queiroz served as Rio's police chief until 20 March 1844, longer than any other person during the empire. During his tenure Queiroz continued to preside over jury sessions as one of the three district judges in the city and in 1842 was elevated to a seat on the court of appeals (*Relação*) in Rio de Janeiro.

He also became one of the founding members of the conservative party and began a political career that overlapped and followed his career as magistrate and police administrator. In 1838 he was elected to the legislative assembly of Rio province and by 1842 he represented that province in the chamber of deputies. In the cabinet formed on 29 September 1848 Queiroz became minister of justice of the empire, whose duties included direct supervision of both the civilian police chief and the commander of the military police of Rio. He held the post until May 1852. The law for which Queiroz is best known as politician and minister of justice declared in September 1850 the transatlantic slave trade to be piracy. The active enforcement of this law effectively brought to an end an activity that had continued with virtual impunity since its legal prohibition by Brazil in 1831.[62] Queiroz became a senator representing Rio Province in May 1854, replacing Francisco de Lima e Silva, father of Caxias, who had died the previous year. In October 1854 he became president of the Rio court of appeals, and in 1855 was appointed to the Council of State. In 1867 he was elevated to a seat on the Supremo Tribunal de Justiça. After a lingering illness he died in Rio in May 1868 at 55 years of age.

The formative experience in Queiroz's public life was his long tenure as Rio's police chief. When he took the position there was no precedent for it. Although Feijó had incorporated the justices of the peace into the centrally controlled institutional network during 1831–32, they retained responsibility for supervising police activity at the local level. The novelty and lack of clear authority of the position may have been one reason it was entrusted to a youth fresh from a new law school. The professional standing and personal connections of Queiroz's father no doubt helped Eusébio get the post, but at the time of his appointment it carried little obvious potential for professional growth.[63]

Like Caxias in command of the military police, Queiroz as police chief took charge of a new agency with a clean slate and untested mandate. Like Caxias, Queiroz was an active and forceful administrator who left a permanent imprint on the institution he headed for nearly eleven years. Like Caxias in the military police, Queiroz built the civil police into an institution oriented by hierarchical, centralizing, and authoritarian principles. The two institutions became effective and mutually reinforcing instruments of repression. These processes of conservative institution building took place while political rhetoric in the parliament, the press, and the public square ran the gamut from radical republicanism to monarchical absolutism, and the political survival of the nation was in question. The successful establishment of the complementary civil and military police systems was a major step in the conservative direction which anticipated national political trends. Caxias and Queiroz were positioned to patrol and regulate the nerve system of the control center of the empire—the streets and public places of the capital city.

Conclusion

From the perspective of traditional historical narrative the motivations for the institutional developments of 1831–32 were political. The mutinies and revolts following Pedro I's abdication were to be put down as a way of preventing opponents of the moderate liberal faction from gaining strength.[64] But fear and uncertainty caused by the revolts had two other effects that made control necessary: they were bad for business, and left person and property open to assaults by the urban rabble, slave and free. The police forces that emerged from the institutional transition of 1831–32 were not merely the partisan creations of the moderate liberals, reflecting their supremacy over the radicals (*exaltados*) and the restorationists seeking the return of Pedro I to the Brazilian throne. They were a more general response to the needs for social control that the institutional hiatus had revealed and exacerbated.

Far from being the result of vaguely shifting ideological winds, or the simple outcome of a game of parliamentary debate, the reversal of the glimmers of liberal legislation of 1827 (creation of the office of justice of the peace) and 1830 (the criminal code) resulted from the conditions in the streets of Rio. Generally under the rubric of "alterations of public tranquility," in the euphemistic rhetoric of the time, these conditions ranged from military sedition and mob violence, to the proliferation of capoeira gangs and their depredations, to slave escapes, to an increase in personal assault and petty theft. To those charged with maintaining order these activities formed a seamless continuum. The task of policing was crowd control and the suppression of armed rebellions, but it was also to maintain an environment conducive to the business of the city, to safeguard property both inanimate and human, and to make the streets safe for "decent" citizens.

In discussing the chronology of political events, a commonality among the range of threats to authority and hierarchy needs to be recognized. Politics was more than ideological debates and votes in parliament and newspaper editorials, and more than armed rebellion alternating with discussion and negotiation. Politics involved the exercise of power, and central to the maintenance of power in the hands of a few was defending it against threats from the many, whether those threats are today labeled political or social. Without the masses kept in their place below, either in service and support roles, or at least obedient and respectful and out of the way, there could be no elite. The mechanisms put into place beginning in 1831 provided the functional equivalent, adapted to the constitutional regime, of the social repression and political control under colonial absolutism—so hated in discourse and rejected in reform legislation. During the ensuing decade those mechanisms were expanded and tightened in practice, leading to another formal and legal stage of consolidation in 1841.

FOUR

Transition, 1833-41

From 1833 to 1841 the public order problem grew along with the city itself as the emerging coffee industry in Rio's hinterland caused increases in the city's commercial, financial, transport, and government administrative services. With economic and demographic growth there were more slaves than ever, and Rio attracted a steady stream of migrants from other parts of Brazil and from Portugal, who were desperate to eke out an existence as best they could, or looking to take advantage of what opportunities might present themselves.

By early 1833, with the chief of police installed, the elements of a new structure of repression were in place in Rio de Janeiro. Its three parts were the national guard, the military police, and the lower-level judicial officials. The latter included the justices of the peace and their ward inspectors and the chief of police with his small but growing staff. Unlike a tripod these three elements did not make for stability because they shared overlapping functions and uncertain lines of authority. Disputes among competing bureaucracies over authority and territory reflected marked differences over how policing the city was to be carried out and by whom. At the beginning of the regency period the basic approach was that the propertied classes would provide their own policing directly, through the national guard, as well as by the local-level application of the law, through the justices of the peace. During nearly a decade-long transition the balance shifted toward the use of full-time professionals in both the military and civilian branches of the system. Although the national guard retained a role as a political symbol and patronage network, as a police force in Rio it became an auxiliary to the military police. The justices of the peace in the national capital were increasingly brought under the supervision of the chief of police, and by an institutional change in late 1841 they were completely removed from their police functions and replaced by appointed officials. Through this process those functions reverted to agents of the centralized state, after a brief period of experimentation with spreading the authority and responsibility for them among sectors of the propertied classes.

While the control of social groups on the bottom occupied the attention of the evolving police system, sporadic incidents of political violence still plagued the national capital and illustrate the selective application of the law during this unsettled time. One notorious example of the early regency was the murder of Clemente José de Oliveira, radical republican and editor of one of the more sensationalistic and politically strident newspapers of the period, *O Brasil Aflito* (Suffering Brazil), published sporadically in Rio between April and September 1833. Oliveira spared few public figures his vitriolic verbal attacks, but Regent Francisco de Lima e Silva and his family were special targets. On 9 September 1833 Carlos Miguel de Lima e Silva, son of the regent and younger brother of military police Commander Luis Alves de Lima e Silva, caught sight of Oliveira as he entered a pharmacy on Carioca Square. The twenty-year-old cavalry lieutenant, seeking redress for the insults to his family, confronted the journalist and, after verifying the man's identity, drew his sabre and mortally wounded Oliveira with a blow to the head. The attack took place in broad daylight in one of the busiest spots in the city. Carlos Miguel subsequently turned himself in to authorities, but when the case came up for trial no witnesses came forward to testify against him, and the charge was dropped for lack of evidence.[1] Such incidents did not happen often, and the explanation for the outcome of this one is obviously related to the status of the murderer and his family, but it also belies any notion that equality before the law was much more than a hollow phrase or abstract aspiration.

The Secretariat of Police

The office staff Eusébio de Queiroz inherited from the intendancy, a holdover from the old regime, had for several years been stagnant and marginal both to the institutional changes and to the political and social crises being played out on the streets of Rio de Janeiro. The clerks and orderlies who had provided support to strong intendants like Viana and Aragão had been relegated to a housekeeping function, maintaining those few records of police activity the various authorities involved saw fit to submit and trying to keep track of the orders and regulations issued as higher powers tried to cope with one emergency after another. When major trouble broke out, those authorities often took personal charge of a crisis team that nominally included the intendant, whose staff was then expected to put the files in order when the situation calmed down.

Queiroz soon gave new purpose and an active role to an office that included a chief clerk (*oficial maior*), who supervised a staff of five clerks (*amanuenses*) whose job was to copy, file, and dispatch reports and correspondence, hand requests and inquiries up and orders and regulations down. One clerk was to keep records on prisons, and another kept track of foreigners entering and leaving the port; both of these became de facto administrative responsibilities of the new chief of the police, as he assumed those duties formerly under the intendant. Another section, headed by an employee who retained the ancient title *alcaíde* (constable), included six duty officers (originally using the old title *meirinho* but soon modernized to *oficial do expediente*) assigned to a variety of police tasks on a rotating basis. The duty officers coordinated attacks on the runaway slave quilombos in the hills of the city, served legal papers, collected evidence related to such major crimes as robbery and murder that were beyond the authority of the justices of the peace, and carried out other liaison and coordination functions. This secretariat of police was the seed from which the civil police of later times grew, and the staffing and procedures Queiroz renovated after 1833 became the basis for a larger and more active institutional apparatus when the chief of police came into his own with the judicial reform of 1841.[2]

As they went about their duties, civilian police officials were more likely to be obeyed if they were accompanied by assistants carrying cudgels and guns. A staff of twelve *pedestres* in the police secretariat provided such armed support, two for each duty officer. These orderlies were the functional descendants of the guardas of colonial times and were extensions of the authority of the state. They had a role in the apparatus of repression similar to the soldiers of the military police, although they were not subject to military discipline or a barracks regimen and in the early years wore no standard uniform. They could make arrests in flagrante, and their presence on the street had a chilling effect on unruly or illegal behavior of the population. They were also similar to the military police in their low social origins and income. As of 1838 when the head administrator of the police secretariat made 700$000 per year, his clerks made 240$000 per year and the duty officers made 200$000, the wage of a pedestre was $400 per day (12$000 per month, or 144$000 per year). That figure was at the lower end of the pay scale free wage workers might expect in Rio in the 1830's and well below the 18$000 monthly wage of a soldier in the military police at the time. Those in charge of this civilian police structure recurrently complained that such low wages made the hiring of qualified personnel very difficult, considering the responsibilities of the job.[3] Under Queiroz the pedestres gradually increased in number and began to patrol the streets independently of the duty officers.

In their new capacity the pedestres often came in contact with military police patrols, and like military police relations with the national guard on the other side of the social scale the encounters were not always friendly. As occasionally happened with police soldiers, pedestres sometimes exceeded the bounds of permissible public behavior, as in November 1833 when one of them beat up several people in Carioca Square, site of the largest public fountain supplying the city and then as today a meeting place for those inhabitants of Rio de Janeiro for whom social life involved gathering in public areas. The military police detachment posted to keep order at the fountain tried to arrest the offending pedestre, who fought them off with a dagger and escaped. The police soldiers were then disciplined for failing to carry out their duty as expected.[4]

Justices of the Peace

The other branch of the civil police structure through the 1830's involved the justices of the peace and the ward inspectors under their direct supervision in each neighborhood. There were sixteen justices of the peace in Rio de Janeiro, two each in the parishes of Santa Rita, Candelária, São José, Glória, Santa Ana, and Engenho Velho; three in Sacramento, and one for the Lagoa district. The number of ward inspectors varied through time, while observing the legal minimum of 25 residences per ward but with no maximum size limit. Through the 1830's there were some 150 to 180 ward inspectors in the city, or an average of about ten per judicial district. The 1832 procedural code gave the justices of the peace broad responsibility for vigilance in their districts, with the ward inspectors' assistance, to guard against crime and investigate those that could not be prevented. As the lowest-level criminal judge with jurisdiction over most minor violations, the justice of the peace followed in the functional footsteps of the intendant of police established in 1808, who also had authority to judge and punish the minor offenders he and his assistants arrested. In this regard the office of the justice of the peace, combining police and judicial attributes, maintained an old tradition. When in 1841 the elected judges were replaced by appointed police officials who were delegated the authority to judge and punish minor offenders, the tradition continued.

Only one intendant had jurisdiction over the entire city. Each of the sixteen justices of the peace could exercise their police authority anywhere in Rio, though they were on another judge's turf if they left their own district. The intendant had undisputed control of the militarized force of the Guarda Real. The justices had no such force at their disposal. Unarmed and unpaid civilian ward inspectors with little authority and their own professions to attend to were no substitute, and although both military police and national guard patrols operated in the judges' districts they were each under separate citywide command structures. Both the military and paramilitary police were expected to deliver to each local judge anyone they arrested in his district and respond to his emergency calls for help. Military police had a rigid duty roster and patrol schedule in addition to frequent additional assignments that stretched their available manpower, however, and after March 1833 they no longer provided orderlies for daily support of the justices of the peace. Sometimes local judges' routine calls for special assistance went unanswered. In July 1837, for example, a justice of the peace in Candelária parish complained that military police Commander Luis Alves de Lima had not fulfilled a request for a squad of three police soldiers for duty at the Carmo church "to contain the disrespect that some young men engage in during the *novena*."[5] National guard units were composed of hundreds of men in each parish, but like ward inspectors most guardsmen had professions and activities to attend to, and it might be difficult to bring a group together in an emergency. They often coordinated their activities with the local judges, but they also responded to calls for assistance from ordinary citizens without the intervention of the justice of the peace.

Revolt of the Kettle Makers

A tragic incident in 1833, early in the history of the complicated police structure of the regency, involved a justice of the peace and the national guard. The former ignored and the latter responded to the call of a man looking for assistance in keeping the slaves in his charge in line. It was no minor case of disrespect at a novena, but one of the few recorded examples of slave rebellion in Rio in the nineteenth century.

On the evening of 14 April 1833, Rodrigo Pinto da Costa, foreman of a kettle factory at no. 70 Alfândega Street, was surprised when some of the slaves he supervised objected to routine disciplinary punishment. Early the next afternoon Costa visited Gustavo Adolfo de Azevedo, justice of the peace of the first district of Candelária parish, and asked for help, saying he feared an uprising of the slaves in the workshop. Azevedo suggested that Costa should appeal to the military police if necessary to control insubordinate slaves because as justice of the peace he could only arrest persons accused of crimes. Disciplinary punishment, the judge reminded the foreman, could be administered at the Calabouço at Costa's request. Later on the afternoon of 15 April, Costa attempted to take into custody those slaves he considered a threat, but they refused to submit, arming themselves instead with tools from the shop. By 5 P.M. things came to a head when the slaves forced Costa from the premises and locked themselves inside. Costa called for help from the national guard, and finding Justice of the Peace Azevedo away from home, he appealed to the justice from the adjacent district to intervene.

Antonio Alves da Silva Pinto Jr., justice of the peace of the adjacent second district of Candelária, arrived on the scene about 7 P.M., and found the fourteen slaves of the kettle shop engaged in a "dangerous and threatening uprising," barricaded in a storage room in the back of the establishment. The doorway leading to their refuge was being watched by an armed national guard detachment that had responded to Costa's earlier call of alarm. The foreman led Pinto to an upstairs room which looked out over the courtyard and the storage area where the slaves had barricaded themselves. Calling each of the rebels by name as these were given to him by the foreman, Pinto tried to talk them into surrender to no avail. The ensuing sequence of events is best related in Pinto's own words:

With peaceful means exhausted, I warned the rebels that there was a large force prepared to repress and contain them, against which their number and strength would be powerless. To this they replied that "we will die when we can kill no more." I told them that despite their stubbornness they would be arrested in any event, and that they could give themselves up when the exit was secured. I then positioned the armed men so as to avoid confusion and maintain calm, giving orders that only an extreme emergency could justify the use of force and that once the passage was opened a new warning would bring the rebels under control.

As it happened, however, when this final warning was passed to the rebels and they were told to come out one by one, they charged out as a group, attacking with hatchets, knives, hammers, stones, bars, and other weapons from among the tools used in the workshop. At that point the national guardsmen opened fire in self defense. I ordered them to cease immediately, and only six or seven shots were fired. As a result the leader of the rebels, who was in front of the group, was killed by a bullet. Some of the others were wounded when, even after being subjugated by force, they engaged in violent resistance in attempting to escape.

Justice of the Peace Azevedo, to whom Costa had appealed in vain at the first stages of the slaves' recalcitrance, soon arrived on the scene. He found Calixto, leader of the revolt, dead, the other thirteen slaves on their way to jail, and calm restored.[6]

The lessons to be learned from this incident were several. For urban slaves it confirmed the difficulty of mounting concerted resistance to their condition, and it helps explain why there are not more of such incidents on record.[7] The first stage of the progression to fatal confrontation came when Calixto and his comrades refused to submit to the routine brutality that those who managed slaves used to reinforce dominance. It was a common practice for owners and supervisors to administer a few strokes with a whip or blows with a *palmatória* (a wooden paddle with holes in the wide end to reduce wind resistance) for the most minor infraction or no offense at all. If slaves objected the next step was to take them to the Calabouço and have the keepers there administer a more serious beating. If the slaves resisted that measure they were in de facto revolt and were to be brought under control by any means necessary. The state provided the means with national guard, military police, judges, and ward inspectors—a multilayered and interconnected network of repression.

While plantation slavery was maintained by the immediate presence of the slave driver and whatever force the planter deemed necessary, the urban master had the coercive power of the state close at hand. In the city the slave owner had an obligation to himself and the surrounding society to maintain the first line of slave discipline, but short of constant imprisonment owners could not be expected to be in direct control of their slaves at all times. As a minister of justice said of the problem of controlling slaves in the city, "one does not guard this property, it walks through the streets."[8] In a city where thousands of captive people were in easy communication, the threat of slave resistance or worse was too important to be left to individual owners. A system of vigilance, control, and discipline had been built up to such an extent that the coercive power of the owner class was pervasive. To expect slaves to engage in open rebellion in such an environment is to expect them to act irrationally, if we assume it was rational for them not to want to suffer intense and prolonged pain, to languish in the fetid dungeons of the Calabouço or the Aljube, or to die. There came a time for Calixto and his companions when rational action was measured by other criteria. Their final decision, as they prepared to leave this life, was to take as many of their oppressors with them as they could.[9]

There is another element of Calixto's revolt that needs stressing. The slaves were being disciplined not simply to enforce some abstract social hierarchy or because foreman Costa was cruel, but so that they would make the kettles upon which Costa's salary and his employer's profits depended. One reason to try to prevent an escalation of events was that the production of pots was stopped at least temporarily, the proprietor suffering considerable direct loss when Calixto was killed and the rest of his workers were carted off to jail. Even if their punishment was to be whipped with the hundreds of lashes usual for such offenses, and they survived that

treatment and were returned to their owner, his business still suffered. Just as it is less costly to prevent fires than to rebuild in their
aftermath, prevention was the key. Control over the behavior of
the slaves and the nonslave lower classes of Rio de Janeiro could
not be total or absolute, and the unrestrained application of arbitrary brutality would have been counterproductive in the literal
sense. The political theories that were helping Europeans redefine
the relationship between the individual and the state in that era,
and which were so talked about in Brazilian political circles, were
of little help in redefining the relationship between master and
slave. The contradictions of authoritarian liberalism were laid bare
in the doorway of the kettle shop on Alfândega Street as Calixto
lay dying from a musket ball of the citizen's militia.

Few people understood this need to refine the techniques of repression better than Diogo Antônio Feijó. In addition to his instrumental role in forming the military police and national guard during his term as minister of justice in 1831–32, he had issued a
series of orders defining the relationship between the emerging
state and the slave owner, as they divided the task of enforcing
discipline. In October 1831 he ordered that the whipping of slaves
in the Calabouço should not exceed a total of 200 lashes for each
offense, and as specified in the 1830 criminal code the maximum
per day would not exceed 50 lashes. Feijó also ordered that correctional punishment in the Calabouço at the request of the slave
owner was not to exceed a total of 50 lashes, "since more than 50
should be understood as excessive punishment and thus prohibited
by law." Feijó made a telling statement justifying these limits on
disciplinary whippings in determining that "the authority of the
slave owner, restricted to the correction of minor faults, should not
be extended to punishment for crimes which are under the jurisdiction of the judicial system. Slaves are men, and the law extends
to them." [10]

The developing state with these and related measures increasingly entered into the area of slave-master relations, imposing the
rule of law and attempting to limit arbitrary and excessive physical
abuse in order to preserve a system thus considered to be more
humane. The apparent compassion of Feijó in this passage must
be understood in the context of the maintenance of an ideological
system and a legal culture that could consider the slave to be a
human being and at the same time regulate brutal techniques of

repression and maintain slavery itself. Being human in nineteenth-century Brazil was not inconsistent with being bought, sold, bound, chained, whipped, or thrown into dungeons with irons clamped on neck and leg.[11] For Feijó and like-minded authoritarian liberals the rule of law, which also meant the authority of the state, should extend to the public behavior of slaves, meeting the authority of the slave owner at the door of his private domain. While punishment was reserved to the state, the master was still allowed and expected to exercise disciplinary control. In a situation in which most workers and many members of public society were also private property, the ideological pretensions of the nation-state to the universal exercise of authority were inevitably circumscribed. Rather than a generalized transition from personal and individualized mechanisms of control to impersonal and standardized systems, in Brazil the two hierarchies of power—traditional and private on the one hand and modern and public on the other—remained complementary and mutually reinforcing.[12]

From the standpoint of the system of repression more narrowly defined, there were also lessons to be learned from the revolt of the kettle makers. That system was adjusted through time in response to a cumulative assessment of many minor incidents. But such outbursts as the one Calixto and his co-workers precipitated in 1833 gave special urgency to such apparently mundane and unrelated matters as staffing levels and standing orders, and the lines of authority among justices of the peace, national guard, military police, and other connected institutions. Specifically, if Justice of the Peace Azevedo had been more responsive to foreman Costa's first call for assistance, the affair might not have reached its fatal impasse later that night. Instead he told Costa it was out of his jurisdiction, to try the military police or maybe the Calabouço, and the beleaguered foreman eventually got a group of national guardsmen to come to his aid as his problem escalated. By the accounting of the second justice of the peace, who was brought from the neighboring jurisdiction, the undisciplined guardsmen disobeyed his orders to exercise restraint, and when the smoke cleared Calixto lay dead. In such a complicated institutional environment some coordination became necessary and Eusébio de Queiroz used the new office of chief of police to provide it. As the decade wore on, coordination grew to resemble control, as the police chief became increasingly powerful at the expense of the putative independence of the locally elected justices of the peace.

Rosa and Agapito, "Free" Africans

During 1836 while Feijó served as sole regent of the empire, several incidents tested his recently refined definition of the border between public and private responsibility for controlling behavior. These cases further illustrate some of the techniques of resistance the subjugated population used and the response of the system of repression.

In early November 1836 two "free" Africans, Rosa and Agapito, appeared at the gates of the House of Correction, the model prison then under construction, demanding protection from mistreatment by their guardians. The fact that they would try to get into prison to escape a domestic situation is a comment on that treatment, and it suggests that "free" Africans understood that the state had a special responsibility for their condition. This peculiar category of people was the result of the selective application of Brazilian law. After 7 November 1831 it was illegal to import slaves into Brazil, and although the slave trade continued on a massive scale, a relatively small number of those brought in from Africa were apprehended in a desultory show of compliance with the law.[13] The question that then arose was what to do with the unacculturated Africans. Most could speak no Portuguese on arrival, and there was little means of determining their point of origin in Africa or transporting them back to their homes. Brazilian authorities decided that although they could not be sold as slaves, neither could they be turned loose in Brazil to fend for themselves.

The solution was to declare the liberated Africans wards of the state. A lower judicial official called a *curador* (custodian) was assigned to keep track of them and collect the rents due for those in private service. Although some were hired out to private individuals for a nominal fee, most were either assigned to labor as servants in government installations or on public works projects. (The House of Correction itself was constructed from 1836 to 1850 largely with the labor of "free" Africans along with prisoners sentenced to hard labor and the slaves sent to the Calabouço, which was transferred to the construction site in 1837 expressly to make use of the imprisoned slaves for labor on the project.)[14] Whether they were servants in a private home or in a government office, the daily treatment of the "free" Africans differed little from that of slaves except that they could not be bought or sold. In 1835, for example, Luis Alves de Lima e Silva requested that fifteen "free" Africans be assigned to cleaning and similar menial duties in military police barracks that the soldiers under his command "cannot be subjected to." He pointed out that the expense of buying or renting slaves for such tasks would thus be avoided and overall expenses reduced. He received twelve. He also provided the *curador* with a list of military police officers wishing to rent "free" Africans as personal servants as they became available.[15] Although the "free" Africans were relatively few compared to the total slave population, the special role of the state in their supervision provides some information on their condition and reveals the attitudes of those who specified the rights and responsibilities of servants and masters as well as the extent of the state's jurisdiction over that relationship.

Rosa, who appeared to the officials involved to be about eleven or twelve years of age, worked as the only servant in the house of Manoel José Simões, and because she fell behind in the many tasks she was assigned, her renter's wife pestered her constantly. When Simões came to fetch her from the House of Correction where she had sought refuge, she refused to return home with him, and the warden ordered a military police soldier to drag her bodily out of the establishment. Rosa managed to wrestle loose of the soldier's grip, run to a nearby well, and jump in. She was hauled out of the hole but then flung herself on the ground and refused to budge. In the warden's words, "there was no way she could be made to accompany Simões," and he ordered her left in the prison until higher authorities could reach some resolution of the case.

The curador brought in to look into the case examined Rosa and found some scars that indicated that she had been whipped but concluded that there was no evidence she was currently being mistreated because the scars were healed and "she seemed well fed." Upon interviewing the parties, however, the curador did note a "great insolence" on the part of Simões's wife, and that Rosa showed "a very strong spirit, and is mischievous and stubborn." The recommendation of the curador to Police Chief Queiroz is a revealing indication of the attitude of the representatives of power:

I think she absolutely must be returned to the custody of her renter, so that her behavior does not become a precedent for serious abuses on the part of others. Nevertheless, in order to keep her in some degree of subjugation, her renter should employ some docility, and he should have his wife assign the girl a less heavy burden of labor. If then she does not submit, I recommend that she be turned over to the authorities so that strong and exemplary punishment might be applied.

The danger of allowing Rosa to succeed in her protest was the example it might provide to others, threatening the stability of the system of subjugation. The example to be set was that members of the dominated class, even "free" Africans, could not successfully resist their condition and that persistent temerity would be met with brutal rebuke—even if the object of the retribution were an eleven-year-old girl.

The case of Agapito was less serious and more easily disposed of. He showed no physical signs of mistreatment but alleged that his renter, Agostinho Feliciano, made the African work even on Sundays and saints' days, delayed what should have been the midday meal until 4 P.M., fed Agapito only crude brown bread, and hit him. Agapito knew enough about free versus slave status to further complain that Feliciano failed to pay him for his labor. Agapito took little satisfaction in the fact that Feliciano, who ran a cartage business located at the edge of the Campo de Santana, was already paying the government a token sum in return for full use of the African's unpaid services. The investigating curador dismissed the charge of mistreatment because he found no signs of physical injury and recommended to Queiroz that "the solution for such cunning is that he be turned over to his renter and be subjected to some punishment, to cure the bad habit of escaping and to correct his errors, for eating brown bread late in the day is not the same as not eating at all, and being mistreated."

Police Chief Queiroz followed the recommendation of the curador in the case of Agapito and returned him to Feliciano without further action. In the case of Rosa, however, Simões and his wife were deemed to have exceeded the bounds of the permissible, and it required a different solution. As Queiroz reported to the minister of justice, the scars the curador found, "supposedly caused by mild correction, indicate the contrary, because mild correction does not leave scars. And as the renter does not treat the African in the humane way specified in the rental agreement he signed when he took her, I recommend she be taken from him and given to someone else who will treat her with the required humaneness." The minister of justice agreed, and the appropriate standard of humaneness was thus served. The resistance of Rosa and Agapito was met by a complex hierarchy of repression directly involving the private individuals who rented their labor, the warden of the House of Correction, the military police on guard there, the custodian of the "free" Africans' welfare, the chief of police, and the minister of justice of the empire. It was no contest.

Graciano, Mina, Capoeira

A few months after Rosa and Agapito attempted their escape to prison, an incident went one step higher in the political hierarchy, involving Regent Feijó himself. On the night of 28 December 1836, a military police patrol arrested Graciano, a Mina slave born in west Africa. He had run afoul of police before for disrespect to authority, illegal weapons possession, and engaging in capoeira, the deadly foot fighting notorious among slaves and the free lower classes of Rio that police authorities were hard pressed to contain. Graciano had a reputation as a sneak thief and was in the habit of carrying a blade, with which he had once tried to attack the cashier in his owner's business. He had also brazenly declared that he was bent on taking away the willfulness of the whites.[16] Taken before Justice of the Peace Luis da Costa Franco e Almeida, Graciano was delivered to his master, Jacomo Rombo, who lived at Conde Street (now Visconde do Rio Branco) in central Rio. Rombo had owned Graciano only six months, but the Mina slave had already tried to escape three times. Rombo decided it was time to teach Graciano a lesson. He had the slave bound so tightly that his hands and forearms were deeply lacerated by the cords and ordered him whipped.

By the next morning the news of the severity of the beating had reached as far as Feijó, regent of the empire, who called for Justice of the Peace Almeida and personally ordered him to investigate the circumstances surrounding it. Almeida in turn brought in two physicians to conduct an examination to determine if a crime had been committed. On the morning of 29 December the doctors found Graciano in his owner's house only able to lie on his side, and unable to stand or walk. In addition to severely lacerated hands and forearms, he had intensely painful open wounds on his thighs and buttocks, surrounded by inflamed tissue, numerous bruises, and lacerations caused by repeated blows of the whip. They declared that due to the seriousness of the wounds and the possibility that his condition would worsen, he would require an extended period of convalescence.

Under interrogation Rombo pointed out that it would hardly be in his interest to kill or seriously damage his own property, so the punishment had been for correctional purposes only. Justice of the Peace Almeida concluded that the laws restricting the authority of owners to punish their slaves were unclear as to the precise limits and decided not to bring formal charges against Rombo. Despite explicit recognition in the language of the interrogation that Rombo had violated the law, he was not submitted to further legal proceedings, much less punishment. Almeida went no further than to oblige the owner to report any deterioration of the slave's condition and not to remove Graciano from the house or otherwise dispose of him for 30 days, after which time another medical examination would be conducted. From Graciano the police had only the mute but graphic testimony of his physical condition.

Seeking the minister of justice's approval of his handling of the case, Almeida recalled the slave revolts in Bahia and Minas Gerais in 1835 and the threat of such an uprising in the province of Rio de Janeiro in January 1836. In this tense atmosphere he argued against a policy of government intrusion into the domain of private residences, which he was required to conduct in the case of Graciano and which would serve to limit the free hand of masters to punish slaves at their own discretion. Beyond what he called a general "state of terror" generated by the threat and reality of slave rebellions, Almeida made specific reference to local incidents that made close vigilance of the slaves essential: "Less than a month ago we had in this city the case of the atrocious and inhuman murder of two unfortunate cashiers, sacrificed by the barbarous Africans, who disgracefully continue to increase among us, and whom nothing will contain short of a healthy terror."[17] He had used the term *terror* twice in the same paragraph of a routine report, first referring to the masters' fear of slave revolt, then to suggest the necessary countermeasures.

In the same memorandum Almeida made more general comments that illustrate essential features of the system of repression that seldom emerge from the bureaucratic formulas and routine police reports. The economy and social hierarchy of Brazil depended fundamentally on slavery, and because people like Graciano were unwilling to submit to their condition without coercion, state authorities and the slave owners found themselves in uneasy collaboration. Justice of the Peace Almeida was caught in this dilemma when Feijó ordered him to look into the case of Graciano.

In restricting his involvement to investigation and supervision of the slave's recovery from a beating Feijó considered excessive, Almeida took a pragmatic position: "There cannot exist, without total subversion of the state, any article of Law which limits the discretionary power of the owners in the correction of their slaves, or which sets the norm or the degree of moderation in the exercise of that power, which after all is indispensable in all countries where slaves exist in such numbers as among us."[18] In the environment of resistance and repression central to Brazilian slave society, state authority had to yield to the traditional obligation and responsibility of property owners. Furthermore, this reasoning went, state power was no substitute for the direct domination of master over slave, and if the state restricted the master's discretion, the state in turn would suffer the consequences of loosened control. Thus the authoritarian liberal state did not represent an ideology or a policy that opposed the interests of slave owners.[19] On the contrary the humane refinements instituted by Feijó, supported by Police Chief Queiroz in the cases of Rosa and Agapito, and contested by Justice of the Peace Almeida in the case of Graciano were intended to streamline the system and specify the roles of the parties involved in the interest of efficiency and predictability.

Other traditional procedures that needed specifying were those related to summary punishment of slaves at the point of arrest. In June 1837 Police Chief Queiroz reported to the minister of justice that he had passed on the minister's instructions to the effect that "justices of the peace are not to continue to order slaves whipped without first submitting them to a judicial proceeding and formal sentencing, in the presence of their owner." But Queiroz asked for further clarification because "the police also normally order slaves whipped without judicial process, either at the request of owners or because the slaves are caught with weapons or engaging in capoeira, so I wish to know if your instructions also extend to the police, or only to justices of the peace." The minister replied that the requirement for formal hearings for slaves only applied to justices of the peace and that police should continue operating under existing orders which permitted "correctional" punishment without a judicial proceeding.[20] Even in the 1830's when the vaguely defined responsibilities of the chief of police did not include that of judging the guilt or innocence of detainees, the police received formal confirmation of their traditional practice of administering summary beatings for minor offenses.

Staffing Problems

Complaints persisted regarding the inefficiency of depending on national guardsmen to respond to public security problems after the fact. As early as January 1833, between the approval of the code of criminal procedure and the appointment of Eusébio de Queiroz, the interim police chief requested that the minister of justice issue instructions to the military police to set up a permanent guard post in the isolated waterfront area of the Saco do Alferes to guard against the activities of "criminals and vagrants" who hid out on the adjacent Nheco hill during the day and "as is public knowledge, go out at night to steal and commit attacks against personal security." The proposed military police detachment would be divided into three squads of three men each with one squad always on patrol and the others in reserve to respond to emergencies. The request was backed by a telling indictment of the national guard that was repeated in some form many times over the next few years. The justice of the peace in the area had called on the guardsmen for assistance, but they "were either not home, or responded to the call more slowly than the situation required." The military police guard post at the Saco do Alferes became one of many such points they staffed around the city, from which patrols provided a police presence in the vicinity.[21]

Honório Hermeto Carneiro Leão, the minister of justice who received this request, subsequently reported that the "patriotic zeal" guardsmen had shown in the political crises of 1831–32 had declined "once the threat of anarchy disappeared" and that the military police had been called to "garrison" the city due to the "laxity of the national guard." He complained of the many exemptions from guard service and the growing practice of members intentionally breaking rules in order to be subject to a disciplinary hearing, pending which the guardsman in question was relieved of patrol duty. The offense then usually went unpunished or resulted in just three days in detention. Many guardsmen simply failed to report for duty, and justices of the peace were reluctant to issue warrants to enter their houses and get them. "It needs to be said," Honório concluded, "that the majority of national guardsmen perform the service now required of them under duress, and thus they perform poorly."[22]

The following year Aureliano de Souza de Oliveira Coutinho, the interim police chief who sent the 1833 request for a police post

in Saco do Alferes, became minister of justice. He made clear that
the problem of the guard was not simple dereliction but one of
specialized function and economic necessity: "It is not possible, nor
is it in the interest of the nation, which needs to accumulate capital,
that industrious citizens continually abandon their commerce and
means of livelihood, to be distracted in such onerous service.
Economy itself demands that a public force be paid, and that it be
used to relieve the national guard."[23] As of January 1835, less than
four years after its founding, the national guard was relieved of
the burden of regular citywide police duty in Rio de Janeiro. After
that time small numbers of guardsmen were given special assignments like ceremonial duty at the downtown imperial palace, sup-
plementing military police patrols on Sundays and more regularly
when there were shortages in police ranks, and responding to
emergencies as called. The minister of justice was quite explicit
about the "valid reasons" for this change: "It was certainly difficult
to take industrious citizens from their profitable work, and put
them in continuous service, for which, far from receiving compen-
sation, their interests suffered and they spent their own funds."[24]

The unpaid justices of the peace had similar problems, as they
were "occupied with their private affairs and do not investigate
crimes because it would take time from their business." The local
judges for their part had their own complaints about the burdens
of the office. They were authorized to appoint up to six bailiffs
(oficiais) to assist them in police duties, but a crucial limitation on
this as on other initiatives was that the local judges had no access to
funds to support a staff. In special circumstances they could request that a pedestre be assigned to serve in their district as a full-
time orderly, but they usually had to make do with the assistance
the police system as a whole provided, subject to a special request
in each case. Faced with many duties and no staff, the judge of the
second district of Santa Ana parish complained in 1836, for example, that he could not find anyone "who would honorably serve"
as an oficial because he had no means to pay them. In exasperation
he said, "I don't know how I am supposed to carry out the many
orders that come down to me, and the requests I receive are piling
up." Queiroz passed this complaint on to the minister of justice for
action, and the latter wondered if it might be possible to provide
one or two pedestres to each justice of the peace. Queiroz responded that the number of pedestres was barely enough to carry

out the normal activities of the secretariat of police and that he could not spare any for duty with the local judges.[25]

In 1837 a staffing problem in Lagoa parish revealed the short-comings of the decentralized police organization made up of un-paid volunteers from among the respectable citizenry and the dif-ficulty the national guard had in filling the gap. At that time the Lagoa district included the suburban area from Botafogo around the Rodrigo de Freitas lagoon and all adjacent points. Ipanema was not used as a separate place name, and Leblon was that part of the area where a Frenchman named Le Blon had a farm. The isolated stretch of sand and brush from Leme rock to Arpoador point was distinguished by a small chapel at the far end where an altar con-taining a relic from the Copacabana shrine in Lake Titicaca, Peru, gave the beach its name. A census in 1838 counted a total popula-tion of 3,319 for the entire district, comprising 392 families. It was divided into twelve wards for about 33 families per *quarteirão*. When women, children, and slaves were discounted there were just 537 adult free males resident in the Lagoa district.[26] Only Botafogo was in reasonably easy communication with the rest of the city along the bay front road, but it was too far from the center of things to be a residential area for people whose business took them downtown every day. The rest of the district was inhabited mainly by small farmers and fishermen, and the botanical garden on the lagoon and the adjacent government-operated gunpowder factory were among the few activities of note. With much of the district covered with wooded hills and isolated beaches, it was a favorite hideout for runaway slaves and men trying to escape forced con-scription into the army. It thus suffered problems of public order and personal safety that belied its sparse population and semirural character.

In May 1837 the minister of justice ordered the lone justice of the peace in Lagoa to circulate through his district every night ac-companied by his personal orderly. Alternatively, a trusted ward inspector could head the patrol. The judge replied that his district was so extensive that a single patrol might barely be able to make one circuit in a dusk-to-dawn shift, but only if they did not stop to look into any suspicious activity or ask questions of anyone. Some of the twelve wards did not currently have inspectors in place, he had no paid pedestres available, and it was difficult enough just to file daily reports, the justice complained, without the burdens of night patrol. If the minister of justice could arrange for some national guardsmen to take on this task, it might be possible to comply with the order. Guardsmen were ordered to report for this duty, but on 27 May they failed to appear. The judge then further specified the frustrations he faced: A patrol of only two men, in isolated circumstances late at night, would be no match for some of the gangs of bad characters they might encounter. Some ward inspectors had jobs or professional obligations during the day and the rest were so "decrepit" that they could not spend all night on patrol. If such duty were forced on them, no one would agree to serve, and because ward inspectors could not be appointed from among those already in the national guard, the pool of candidates was quite reduced. As for the national guardsmen, they also had daytime occupations that kept most from doing night patrols on a regular basis. Those assigned to this task were "old men, invalids from the reserve rolls, men who fail to show up for duty, or when they do appear they are so tired that they cannot cover the whole district, so they usually report they found nothing unusual when in another part of the district all sorts of things are going on." The local judge requested permission to continue policing his district as in the past, with ward inspectors keeping an eye out for trouble and circulating now and then in their local neighborhoods, "especially on holidays or when there is a public festival," and requesting additional force as circumstances required.[27]

The sparse population and extensive area of the Lagoa district made for special circumstances, but it was an extreme case of a more general problem. As the city grew in population and area, it was increasingly difficult for the people who wanted protection to supply it for themselves in their spare time. These reports from Lagoa were part of a citywide effort by Minister of Justice Gustavo Aguilar Pantoja to take stock of the police system in 1837. Of particular importance was the issue of service as ward inspector versus the national guard. Those in charge of the guard repeatedly complained that the many openings for ward inspectors—about 180 in the city as a whole—created too many exemptions from guard service. Most justices of the peace, in contrast, reported that there were wards in their districts for which they could not keep inspectors and that reducing the number of *quarteirões* was no solution because it was even more difficult to get men to serve in the larger wards. Exemption from national guard service was no advantage if the tradeoff was dealing with a disrespectful public, risking injury in confrontation with dangerous characters, and being called out at all hours to deal with everything from a riot to noisy drunks.

A justice of the peace in Santa Ana parish was more explicit about the relationship between poverty and public order. Though he recognized the importance of the inspectors as "the right arm of the justices of the peace," few men with the necessary competence wanted "to take on such a burdensome job" as unpaid ward inspector because it "provided no reward other than bother and intrigue." In his own district on the outskirts of the city there were "terrible" wards where "due to the low cost of housing, there are many people with bad habits, and even those who commit disorders, making it essential to have an inspector who is both active and prudent, and respected by his neighbors." It was important that inspectors live in their wards in order to provide direct supervision, but in some neighborhoods, "fertile in disorders and disturbances," the national guard and the police system competed for the services of those few residents with the appropriate qualities.[28]

Thieves and Foreigners

Among the phenomena that the chief of police and his staff of duty officers and pedestres were better equipped to respond to than were local judges were the relatively few major crimes against property that were reported in these years. On 7 August 1837, for example, Queiroz got word that at four o'clock that morning a tavern was broken into by what appeared to be a skillful gang that got away with more than 2:000$000 in cash. There were indications that the thieves might strike again, so the chief gave orders for the military police to be on the alert and sent squads of duty officers and pedestres in search of the culprits. They launched a citywide dragnet that was beyond the authority of both the local justice of the peace and the military police commander, and it worked. The next day a military police patrol captured two members of the gang, one of whom was carrying a pistol, and a squad of pedestres discovered another of the thieves disguised as a beggar and lying about with other mendicants on the street to avoid detection. He resisted the arrest but was not armed. Three weeks later Queiroz's staff foiled a robbery when they received reports of a plan to rob a house on Santa Luzia beach, but the gang fled when they in turn got wind of the approaching squad of pedestres. Only one was captured, and the tools of his trade, a crowbar and a knife, were found at the site.[29] Such incidents were uncommon, compared to the on-going task of dealing with minor and usually victimless public order offenses, but when major crime did occur, a centralized bureaucratic structure like the one Queiroz was building was helpful in the response.

There were also occasional public order problems that spread across several judicial districts or involved disparate institutions and required the coordinated response the chief of police was increasingly able to provide. Such were the periodic disturbances caused by patrons of the string of *publicaos* along the city's waterfront. (The word is a phonetic rendering of the English public house.) These pubs catered primarily to foreign sailors on shore leave. The increase in this social category—undesirable for the forces of order but welcome for the proprietors of the pubs and others who offered services in demand among sailors fresh from several weeks before the mast—was an unavoidable result of the commerce attending the growth of the coffee industry in these years. If the people who administered Rio de Janeiro wanted to maintain the lifeblood of the regional export economy, they were going to have to deal with carousing sailors.

On 14 January 1838 a crowd of about forty English-speaking sailors, most of them feeling the effects of sugarcane brandy, roamed along Misericórdia Street and environs, beating up on each other and passersby. The ward inspector in the area ran for the guards at the nearby royal palace, who fixed bayonets and managed to arrest several of the miscreants. The inspector then ordered all the pubs in the area closed to help restore order. This temporary halt to one of the important commercial activities of the area was approved by the local justice of the peace, who then recommended to the chief of police that every offending publicaos in the city be closed for good. Queiroz met with the consuls of Great Britain, the United States, Holland, and Austria, and together they drafted a petition requesting the city council, which had authority over retail commerce and public accommodations, to issue the ban. The petition, written in English for the benefit of the principal parties, defined the pubs as rooming houses and drinking places that facilitated desertion by sailors and generally "disturb shipping."[30] It was important that shipping not be disturbed for the same underlying reason it was important that the public order in Rio de Janeiro not be disturbed. The retail trade of the pub owners, not to mention the recreation available to foreign sailors, had to yield to a higher good that the chief of police of Rio and the representatives of Brazil's major trading partners agreed upon.

Another type of foreign presence was not a necessary by-product of international commerce but a problem many major seaports have encountered in history. Professional thieves, confidence men, and gamblers lived an itinerant existence exploiting whatever opportunities they might find, until they prudently moved on to the next port or the police caught up with them. As minister of justice, Feijó had ordered that after 1 January 1833 no foreigners would be allowed to disembark in Brazilian ports without a visa from a Brazilian consul attesting to their honest habits and capacity to earn a respectable living.[31] An official of the Rio police was supposed to visit every ship that entered the harbor and verify the bona fides of all passengers before they disembarked, and for the rest of the empire period the port inspection service (*visita do porto*) was a permanent branch of the city police bureaucracy. It was apparently fairly easy to slip through this surveillance, and the device police used repeatedly over the years to rid Rio of such undesirables was summary deportation, for which permission needed to be obtained from the minister of justice through the chief of police. In 1836 Queiroz deported an Italian named Vicente Andrini, a.k.a. Dentista Perna de Pau (the peg-legged dentist), who was operating an illegal gambling den that was "corrupting the sons of good families" and who had been deported in 1833 for the same offense after police destroyed his roulette wheel. Twenty-three people were arrested in the raid, which was conducted undercover by military police in civilian disguise. Among those Queiroz deported in 1838 were Antônio Joaquim da Silva, a.k.a. O Galego, who "with the two Souzas already deported, robbed Meirat's jewelry shop in Santa Teresa after murdering his slave"; Francisco José de Amorim, "known slave thief and also a bandit," who had already been deported once and dared to return; and José Joaquim Pereira de Carvalho, who had been arrested several times and had used his considerable facility with several languages to engage in "evil and fraudulent practices."[32]

Another alien presence was Gypsies. The Campo de Santana, that all-purpose open area on the edge of the city, also served as the gathering point for mule trains arriving from the interior and a place where country folk could water their horses around the large fountain where slave women did laundry. Merchants and peddlers catered to the travelers and passersby who also received attention from Gypsies that was not always welcome. So many Gypsies had frequented the area for so long that one of the streets entering the Campo was named after them (now rua da Constitui-ção). In 1837 Queiroz received a request from the justice of the peace whose district included the Campo de Santana for permission to charge the worst offenders among the Gypsies with vagrancy to get them out of circulation. They had an occupation to be sure, but it was "to deceive the credulous *Mineiros* [people from the province of Minas Gerais] and farmers" who passed through the Campo, "selling yellow articles as made of gold, enticing slaves away, and by insidious methods filching money from people's purses while they haggled over the fake jewelry." The judge had tried to catch them in the act or with the evidence, but among the Gypsies' many skills was covering their tracks. By charging them with vagrancy the judge could sentence them to labor on public works for a month, which might be more effective than the fruitless warnings he had issued. He had communicated directly with Caxias requesting that a detachment of five police soldiers report to him in civilian clothes, so they could surround the Gypsies and take them by surprise, but he asked Queiroz to inquire of the minister of justice regarding the plan to charge those caught with vagrancy. Queiroz passed on the inquiry with a positive recommendation, which the minister approved.[33]

Beyond intriguing hints about members of an ethnic group still plying their profession today in Rio de Janeiro, with appropriate updating from the way it was described in 1837, this case provides other clues about policing the city. Vagrancy became a catchall charge that authorities used when more specific criminal acts were difficult to prove, or when they wanted to get someone off the streets and teach him or her a lesson. And it was not uncommon for the military police to send out squads in plain clothes, the urban equivalent of a soldier's camouflage. Two months after the operation against the Gypsies, for example, Caxias reported on the undercover surveillance his men had conducted on an army captain whom a justice of the police had jailed as a chicken thief and whom "our spies circulating in gambling dens and *botequims* always mention as one of the most inveterate gamblers in the city, and of very bad habits."[34]

Beggars, Vagrants, Abandoned Children

One old problem for which Queiroz thought he had at least a partial solution was begging in the streets. "Begging is a matter that occupies the attention of police in all civilized countries," he declared in 1838. "Its extinction is impossible, however, and the most that can be sought is to diminish its bad effects." At the time he took over as police chief six years earlier, the standard practice had been to deposit beggars in the common jail, which was recognized as "a school capable of converting those who were merely vagrants and beggars into criminals and thieves." That situation made justices of the peace reluctant to do anything about the proliferation of such people on the streets. Since that time Queiroz had established a series of shelters where homeless people could spend the night, attempted to create a workshop where they might be usefully occupied, and ordered some arrested now and then, thus "reducing the number of those who habitually sleep in the streets and in the doorways of churches."

In September 1838 an opportunity arose for a new push against the chronic problem when space became available in the prison on Santa Barbara island for holding those beggars incapable of working. With undue optimism Queiroz told the minister of justice that he "did not want to lose the opportunity to end the problem of street beggars." In a stance on the issue now called civil liberties that was characteristic of the time, Queiroz said that those affected by the police sweep "would not be deprived of their freedom, because they will be permitted to leave upon signing a promise to stop begging, and they would only be locked up at night. Thus those who are invalid and truly in need will find a way to satisfy all the necessities of life, without luxury it is true, but in a way analogous to their condition, without having to wander the streets of the city—an activity enjoyed only by those addicted to begging." He confidently anticipated one criticism of the plan, providing at the same time his own view of the mind-set of poor people and the socioeconomic conditions in Brazil:

We should not be concerned that the very existence of an establishment where beggars are provided for will make their numbers increase, and that people without urgent need will want to enter. Living in one of the bays of [the former jail on] Santa Barbara [island], with meager sustenance and nightly lockup, may be considered a benefit for the truly invalid, but it is not the sort of life to be envied by the vagrants and unemployed of a country, such as this one, where anyone who wants to work, however proletarian he may be, does not die of hunger. Such concerns might be valid in some countries of Europe, where the strongest desire to work at times is insufficient to provide a living.

In justifying the new approach to an old problem, Queiroz mixed high-minded paternalism with ruthlessness, saying it was a plan "by which, with the humanity due to the truly unfortunate, we will purge the beggars from the streets of this city."[35]

To put the scheme in operation Queiroz issued a general warning that after a grace period of a few days beggars would be rounded up. He then ordered justices of the peace to arrest everyone who fell under article 296 of the criminal code, which declared public begging a crime punishable by up to one month prison with hard labor. Those unfit to work were to go to jail on Santa Barbara island, and able-bodied detainees to the House of Correction for a month, after which they would be sent to the officer in charge of military conscription, for selection of those fit for service in the army or navy. The navy had certain standards of physical fitness for conscripts who were to join ships' crews, but Queiroz suggested that useful employment might also be found on unarmed vessels or on the grounds of the naval arsenal for those unable to serve on men of war, and "in this way not only will we remedy the manpower shortage our navy suffers, but the city will also be free of the vagrants and false beggars who flood it." The director of the arsenal, less enthusiastic about the prospects, responded that he would be able to accept only men fit to sail.[36]

The roundup of undesirables was a short-term success, primarily due to the reward of 10$000 for each able-bodied beggar brought in. With a bonus amounting to about two weeks' normal pay per mendicant arrested, police "spared no effort in discovering them." The cost of paying these rewards would soon decline, Queiroz assured the minister of justice, when "the number of such vagrants and beggars will drop to almost nothing, because of the arrests themselves and because people will either hurry to find honest work or leave the city." The police chief reported that in less than a week no fewer than 104 beggars fit for work had been removed from the streets and were serving their one-month term of prison with labor at the House of Correction, the new model prison then under construction. Their work assignment was breaking rock for use in the nearby fill of swampy land of the Mangue (now Cidade Nova).[37] If the full 10$000 bounty was paid for each beggar brought in, the secretariat of police disbursed enough in bonuses in one week to pay the wages of a police soldier (at $640 per day) for almost four and a half years, and a pedestre (at $400) for more than seven years. Other rewards paid in this period were 4$000 for apprehending a runaway slave and 5$000 for capturing a conscript fit for military service, so 10$000 for a beggar was indeed an extra incentive.

In several long memos on the scheme, the root cause of the profusion of beggars and vagrants was not specified beyond invoking a series of negative terms. Beggars "infest" and "flood" the city, with "bad effects," but the underlying nature of the problem was considered so obvious and unquestioned as to dispense explicit comment. The sweep of 1838 illustrates how the political and social elite perceived the issue, the associations they made among poverty, charity, the obligation of the able-bodied to work, and the obligation of the state to remove the social detritus from public view. It was not the last of similar efforts by police authorities, nor did it end the presence of beggars in Rio de Janeiro.

In 1821 Intendant Viana could order the arrest of a man for behavior called capoeira, have him whipped with three hundred strokes of the lash if he were a slave, and have him spend three months working on a road gang for the department of public works Viana also supervised. In 1838 after independence, a new constitution, a new system of laws, police, and procedures, Police Chief Queiroz could order the justices of the peace to arrest beggars, process them under the provisions of the liberal criminal code, and send them to the modern prison, the House of Correction, where they would spend the next month working on the construction of the prison or breaking and hauling stone to fill in wetland onto which the city could expand, in coordination with the city department of public works. The advantages of liberal institutions and modern administrative structures were probably lost on the people whose coerced labor made the roads and landfills onto which Rio de Janeiro expanded, or who literally built their own prison.

Yet another initiative Queiroz took in 1838 was to address a social issue already growing at that time—abandoned children. His assessment of the nature of the problem and its origins reveals much about his outlook on policing Rio de Janeiro. The target group was "the great number of boys who, barely past their infancy, wander the streets acquiring the bad habits of idleness, gambling, etc., preparing themselves for a youth that, far from being advantageous for the state, will on the contrary be harmful, due to the crimes they will probably engage in." His proposal for dealing with these "poor orphans and the sons of people whose poverty prevents them from providing the proper training" was to set aside a separate space in the House of Correction where boys between the ages of twelve and seventeen could learn a trade. Queiroz's modest intent was to address a social problem before it became a criminal problem, rather than to form some grand plan to replace slaves with free and skilled proletarians. The director of the House of Correction did point out, however, that there was great demand for men with skills the boys would learn—carpentry, masonry, plumbing, and blacksmithing—because for the most part "only captive people are employed in those professions."[38] In any case not much came of this suggestion, and although some years later such a combination shelter/workshop was set up in the House of Correction, it was soon disbanded and did little to treat the symptom of street urchins, much less the underlying social disease.

After five years as police chief, Eusébio de Queiroz was ready to give his assessment of the organization set up by the 1832 procedural code. "As weak as it is," he said in an 1838 memo to the minister of justice, "our police system continues to provide some utility." For the most part the local justices of the peace were cooperative and responsible, usually coordinating their activities with the several other institutions with whom they shared a common purpose. But incidents involving jurisdictional disputes, laxity, and pretensions to independence on the part of justices of the peace were frequent enough to cause recurring inefficiencies from the government's perspective. In the view of Queiroz, "today the need to increase the authority of the police is so generally recognized that further comment is unnecessary."[39] The authority of the police was increased substantially in late 1841, and Queiroz was maintained in charge of the stronger system he had advocated for several years.

Military Police

One institution little affected by those changes was the military police, which from its October 1831 beginnings as a replacement for the Guarda Real de Polícia had been tested early on in armed clashes with political rebels and by 1841 had become the all-purpose instrument of force in the hands of those who controlled the state.

Soon after it was established, the military police found itself overextended and understaffed, a situation commanders frequently complained about and civilian authorities recognized but did little to correct. Authorized at a level of 400 soldiers at the time of its founding, the corps was considerably larger than the old Guarda Real had been, and the new unit often had trouble keeping its ranks filled. By June 1832 it had 163 cavalry and 191 infantry, plus a staff of 7 in the general headquarters, totaling 361. The headquarters and main infantry barracks was located then as today on the site of an old monastery on Borbonos Street (now Evaristo da Veiga), near the Passeio Público, the city's oldest public park. The main cavalry barracks was in a complex used for the same purpose by the extinct Guarda Real, adjacent to Espírito Santo Church on Mataporcos Street (now Haddock Lobo) on the outskirts of the city. By 1834 there were 9 men on the headquarters staff, 169 cavalry, and 279 infantry for a total of 457. Assigned to be on guard or patrol duty 24 hours a day, seven days a week, in a variety of situations, the military police had some 235 infantry and cavalry assigned to duty at any given time by 1832. The largest detachments were 30 men on ready alert for emergency service in case of public disturbance (the predecessor of today's crowd control unit, the *tropa de choque*), 30 cavalrymen on dusk-to-dawn night patrol, 30 infantry troops stationed at the navy arsenal and 20 at the army arsenal to guard the downtown area, and 25 assigned to duty at the orders of the justices of the peace around the city. Among the many smaller duty stations were the 10 guards at the Aljube jail, 9 assigned to guard *galé* prisoners, and a squad of 3 in Carioca Square. Each detachment of more than 2 or 3 men had a corporal in charge, of which there were 10 in the cavalry and 18 in the infantry by 1834.[40]

In November 1835 not long after the national guard had been relieved of routine police duty, the minister of justice instructed the military police to "exercise greater care to ensure that the city is duly patrolled," by sending men into areas where several disturbances had recently been reported. Caxias reacted with characteristic bluntness, pointing out that adequate patrolling, however desirable, was impossible "as long as the corps under my command is charged with guard duty throughout the city, in which all the infantry is occupied, leaving only cavalry for mobile patrols." He further pointed out that the high crime areas, full of hideouts and blind alleys, were not accessible to mounted cavalry. The minister accepted Caxias's objections, suggesting that when the military police was staffed at the full authorized strength and regular army ranks were again built up through conscription, the policing of the city could be improved.[41]

In addition to routine posting and patrolling to maintain what regulations called a "preventive and repressive" presence, wherever a disciplined armed force was needed a squad of military police was sent. These orders illustrate the range of duties the police soldiers performed and give a sense of the nature of the problems they were intended to solve. In February 1833 a corporal and nine men were sent to patrol one of the hills of the city, "to prevent vagrants and criminals from hiding there." In May of that year six men were sent to assist in capturing conscripts for the coast artillery and navy. In July the corps was ordered to send six men and a corporal to guard a theater located near the arches of the Carioca aqueduct, "whenever requested by the director of the *Companhia Cómica*." In August 1833 patrols in the suburban Engenho Velho district were ordered to increase the size of each squad from three to five men for better protection against "the blacks who roam there in large groups, armed with knives." The enlarged patrols were to "take the greatest care to stop and search anyone who might be carrying a weapon, not allowing any gatherings on the roads or in taverns." The usual weapons police looked for were daggers, razors, and clubs, but in November 1833 they were ordered to take some care examining walking sticks (*bengalas*), the nineteenth-century equivalent of the gentleman's sword of former times. No special courtesies were expected when searching blacks for weapons, but in examining walking sticks for hidden and illegal blades police soldiers were to "employ all decency and civility." A similar indirect reference to the social categories requiring special vigilance came in November 1835, when patrols were ordered to stop any persons who "by their status, the time, or the place become suspect," and "scrupulously search" for illegal weapons.[42]

Increasing the size of a squad was considered adequate protection for suburban patrols, but concerted raids against encampments of runaway slaves required a larger force. In January 1835 a justice of the peace organizing such an operation in an isolated beach area requested a detachment of 30 police soldiers, "appropriately armed," who were to assemble at 3 A.M. for the march to the site of the quilombo in order to attack at dawn. If 30 soldiers were adequate for such a mission, it was considered prudent to assign twice that number for crowd control at a hanging, which would be far beyond a symbolic presence of the state on such an occasion. When Dyonisio, a slave convicted of murder, was to be executed on 26 September 1837, the military police was ordered to provide a cavalry squad to escort him from the Aljube jail to the gallows erected in Rocio Pequeno Square where 60 more military police were to be posted "in order to avoid any disorder that might occur, as happened at the last execution."[43]

The following are examples of the special problems brought to the attention of the military police for increased surveillance. In August 1836 the justice of the peace in Santa Ana parish reported that gangs of capoeiras were gathering in the Campo de Santana with some frequency, armed with iron bars and committing disorders and attacks. Military police were ordered to coordinate with the local judge and go after the gangs whenever word arrived that they were gathered. In May 1837 shadowy figures were seen tampering with the windows on the roof of the royal storehouse near the downtown palace, and in the entryway of the building "slaves, vagrants, and many other idle and suspicious persons gather." Graffiti artists also were a problem for police 150 years ago: In January 1840 Queiroz ordered a military police patrol to the isolated waterfront area of Saco do Alferes, where "groups of idle people with evil intentions have roamed the area late at night, shouting and disturbing the peace, writing and painting indecent figures on the walls of houses, and there have even been some attacks on peaceful citizens passing through the area."[44]

In December 1840 a major disturbance involving slaves and street people gathered around the fountain in front of Santa Rita Church showed the dangers of loosened vigilance. It was a Sunday afternoon, the day of rest, and a sizable crowd was gathered in the small square. About 6 P.M. a fight broke out, and soon a major melee was in progress, "with people attacking each other with clubs and stones, causing an immense confusion." The local ward inspector was the only authority in the area, and with no police available he was able to take only one man, José, a Benguela slave into custody. Civilian authorities from the justice of the peace to the minister of justice of the empire later criticized the military police for not being available to reestablish calm in Santa Rita Square. They issued orders for renewed vigilance to "prevent future gatherings of blacks, and to arrest those found in groups because such meetings are a serious problem that must be nipped in the bud, using strong measures." To avoid similar outbursts police were to "arrest and punish, according to the law, any slave found engaged in disorderly conduct, and those who fail to show due respect to sentinels and patrols."[45] The agents of the slave-holding class clearly perceived a chain linking disrespect to disorderly conduct to menacing gatherings to uncontrollable outbreaks of violence, which could have unpredictable and dangerous consequences. A central, recurring mission of the military police was to see that the progression never got started.

Hostility, Discipline, Solidarity

As the replacement for the brutal and hated Guarda Real de Polícia and as the main instrument of force available to the new state struggling for control of a hierarchical social order based ultimately on coercion, the military police occupied an unenviable position. There were many indirect indications in these early years that fulfilling their assigned role in the system was not going to win the military police many friends. Hostility between members of the corps and the society they were delegated to keep in line emerged early and persisted. One form of this hostility was physical—the recurring attacks military police soldiers made on people on the streets both before and after arrest. Early on, Feijó had warned the corps he created against arbitrarily beating people, and since 1831 there were regulations on the books restricting military police to applying only the force necessary to effect a lawful arrest. The acceptable level of force and the circumstances under which force should be applied have been recurring issues ever since.

An incident in October 1832, within a year of the founding of the corps, suggests how far back the hostility between police and public extends. Two military police soldiers were going past the São José seminary when they were insulted by a group of the students there who threw stones and shouted "scoundrel" (*caim*) and "slaves of Feijó." The uniform of one of the soldiers was torn in the scuffle.[46] In a similar incident involving the sons of the elite a few years later, the director of the medical college adjacent to the charity hospital was instructed to order his students to refrain from insulting the police soldiers on guard duty there.[47] Extra police had been assigned to the Santa Casa de Misericórdia to prevent a special kind of theft: there had been several attempts to steal slaves who were patients in the hospital, who were outside the direct vigilance of their owners and too ill or weak to resist abduction.

An incident in October 1833 put the permanentes involved clearly beyond the bounds of the permissible exercise of force. For those in charge of the new police system it was an example of the risks of giving guns and control over others to men with little to risk themselves and allowing discipline to slacken. Late on the night of 8 October, Minister of Justice Aureliano de Souza Coutinho received a note written on wrinkled paper in the cramped scrawl of someone not accustomed to drafting formal correspondence. It had come from the Aljube jail, and the contents were alarming. "Our lives are threatened," the note said, "and we are all in danger of being killed tonight, because the permanentes are shooting into the cells—they say they have orders to do this." Pleading for the minister to do something "so that we are not victims of these murderers," the message concluded hastily, "I cannot say more, because I also expect to be shot, but I can only trust in Your Excellency's humanity." The next day Police Chief Queiroz received a fuller report from the jailer at the Aljube, confirming the contents of the note Coutinho had received and giving fuller details of the terrible night.

By the jailer's account, about 8:30 in the evening as he was putting out the lights in the entryway of the building, one of the guards exchanged sharp words with a prisoner in the *sala livre*, the holding room for those in short-term detention. Suddenly another guard appeared and fired his musket through the window into the cell. The first guard then followed suit. Thinking there was a breakout attempt in progress, the rest of the military police on duty that night came running, and the jailer asked the sergeant in charge to do something to stop such reckless behavior "which was nothing less than an attack on the lives of many men." The sergeant said nothing in reply and left with the other guards when he saw there was no mutiny among the prisoners. The shooting started again with four more shots into the sala livre. No one was killed, but one prisoner, José Bento Jorge, was seriously wounded. One of the wayward guards then waited with his musket ready to shoot at any prisoner who might appear at the windows. When the jailer ventured to ask him what he was doing, the police soldier replied, "I'm hunting." The crash of a bottle breaking in the patio confirmed the jailer's suspicion that the guards had been drinking, and the armed police soldiers milling around the jail stopped all traffic in the street outside from where residents and tavern keepers watched the scene in horror. Through all this the prisoners in the two cells that were fired upon lay low and stayed as calm as they could under the circumstances, but one who could write managed to slip out the desperate note calling for help from higher authority. The situation finally settled into a tense calm until the guards were relieved by another military police squad. In his memo to Caxias deploring the incident, Coutinho urged the military police commander to proceed as regulations required against those involved, "making them aware of the extent to which such behavior destroys order, the public trust, and discipline of the corps."[48]

Such extreme cases of dereliction were rare, and they became even less common as Caxias, with the strict and ruthless measures for which he became renowned, tightened discipline in the unit and weeded out the bad actors. True to the corporatist spirit of the military, as long as the soldiers under his command gave him unquestioned loyalty and commitment to duty they would be in his good graces. In return he was jealously protective of his men and the reputation of the corps. An example of this corporate solidarity came in an incident just a few blocks away from the Aljube jail, a little more than a year after the inebriated guards went "hunting" in that squalid establishment.

On the night of 3 November 1834 a ward inspector was called on by his neighbors to do something about the loud goings-on at the house of Candida Luiza Joaquina do Amparo, at no. 47 Conceição Street. As the inspector reported, this woman, "by her terrible behavior and execrable life of prostitution has stirred the general indignation of the residents of that ward." He had warned her to change her ways to no avail. This time there was little he could do beyond threaten from the street, because the people creating the ruckus were all inside the house and he had no authority to force entry into a residence. One of those in the house, a police soldier named Manoel Joaquim Coelho, shouted back, insulting the ward inspector. This created a problem for the inspector because his honor had been impugned and the respect of his observing neighbors was at stake, but no civilian was allowed to arrest a member of the military. Fortunately for the ward inspector, some national guardsmen had appeared on the scene, and he asked them to arrest Coelho.

At that point a group of police soldiers from the guard detail at the nearby Aljube jail arrived, and they announced they would take their colleague Coelho in custody to military police headquarters. The ward inspector tried to insist on the course of action he had begun, but the military police had their way after drawing their pistols against the inspector and the national guardsmen. The best the inspector could do was to tag along to make sure Coelho was not released after he and his comrades had gone out of sight. The justice of the peace in whose district the confrontation had taken place asked the minister of justice later to take action in this matter "because otherwise it will be impossible to enforce the law, which is the only safeguard of the people." Caxias's laconic reply to the minister's request for an explanation was that the incident was "greatly exaggerated" and the report contained "many falsehoods." The offending Coelho was off duty and in civilian clothes at the time and in any case had already been turned over to the justice of the peace for judicial action. But the commander declined to discipline the squad that had come to Coelho's aid and confronted the ward inspector and national guardsmen with pistols drawn.[49] The form of recreation that police soldier Coelho was engaged in at the time the incident began was not an issue, nor was the professional activity of Candida do Amparo at no. 47 Conceição Street. That was a matter for the ward inspector to deal with in the interest of his neighbors' moral principles and a full night's sleep.

Guards taking potshots at prisoners in their cells might indicate the low regard military police had for the men in their custody, but it was clearly outrageous to their superiors. Coming to the aid of a comrade in arms, and rescuing him at gunpoint from arrest by another branch of the network of authority was for Caxias a borderline case. He acknowledged that Coelho had been in the wrong, but because he was off duty and out of uniform he had not brought overt disgrace to the corps and thus was eligible for the protection his comrades provided. The abstract legal principle the justice of the peace had invoked was just that—an abstraction that may or may not be useful in interpreting a situation that had more to do with the protection of loyal subordinates and corporate solidarity than with ink in law books. To Caxias's military mind corporate solidarity was not an abstraction nor a vain or antiquated pretension rooted in the *foros* of an earlier era. It was a conscious technique related to regimentation, building morale, and esprit de corps for ensuring faithful compliance with orders, adherence to duty, and mutual support in the face of the enemy. Those attributes were useful to an army on the field of battle, and they were similarly useful to the military police on the streets of Rio.

Those streets were a difficult environment in which to determine the acceptable levels of official violence, as police soldiers were expected to deal with the general public applying only the "necessary" force. Depending on a shifting combination of circumstances, prudent application of force in one situation might be police brutality in the next. As regent of the empire in January 1836, Feijó intervened in one such case, that of a police soldier on guard at the Passeio Público who had injured an innocent passerby in an altercation. The administrator of the park at Feijó's request asked the military police commander to discipline the soldier in question "so that the public order is not at the mercy of any ruffian." Liberal sensibilities at the time saw such incidents as unacceptable brutality. Whatever value judgments one applies it should be kept in mind that the military police soldier has always lived and worked in a hostile and violent world where he was expected to exert force to carry out his duty. While he was not to behave like "any ruffian," he was in the Passeio Público for a reason, as made clear in another order for increased patrols in the park to prevent "vagrants and those with bad intentions from damaging the restoration work currently going on there."[50]

In February 1836 several men were arrested by a military police squad and brought into the headquarters barracks for processing. They repeatedly insulted the arresting soldiers as well as the officer on duty at the central station. When Caxias came in to see about the commotion, one of the detainees tried to attack him. The corps commander pushed the would-be assailant down with a chair, and the mutinous prisoners were soon subdued. Later the minister of justice informed Caxias that he had instructed Eusébio de Queiroz, into whose custody such prisoners were remanded, "not to loosen vigilance over them for any reason, and to repress them and punish them so that their audacity does not acquire new strength, and they do not dare to commit greater crimes."[51] Not many of such incidents involved the commander of the corps, but this case illustrates a constant if unstated operating guideline of Rio's police system: meet force with superior force and insult with subjugation. To maintain the hierarchy it was not enough to fight to a draw. Every battle in the social war, large or small, had to be won.

Bribery and Corruption

The military police faced the perennial problem that occurs when police interact with thieves—bribery. There are cherished canons at issue that make any discussion of the subject a sensitive matter. Honesty was supposed to be a prerequisite for employment in the police. Dutiful service was the pledge made by each member of the force, and the opposite of integrity was corruption—also a medical term for rot and decay. These are powerful words evoking strong feelings and expressing principles that many well-intentioned people might agree are worth upholding for the common good. In a failure to proceed diligently out of laziness or lack of dedication, there was a large grey area between right and wrong. How fast was a patrolman required to run in pursuit of a suspect? What were the criteria for deciding whom to stop and question and whom to let pass? In Rio the criteria were largely determined by the "condition" of the objects of police attention, which referred to the racial identity, manner of dress, speech, and behavior of the suspect as well as the location and time of day.[52] But the decision to stop and search was discretionary. On the other end of the scale, the point at which zealous and even courageous commitment to duty became arbitrary and unjustified brutality and repression varied according to an often subtle combination of circumstances and the point of view of the person evaluating the incident.

With bribery, on the other hand, the principle was as clear as it was absolute. If an agent of the state's monopoly on force received some personal advantage directly from a person suspected of offending the state's rules in return for not applying coercive force and sparing the suspect punishment, then that agent was guilty of breaking one of the cardinal principles on which the impersonal apparatus of the state was based. In nineteenth-century Rio de Janeiro this offense could hardly be called the violation of a public trust in anything more than a euphemistic sense. By accepting a bribe a police soldier violated the terms under which he accepted the role of an agent of the coercive power of the state. If he were caught he would be punished severely, both in retribution for the offense and as an example. Such was the situation in which three men found themselves late in 1837.

Late on the night of 4 December, military police Corporal Francisco das Chagas, accompanied by police soldier João Francisco de Andrade and Silvério José Lopes, a national guardsman on temporary assignment with the military police, were on night patrol in downtown Rio. On Ouvidor Street they stopped two men on whom they found a number of pocket watches, jewelry, and coins. The police agreed not to arrest the pair, in return for a share of the loot, which it was later discovered had been stolen from the shop of a French jeweler named Meirat. Another member of the gang of jewel thieves, Antonio Justino da Costa Ramos "better known by the nickname Panaquinha (Little Fool)," was later arrested in the case. Upon interrogation, the three members of the police patrol confessed their offense. Corporal Chagas said he received one silver watch and five gold coins, Andrade received a silver watch, and Lopes a gold watch. The three were tried and convicted in court martial. Chagas was sentenced to three years in prison at labor plus nine months of simple prison; Andrade got eighteen months in prison, and Lopes fifteen months in prison. For the last two, one year of the sentence was to be served at labor. With a sentence of that severity, all three were expelled from their respective military units.[53]

In this case and others like it over the years the police agents clearly violated legal and moral strictures. Another aspect of their behavior to consider might be called political, in the sense that the police used the power they were delegated for personal gain. The military police soldier patrolling the streets was paid just enough to make such employment a reasonable alternative to the sorts of disruptive, marginal, and parasitic activity he was supposed to repress. He was sworn to uphold certain principles, given a uniform, two pistols, and a sword, and sent onto the streets of the city. As long as he did his sworn duty he was taken care of. In the course of most of what he did on the job—stopping arguments before they escalated into injury and tumult; arresting drunks, vagrants, beggars, or suspicious people on the street after curfew; then seeing animated groups of people grow quiet and assume a sullen silence as he approached only to revive talk of the world from which he was excluded as he passed—there was little chance for serious bribery or corruption. He could scowl, then verbally threaten, then brandish his sword, then strike an offending party with impunity and make an arrest for disrespect or resistance or disorderly conduct. But there was not much chance of a payoff. Those people had little that he wanted except the submission they begrudgingly gave to avoid the sword of the law. For the most part the only people that could be the source of a corrupting influence were those who had something that by the police soldier's calculation was worth the risk. The opportunities to take material advantage of his authority came infrequently, and when they did it should not be surprising that sometimes police soldiers yielded to the temptation.

Seeing this incident in such a light is not to excuse the action of Corporal Chagas and his accomplices, nor is it to suggest that the thieves had a right to steal the watches and jewelry in the first place. It is to suggest that there is more to corruption, as to brutality, than meets the eye, if that eye is looking through a tunnel of definitions and principles established and perpetuated by one class for use in controlling another in a society that is based essentially on the co-ercion and exploitation of the many by the few. One incidental cost of authoritarian liberalism was that a police soldier might risk years in jail at hard labor and expulsion from the military corps that gave him identity and authority in return for a silver watch and five gold coins from a thief's hoard. Although that cost could not be elimi-nated, one way to keep it within acceptable limits was to give police soldiers the support of corporate solidarity, which in turn gave them an incentive for accepting the rigid discipline under which they were punished if they were caught in egregious rule violation.

Another aspect of the police soldier's condition that relates to the temptations of a payoff is the desperate poverty of the social stratum from which such men were drawn. The assurance of a minimal but living wage could be a powerful incentive for members of the free lower classes, who had few other opportunities, to sub-mit to the discipline and social isolation that was the fate of a mili-tary police soldier. Their separation was physical as well as social since they were billeted in a garrison-style regimen, but many used their salary to support family members they saw only infrequently after joining the corps. A case in 1839 illustrates the economic and social cost soldiers might incur as they balanced family obligations against the rules of service and shows the plight of the patronless poor of Rio de Janeiro. Police soldiers José Victor dos Santos and his cousin Francisco José da Costa were the sole source of support for Santos's poor and widowed mother Simpliciana Rosa dos Santos and her three daughters, two of whom were children. When Simpliciana and her older daughter fell ill, the two police soldiers went home to nurse them and care for the children. When they had been absent for more than three days, which constituted desertion, a squad was sent to arrest them. They were convicted in court martial and received the standard sentence of three months in the guardhouse without pay. Ten days after the arrest of the two deserters, Simpliciana sent a desperate plea to Caxias, as "father and protector of the helpless," to commute their sentence and restore them to service with pay, "so that the petitioner and her miserable family might continue to receive this aid, their only source of sustenance, and not be forced to beg for survival from door to door."[54]

Rivalry and Revelry

Examples of how the sense of corporate identity in the military police was built up during the regency period come from one of the types of duty the soldiers of the corps found near the bottom of their dignity, if not beneath it—keeping order around public fountains. Most of the thirteen thousand households in the city sent someone to one of the fifteen public fountains to fetch water usually every day.[55] Much of the movement on the streets at any given time was of servile people going to and from water fountains, and a major task for police was keeping lines in order and discussions in the constantly circulating crowd from escalating into conflict. During periodic dry spells when the supply of water was reduced, lines grew longer and tempers shorter. The potential for trouble was shown in April 1833 when a mulatto slave named Herculano entered Carioca Square supervising a group of slave water-carriers, found the line too long for his liking, and attacked other slaves ahead of him with an axe handle. Herculano was sent to the Calabouço.[56]

After the water went into the houses in jars or kegs, most of it came back out in a similar vessel because there were no sewers. The waste water produced by nearly 100,000 people was tossed into the bay at certain designated spots and times of the day or into any handy ditch or drain. In June 1836 the inspector of public works asked the minister of justice to order the military police in Carioca Square to be especially vigilant to the practice of emptying chamber pots into drains around the water fountain there. Caxias complied but under protest. When he gave his men these instructions, he said they replied that they had enough trouble "preventing the disorder the blacks continuously engage in at the fountain." Besides, Caxias went on, the city public works department had inspectors in each neighborhood whose job it was to prevent use of the drains around fountains for sewage, "and they have guards available to assist them."[57] Caxias in this case was objecting on behalf of his men to the minister of justice and the minister of the empire who supervised the water supply and was passing on his troops' complaints about the indignity of such duty when their first priority was to preserve order.

The problem did not go away nor did military police brutality or disputes with the public works department. In August 1840 a police soldier on duty in Carioca Square tried to stop a slave from dumping garbage in the area, and when the offending slave began to insult the soldier, he hit the slave twice. A public works department crew was installing a new water pipe nearby, and the foreman, witnessing the beating of the black by the police soldier, came over and reproached the latter in "very offensive terms." The soldier then arrested the foreman, who called his supervisor, the city inspector of public works, who in turn proceeded to arrest the soldier and take him to the nearby military police headquarters. The head of the public works department could arrest a soldier because he was an army officer himself—Lieutenant Colonel Miguel de Frias, the same man who announced Pedro I's abdication in April 1831, involved himself in the massacre by municipal guards at the theater in September of that year, led the Abrilada rebellion that Caxias crushed in April 1832, escaped into exile in the United States, and returned to Brazil after an amnesty decree in 1833. The upshot of this case was that the minister of justice sent a formal protest to the minister of the empire (who supervised public works in the city) asking him to ensure that military police soldiers "are not subjected to punishment for the offense of doing their duty."[58] No one claimed the soldier had not hit the bad-mouthing slave—the duty the minister was alluding to.

An incident during the pre-Lenten carnival of 1836 pitted a military police patrol against a justice of the peace and the national guard over the enforcement of municipal ordinances restricting public revelry. For most of the nineteenth century, carnival was not an officially sanctioned festival, as were the Epiphany on 6 January, the day of Saint Sebastian, the city's patron, later the same month, and other occasions on the religious and civil calendar. Lack of official sanction meant that rules against behavior that might break the normal routine were still in place, but informal fun and games went on during the days before Lent despite restrictive ordinances and police efforts at enforcement. One of the most widespread of prohibited activities was the game of *entrudo*. This involved making hollow wax balls about the size of a lemon, filling the balls with perfumed water and resealing the opening, and then throwing them at passersby. The *limão de cheiro* might be followed by a net bag of powdered manioc starch or flour. The result of such an attack was that the victim, although not permanently injured, smelled like cinnamon tea, was soaked, and looked as if covered by a layer of white mud. Whether it was all in fun or a barbarous assault depended on the point of view. The top hats favored by men who could afford them made inviting targets for people wielding wax balls, and entrudo was the bane of the "respectable" population of Rio de Janeiro.[59]

On 17 February 1836 a military police squad on duty in the cathedral square detained a man for engaging in entrudo. As they were making the arrest, a national guard captain approached and criticized the police soldiers in insulting tones, so they arrested him too. Following standard procedures, the soldiers took the two men to the local justice of the peace for judicial action and punishment. Instead of proceeding as the law required, the justice ordered the detainees set free, and when the police soldiers objected he ordered them disarmed and arrested instead. When the patrol's report of this demeaning incident reached Caxias, he shot off to the minister of justice a copy of the report and the demand that justice be done his men, who were only trying to do their duty. The minister looked into the matter and sent a formal reprimand to the justice of the peace criticizing his conduct in "failing to proceed with vigor and energy against those who dare to violate the law and police regulations."[60]

The influence Caxias had acquired by that time, his active defense of the prerogatives and dignity of the military police, and the discipline he imposed on the soldiers under his command were important in securing respect for the corps in the eyes of the governing elite. But that respect was also based on the efficacy of the military police as an instrument of repression. Caxias in effect made a pact with the political leaders who had ultimate command of the military police: The police corps would do what was expected of it efficiently and with dispatch. In return they expected to be given the operational autonomy, material resources and personnel to carry out their mission—and the respect and status due to a loyal retainer. Other police forces were proposed, some were established and later disbanded, but only the military police can claim institutional continuity from 1831 to the present. In that long trajectory they maintained a sense of corporate identity and internal solidarity that stood them well as they carried out their end of Caxias's bargain.[61]

Military Police vs. National Guard

The entrudo incident during carnival of 1836 was no watershed event. It was similar to myriad other small encounters over the years and is used here to illustrate how Rio de Janeiro was policed. But it also contained elements of the more general historical development of the institutions with which the military police shared the task of repression. The justice of the peace as a relevant part of that system barely survived the regency, and the national guard was eventually relegated to a marginal role. The strained relationship between the guard and the military police dated virtually from the time of their founding. Under the command of Luis Alves de Lima e Silva, the police troops held their own in this institutional rivalry and emerged from the transition of the regency with their status as a military unit established and the burdens of daily policing in their hands.

The initial orders of 1832 placing the military police under the temporary command of the national guard during public emergencies did not last long, and in any case after April of that year the point was moot. There were tumults involving slaves and street people, near-riots at contested elections, and popular protests over tax increases and similar issues later in the century. Major regional revolts continued to flare up elsewhere in the country for more than a decade, but in the city of Rio major rebellions by armed mutineers numbering in the thousands, like those occurring during the year from Pedro I's abdication to the 1832 Abrilada, were a thing of the past. After his successful performance in those battles, the new commander of the military police was one of the foremost guardians of government's monopoly on armed force. That principle, as Caxias defined it, was not universally accepted as of 1833. He considered the arrogant pretensions to autonomous authority exhibited by some national guardsmen to be unacceptable, particularly when the legitimate forces that suffered at the hands of these wayward guardsmen were Caxias's own permanentes.

On 22 September 1833 two military police cavalrymen were riding along Sabão Street in Santa Ana parish when they were confronted by a group of four mounted national guardsmen who told the military police to retire, that they were on patrol in that district. The guardsmen who "were in the habit of insulting the permanentes, said they had run off a military police patrol the night before, and maybe they would do the same" with this pair. Outnumbered, the police soldiers returned to their barracks to report. Caxias thereupon sent a new patrol of three men and an officer to the site of the encounter with orders to disperse any groups gathered there and to arrest any national guardsmen who interfered. The police patrol met the offending guardsmen and after another exchange of words sent them on their way.[62]

After a similar confrontation a few weeks later, Caxias made clear the basis for his criticism of the guard. A patrol of permanentes had been accosted by members of the guard battalion in São José parish. Among the epithets the guardsmen shouted were "Death to the Chimangos!" "It is a great honor for us to kill Chimangos!" and "This is our territory, you scoundrels (*cains*)!" Chimango was the nickname their political opponents gave the partisans of the moderate liberal group who by 1833 had emerged victorious in parliamentary politics, including Feijó, Bernardo de Vasconcelos, and Evaristo da Veiga. By their slogans the unruly guardsmen were associating the military police with that political faction. Caxias reported the insults, but what really bothered him was that many of the rowdies in question were not legitimate members of the guard but were "profiteering anarchists using the uniform as a disguise so they can get away with their slander." His proof was that the most vocal man in the group, Antônio Ferreira, had already been expelled from the unit Caxias commanded "for drunkenness and bad conduct, and he lives off the pay he gets from service in the guard."

Some men required to serve as national guards, Caxias accused, were paying unqualified substitutes to take their place. Besides setting a bad precedent by violating the regulation requiring substitutes to meet normal eligibility requirements, there was a clearer danger in such a practice. Anyone who did not have the income to qualify for guard service was "of the lowest class of the people, and consequently only capable of committing and promoting disturbances, as has already happened." The guard, he felt the need to point out, had been established to prevent that sort of occurrence. Caxias asked the minister of justice to stop this abuse and bring charges against the unqualified guardsmen under the article of the criminal code prohibiting unauthorized use of weapons and insignia of office.[63] Beyond the technicalities of regulations, a fundamental principle was at stake. The income requirements for guard eligibility were intended to ensure that those who had material interests to defend would have the duty of preserving the social order on which their status depended. Any man lower on the economic ladder, by Caxias's assessment, could be expected to attack the very hierarchy of which, with the exception of slaves, he occupied the lowest stratum. There was no income requirement for service in the military police, but the crucial distinction was that fulltime police soldiers were under strict military discipline. The effective exercise of that discipline was revealed in this same incident, as the most vocal troublemaker was identified as a man Caxias had expelled from his corps for misconduct.

Another clash in 1836 came over what many civilians consider a minor matter, but which symbolizes much of the defense of corporate identity so central to the military tradition. A military police corporal had been in charge of the detachment on duty in Carioca Square when a national guard captain approached. The corporal failed to salute and was taken to task for disrespect to a superior officer, who asked him if he realized whom he was talking to. "Yes," the corporal replied, "a national guard officer with no commission."[64] A heated discussion ensued. The corporal was referring to the fact that officers in the guard were elected by their peers or appointed but did not receive the *patente* that was the basis for the status and corporate membership that a commission in the professional military gave its holders. In the sense of permanent membership in a professional group set apart from other members of society, a patente for a Brazilian officer is similar to the ordainment of a priest. It confers special status, privileges, and obligations that no one else can claim. Caxias pointed out in his reply to the minister of justice that no law required military police to salute national guard officers, even though they continued to insist on that deferential treatment, and he asked the minister to give the guard orders to desist from such demands in the future. Coming from Caxias, who as of 1836 had been in the army for 28 years, since he was five years old, who received his patente on his fifteenth birthday, and whose father and uncles were all generals, the message was clear: The guard was not a real military unit, and its members did not deserve the respect the professional military reserved for its own. While noncommissioned officers and soldiers had no equivalent document, they had the uniform itself, and the protection of their officers—as shown by Caxias's defense of the police corporal who refused to salute a national guard captain.

The military police under Caxias began to build a corporate tradition that set them apart from civil society and gave the corps an us-versus-them mentality not only in relation to such competing institutions as the national guard but to the surrounding society in general. While some critics of the modern police have criticized such separateness, the advantages of that development were not lost on the civilian authorities who maintained close oversight of police practices and overall control. In 1837 the minister of justice congratulated the Rio military police for a job well done, explicitly stating the civilian political elite's rationale for maintaining a militarized force: "The police are one of the first columns of support for public peace and the tranquility of a people, and they would not be able to achieve that purpose if military discipline did not provide the good order, neatness, and precision on the job."[65] That rationale was not unthinking tradition, nor a vaguely defined militaristic approach to organization generally, nor did Caxias singlehandedly create a militarized police by force of will, important though his personal role was. The military police represented a deliberate effort to provide as close to a precision instrument for ensuring control as could be achieved, given the raw material there was to work with and the problem to be resolved. Nor could militarization be called the result of some propensity toward structure and discipline in Brazilian culture. On the contrary, the perceived unruliness, rebelliousness, lack of discipline, and lack of respect for authority of that part of the population that occupied the streets and public places of the city made a police force with opposite characteristics an appropriate response.

If many guardsmen were reluctant to serve on active duty police patrols as originally intended, there were still important motives for those eligible to maintain guard membership, including the sense of belonging to an elite institution sanctioned by the state and access to patronage networks. Guardsmen were also exempt from being drafted into the regular military. Justices of the peace were in charge of conscription in their districts, and in 1836 a national guard battalion commander in Santa Rita parish accused the local judge of drafting several members of his unit into the army in an act of "personal revenge." Police Chief Queiroz passed the complaint on to the minister of justice, who rebuked the offending judge. Two years later Queiroz himself wanted to use the draft to remove from the streets "some vagrants and reprobates, even suspected of connivance with thieves, but as they are members of the national guard, where they are easily admitted, they cannot be conscripted." He asked for special permission to draft the worst of the guardsmen in question, "which would greatly benefit the tranquility of this city." The minister's decision was that, "for the time being," the order exempting guardsmen from the draft should stand.[66] This time there was no rebuke, but guard membership still provided protection not available to others.

Caxias might have said that clerks and cobblers had no business trying to act like soldiers, and Queiroz might have wanted to remove the shield of patronage that protected some of the bad apples in the guard. The transition from policing the city by a citizens' militia to depending on full-time militarized corps, however, was made for another reason. National guardsmen, as unpaid volunteers who had to earn their living elsewhere, would be better off working at their regular professions. The minister of justice claimed in 1835 that it was not a problem to get guardsmen to serve in Rio de Janeiro, where "civilization and the love of property guarantees the moral standing of the guard, and the regularity with which it performs its duties." Recurring problems of staffing, laxity, and failure to report for duty, however, suggest that the minister's statement expressed little more than his hope that the individual guardsman would want to protect the property of the civilized haves against the depredations of the barbarous have-nots. By 1841 the tone of the minister of justice was different from that of his predecessor when he urged a solution to the burdens of supplemental police work, especially in outlying suburban districts where active duty in the guard was "prejudicial to agriculture, where most guard members are employed." Not only would guardsmen prefer to be free of active duty patrolling, but the productive activities they engaged in or supervised would be better off as well. From the standpoint of the system as a whole, they were too valuable to dissipate their time and energy on police work, which should be left to those specialized in that function.[67]

The Urbanos Proposal

At the same time as the minor entrudo incident that brought institutional rivalries to the surface, a major new initiative clearly pointed to perceived deficiencies in the existing police structure. In February 1836 Feijó, then sole regent, used his constitutional authority to decree the formation of an additional police force in order to "better guarantee property and individual security" in the city. Although the proposal got well into the planning stage, its fate was similar to the 1825 plan for police comissários in that it was not brought to fruition. In discussing several of the innovative features of the plan, authorities explicitly referred to problems it was to address, as they continued to seek ways to institutionalize an adequate level of repression. The discussions at the time also reveal some of the problems of using national guards as police at this early date and the confusion of public funding of the police for the general good versus private financing of security by those who needed it and could afford to pay for it.

Members of this new unit were to be called *urbanos*. They were to be attached to and administered by the military police, and they were to be similarly uniformed and armed with the standard pair of pistols, a short sword, and a whistle for calling reinforcements. They would be allowed to carry their sword while off duty as long as they were in uniform. Once again the uniform, a symbol of authority, and the sword, its instrument, were a unit. In recruitment, preference would be given to current members of the military police or the regular army, especially those who were by age or infirmity less able to carry out the "active and heavy" duties of the existing corps. They were to be paid the same as soldiers in the military police, which in 1836 was $640 per day. Their proposed strength was two hundred men, to be divided equally among the sixteen judicial districts of the city, or twelve men per district. With normal duty from nightfall until morning on alternate nights, there would be six urbanos, patrolling in pairs, in each district each night.[68]

In the existing military police, patrol duty was assigned according to the number of men available at any given time, but there was no effort to keep the same individuals in a consistent area of the city. Also, military police patrols covered large areas. Miscreants, knowing that a patrol passed by at intervals, took advantage to commit their evil deeds. As the minister of justice pointed out in discussing the proposed urbanos, "It is indispensable, in order to contain these turbulent and perverse men, that they fear with some probability firstly being discovered in their attempts, and then that they will not easily escape arrest."[69] The urbanos were intended to remedy that deficiency by assigning each two-man team permanently to a specific district (called a beat in British and U.S. police slang) small enough so that they were never far from any point in their area. From nightfall until morning, each urbano was to circulate continuously in his assigned area while his teammate circulated in the opposite direction, never stopping for more than five minutes at a time to observe alleys and intersections.

While on duty they were to have virtually the same operating guidelines as the military police. They were to "be observant for any crime that might be committed and prevent it from happening if possible." Upon witnessing altercations they were to issue warnings, impose silence, and order any dangerous or suspicious meeting to disperse. They were not to allow any unknown person to approach, instead ordering them to stop, searching them for weapons "in a civil manner," and arresting them if weapons were found. Urbanos were to use their own weapons only to carry out their mission or in self-defense and to blow their whistle for help or fire a shot in the air if the matter were urgent. The military police were to have cavalry squads posted at convenient points around the city every night in order to respond quickly to the urbanos' calls for assistance. Military police officers would be detailed to make random visits to urbanos on patrol to make sure they were carrying out their instructions.

Among the more revealing aspects of this proposal was the way the members of the community with a stake in public order and the protection of property were brought into the system of control. This recalled the role of the short-lived civilian municipal guards and Feijó's order during the disturbances of 1831 that owners of businesses be armed and directed in their collective defense by police authorities. By the 1836 decree ordering the formation of the urbanos, any national guardsman, as well as owners and employees of "stores, bars, taverns, or business establishments, of whatever nationality," were required to "go armed into the street" in response to an urbano's call for assistance. To facilitate such participation the chief of police was to issue two wooden lances to each place of business, which would be under the responsibility of specific individuals there. Justices of the peace and ward inspectors were also obligated to respond to such a call for aid, but they would take charge of the situation as officials superior to the urbano. The chief of police was given operational authority over urbanos, and justices of the peace and ward inspectors were required to report any irregular conduct of the patrolmen to the chief of police.

The propertied classes were to be directly involved in the functioning of the urbanos by paying for this additional police force. Funding for Rio's post-1831 military police came from the general revenues of the national government as part of the budget of the ministry of justice. The urbanos, in contrast, were to have their salaries and operating expenses paid by a "voluntary subscription" of direct contributions from residents in each district. The amount each person might pledge was left open, but residents were urged to make an initial one-time donation as well as a regular monthly contribution for ongoing expenses. Potential donors were assured that no pledge would be due and payable until the urbanos thus organized were actually on duty in the donor's neighborhood. That promise was intended to overcome suspicion that any money paid into the fund before the patrols went into operation might be lost, but it also reflects the sense that those members of society who wanted and felt the need for more police should pay for them directly. This method of financing looked remarkably similar to the private loans and grants by which Intendant Viana had financed the Guarda Real de Polícia in 1809.

Funding the police through direct contributions by those receiving protection contradicts the modern notion that the state should provide police services for the general welfare from general revenues. But it also belies the older absolutist (and in Brazil's case, colonial) idea that the police were little more than the instrument of state authority, pitting the autocratic regime and its military or judicial representatives against the people. In an explicit and direct sense, the state was offering to be the facilitator and organizer of a system by which the propertied classes would give up some of their property in exchange for increased security, very much like hiring private guards directly. Less explicit was another crucial contribution of the state to this scheme that would make the urbanos, like other police, distinct from private guards. That contribution was the state's theoretical monopoly on the use of force and its related authority to define behavior as unacceptable and arrest and punish transgressors through the judicial system.

The promise of increased security of person and property was a positive incentive to ensure voluntary contributions, but there was a further negative inducement to ensuring an adequate level of funding for the plan. All were warned that anyone "who chooses not to contribute to this subscription will, as national guards, be the first called up for patrol duty that might become necessary due to the lack of urbanos." This was publicized in city newspapers and in a circular from the commander of the Rio national guard to all his subordinates.[70] Discussion of the scheme made recurrent reference to the perceived shortage of military police and the burdens long and frequent patrolling placed on them. Of the total military police contingent of 456 in 1835, about 275 were available for duty on any given day, so the proposed addition of 100 urbanos on duty each night would be a significant increase. But the plan was also intended to "relieve the national guards of the onerous service to which they are presently subject, so that they can dedicate themselves more freely to their recreation, or to the exercise of their industry and commerce."[71] The guardsmen were being given the opportunity for relief from active duty, but only if they paid for their replacement by personally contributing to cost of the urbanos. The role of the urbanos in relieving national guardsmen from active police duty was thus explicit in the proposal, and there was a clear connection between the urbanos plan and the earlier citizen police, the municipal guard of mid-1831. In 1836 the propertied classes, instead of serving themselves, were to pay directly for hiring men who would provide some protection in return for a subsistence stipend. In case of emergency the owners of businesses were to grab their government-issue spears and respond to a guard's call for help, recalling the earlier order for municipal guards to come for duty armed with a lance if they had no gun available.

Commissions formed in each district were composed of residents of "recognized probity and influence" to administer the subscription drive and collect funds in their local area. After several months of effort they had pledges of financial support from 798 people, but there was enough resistance to the plan, especially from national guardsmen, that it was abandoned. The newspaper that reflected the position of Rio national guardsmen, for example, objected to yet another "voluntary" burden on the citizenry, an unconstitutional throwback to colonial absolutism. "The government has the regular army, military police, and other persons to police the city," the newspaper said, "and at its pleasure creates this corps of urbanos, to the detriment of artisan activities." The paper concluded that its readers, many of whom earned their living from such artisan activities, "should not give even ten réis" to the funding drive.[72] Without the support of the citizens subject to national guard service, the "voluntary" funding drive could not be sustained. The minister of justice blamed its failure on the fact that the subscription drive "produced almost nothing."[73] Regular policing continued to be done by the military police, the few pedestres auxiliary to civilian police authorities, and national guard units on part-time auxiliary duty. The Guarda Urbana eventually established in 1866, when large numbers of military police troops were sent to the war in Paraguay, was separate from the failed attempt in 1836 and was funded from general revenues.

Police and Politics

As a disciplined armed force available to those in control of the state, the military police would inevitably find themselves in the middle of factional disputes pitting the political "outs" against the "ins." A member of the upper strata of society might feel the flat of a police soldier's sword against the side of his head only when a detachment was sent to "establish order" at a contested election or an opposition political rally. Such incidents were reason enough for some to want to rein in the police until the party they favored could gain the upper hand, and they had the opportunity to use police power in a similar way.

Gaining control over the police was one of the main advantages the dominant faction had in political rivalries. During the first few months after the establishment of the corps, several armed confrontations against politically motivated rebels had shown the value of such a force being at the government's disposal. By 1833 the main political task, at least in the capital of the empire, was to ensure that the periodic elections for city councilmen, justices of the peace, and members of the electoral college all proceeded in a manner favorable to the interests of the faction in power. "Maintaining public tranquility" meant controlling the behavior of slaves, free lower classes, sailors on shore leave, and those young men of higher social status whose predictably rowdy behavior exceeded acceptable bounds. At election time, in contrast, maintaining public tranquility meant keeping rivalry from breaking into uncontrollable physical confrontation and ensuring that the results of the election satisfied those who supervised the electoral machinery and had control over the military police. This political mission was in many ways an extension of the social mission, and the police would continue to be associated with it.

Parish churches served as polling places. The supervising electoral board, with the justice of the peace presiding, sat in the middle of the nave with the list of eligible voters on the table before them. Voters approached the table, their eligibility was verified, and they publicly deposited their ballots in the sealed box. The board members were surrounded by representatives of the various political factions and their supporters. Those in the crowd were present to see that the proceedings went according to regulations, but if the election were contested they turned into cheering sections or intimidation squads as dictated by the turn of events.[74] In normal circumstances a few police soldiers were detailed for sentry duty inside the polling place as a symbolic presence and precautionary measure. Thus, when the justice of the peace in Santa Rita parish requested a squad of twelve police cavalry to be present during the election of 13 March 1833, it meant he was expecting trouble. When police Lieutenant Jorge Castroito arrived in Santa Rita Square at the head of the cavalry contingent, he found a large group of national guardsmen in uniform already in place around the church and others in civilian clothes in the crowd. The commander of the national guard unit confronted Lieutenant Castroito, saying in menacing tones he was surprised the justice of the peace would commit such a provocation as to request a detachment of military police. The judge, after assessing the situation, ordered that "no armed force should approach the polling place, especially not military police."

When Caxias got Castroito's report of this affair, he wrote a strongly worded memo to the minister of justice, saying that the action of the local judge had no legal basis and that favoring the position of the guardsmen had exacerbated their rivalry with the military police, which was "prejudicial to public tranquility." Caxias pointed out that the judge's abuse of authority had the effect of "stripping from the citizens enlisted in this corps the right to be present, like any other citizen, at the verification of the votes." The implication of such an action, he concluded, was to suggest that the military police were the ones disturbing the peace "when on the contrary, they have always maintained order, at the risk of their own lives."[75] It was technically correct that police had a right to watch the vote count, but it was specious for Caxias to claim that soldiers present during an election were "like any other citizen." They were in uniform with pistols at their belts, swords at their sides, and standing orders to use their weapons if necessary. But he was also saying that as long as military police troops were risking their personal safety in order to create a social and political environment those in authority wanted to establish, they objected to being belittled and contradicted by an official who was supposed to represent that same authority—particularly with a group of mocking national guardsmen observing the entire scene.

The police force served in the interest of the political "in's" on 7 April 1835, the fourth anniversary of the abdication of Pedro I. The Society for the Defense of Freedom and National Independence, a political organization dominated by the moderate liberals who had emerged victorious from the upheaval following the abdication and the closest thing there was to a political party in 1835, scheduled a celebratory Te Deum mass at São Francisco de Paula Church, one of the largest in downtown Rio. Police were ordered to stand guard at the church and also at the city council chambers during the event. Permanentes were called out any time a crowd was anticipated and posting such a guard during a Te Deum was not unusual. But in this case the sponsors anticipated trouble from political opponents. The government, which was dominated by members of the Sociedade Defensora, ordered police to "arrest any individual who might engage in any act of disrespect against the Sociedade."[76]

Such use of the armed force of the state can be called partisan in a narrow political sense, but it also illustrates the similarity between the political and the social function of the police. Military police were routinely deployed to repress the behavior or arrest those who showed disrespect at officially authorized events, whether the sponsor was the Catholic Church, one of the elite lay brotherhoods such as the Third Order of São Francisco, the state, or a semiofficial group such as the Sociedade Defensora. All these organizations were in some way part of the domination of the many by the few, and the disrespectful acts police were to repress were a form of resistance to that domination. There were many public events in Rio attended primarily by slaves, free people of color, and other members of the lower classes. These included nighttime *batuques* at which large numbers of people danced to throbbing percussion instruments, drank, and socialized, as well as smaller gatherings in public squares, especially around fountains and at the marketplace along the waterfront, and in taverns, *botequins*, or publicaos. For people engaged in these activities there was no police protection. On the contrary, if a gathering grew too large, seemed threatening, or occurred after curfew, military police were called to disperse the group and arrest anyone who objected. One example among many was the arrest of a tavern owner and the closing of his business near the Campo de Santana in September 1833. A military police patrol found the place bustling at 2 A.M., after the owner had been repeatedly warned to observe the 10 P.M. closing time. "He, however, continues to allow large gatherings of vagrants there, who get drunk," the patrol reported.[77] Fights were often broken up and those involved taken into custody, especially when blades appeared and blood flowed, so it might be asserted that the police protected the antagonists from further mutual injury. But the problem police had with such altercations was not so much with the fight itself but with the crowd that inevitably gathered. Crowds—impersonal agglomerations of people not restrained by the hierarchy of respect and submission that usually governed relations among individuals—were always an unpredictable challenge to the police.

Political rivalries came to a head at elections for city council and justice of the peace, and military police details were posted to prevent partisan gangs, who were often armed with clubs, from injuring those voters "opposed to their sentiments." In 1836 police on duty at polling places were instructed to take the necessary measures "to prevent, with all moderation and civility, any altercations or other activity that would be inimical to public and individual security and order."[78] A police presence at tumultuous elections would not have been found objectionable except by those who wanted to take advantage of the chaos to make the results go their way. In 1840 the members of the cabinet of the national government used the police they controlled to make just such an attempt.

The notoriously violent elections of September 1840, dubbed by historians the "elections of the cudgel," followed a parliamentary coup in July of that year by the Liberal party minority. In a bold effort to stem the growing power of the Conservative party, the Liberal cabinet tried to manipulate the next elections in their favor. They removed many of the appointed judges who had control over electoral machinery and put their own supporters in the judgeships, handed out high appointments in the national guard and similar favors to their partisans, sent club-wielding gangs to the meetings that determined the composition of local electoral boards, and in some Rio precincts sent in squads of military police to confiscate the voting lists when all else failed. The government sent messages of praise to the police for their actions in limiting the disturbances during the first round of voting in early September and issued detailed instructions on policing polling places in the future.[79] A petition from citizens whose candidates lost those elections, in contrast, claimed that the action of the military police was less than neutral. According to their complaint, police soldiers "invaded" a church being used as a polling place in Engenho Velho, provoking a "massacre" in which blood flowed, as the police attempted to confiscate the electoral rolls. The petitioners pinpointed a problem that could be applied to the police as an institution through history and to the political class that created it and has always maintained it: "No government can gain the sympathy of the nation through the power of force." The blunt reply of the minister of justice, intending no irony, could also be taken as an epigrammatic statement of the truculent position of those in power in the face of such criticism: "The imperial government knows sufficiently well the obligations it must fulfill, and the means to achieve those ends."[80] One of the principal means was the military police.

Caxias, the strict guardian of principle and discipline, had been sent to put down a rebellion in the northern province of Maranhão the year before, after he had spent eight years in the Rio police, and he took no part in this unedifying affair. Eusébio de Queiroz, a Conservative party candidate for reelection to the provincial assembly of Rio de Janeiro in these elections, was dismissed from his post as police chief by the Liberal cabinet after the first phase of the voting, on 28 September. He won reelection anyway, and on 24 March 1841, the day after a Conservative ministry took over from the discredited liberals, Queiroz was reinstated as Rio's chief of police.[81]

Conclusion

During the regency period as Rio de Janeiro grew, the business and professional activities of the propertied and powerful class became more specialized and more demanding. The old strategic seaport and seat of colonial government became a center of commercial capitalism and specialized bureaucratic administration. Contributing most fundamentally to those changes were increasing shipments of coffee passing through the port and the institution building associated with the consolidation of the independent state. Patriarchal traditions and personal social relations were increasingly surrounded and supplanted by an impersonal and individualistic urban environment. The administration of the city itself needed to adapt to these changing circumstances nowhere more obviously than in the network of formal institutions that substituted for the control previously exercised by a more closely knit hierarchy of personal obligation, discipline, and deference.

A coffee broker involved in large-scale financial and commercial dealings did not want to come home in the evening, put on a ward inspector's sash, and walk the streets rounding up vagrants and breaking up fights between drunk sailors and capoeira ruffians. And he was too valuable to the newly expanding complex of export agriculture to be used in such a way. A store owner did not want to take a government-issued lance out of his broom closet and go running into the street in response to a patrolman's whistle for help. He paid his taxes—let the government provide an adequate protection service in return. A shoemaker was gratified to be able to put on his crisp blue uniform and tasseled shako and join with similarly attired men in an occasional parade of the national guard. He would be identified with the forces of order and control and have camaraderie of his social betters while gaining access to an important patronage network. But he had to devote himself to running his shop if he wanted to avoid falling into the stratum that had to be content with watching those parades from the sidelines. It was a burden for him to patrol the streets or stand guard on a corner, especially if a *beleguim* of the military police could challenge his authority with impunity.[82]

On the other side of the social divide, Rio de Janeiro had tens of thousands of slaves chafing at the restrictions of their condition in many ways, from suicide to subtle sabotage to illicit recreation to violent outbursts against their oppressors. Former slaves and their descendants, along with propertyless mulattos and mestizos, indigent Portuguese immigrants, transients and drifters from other parts of the country, sailors off merchant ships, invalid former soldiers left adrift made up a diverse group that might for shorthand be called the free rabble, or in Patricia Aufderheide's appropriate term, the patronless poor. Slaves are known to have comprised something over 40 percent of the city's population in this period, but it is much more difficult to estimate the proportion of the population that might be lumped as free rabble, particularly because many would have been left out of census counts that focused on the household as the relevant social unit. Certainly the slaves and free poor added together made up the majority of the inhabitants of the city by a considerable margin.[83] The police system born of the political crisis of 1831 settled into a routine of surveillance and repression of the behavior of the lower social orders, expanding and refining the mission launched by the intendancy and the Guarda Real in 1808-9.

By 1841 the Rio police system had evolved considerably from those beginnings. The police chief, with an enlarged staff, de facto supervision of the justices of the peace and ward inspectors, also had considerable influence over how the newly efficient military police were to be deployed. Supreme in his jurisdiction, Eusébio de Queiroz was at age 29 referred to in Parliament as a "police celebrity, whose gaze penetrates everything."[84] He advocated and implemented the 1841 reform which removed the anomaly that the chief and most other officials were appointed by the central government while the justices of the peace were elected by their neighbors.

Those who wanted to streamline the organization nevertheless recognized one advantage of the system of the regency period: by judging and sentencing most petty offenders in a local judicial proceeding immediately upon arrest, the justices of the peace took the brunt of the task of processing malefactors from the streets to the jails, without the intervention of a cumbersome criminal court structure. When in late 1841 appointed police officials replaced the elected judges in local districts, the new officials were delegated the authority to investigate, arrest, judge, and sentence petty offenders right in the police station, without the intervention of lawyers, prosecutors, or higher judicial authority.

FIVE

Maturity, 1842-65

A year after the "elections of the cudgel," Parliament passed a law that significantly changed the institutional structure set forth in the 1832 code of criminal procedure. Named for the day of its approval, the 1841 reform became known as the Law of 3 December. It confirmed the principle that authority should be centralized in the hands of the appointed police chief, a goal Eusébio de Queiroz had already achieved by that time. Queiroz was reconfirmed as chief under the new guidelines on 28 January 1842, and three days later detailed regulations were issued for carrying out the changes approved the previous month. The legal and institutional transition was complete, and the police and judicial system of Rio de Janeiro entered a period of maturity that lasted with only minor alterations for the next 24 years. In 1866 the creation of a new police force changed the structure, if not the function, of the system of policing the city. The delegation of judicial powers to the civilian police hierarchy lasted to 1871. Despite some further changes after the proclamation of the republic in 1889, important features of the institutional structure created in 1841, along with informal police attitudes and procedures that matured in the middle of the nineteenth century, are still in place today.

As early as 1834 the minister of justice had called for a centralized system by making the justice of the peace an appointive office. That change also became a pet project of conservative minister

Bernardo Pereira de Vasconcelos, who in 1827, as a member of what was then called the liberal faction in Parliament, had advocated establishing the justice of the peace as a "police judge."[1] From the perspective of national politicians, the justice of the peace had proven a nearly unmitigated failure for controlling unlawful activity. The locally elected judge was a principal casualty of the reform, but the office had by that time become thoroughly discredited in influential political circles. As the minister of justice put it in 1840 while advocating the reform approved the following year, "Police agents are the front-line organs of government, who are party to the confidential workings of the state and authorized to use force. To have them elected independently of the government, or even contrary to the wishes of the government, is certainly an anomalous, if not an absurd, institution."[2] In short, the political elite of Brazil concluded that electoral democracy was incompatible with the interests of the state, which they closely identified with their interests as a class. After December 1841, stripped of all police authority and nearly all authority in civil cases, the justice of the peace became a vestigial remnant of the original 1827 model.[3] In the city of Rio, which was directly controlled by the central government, the justices of the peace had long since been effectively subordinated to the ad hoc authority of Police Chief Queiroz. Despite the lingering inefficiencies of competing local authorities, the centralized hierarchy that had been established in Rio during the 1830's provided a model for a system that was, by the law of 3 December 1841, formally secured in the city and extended in principle over the entire country.

The new national structure was to have a chief of police in each province. In Rio de Janeiro he was to be appointed by the emperor (in practice by the minister of justice) from among those district judges with at least three years' experience on the bench. The police chief of the city of Rio de Janeiro reported directly to the minister of justice, as Queiroz had been doing since 1833. He nominated his subordinate delegados and subdelegados for formal appointment by the emperor. They, in turn, nominated neighborhood ward inspectors for approval by the police chief. In the apt words of the nineteenth-century liberal legal scholar Tavares Bastos, the law of 3 December 1841 "established a centralizing apparatus, which descends from the emperor to the ward inspector."[4]

Along with the centralization of the authority hierarchy, the most significant effect of the law of 3 December was to formally extend judicial powers to the police. Under the 1841 reform, for violation of municipal ordinances and for all misdemeanor offenses the police chiefs, delegados, and subdelegados had full authority to issue warrants for search and arrest, to carry out the arrest, bring formal charges, set bail, hold summary judicial hearings, pass sentence, and supervise punishment—all without the intervention of any other authority.[5] For all but the most serious crime, the police chief or his appointed delegate down to the neighborhood level became accuser, investigator, arresting officer, and prosecutor, as well as judge, jury, and jailer. As a contemporary legal scholar justified subsequent "summary correctional or repressive police procedures," the law granting judicial authority to the police "is useful both to society and to the accused: minor crimes, and thus minor punishments, do not require so many guarantees, nor a trial full of formalities and delays that would involve more time and expense than the matter requires." He further explained that the police had a correctional role, authorizing them to "punish minor offenses, in order to prevent them from developing into bad habits and more serious crimes."[6]

In the national capital, extending local judicial powers to appointed police officials was not an authoritarian innovation in violation of previous practices, as liberal critics later suggested. The intendant had been expressly granted such powers in 1808, they were transferred to the justices of the peace in 1832 and in 1841 were passed on to the police chief and his delegates. There was considerable continuity in this regard from the enlightened despotism of the late colonial era through the interim period of institutional experimentation to the centralized bureaucracy of the consolidated state. The anomaly was the 1827–41 period when locally elected judges had such authority, and in Rio de Janeiro their autonomy existed only in principle. Under the stewardship of Eusébio de Queiroz and actively abetted by a series of justice ministers during the regency, the locally elected judges had become extensions of the centrally controlled police and judicial structure. The effect of the 1841 reform was to restore centralized authority by removing that anomaly.

Police Chief Queiroz quickly moved to marginalize the justices of the peace in his jurisdiction. The justices were still allowed to require habitual drunks to sign promises of good conduct and to "keep watch on their subsequent behavior." The standard punishment for violation of such a promise was a jail term. When in April 1842 a justice of the peace took the next step and sentenced two men to 30 days in jail for breaking their pledge not to appear drunk in public, he went too far. Queiroz reported the violation to the minister of justice, who ruled that under the new system, "justices of the peace may not bring charges and pass sentence . . . as their police and criminal jurisdiction is very expressly and strictly limited" by the provisions of the law of 3 December and its subsequent regulations.[7] For the city of Rio de Janeiro, the practical effect of the Law of 3 December was to eliminate the elected justices of the peace as significant cogs in the mechanism of repression and to replace them with appointed subdelegados.

The Civilian Police System at Midcentury

By the mid-point of the nineteenth century, with a total population of about 200,000, Rio de Janeiro had more than 850 men in its police institutions, supplemented by several auxiliary and emergency forces. At the top was the chief of police, appointed from among sitting district judges. The chief was assisted by two delegados who had citywide jurisdiction and a staff of some 20 clerks, bailiffs, and duty officers in the central police secretariat. In 1850 there were 32 pedestres, or civilian patrolmen, subordinate to the secretariat of police. They backed up subdelegados and duty officers as they conducted police business, then patrolled their assigned parishes from 6 P.M. to midnight with duty officers as squad leaders. The pedestres on the street were usually armed only with clubs, uniforms were a sometime thing, discipline was lax, and consequently pedestres received little respect from the public. Pedestres were drawn from the lowest social stratum above slaves, men with few skills, aspirations, or opportunities. Each patrolman received $560 per day, or 204$400 per year, and the police chief requested an increase in the size of the force and in wages, saying the low current rates "do not attract anyone with the attributes that would make a good pedestre, and those who take the job for lack of alternative employment do not serve with the positive spirit that a well-paid employee always shows." The chief decried the low quality of men in the pedestre force because "as a general rule," those who are "strong, outgoing, and active easily find many other ways of making a living with higher pay and more leisure." Chiefs of police in the late 1840's repeatedly argued for a larger and better-paid staff of patrolmen. The response from the ministry of justice was favorable, and by 1858 there were 129 men in the force, including the commander and his assistant, 96 full-time pedestres, and 31 part-time auxiliaries.

Pedestres' pay was increased in 1853 to $800 per day, a 43 percent increase over 1850, and in 1858 it was raised again to 1$100 per day after the police chief complained of the increase in the cost of living and "the impossibility of obtaining good pedestres . . . with the meager salary they make."[8] An 1856 report on wages paid to artisans and laborers working on repairs to the House of Correction provides a comparative context for such a complaint. A master mason got 3$500 per day, a master carpenter got 3$000, and journeyman carpenters between 1$600 and 2$000. Overseers (*feitores*) of slave laborers were paid from 1$280 to 1$800 per day. A cartman got 1$100, the same as pedestres received after the 1858 raise. These rates for free workers compare to wages paid to slaves hired for the project: Cassiano, a slave mason, was paid 1$120 per day at a time when a police pedestre still made $800; Carlos, a slave carpenter, was paid $500; and Firmina, a slave laundress, received $400 per day.[9] In other words, the pay of rank-and-file members of the police force was lower than that of free skilled workers and slave drivers, as well as of skilled slave artisans. Only slaves-for-hire engaged in menial labor were paid less than policemen.

The subdelegado in charge of each district was the functional successor to the justice of the peace in terms of territory as well as authority. At mid-century the city was divided into sixteen police districts, the same as those the justices of the peace oversaw during the regency, with three in Sacramento parish, two each in Santa Ana, São José, Santa Rita, Engenho Velho, Candelária, and Glória, and one in Lagoa.[10] Each of the two delegados and sixteen subdelegados was backed up by six alternates (*suplentes*) for a total of 108 men who often filled in for the subdelegados in their absence or joined in police operations. The experience the alternates thus gained made them likely candidates to succeed subdelegados who retired or moved to another position. Subdelegados also appointed bailiffs (*oficiais de justiça*) to assist them or sometimes simply to reward friends and clients with a public post which, although unpaid, at least got them exemption from service in the national guard. As of 1850, in addition to 36 bailiffs attached to the three municipal courts, there were 32 attached to the various subdelegados' offices. Like the duty officers in the central police headquarters the bailiffs had arrest powers, and they often participated in police operations on the street where they established a hostile relationship with the targets of police repression.

The smallest administrative subdivisions were the 195 wards, with a resident appointed as ward inspector in each, which were under the orders of the subdelegado as they had previously been auxiliary to the justices of the peace. As the front line of the civilian police structure, the unpaid ward inspector was expected to be alert for suspicious, disruptive, or illegal activity in his local jurisdiction, could arrest in flagrante, and was to call for help from other authorities as necessary. The average population of a ward in 1849 was 1,056 in 111 residential units, but they varied greatly, from the second ward of Santa Rita with 3,828 inhabitants (which included the naval arsenal with the marines and sailors stationed there along with the São Bento monastery) to the seventeenth ward of Glória with just 194 people, most of them patients or staff in the veterans' hospital in São João fort on the point extending from Sugarloaf rock into the entrance to Guanabara Bay.[11]

Secret Police

One of the areas of police activity begun by Queiroz in the 1830's, which was expanded after the 1841 reform and again in the 1850's, was secret. It began as a discretionary fund at the chief's disposal that he used to pay the substantial monetary rewards deemed necessary to encourage both private individuals and members of the police system to report crimes and assist in the capture of delinquents. This followed common police practice in the era before the development of "scientific" investigative techniques and detective procedures. In Rio the practice was at least as old as the rewards to the Guarda Real de Polícia for capturing runaway slaves in the 1820's and the bonuses Queiroz instituted to clear the streets of vagrants in 1838. This system of rewards led to payoffs to informers and retainers paid to spies, all of which was done in confidentiality and completely at the discretion of the chief of police. In justifying these expenses to skeptical members of the chamber of deputies scrutinizing the annual budget request in 1841, the minister of justice claimed that jail breaks, robberies, and other crimes had been reduced because the knowledge that rewards were available to informants served to "introduce mutual distrust" among the potential perpetrators. "Without rewards to informants," he asked rhetorically,

How will it be possible to solve certain crimes in a capital as populous as this one? If an individual of the lower class knows, for example, that counterfeit money is about to be distributed, is he going to report it for nothing without the incentive of a reward? Some police employees receive a salary of 300$000 per year. Many times they are put in charge of risky missions, in which they must put out considerable effort. Do you expect them to carry out these duties with no more incentive than the salaries they normally receive? [12]

Such rewards and bonuses were based on the assumption that private individuals with no personal stake in the issue would have no reason to assist those who represented the power of the state and that poorly paid police employees required supplementary pay to ensure that they would carry out the tasks they were assigned. The notions that an ordinary citizen might feel an obligation to the common good that would lead him or her to cooperate with the police or that a public employee accepted certain responsibilities along with his salary were alien to the political culture of nineteenth-century Brazil.

The annual sum allocated for these purposes was already 20:000$000 before the 1841 reform. As of 1851–52 that amounted to nearly one-third of the annual budget of the secretariat of police, which totaled 61:073$000. (The salaries of the entire corps of 32 pedestres in that year, in contrast, came to less than 7:000$000.) [13] Several individuals were put on a regular retainer paid from the chief's discretionary fund. In November 1857, payments representative of allocations to the same men over several months and totaling 290$000 were made to "agents of the secret police" Fidelis Carboni, Graciano José de Carvalho, José Maria Candido Ribeiro, and Luiz Muniz Tello de Sampaio. In the absence of any employees assigned to the investigation of criminal activities, the secret agents became a rudimentary detective force, as when in January 1854 the chief sent several to investigate a robbery reported in the suburban area of Andaraí. Traditional uses for the "secret" fund also continued, as in November 1858 when four pedestres and one slave shared a reward of 100$000 for the capture of a slave accused of murder. Continued discretionary allocations paid for a variable staff of plainclothes investigators and informants who lived in the shadow of the law and worked on the thin boundary dividing the forces of repression and the sources of resistance.[14]

The Military Police

Parallel to but distinct from the civilian police hierarchy comprising about 450 men, the military police corps created in 1831 also had over 400 men in its ranks by 1850, including a headquarters staff of 10 officers and senior noncommissioned officers, 123 cavalry, and 286 infantry. Like the civilian chief of police, the commander of the military police was subordinated directly to the minister of justice of the empire. Rank-and-file soldiers continued to be drawn from the lowest ranks of the free population, although the salary of a police soldier of $640 per day was significantly more than the pedestres at the bottom of the civilian hierarchy. In 1851 Minister of Justice Eusébio de Queiroz urged a raise to $800 per day, noting that "any common laborer makes equal or better pay, and is not subject to the rigor of military discipline." By 1865 a soldier's base pay was still $800 per day, but that had been increased by a $160 supplementary stipend and a $300 subsistence allowance for a total of 1$260 per day. Military police were supplied with uniforms and equipment, and in contrast to pedestres and other members of the civilian hierarchy they were housed and fed in barracks where they lived under strict military regimen.[15]

Officers were Brazilian nationals, but foreigners were allowed to enter the enlisted ranks after two years' residence in Brazil, and significant numbers were Portuguese immigrants. In 1865, of a total force of 633 corporals and soldiers of the lowest rank, 231 (36 percent) were Portuguese; there were also 6 Spaniards and 2 Italians in the service. The proportion was roughly similar to that of free foreigners in the male population of the city.[16] On the other hand there were recurring petitions by owners requesting the return of their slaves who had managed to enlist as soldiers in the military police by passing themselves off as free men. In March 1853, for example, João Estévão da Cruz requested that the military police release from service his slave, Marcelino. The commander of the corps reported that the man in question voluntarily entered the headquarters barracks to enlist, saying he was a free man born in Rio de Janeiro and a tailor by profession. He was well dressed, of robust physique and good appearance. Furthermore he had been wearing shoes, a sign of free status. When questioned following Cruz's request, the new soldier, who gave his name as José Soares, insisted he had once been a slave but considered himself free "in principle" because his owner had died. Cruz, however, included ample proof of ownership with his petition, and the military police released Marcelino to him. In a similar case in 1856 the military police commander, upon interrogating a new recruit claimed by João Luiz Pereira de Souza as his escaped slave, concluded the man may have been enslaved illegally, as he described how his mother, a free mulatto woman, had apprenticed him to his godfather, a baker, in his home province of Bahia. He had subsequently served several masters before one sold him to a slave dealer in Rio de Janeiro who then sold him to Souza. The recruit in question was turned over to a civil court judge for disposition of the case.[17]

The fact that such men were accepted for enlistment suggests that there was considerable racial and ethnic diversity in the ranks of the military police, who accepted black and brown men without question along with those of European stock, including many of Portuguese birth. In the several sets of general regulations issued during the nineteenth century and in operating guidelines or documented practice, there is no clear indication that racial discrimination was practiced in recruitment or conditions of service. What military police soldiers shared in common in addition to reasonably good health and free status was their origin in the lower end of the social pyramid—the same social category that was the main target of police action.

Police soldiers were imprisoned in the corps' own guardhouse for disciplinary infractions or offenses committed while on duty. Soldiers deemed "incorrigible" after repeated minor offenses, most commonly habitual drunkenness or being absent without leave, were sometimes simply expelled from the corps, as were three men in 1866 who "forgetting their duty, engaged in the horrible vice of debauchery and promoted disorders, when they should be the first to avoid such behavior." But more often they were sent to regular army service—poorly paid, considered more rigid, and generally less desirable—in exchange for army soldiers selected for desired qualities. In April 1848, for example, the military police exchanged 34 soldiers for an equal number of army troops "of good conduct."[18] As for criminal offenses committed while off duty, questions occasionally arose as to the appropriate procedure. One general rationale for a separate military punishment system, with courts-martial conducted by regular officers and internal detention, was that during the isolation of the military campaign or in the press of battle, sending offenders to civilian courts and jails would be unduly encumbering. A request from 1847 reflects another reason for separating the punishment of military offenders from the general prison population, when that same population is the adversary. Civilian authorities had sentenced a police soldier for a minor crime to one month behind bars. Such a sentence would normally have been served in the Aljube jail, but the military police commander requested that the soldier be allowed to serve his time in the internal guardhouse of the corps instead, pointing out that "military police soldiers serve as guards at the jail, and they have pursued and arrested many of the prisoners there. They thus incur the wrath and rancor of such criminals, and they would be massacred and subject to all sorts of revenge, if they were put in the company of the prisoners in the public jails."[19]

Military police were assigned to a variety of tasks wherever authorities deemed the public order problem to be more serious. For example, in 1844 the chief of police, lamenting the "continuous disorders, insults by blacks, and capoeira activity on the docks" in the Saco do Alferes, ordered the military police to place a detachment there. Such a measure, the chief noted, "along with orders that after a certain time of night no loading or unloading will take place and that the blacks must get off the streets and spend the night in their owner's houses will do much to prevent the frequent disturbances they often cause." Along with this recognition that many slaves were abroad in the streets at night beyond the control of their owners, the chief noted that "the beaches of Prainha and Peixe are, without a doubt, the sections of this capital where there are the most daily occurrences of disorders of all types. Personal injury, theft, and many other crimes are very frequent there, due to the concentration of slaves and of men of the lowest class, disembarking at all hours. There would be great advantage in placing a small detachment of three to five men in each of these sites, to police the area day and night."[20] To such problems involving sailors, slaves, and the "disorderly" population of the city, the military police provided an all-purpose response.

Armed with two pistols and a sabre, a whistle for calling reinforcements pinned to their tightly buttoned blue uniform jackets, their tall blue caps visible from a distance, military police soldiers patrolled the streets in small units. (See Frontispiece for the look of a police soldier and a hint at his relationship to the lower orders of urban society, slave and free.) As two North American residents of Rio observed, military police were "fortified with plenty of authority and take care to use it." Specific assignments changed through time in response to perceived threats to public order, but as of 1848 there were about 70 men on patrol duty with 11 squads on the streets from 7 A.M. to midnight and an additional 3 squads from 2 P.M. to 10 P.M. in the extensive and turbulent waterfront area. From midnight to dawn only 5 squads circulated.[21] Another 30 or so in detachments of 4 or 5 men each staffed guard posts around the city, and others served as guards at the Aljube jail and the House of Correction as orderlies and staffed the headquarters barracks and cavalry stables where the corps' 200 horses were kept. A force of about 30 was held in readiness in case of civil disturbance or similar eventuality, but this backup force often found itself occupied in more mundane extra duty at the behest of a variety of elite institutions, some public and some private. One of the public institutions meriting special consideration was the monarchy itself. Whenever the itinerary of Emperor Pedro II took him out in public, police were ordered to clean up the area in advance, as when in May 1845 he was to attend a concert in Constitution Square, and the military police were ordered to post cavalry troops at the various entrances to the plaza "so that no barefoot persons, such as slaves etc., should be in or enter the square, and no carriages pass through it from six o'clock on."[22]

Auxiliary Forces

In addition to these full-time civilian and military police institutions, the city government employed a staff of about 60 park watchmen, market inspectors, and guards for public buildings and other facilities who had very restricted authority. The municipal guards were not integrated into the police hierarchy, although they might be considered auxiliary to it.[23] The other auxiliary force was the national guard of which there were 6,544 members in Rio in 1849, the equivalent of nearly 13 percent of the 51,077 free male Brazilians of all ages in the population. Although they were not integrated into the operational command structure on a consistent basis, the guard continued to provide some support for police activities, including street patrols when the military corps was shorthanded. Such detachments were small compared to the total numbers of men in the guard but could be important supplements to the full-time police structure. As of 1841 a group of 250 national guardsmen was assigned to assist in policing the city. Only a small number of that total was on duty at any given time, but authorities still complained of absenteeism and laxity in service. The problems of relying on unpaid guardsmen were the same as those of the mid-1830's, when they turned over most regular patrolling to paid professionals. As the minister of justice reported to parliament in 1841, it was very difficult for members of the guard to do street patrol because it "is made up of men who live from their daily labor, and for them the loss of one or two days [normal income] is a great sacrifice." Despite such complaints small numbers of guardsmen continued to be called upon. In 1858, with some five thousand men in the national guard in the city of Rio, an average of 90 guardsmen were assigned to supplement police patrols on any given day.[24]

Finally, there were several hundred men stationed in navy, marine, coast artillery, and regular army units, some of whom could be called on in case of a general emergency or for temporary duty. A confrontation in 1848, for example, provided civilian police authorities an opportunity to elicit army assistance. José Urbano, a soldier in the first light cavalry regiment, was escorting a group of captured deserters through Santa Ana parish toward army headquarters when one of the detainees escaped. When Urbano gave chase his cap blew off, then he drew his sword and dropped his encumbering equipment harness as he ran. He entered a tavern where he thought the deserter had hidden, waving his drawn sword and shouting that he would cut off the ears, or even the head, of the man he was after. The deserter, meanwhile, went through the back door of a butcher shop next door and made good his escape. Back in the tavern, a police pedestre called the local ward inspector, who arrested Urbano for his unusual conduct and for being out of uniform and delivered him to the district sub-delegado. This action prompted memos from army authorities highly critical of the inspector's presumptuousness in obstructing a soldier in the line of duty on a frivolous pretext. The subdelegado replied that he hoped that the army would henceforth do more to help capture common criminals in reciprocity for civilian assistance to the military in catching deserters. For lack of such aid, he said, several suspects had recently avoided arrest when army personnel in the area refused to help "on the pretext that that they do not belong to the police."[25]

Such cooperation was easier to promote in principle than it was to enforce in practice, but sometimes police got more than they bargained for. In November 1849 the commander of the first artillery battalion ordered his men to round up the beggars and drunks in the vicinity of their barracks in São José parish. They picked up nineteen such people and marched them directly to the Aljube jail with a note listing the subdelegado of São José as the arresting authority, because an army officer had no legal right to arrest civilians on his own. When the subdelegado whose name was on the note found out about the action, he suggested it was bad precedent to conduct such an operation without at least informing him of the plan and the results. The problems were related to violations of the chain of authority and standard operating procedures, not with the propriety of jailing nineteen people who happened to be in the vicinity of the artillery barracks when its commander decided, on his own, to clean up the area.[26]

Civilian police authorities routinely requested and received supplementary manpower during periods of peak demand. Before Christmas in 1851, for example, the chief of police asked the minister of justice to request army troops to supplement military police patrols "in the interest of security of the public and of property" during the holidays. The request was duly passed to the minister of war, then to the commander of the military garrison of the capital city, who agreed to supply a force "as large as possible" for duty from the morning of 24 December through 6 January. Before Carnival in 1854 the chief requested one hundred infantry troops of the regular army to supplement military police patrols from 8 A.M. to 8 P.M. during the four days preceding Ash Wednesday. The troops were needed because "during those days the lower population of the city, engaging in excessive consumption of alcoholic beverages, shows disrespect and provokes disorders, violating the municipal ordinances prohibiting the game of entrudo."[27]

Control of the city's population was never total, authorities often complained of inadequate staffing and the low quality of front-line personnel, and bureaucratic inefficiency continued to plague the system. Still, the military and civilian police structures established during the 1830's, consolidated in the 1840's and 1850's, and supplemented by several other institutions provided an extensive network of surveillance and control. It covered overlapping territory with interconnected jurisdictions. At any time of the day and most of the night and most anywhere in the public space of the city, a representative of the state or officer of the law was never very far away or would soon pass on patrol, and a whistle or shout could quickly bring reinforcements. Institutionalized surveillance and control over the public behavior of the patronless poor as well as slaves was well advanced by the middle of the century.

Institutional Rivalry

Rivalry between military and civilian police institutions that bordered at times on hostility has also been a recurring feature of Rio de Janeiro's police system. From the colonel commandant to soldiers on the street, military police repeatedly contested civilian domination in formal and informal ways, but the principle of the supreme authority vested in the civilian chief of police after 1841 was not directly or successfully challenged. The usual points of tension were low in the chain of command, at the level of delegado, subdelegado, and ward inspector. The powers of these officials were derived from the chief of police in principle, and their efforts to exercise control over military police revealed the persistent ambiguities in the chain of command in practice. Civilian authorities were able to maintain civilian control at the top through the same discipline and hierarchy that gave the military police its internal unity. But the contradictions persisted of a militarized force existing in the midst of a society to which it was assigned an adversarial relationship. The flurries of memoranda attending interorganizational conflicts reveal not only the rivalries themselves but much about police practice and the broader context of repression and resistance in which these overlapping institutions operated.

An incident early in the history of the post-1841 police ma-

chinery reflects several persistent themes, including the treatment
of slaves, race relations, attitudes of the military police toward society and vice versa, and the antagonism among various branches
of the system. This event and the subsequent exchange among the
authorities involved show how these and related themes were part
of a web of relationships that reflects the central role of the police
institutions in the life of the city and in the broader culture that
produced and maintained them.

Around 7 P.M. on 2 October 1844, Mamede José da Silva Passos
was walking down Vala Street (now Uruguaiana) in central Rio
de Janeiro. As a ward inspector of Sacramento parish, he was expected to keep an eye on things. That Wednesday evening Passos
was dismayed to encounter a patrol of the military police "beating
without provocation any blacks that passed and even a white man,
who was wounded on a finger." When Passos asked the head of the
patrol for an explanation of such unwarranted behavior, the police
corporal replied with an insult. Despite the broad green-and-yellow
sash of a ward inspector across Passos's chest, the military police
said they did not recognize his authority, claiming that they had
orders from the chief of police to beat the blacks. João Francisco
Pereira, the injured white man, declined to lodge a complaint
against the police, so that same night Passos took it upon himself to
denounce the incident to his immediate superior, Antonio José de
Souza e Almeida, subdelegado of Sacramento parish. Passos said
that this was not the first time military police had shown disrespect
to himself and other ward inspectors, and he took the trouble to
append a list of witnesses to the incident, including the injured
Pereira, a national guard captain, a ward inspector from neighboring Santa Rita parish, and five other men.[28]

Meanwhile, the military police lost no time in entering their version of the events of 2 October into the records with a memo from
the commander of the corps to the minister of justice demanding
the dismissal of Ward Inspector Passos for abuse of authority and
insulting the military police patrol and accusing him of protecting
from police action the slaves who gathered in taverns in his jurisdiction. The military police version of the original encounter was
that a patrol, following standing orders to break up gatherings of
slaves, was taken to task when a lowly ward inspector objected to
their methods. But ward inspectors had no authority over military
police, and Passos, at other times tolerant of misbehavior by slaves,

seemed at least as concerned that a white man was injured on the finger—an apparent accident—as with what he initially interpreted as unjustified physical abuse of slaves by the military police patrol. On 3 October the minister of justice asked the chief of police for clarification, suggesting that if the military police accusations were true then Passos should be dismissed. The chief of police asked subdelegado Almeida for a report which he submitted on the following Monday, 8 October.

Almeida took the side of the ward inspector, referring to the "many witnesses to the irregular behavior of the military police patrol, and the wound suffered by João Francisco Pereira, also verified by two witnesses of credit and public esteem." As for the suggestion that Passos was complicit in illegal slave gatherings, Almeida noted that "he has, on the contrary, been very diligent in his duties, and only a few days before the incident with the military police patrol he reported to me the name of the owner of a tavern where such meetings took place, who yesterday responded to charges in this office for violation of municipal ordinances." Almeida provided detailed examples of what he considered previous acts of dereliction by military police patrols and their refusal to accept direction from civilian police officials. With some irony, in view of the long history of such disputes, he lamented that these incidents "could cause misunderstanding among police authorities, which must be avoided." The eventual censure of the military police in this case illustrates their isolation and subordination, as civilian authorities from ward inspector to minister of justice were unanimous in contradicting the military version of the incident.

More than twenty years after the altercation on Vala Street, on the night of 7 January 1865 during Epiphany observances, an incident took place that reflected the persistent tension between military police on the street and the ward inspectors and the low regard in which the former held the latter. It also confirms that people were routinely beaten at the time of arrest and that military police continued the undercover operations begun by Caxias in the early days of the corps. During the street celebrations that made the Festival of the Kings the nineteenth-century analog to Carnival in more recent times, Benedito Ferreira do Amaral was arrested for instigating public disorder by several military police in civilian clothes. A crowd gathered to protest the arrest, saying that another man who had escaped was the perpetrator of the disturbance, not

Amaral. A ward inspector approached to look into the incident but in the tumult could do little more than accompany the military police and their prisoner toward the police station. On the way the soldiers beat Amaral for no apparent reason, and when the ward inspector protested such treatment he was arrested as well. At the police post the plainclothes military police turned the two prisoners over to Corporal Francisco Antonio Duarte, and when the ward inspector requested permission to speak to someone in authority the corporal told him he "had nothing to say to any authority, that he was going to jail." The inspector showed his sash of office which Corporal Duarte seized and ripped, repeating that the inspector was going to jail in any case. The delegado who later investigated the incident concluded that "there seems to be much to censure in this case, both in the behavior of the plainclothes military police who arrested Amaral, and in that of the corporal" in his treatment of the ward inspector. As for the latter, the delegado vouched that "he is a well-mannered man, whose word I have no reason to doubt."[29]

Such examples of corporate solidarity and subordination to the control of civilian authorities, confirmed by similar incidents through the years, say much about the historical role of Rio's military police. They retained the separateness from civilian society that Caxias had established in the 1830's. They were the largest single unified part of the police system and more than any other part they maintained internal discipline and regimentation, subjecting members of the corps to onerous patrol duty at all hours in any weather, facing a hostile and often dangerous adversary— the public. Thus the military police constituted a relatively efficient instrument for carrying out the objectives of the civilian political elite that created the corps and maintained it from the 1830's onward. Military regimentation provided internal discipline and a source of morale but not real independence. Under the active command of Caxias, when the chief of police had little power and the justices of the peace acted as police authorities, the corps had exercised considerable autonomy. That situation was changed by regulations issued in July 1842 following the judicial reform of 3 December 1841, and civilian control was strengthened further by new regulations in January 1858. Civilian authorities carefully monitored and regulated the military police regarding their level of staffing, legal mandate, operating procedures, and relationship to other elements in the police structure. The point is not that "so-ciety got the police it deserved," to paraphrase an aphorism some-times used in evaluating the Brazilian police in modern times, but that the ruling class created, maintained, and controlled the police it wanted.

Patterns of Repression

The hundreds of men in the complex and contentious web of police institutions, the direct predecessor of today's civilian and military police organizations, engaged in a wide range of activities related to controlling the behavior of the population. Some of that behavior was formally outlawed, some was defined as unaccept-able by police operating guidelines and informal consensus among those in authority. Other police activity had the purpose of intimi-dating the public and ensuring respect for those who represented power of the state on the streets.

Much of what police did was not intended to result in detention and judicial processing. One of the main goals in developing police institutions after 1831, following practices the Guarda Real had begun under Vidigal, was the preemptive repression of unaccept-able behavior, rather than simply reacting after a problem had oc-curred. If the "ostensive and repressive" mission of the military police was successful, the results would not show up in arrest re-cords but in reports of action on the street. In commenting on a relatively low number of crimes reported during 1838, Eusébio de Queiroz had waxed almost philosophical on what made good policing: "Just as times of good fortune for nations are those which offer less material to the historian, so also when preventive policing is successful, the facts related to policing are fewer."[30] Squads of police soldiers were repeatedly and routinely sent to problem areas with explicit orders to prevent, by their presence, behavior that authorities considered to be criminal, dangerous, or merely threat-ening to the social order.

From 1831 onward military police were also admonished in reg-ulations to use moderation in dealing with the public and to use their weapons only when necessary to defend themselves or bring a dangerous adversary under control. The new guidelines of 1858, for example, following a long list of conditions in which arrests were to be made, urged patrols to "use all temperate means (*meios brandos*) to prevent disorder, separate arguments, stop shouts and loud noises that threaten the public calm, and warn violators they will be arrested if they persist." They were also to disperse gatherings of slaves in taverns or other places of business and ensure that taverns and botequins closed at ten o'clock. For such minor but recurring public order offenses, arrest was to be used only as a last resort, to make good on threats. It was "absolutely prohibited" for patrols to "discuss or argue with any person regarding their professional conduct, insult those arrested in any way, whether through words or gestures, much less physically mistreat them. They may use only the degree of force necessary to contain resistance."[31] The repetition of such warnings over the years suggests that violations were also recurrent, as they were confirmed by numerous documented cases of what is today called police brutality and the violation of human rights.

Such an incident occurred on the afternoon of 14 September 1849 in an isolated area near the Botanical Garden in the southern zone of the city, where police patrols could usually assume they were beyond the scrutiny of competing or supervising authority. Several slaves-for-hire were traveling along the road, one carrying a pole with a dirty scrap of white cloth attached to the top. A military police cavalry squad stopped the group, and the ensuing confrontation was later described by Ward Inspector Carlos Augusto D'Antenil, who watched from his nearby house as the soldiers demanded the slaves give them the "flag." The inspector thought this was unnecessary because police soldiers should have been accustomed to seeing coffee carriers and other teams of slaves with similar banners, "a very frequent sight around the city." The slaves immediately stopped when so ordered, indicating deference by asking the soldiers for their blessing, a ritual of submission in the relations between master and slave, parent and child, priest and parishioner, and by extension those in authority and those subject to it. When the slave holding the flag declined to give it up, the sergeant in charge grabbed the staff and hit the black with it so hard the pole broke in several places. Then two other soldiers in the mounted patrol charged the slaves with swords drawn, apparently for the fun of seeing the blacks cower and run. This was too much for the observing ward inspector, who approached and told the cavalrymen their behavior was disturbing the peace instead of maintaining it and that "a soldier should never draw his weapon" except to overcome resistance to arrest. To this the sergeant declared to the inspector, "in a quite insolent manner, that he was only following the orders he was required to carry out, whether it was with blacks or even with whites." The orders he referred to required police squads to break up suspicious gatherings, but the blacks being harassed were obviously not capoeiras nor bent on mischief. Their dress, cargo baskets, demeanor, and even the flag, the ward inspector pointed out, clearly marked them as the sort of slaves who routinely hired their services around the city.[32]

Military police could use the authority represented by their uniform and the threat of their charging horses and flashing sabers to intimidate people without the necessity of arrest, and civilian police continued to use a variety of tactics other than imprisonment to clear the city of undesirables. As a former minister of justice proclaimed in parliament in one of the periodic discussions on policing the city, "There are two means of preventing and punishing crimes—deportation and conscription."[33] Summary deportation was the method of choice for foreigners, although many non-Brazilians were also forcibly conscripted into the military along with the natives caught in periodic roundups of "troublemakers." In 1844, for example, the chief of police was frustrated by a string of petty thefts. His men made some arrests, but the detainees had to be released for lack of evidence, whereupon the thefts continued. The chief decided that since he had identified the culprits to his own satisfaction, he could solve the problem by "giving employment to some vagrants who had no licit means of support, which they found instead in their criminal activities." Over the next five months he sent 57 such individuals, some of whom had been sailors, to the navy as conscripts. With this roundup reports of theft fell back to the level one would "ordinarily and inevitably expect" in a large city "where many foreigners disembarked daily."[34]

In the 1830's deportation was usually a recourse applied to those deemed incorrigible by virtue of their long criminal histories, and each case required the approval of the minister of justice. After 1841 the newly empowered police chief could order such expulsions on his own authority, and summary deportation had the advantage of expediency. No formal charges were required; the signature of the police chief sufficed. In a brief period in 1849 Police Chief Antonio Simões da Silva ordered fifteen foreigners deported, including thirteen Portuguese, one Austrian, and one

Chilean. In justifying this action he claimed that the deportees were of "terrible habits, incorrigible, drunks and troublemakers who had been convicted and served jail time for various crimes." Some of those deported "carried depravation and immorality to such extremes that they ran the most repulsive and scandalous houses of prostitution, where orgies were constant and where turbulent and vicious vagrants gathered, engaged in all manner of illegal gambling, stole from each other, and ended up in fights." By closing down such establishments, "expelling those foreigners and dispersing, terrorizing, and repressing their colleagues by all means the law allows me," the chief proclaimed the problem "cut out by the roots."[35] In this self-congratulatory but otherwise routine report, the chief explicitly invoked two mechanisms central to the policing of Rio de Janeiro: instilling terror in the population and repressing undesirable behavior.

The chief of police expected praise from his superiors, respect from his colleagues, obedience from his subordinates, and subservience from his adversaries. With such an attitude from the man in charge of the entire system, himself a trained lawyer, appointed judge, and thus a member of the political elite, it is little wonder that some of the hundreds of subordinates under his command would engage in arbitrary and brutal behavior. Nor is it surprising that his thousands of adversaries responded with hostile tactics of their own.

One incident involving foreigners in 1850 had the potential of becoming a major diplomatic confrontation at a time of extreme tension between Brazil and Great Britain, and the resulting stack of accusations and explanations reveals much about the everyday workings of Rio's police. The case turned out to be unusual, but the procedures and relationships it reflects among elements of the police system and between police and public were not far from the ordinary. As with many other such stories there were two sides to this one, but because the men arrested were under the protection of the queen of England, their version became part of the documentary record along with that of the Rio police.

First, the Brazilian perspective: About the time of the 10 P.M. curfew on Saturday night, 31 August 1850, Carmelo Ferreira de Andrade, a ward inspector in Sacramento parish, heard a disturbance in the street. Accompanied by a lone pedestre, he stepped out and found a group of foreigners dressed in rough clothes, covered with mud and dust, armed with cudgels, and shouting boisterously as they walked up Vala (Uruguaiana) Street. Andrade approached, told them they would have to quiet down and quickly disarmed them to prevent any "act of disrespect." One of the group, dressed in a dark blue jacket different from the sailcloth waistcoats of the rest, became quite recalcitrant, refusing to yield his club. He was immediately detained, and although the others tried to prevent the arrest, an unarmed military police soldier happened by and assisted the inspector. The latter blew his whistle for reinforcements, but none immediately appeared. Outnumbered, he decided he had no means to put the entire group of eight men under arrest, so the inspector, pedestre, and police soldier made their way to the central police station on Constitution (Tiradentes) Square with the blue-jacketed foreigner in tow and the others tagging along. When they arrived outside the station, another of the foreigners, dressed in a dirty white vest and broad-brimmed hat, tried to push aside the police soldier accompanying the first prisoner and free his comrade. By this time a squad of pedestres on duty in nearby São Francisco Square had come on the scene, and they assisted in the arrest of the second stranger, engaging in a minor scuffle in the process.

The inspector presented the two prisoners to Quintiliano Ferreira da Costa, the duty clerk who normally entered arrests into the station log on the night shift. But when he made out from their halting attempts at communication that they claimed to be officers and that the first arrestee seemed to be in some sort of uniform, Costa refused to accept them into his custody. He wanted none of the trouble that might arise from an encounter with the military, native or foreign. In exasperation, Inspector Andrade sat down at the desk, found a slip of paper, wrote out a note remanding the two prisoners to the custody of the military police, and sent them with the pedestres to the corps headquarters on Borbonos (Evaristo da Veiga) Street, a considerable distance away on the other side of Santo Antonio hill. When the party arrived there it was after 11 P.M., and the officer of the day, Captain José de Oliveira, refused to accept the two foreigners. Dirty and poorly dressed as they were, with no insignia displayed, he doubted they were military officers as the accompanying note claimed. That note, moreover, did not conform to regulations—it was written on less than a full sheet of paper and was addressed to the Police Prison rather than to the

Headquarters of the Permanent Municipal Corps of which Oliveira was in temporary charge—and in any case there was no cell available. The pedestres then took the two prisoners back around to the central police station on Constitution Square, where they were held until the arresting ward inspector could be brought back to dispose of the case.

While they were waiting for the inspector to reappear, the man in the blue jacket lay down on his back on the stair landing leading up to the offices of the police secretariat. Duty clerk Costa told the man he should not stay in that harmful position and offered him a bench to sit on. When the detainee said he was all right where he was, Costa concluded he must have been slightly touched in the head (*tonto de cabeça*). When Inspector Andrade arrived back at the station, he decided that the two were ordinary men or probably sailors, so he and two pedestres took them to be locked up in the Aljube jail some twelve blocks away on the other side of the city. They arrived at the Aljube after midnight, and the jailer put the men in the holding cell called the Sala Livre, accepting Inspector Andrade's declaration that they were in custody on the authority of the subdelegado of Sacramento parish. They asked that someone be sent to get them something to eat, but the request was denied. To hinder escapes, jail regulations specified that at night the doors could be opened to let people in, but no one could leave. Besides, the jailer pointed out, there was no place open at that hour where one could buy the bread they requested.

The next morning Inspector Almeida sent a detailed report to his superior, Subdelegado Antonio José Gonçalves Fontes, along with the cudgels he had taken from the dirty group on Vala Street the night before as evidence. Also that morning an English civilian appeared at the Aljube and informed the jailer that the two men were officers in the British navy, whereupon the keeper had them brought to the more commodious interrogation room to await the arrival of Subdelegado Fontes. Meanwhile, a British naval officer visited Fontes, requesting that he order the release of the captain of the frigate *Southampton* and a navy lieutenant, son of an admiral, who had been jailed on the authority of the subdelegado. The visitor requested that the two be released if at all possible in order to avoid the lodging of a formal complaint by his government. When the subdelegado went to the Aljube and ordered the two detainees to his presence, he saw that one, said to be the commander of the frigate, was dressed in dirty and rumpled sailcloth; the other was wearing a dark blue jacket but was so dirty and disheveled that at first glance he did not seem to be in uniform, if one did not notice the single gold band on each cuff. They told the subdelegado their story, apologized for the inconvenience, and requested permission to go, as their vessel was scheduled to weigh anchor and they were due on board. Subdelegado Fontes hastily concluded that their offense amounted to a simple violation of city ordinances due to their ignorance of local laws, and he ordered them released at once. He then sent the confiscated cudgels along with his report to Police Chief Antonio Simões da Silva as evidence.

The British version sketched for the subdelegado was subsequently filled out in some detail in protests passed on by Rear Admiral Reynolds, commander of the British South American squadron, to the Brazilian ministers of foreign affairs and justice. It ran as follows: While idle in the port of Rio, eight officers of the frigate *Southampton*, flagship of the British squadron, decided to climb Gávea rock, a massive flat-topped promontory more than ten kilometers from the foot of Botafogo Bay, where a launch put them ashore at 6 A.M. on the Saturday in question. At 7 A.M. they ate the only food they had with them and hiked and climbed through the day, often through thick forest and over steep slopes. Around 10 P.M., hungry, dirty, and exhausted from their adventure, they were quietly walking single file through the downtown area within a few blocks of the dock where a launch awaited them when they were rudely accosted by an unidentified individual who demanded they give him their walking sticks. The individual making demands of them had taken a green-and-yellow sash from his bag and draped it across his chest, from which the Englishmen concluded he must be someone of authority. Commander James West, captain of the *Southampton*, turned over his stick upon perceiving that the aggressors were members of the police. Most of the Englishmen in the group were dressed in rough clothing appropriate for their excursion, but Flag Lieutenant Frederick Woollcombe was in uniform. He refused to give up his walking stick to a civilian, demanding instead to be taken to the presence of the chief of police "so that, if such an extraordinary procedure was really legal, he could at least hear that fact from a higher authority." The man in the sash responded that this had nothing to do with the chief of police. (Little did Andrade realize that within a week, as the ripples from this encounter spread, Police Chief Silva would summarily order Subdelegado Fontes to dismiss him from his position as ward inspector.)

Commander West tried to present the man in the sash with his calling card as identification, but he rudely threw the card back in West's face, saying he did not believe Woollcombe was an officer because he was not carrying a sword. The man in the sash had blown a whistle at the start of the incident, and when soldiers arrived they surrounded the Englishmen and took them toward a police post, gripping Woollcombe by the arm and pushing him forward. When they arrived the soldiers forcibly yanked the walking stick from Woollcombe's grip and grabbed the lieutenant by the arms and the collar of his jacket to take him into the station. Commander West, not wanting to leave his subordinate to an uncertain fate, refused to leave him as the Brazilian official had ordered. Soldiers then surrounded West and struck him several times on the shoulders and chest, and took him along with Woollcombe into the station. The others of the British group left to report the affair as soon as they were safely aboard their vessel.

The two officers taken into custody poorly understood why they spent the next two hours being forced to march from one side of the city to another, but they were in little condition to focus their attention in any case after all they had been through that day. When they objected to the indignity of being led around by their collars, they were allowed to walk unhindered, but the accompanying policemen kept their swords drawn in readiness. At the military police headquarters they complained of their mistreatment, but the officer in charge ignored their entreaties and sent them elsewhere. Back at the central police station they asked for a place to sit down as they were very tired. The duty clerk pointed to a stone block and said they could sit there if they wanted. Arriving at the Aljube jail at one in the morning, they were tossed in a filthy cell with seven or eight other prisoners accused of various offenses. They told the jailer they had not eaten all day and asked for something, offering to pay for bread, but were refused. After "passing through all the degrading formalities to which criminals of the lowest caste are subject," they were finally released at noon the next day, still without being given anything to eat.[36]

This case is pregnant with information related to international politics, linguistic barriers and ethnocentric bias, social hierarchies, and more. If any member of the British party had been reasonably fluent in Portuguese, much of the misunderstanding leading to injured dignity, physical assault, a night of confusion, and a minor diplomatic incident might have been avoided. If either Inspector Andrade or Lieutenant Woollcombe had been less insistent on what each considered the prerogatives of his status, the initial encounter could have ended quickly and calmly. Some of the Brazilians must have wondered why naval officers would dress like common sailors and tramp through jungle and climb mountains all day and half the night for recreation.

But as far as police institutions of Rio are concerned, this case does little more than specify and confirm the impressions gleaned from myriad other cases of lesser note. Noise in the street brings a ward inspector and a pedestre out into the night. A gang of loud and unkempt sailors with clubs are quieted and disarmed. Resistance brings the immediate arrest and physical subjugation of the culprit. A police soldier arrives to assist, and a whistle soon brings more pedestres. A comrade tries to help the first detainee escape and is beaten and taken into custody as well. The clerk on duty at the police station refuses to take responsibility for the detainees when the case seems irregular. The military police officer of the day, strictly adhering to regulations, rejects what the ward inspector thinks is a legitimate order. The two men, marched all over the city by sword-wielding pedestres, spend what is left of the night in the holding tank at the Aljube jail in the company of other men of lesser status. It was a case of mistaken identity, but the identity in question was not individual but social. Police Chief Silva made a telling assessment of the relevant context of the incident when he pointed out that the two men were "found after curfew, dirty, poorly dressed in civilian clothes, armed, making noise, so they were arrested with good reason. There was no way to recognize them as persons of status."

Arrests in 1850

We know the arrests of Woollcombe and West went unrecorded because the central police station ledger book for 1850, which duty clerk Costa presided over on the night he refused to assume responsibility for the Englishmen, still exists. There are five arrests listed in it for 31 August 1850. All five were slaves, four of whom were Brazilian-born and one an African from the Inhambane region of southern Mozambique. The Inhambane, the only one of the five with the reason for his arrest recorded, was detained by a pedestre in São José parish for weapons possession, spent four days in the jail at the police station, and was then released to his owner. Three of the others were released after eleven, two, and two days respectively in the police station jail. The fifth, after ten days in jail, was sent on to the House of Correction for further punishment. That was a fairly typical day's traffic through the station for 1850. There were 1,676 arrests recorded for the year, an average of 4.7 per day. The last day in August is unusual in that over the entire year just under one-third of all detainees were slaves.

The blotter of the central police station is not a complete listing of all people arrested in Rio during 1850. Some, like West and Woollcombe, might have spent time in custody and their passing might not have been recorded in that document. The Aljube jail where the English officers spent the night continued to serve as a temporary or short-term detention center as well as a long-term prison for some people serving sentence. In September 1851, for example, in response to an inquiry as to why so many people were held in the Aljube, the chief of police said that some were brought in as suspects in general sweeps after a crime was committed and later freed; others were arrested at periodic public civil and religious celebrations, "where there are always disorders of greater or lesser scale, which oblige the police authorities and patrols to bring a few people into jail."[37]

Immediate lodging in the Aljube or the House of Correction upon arrest, without their passing through the central police station, was sometimes the fate of those apprehended for more serious crimes, particularly offenses defined in the 1832 code of criminal procedure and the 1841 reform as out of the judicial purview of the chief of police or his delegates. For example, no arrests for murder were recorded in the police station ledger, yet there were three people tried by jury in Rio for murders committed in 1850. There were 45 people tried for the crime of inflicting physical injury on another person, yet only 36 of the ledger entries could be interpreted as falling under that offense.[38] Slaves captured after escape, as well as those arrested for a variety of offenses bringing immediate punishment, were often taken directly to the Calabouço slave prison. There were many cases similar to that of Januário, slave of the Viscountess of Merandela, whom pedestre Joaquim Lourenço arrested at 11:30 one night in May 1845. Besides the curfew violation Januário was carrying a straight razor. On standing orders from the chief of police, he was arrested for what police defined as capoeira, taken to the Calabouço, and immediately given 50 strokes of the lash, with another 50 due to complete the sentence, and was registered for a 30-day term in the slave jail besides. The police chief was routinely informed after the fact of such actions taken on his judicial authority.[39] Keeping in mind the limitations posed by arrests not recorded in it, one can regard the ledger as still a rich source for understanding how Rio de Janeiro was policed in the middle of the nineteenth century, who was affected by the system and in what way, and what sorts of behavior police were seeking to control. (To provide context for the following discussion, summary data from the police station log for 1850 are in Appendix 4.)[40]

In some ways, the information not recorded in the 1850 ledger is as revealing as the data that are available, frustrating though missing data may be for quantitative analysis. The most pervasive example is that for more than half the people brought in (911 out of 1,676, or 54 percent) the reason for detention was not recorded. From the time spent in jail and other known information, there is little to distinguish clearly those for whom a reason for arrest was provided from those for whom it was not. We can assume that most of the people for whom no cause of arrest was recorded were, in fact, brought into the station for some offense (although a small proportion were probably in detention for "neutral" reasons, discussed below). The missing information must be attributed to a lack of concern on the part of the police clerks and the chief of police to whom the ledger entries were formally addressed regarding the cause of arrest. The nature of the specific offense did not seem to matter very much to people who were not accountable to any higher or outside authority for the arrests they made for minor offenses and disciplinary purposes.

Other bits of information that appear much more frequently than the alleged offense of the detainee measure what police clerks considered important. Such data help elucidate which parts of the system were engaging in what types of repressive activity, who was on the front lines of the social war, and which parts of the system were in backup and support roles. The person who made the arrest, for example, was recorded for 1,421 cases, 85 percent of the total of 1,676. (Appendix 4.3 lists data on the individual carrying out the arrest for all known cases.) Keeping in mind that some detainees were not brought to the central station, it is clear that pedestres—the relatively small force of foot patrolmen in the downtown area—were the most important single category of police personnel bringing people in, accounting for 642 arrests in 1850, or 38 percent. Although military police detained a significant number (225 or 13 percent), the other parts of the civilian police structure—subdelegados, duty officers, bailiffs, and ward inspectors—together accounted for 377 arrests, or 22.5 percent, nearly twice as many as did police soldiers. The national guard was marginally represented in these data (41 arrests), in about the same numbers as guards employed by the city government (47 arrests) and regular army personnel (35 arrests). Of 19 arrests made by "owners," 16 were of slaves and 3 were "free" Africans. Of 21 arrests made by civilian private individuals, in contrast, 13 were of free people, followed by 5 slaves, 2 freedmen, and 1 "free" African. Two arrests were made by slaves to capture other slaves, one for escape and the other with no offense listed. Both those detainees were sent on to the Calabouço.

In exploring the operation of the police system, intriguing hints emerge from data on patterns of arrests by month and by day. Figure 4 illustrates the monthly distribution of arrests in the course

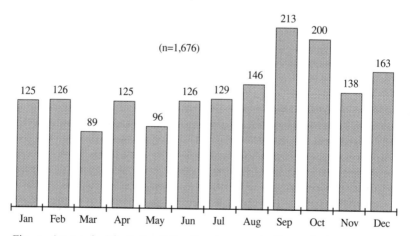

Fig. 4. Arrests in Rio Police Jail, 1850, by month. N = 1,676. From Arquivo Nacional do Rio de Janeiro, Códice 398, Prisões no Rio, 1849–50.

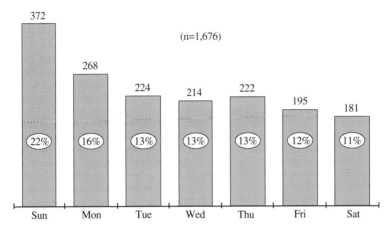

Fig. 5. Arrests in Rio Police Jail, 1850, by day of the week. N = 1,676. Same source as Figure 4.

of 1850. The months of markedly more arrests than the average, September and October, are not clearly associated with holidays when police routinely called for supplementary reinforcements and reported more problems, such as the pre-Lenten Carnival, or the period from Christmas to Epiphany. A closer look at September and October reveals that of 66 cases in all of 1850 in which men were arrested in order to forcibly conscript them into military service, 59 took place in September and October. During the four days from Monday, 16 September to Thursday, 19 September there were 40 recorded arrests. One was for beating and 25 were forced conscription, interspersed with 14 entries for which no reason for arrest appears. Two of those arrested without reason were women not subject to military draft, but it is possible that some of the others of the 14 were also being forcibly conscripted in what amounted to a four-day sweep of the city. Thus much of the apparent anomaly of an increase in arrests in September and October is explained by changes in the intensity and focus of the police system in operation, not necessarily by real levels of criminality.

The distribution of arrests by days of the week in Figure 5 is easier to explain. More people were arrested on Sunday because it was the only day of relief from work for most of the population. Leisure involved gathering in public squares and taverns for socializing and drinking, which was accompanied eventually by rowdiness, gambling, fighting, and other acts that violated the authori-

TABLE 2

Arrests in Rio Police Jail, 1850: Selected Categories of Detainee, as Percentage of a Total 1,676 Arrests

Detainee	No.	%
All Free	1,057	63.1
Free Brazilian	638	38.1
All foreign (except African)	360	21.5
Portuguese	288	17.2
Spanish	23	1.4
North American	14	0.8
All unfree	617	36.8
Slaves	530	31.6
Former slaves[a]	56	3.3
"Free" African	31	1.8
Brazilian-born	280	16.7
African-born	305	18.2
Mina	53	3.2
Angola	47	2.8
Cabinda	43	2.6
Moçambique	34	2.0
All women	122	7.3
Free women	32	0.7
Slave women	66	3.9
Former slave women[a]	17	1.0
"Free" African women	7	0.4
With age recorded	664	39.6
Free-age recorded	638	38.1
Slave-age recorded	26	1.6

SOURCE: Arquivo Nacional do Rio de Janeiro, Códice 398, Prisões no Rio, 1849–50.

[a] Although former slaves (*forros*) were legally free, they were listed separately, and they are included here because they were classified by the same categories of ethnic origin as were slaves.

ties' sense of permissible behavior. Much of what people did for recreation brought them into confrontation with the police, who in turn redoubled efforts to ensure public order.

From how the police system operated, we now focus on what sorts of people were arrested in 1850. As context for the eventual discussion of the types of offenses reported, Table 2 shows the total number of arrests for selected categories of persons and the percentage of each category in the total. (Appendix 4.1 provides fuller information on national origin of free and African regional origin of slave arrestees.)

In order to explore who was arrested for what type of offense, it is necessary to discuss how the 765 offenses mentioned in the ledger have been grouped for purposes of this analysis. The five

categories to be considered are those offenses applicable only to
slaves, victimless "public order" offenses, physical injury to another
person, crimes against property, usually through theft or damage,
and "neutral" arrests in which the reason specified could not fit in
any other category.

The total of 54 arrests for slave offenses (7 percent of those for
known causes) includes eighteen for escape and fifteen for suspicion of escape as well as twelve arrests of newly arrived Africans
illegally imported after the 1831 prohibition on transatlantic slave
traffic—after legal processing such people would be declared free
and wards of the state. Also, five slaves were arrested for disobedience, classified here as a slave offense even though the criminal
code does not restrict its application to slaves. Finally, four people
were brought into the police station for "irritating" their owner (*por
descompor seu senhor*). One free man and one former slave (*forro*)
were arrested for escape, and two other free men were brought in
for suspicion of escape, probably from jail rather than from
enslavement.

By far the most important type of activity for which people suffered arrest was the diverse range of public order offenses—
behavior which in itself did not directly jeopardize property or
other people, but which was either illegal or merely unacceptable.
Of 499 arrests for public order offenses (65 percent of all arrests
for which the offense was recorded), Table 3 presents data on the
ten specific offenses accounting for the most arrests. (The 402 arrests in these top ten categories account for 81 percent of all public
order arrests. A full listing of the 33 specific categories of public
order arrests is in Appendix 4.2.)

All the groups shown were arrested for disorderly conduct—the
most common single category of arrest in these data—in proportions roughly similar to their presence in global arrest data (shown
in Table 2), but there are significant deviations from that proportion in the case of some other offenses. Arrests for drunkenness,
insults, vagrancy, and absenteeism (*faltar ao serviço*) were proportionally more often the fate of free Brazilians than of the other
groups shown. The men arrested for capoeira were nearly all slaves
and overwhelmingly African-born. They also had a much higher
rate of arrest than the norm for weapons possession—an offense
that frequently accompanied capoeira. Recent arrivals from Africa
were more dangerous, or at least the police considered them so.

*Arrests in Rio Police Jail, 1850: Selected Public Order Offenses
by Selected Categories of Arrestees*

Offense	Total	Free Brazilian		Portuguese		Slave Brazilian-born		Slave African-born	
		No.	%	No.	%	No.	%	No.	%
Disorder	86	33	38.4	16	18.6	12	14.0	13	15.1
Drunkenness	73	33	45.2	11	15.1	7	9.6	9	12.3
Capoeira	69	3	4.3	0	0.0	19	27.5	40	58.0
Insults	55	19	34.5	9	16.4	3	5.5	9	16.4
Curfew violation	26	6	23.1	0	0.0	10	38.5	9	34.6
Weapons possession	22	4	18.2	2	9.1	3	13.6	10	45.5
Vagrancy	20	13	65.0	6	30.0	0	0.0	0	0.0
Gambling	20	3	15.0	1	5.0	9	45.0	3	15.0
Quarreling	18	7	38.9	4	22.2	3	16.7	2	11.1
Absent from work	13	12	92.3	0	0.0	0	0.0	0	0.0
Other	97	53	54.6	24	24.7	5	5.2	6	6.2
Total	499	186	37.3	73	14.6	71	14.2	101	20.2

SOURCE: Same as Table 2.

Curfew enforcement affected a higher proportion of slaves than free people, and no Portuguese were detained for violating curfew. Curfew restrictions were routinely applied primarily to black or brown people; many free Brazilians would thus be subject, but no European immigrants. Here as elsewhere, however, the record is tantalizingly silent regarding the racial status of free people. Distinct from curfew violations were six arrests for sleeping in the street, which was the fate of four free people and two former slaves.

The preponderance of creole slaves in arrests for gambling was the result of a single raid. On 22 October a ward inspector in São José parish brought in eleven slaves for that offense, thus accounting for more than half the recorded gambling arrests for the entire year. Eight were Brazilian-born, and three were African—a Mina, a Congo, and a Quiçiman—the only African-born slaves brought into the central police station for gambling during 1850. One of the Brazilians was a ten-year-old boy, the only one in that group whose age was listed. He was one of three slave boys about ten years old arrested in 1850, the youngest age among the 664 arrestees whose age was listed.

One group of 26 public order arrests had to do with violations of traffic rules or rules to which coaches for hire were subject, based on the first detailed regulations for cabs and omnibuses issued in November 1848. Besides refraining from "obscene words and indecorous acts," drivers were not to exceed a slow trot and were required to have a lantern on each side of their coach "except on moonlit nights." Arrests in 1850 for violating traffic rules included eleven for leaving a carriage unattended, nine for stopping at a point other than Constitution Square (now Tiradentes) and Direita Street (now Primeiro de Março), the two points designated for passenger pickup, three for excessive speed, two for refusing to accept passengers, and one arrest of a slave for attempting to hire out a coach without a license.[41] A related violation recalled earlier forms of transportation still in widespread use in 1850 and the sumptuary regulations governing their use: an Inhambane slave named Caetano was arrested on 27 April for carrying a newly arrived African man in a sedan chair.

Another grouping of 82 public order arrests is more directly related to the response of the people of Rio to the police in their midst, or perhaps to the combative nature of a segment of the population. To the 55 arrests for insults shown in Table 3, we might add eight for disobeying police orders, eight for indecent words, five for disrespect, five free people for disobedience, and one for resistance. Of the 82 people arrested for this grouping of acts of defiance that stopped short of physical aggression, 54 were free people, and 28 were slaves.

Physical aggression is the determining characteristic for a third general type of offense: crimes against a person. There were 40 such cases identified in the arrest ledger for 1850 (5.2 percent of the 765 arrests with reason for arrest recorded). Thirteen of the 40 were moving traffic violations, including twelve cases of running over a person with a vehicle, and one in which a running horse inflicted the injury. Assuming that those cases were accidental or the result of negligence, 27 cases of arrest for this type of offense were probably for deliberate acts. They include twelve for beating another person, six for the crime of personal injury, which was defined in the criminal code as physical offense that caused pain, wounds, or cuts to any part of the human body; three cases of whipping a free person; two for serious personal injury, defined as causing permanent mutilation of the victim; two for attempted serious injury; and one each for attempted murder and attempted

TABLE 4

Arrests in Rio Police Jail, 1850:
Offenses Against Property

Offense	No.
Theft (*furto*)	11
Trespassing (*entrar em casa alheia*)	10
Robbery (*roubo*)	8
Suspicion of theft	7
Breaking and entering (*arrombamento*)	2
Property damage (*estragos*)	1
Accusation of theft	1
Counterfeiting	1
Not paying taxes	1
Arson	1
Bribery	1
Total known cases	44

SOURCE: Same as Table 2.

suicide—a creole slave was found with a knife with which he had opened two deep cuts in his own throat. Subtracting the attempted offenses, there remain just 23 known cases of arrest for deliberate physical injury to another person, or 3 percent of the 765 arrests with a reason recorded. One of those arrested was Policarpo Bernardo da Rocha, a police pedestre, for "beating a black in the police station after arresting him" on 27 October. Rocha also failed to show proper respect to the duty clerk working at the time, and he spent three days in jail. In a similar incident on 10 November, Pedestre João de Arruda was arrested for "unjustly arresting and beating" several people.

Another general type of crime involves an offense against property. Like physical assault, theft loomed large among the concerns of those with property to protect. But also like crimes against a person, relatively few arrests were recorded in the central police station ledger for theft or property damage. The 44 arrests that can be classified as this type (5.8 percent of the 765 arrests for known offenses) are listed in Table 4. The technical definition of theft was to take property without the knowledge of its rightful owner; robbery, in contrast, involved confronting or assaulting the owner of the property as well. Those two offenses together totalled nineteen arrests, or 2.5 percent. Keeping in mind the problems of missing information, the conclusion is still inescapable: despite the alarms of the propertied and powerful, very few people were arrested for criminal offense to person or property. Victimless public order offenses absorbed most of the energies and attention of Rio's police. Police activity was primarily devoted to disciplinary, preventive repression of behavior that authorities considered threatening, unacceptable, or which they concluded might lead to a more serious offense.

There remains one more type of entry into custody for which some information is available, but not enough of it to determine if an offense was committed. Such "neutral" arrests included 66 men brought in for forced conscription into military service. Most of this activity, as we have seen, took place in September and October. Thirty-one of those were released, probably after it was determined that they were ineligible or unfit for service, or perhaps after the intervention of influential patrons.[42] Twenty-six were sent to the army, five to the navy, and three were turned over for service in the military police. Another neutral category comprised the 39 cases of entry into custody for unspecified "investigation" (*averiguações*). Sometimes this referred to verifying the story of people who were not arrested but who walked into the station to lodge a complaint and were held until the matter was resolved. Such was the case of Bernardino and Bartolomeu, slaves of Francisco de Paula Correia Saião, who escaped from their owner on 2 December 1850 and made it into the police station to report that Saião had threatened to hang them in an isolated beach area. Bartolomeu was wearing handcuffs when he entered the station. Both slaves were released the next day, but the blotter notes say no more about the case. Other neutral cases involved ten arrests for unspecified "suspicion," five for insanity, four for unspecified violation of municipal ordinances, three on unspecified "complaint," and one on unspecified "request."

With this grouping of arrests into slave, public order, person, property, and neutral, we may examine the profile of recorded offenses by specific type of detainee. Table 5 shows these data broken down by the legal status of the people arrested. Except for the relatively small number of free Africans in this sample, one remarkable aspect of these data is the consistency of the proportion of public order offenses across the four categories. This consistency is continued when the analysis is extended to the categories shown in

TABLE 5

Arrests in Rio Police Jail, 1850: Type of Offense by Legal Status of Detainee

Offense	Free		Slave		Freedman		"Free" African		Total	
	No.	%	No.	%	No.	%	No.	%	No.	%
Public order	291	68	183	63	19	66	6	43	499	65
Slave	3	1	43	15	1	3	7	50	54	7
Against property	18	4	24	8	2	7	0	0	44	6
Against person	27	6	11	4	2	7	0	0	40	5
Neutral	93	22	29	10	5	17	1	7	128	17
Total	432	100	290	100	29	100	14	100	765	100

SOURCE: Same as Table 2.

TABLE 6

Arrests in Rio Police Jail, 1850: Type of Offense by Selected Groups of Detainees

Offense	Free Brazilian		Free foreign		Slave Brazilian-born		Slave African-born		All women	
	No.	%	No.	%	No.	%	No.	%	No.	%
Public order	186	68	98	68	74	55	101	69	33	63
Slave	2	1	0	0	22	16	21	14	8	15
Against property	7	3	9	6	12	9	12	8	4	8
Against person	17	6	10	7	7	5	4	3	3	6
Neutral	61	22	27	19	20	15	8	6	4	8
Total	273	100	144	100	135	100	146	100	52	100

SOURCE: Same as Table 2.

Table 6, which divides free detainees into Brazilian and foreign, slaves into Creole and African-born, and presents data on the 52 women arrested for whom the nature of their offense is known. The exception in Table 6 is that Brazilian-born slaves were arrested for a significantly lower proportion of public order offenses than were other categories. This may have been because Creole slaves were somehow more docile or tractable, as many of the master class believed. It also may have been because native Brazilians knew better Portuguese and had a better command of the social landscape of the city and thus managed to stay out of the clutches of pedestres and police soldiers more successfully than recent arrivals from Africa. Another possibility is that because of their reputation for making trouble, African slaves were under more strict surveillance and suffered a higher proportion of arrests for minor public order offenses. Throughout this discussion it is well to keep in mind that these data measure police activity directly, but any extrapolation leading to a characterization of the general behavior of these social groups is quite tenuous and probably unwarranted.

In many ways the quantitative data from the 1850 police blotter confirm and specify what appears in police operating guidelines and the record of operations on the street. Most police activity was directed at controlling behavior that in itself was not injurious to other people nor damaging to property but which actually or potentially violated arbitrary rules or disturbed calm and order. Furthermore, with some clear exceptions there is little marked differentiation in the types and proportions of offenses that the various categories of people were arrested for. The street people of Rio were heterogeneous when measured by national origin, race, and legal status, but from the perspective of the police system and its operation they were remarkably similar. In the eyes of the police, disorderly conduct was disorderly conduct whether the perpetrator was free Brazilian, Portuguese immigrant, Creole or African slave, man or woman.

For 1,616 of the 1850 detainees (94 percent of the 1,676 total), it is possible to determine how long the individuals spent in the police jail and whether they were released or remanded to some other police or judicial authority. Of those, 1,024 (63 percent) were released after an average of 2.4 days in the police jail. One hundred twenty-four (8 percent) were sent on to the Aljube jail after an average of 2.8 days in the police lockup, and 117 (7 percent) were sent to the House of Correction prison after an average of 1.9 days in the police jail. Only ten slaves were whipped in the police jail and immediately released in 1850, but most such corporal punishment of slaves still took place in the Calabouço. (A full listing of destinations is in Appendix 4.4.) The police station lockup, then, was the point of entry into the system that included other prisons for long-term sentences. But for the majority of people arrested, most of whom were detained for victimless crimes against public order, the police jail was a place for temporary disciplinary confinement. Under procedures established by the 1841 judicial reform, traffic through the police station jail was wholly within the administrative and judicial authority of the police chief and his appointed delegates.

Other Prisons, Other Punishments

The Aljube jail also continued to be an important short-term detention center for those held for minor offenses. In 1853 when 1,740 people were processed through the central police station, 5,427 spent short terms in the Aljube. And through all of 1854, while 2,642 people passed through the holding cells at the central police station, 5,660 spent time in the dank cells of the Aljube. Most of them were sent by police officials, and victimless public order violations constituted the most important category of offense.[43] Despite some efforts to improve sanitary facilities in the old ecclesiastical jail, in early 1856 an inspection commission submitted the last of a long series of reports on the unhealthy conditions there along with a costly estimate for needed repairs. The police chief passed on this report with a ringing condemnation, making clear that the problem was not just the absolute level of squalor but the contrast with the political and cultural position of Rio de Janeiro in his eyes: "In the capital of the empire, the center of our civilization, [the Aljube] is in flagrant contradiction with the humanitarian sentiments that distinguish the Brazilian population." Calling the old ecclesiastical jail "a living protest against our moral progress," he recommended that it be closed down and its functions transferred elsewhere.[44] Accordingly, in mid-1856 the Aljube's functions were assumed by the newly established House of Detention, part of the prison complex where the House of Correction and the Calabouço were also located.

The House of Correction, which began construction in the mid-1830's, was formally opened in August 1850. It had been planned on the Auburn system of individual cellular confinement at night and group labor in workshops during the day for people sentenced to prison with labor, and it was originally built with a capacity for two hundred prisoners in single cells, along with carpentry, metalworking, and other workshops. In mid-1859 the last of the old military dungeons, part of Santa Cruz fort on the entrance to Guanabara Bay opposite the city of Rio, was closed. The 80 inmates, all sentenced to lengthy terms or life in prison for major crime, were transferred to a newly opened wing of the House of Correction. The Calabouço slave jail was moved to the site in 1837 for two nicely complementary reasons: it meant an improvement over the terrible conditions of the old dungeons on what was still called Calabouço point and it increased the availability of slave inmates' labor for the construction of the prison itself as well as for other public works. (Figure 6 suggests the methods a slave owner or member of the civilian police structure might use to conduct a black to the facility then being built.) Once the prison was completed, inmates of the slave jail were employed mostly in building roads and carrying crushed stone fill to the wetlands being reclaimed in what became known as the Cidade Nova district, which was drained by the Mangue channel, where they "changed swamps into elegant streets." By the 1850's some prisoners still labored on public works, but *libambos*, the gangs of chained water bearers and porters common on the streets of Rio earlier in the century, had been eliminated in the late 1830's in order "to remove the sight of chained men from the view of the public." Public whipping of slaves also ceased in the transition, and both punishment for crimes and disciplinary whipping took place within the new prison compound. By these measures Brazil participated in the general change from the degradation and physical torment of offenders in public to the private meting out of punishment in measured doses behind prison walls.[45]

The Calabouço at the House of Correction consisted of two large rooms which together could hold 300 men, plus a smaller room upstairs with space for 30 to 40 women. A record of all slaves who passed through the institution from June 1857 through May 1858 provides a portrait of how the Calabouço functioned during this period of enlightened administration. There were 329 people sent through the place in that year, but 41 of them were not there for punishment, but were held "on deposit," were being transferred from other parts of Brazil to Rio and temporarily held until their new owner could retrieve them—a service the state provided to buyers and sellers. Data on the offenses of the remaining 288 (an average of 24 entries per month) are shown in Table 7.

During 1826, when there were about 50,000 slaves in Rio de Janeiro, masters had sent 1,786 of them into the old Calabouço for correctional punishment, and only 58 of that total endured less than 100 lashes, 778 got 200 strokes, and 365 got 300 strokes.[46] Thirty-one years later the total slave population of the city was roughly the same, but just 69 of them were taken to the Calabouço for correctional punishment. Of that number, 4 received 25 lashes, 15 got 50 lashes, 5 got 100 lashes, and 2 got 150 lashes. Others received lesser punishments, including beatings with a strap or blows to the hand with the *palmatória*.

Fig. 6. "Going to the House of Correction" (Indo para a Correcção). Lithograph from a collection by the Ludwig and Briggs studio in Rio de Janeiro, 1846–49. From Briggs, *The Brasilian Souvenir*.

TABLE 7

Slaves in Rio Calabouço, 1857–58

Offense	Total	%	Origin		Sex	
			Brazil	Africa	Men	Women
Capoeira	81	31.0	27	54	81	0
To be punished	69	26.4	18	51	62	7
Escape	28	10.7	9	19	25	3
Curfew violation	25	9.6	7	18	24	1
Disorder	14	5.4	4	10	13	1
Theft	12	4.6	5	7	12	0
Weapons possession	7	2.7	1	6	7	0
Insults	7	2.7	4	3	5	2
Investigation	6	2.3	3	3	6	0
Drunkenness	4	1.5	2	2	3	1
Trespassing	3	1.1	1	2	3	0
Disobedience	2	0.8	1	1	2	0
Beating another person	1	0.4	0	1	1	0
Insubordination	1	0.4	0	1	1	0
Gambling	1	0.4	1	0	1	0
No information	27	10.3	10	17	25	2
Total	288	100.0	93	195	271	17

SOURCE: Arquivo Nacional do Rio de Janeiro IV7 2 (Calabouço-Matrícula de Presos, 1852–58).

Clearly a significant transition took place in both the rate and severity of state-sanctioned slave punishments during those three decades. Part of the change is related to the ethnic composition of the slave population. Those born in Africa were punished more frequently and more harshly than natives of Brazil, and the proportion of Africans in the slave population was lower in 1857 than in 1826. But the change also has to do with other data from the 1857–58 Calabouço records. Of the total of 288 slaves, punishments were ordered by owners in only 23 cases. The other 265 were sent to the slave jail and ordered punished by the chief of police or officials subordinate to him. In other words, punishment in the Calabouço was no longer primarily a service the state provided to serve the needs of private owners. It had become primarily a specialized institution through which the state itself exercised control over the slaves in the city. It had to be maintained in order to make good on the threat of brutal retribution for violating the bounds of acceptable behavior, but by the 1850's that threat was carried out in relatively few cases. If the system of repression was functioning smoothly, there was less need for arbitrarily excessive punishment that was likely to stoke the smoldering fires of resistance.

This is not to belittle the horrible suffering of those relatively few who still felt the lash, and the precipitous decline in judicially ordered or officially sponsored whipping of slaves during the second quarter of the nineteenth century cannot be attributed to generalized reluctance to impose such punishments. The aggregate scale of such whipping declined, but extreme cases belie the notion that the rules had changed. In August 1844 João, a Creole slave, was sent to the Calabouço to be punished with 700 strokes of the lash, a sentence imposed in a jury trial for inflicting serious physical injury on another person. After receiving a total of 500 strokes in the standard blocks of 50 at a time—a result of the "humane" reform of the early 1830's—interspersed by periods of recovery, João died on 3 April 1845 "of wounds and contusions in the gluteal region, complicated by dysentery." Claudina, also Creole, entered the Calabouço on 22 May 1855 sentenced by a jury to 300 lashes, which she received. On 1 July 1857 while still in the slave jail, she gave birth to a daughter, also named Claudina, with the Virgin Mary designated as godmother. The mother died eight days after giving birth, and the daughter died on 21 March 1858.[47]

The nature of the disruptive threat slaves still posed is revealed by separating the 69 cases of imprisonment during 1857–58 to be punished for unspecified disciplinary reasons and grouping the remaining 192 by type of offense, as shown in Table 8. It can be seen that very few slaves were in the Calabouço for escape, often considered the typical slave offense. Furthermore, this distribution looks remarkably like the breakdown of all arrests in the central police jail in 1850 shown in Table 5, except that victimless public order violations are even more predominant and offenses against person and property correspondingly less salient. This confirms a general pattern of the relationship between the institutions of repression

TABLE 8

Slaves in Rio Calabouço, 1857–58: Type of Offense

Offense	No.	%
Slave (escape)	28	14.6
Person (beating another person)	1	0.5
Property (theft, trespassing)	15	7.8
Public order (all others from Table 7 except "to be punished")	148	77.1
Total	192	100.0

SOURCE: Same as Table 7.

and the population of the city after midcentury. Except for the lingering distinction in the form of punishment, there were more similarities than differences among slaves, free Brazilians, and free foreigners when it came to their policing and punishment. Slaves, free black and brown people, and immigrants were arrested for similar offenses and suffered similar fates. Yet only foreigners were deported, only slaves were whipped, and most of those arrested for capoeira activity were slaves, although in subsequent decades increasing numbers of free people engaged in activity police classified as capoeira.

Expanding the System of Repression

By the 1860's Rio de Janeiro's repressive institutions had been modernized and standardized both on the streets and in the office, as clerks began to be more careful about logging information on arrests and compiling the statistical record that is a hallmark of the modern bureaucratic state. The chief of police proudly reported that following a reorganization in April 1856, record keeping was improved, and the number of documents produced by the police secretariat increased from 52,066 in 1857 to 98,527 in 1860 to 107,254 in 1862.[48] Administrative control over policing the city had moved far beyond the days when Major Vidigal had been given free rein to terrorize the vagabonds and troublemakers of the 1810's and beyond the fledgling institutions left largely to the discretion of strong commanders like Caxias and Queiroz in the 1830's. After a reorganization in 1853 the numbers of pedestres available to civilian police officials rose from about 30 to 100, and the military police were expanded and brought more firmly under civilian control by new regulations in 1858. The agents of repression could examine the results of these changes in the burgeoning statistical record of the system, and they and their supervisors in the political elite had reason to congratulate themselves.

The place to measure those successes was not in the few court cases involving major crime, nor in the relatively small populations of prisons where people serving long sentences accumulated. The success was on the streets in the surveillance and control of unacceptable behavior. That control was supported closely by increasing numbers of arrests primarily for the victimless violation of acceptable norms of public order or as a preemptive measure during disturbances and during dragnets. In 1862 there were 7,290 de-

TABLE 9

Arrests in Rio Police Jail, 1862 and 1865: Category of Detainee

Detainee	1862		1865	
	No.	%	No.	%
Free men	4,132	56.7	5,330	71.2
Free women	74	1.0	312	4.2
Slave men	2,875	39.4	1,509	20.1
Slave women	209	2.9	340	4.5
Total	7,290	100.0	7,491	100.0

SOURCE: Relatório do Chefe de Polícia do Rio de Janeiro, 1862 and 1865, annex to respective Relatórios of the minister of justice.

tainees brought into the central police jail, a more than fourfold increase over 1850. In 1865 the number was 7,491. Table 9 shows arrests for those two years according to sex and legal status.[49]

Table 10 shows the numbers of people Rio police arrested during those two years for public order offenses. Arrests in 1862 for the most common reasons—vagrancy and curfew violation—total almost as many as all arrests recorded in 1850. Comparisons of many of the specific reasons for arrest during these two years suggest that police activity focused on different behavior at different times or that arresting officers and duty clerks used changing criteria for classifying arrests that might have resulted from complex circumstances and variable definitions. It does not seem likely, for example, that only one-fourth as many people practiced capoeira in 1865, that patronage at brothels in the city dropped by as much, that in some strict sense the incidence of verbal insult doubled in 1865 over 1862, that half as many people were actually disobedient in the later year, that acts of insubordination in 1865 dropped to one-fifth their 1862 level, or that no illegal obscenities were uttered on the streets of Rio de Janeiro in 1862 but 32 were in 1865.

It also is quite unlikely that no beggars worked the streets of the city in 1862 and that police came across only fifteen during 1865. These and subsequent arrest statistics reflect a de facto decriminalization of begging as a punishable offense in this period, after many years of searching for a solution to what authorities concluded was an intractable problem. The problems with beggars were several, and they persisted despite a variety of efforts by police authorities over the years that were by turns paternalistic and repressive. Beggars were unsightly, unseemly, unsanitary, and made a bad impression on visitors to the city; life on the streets was detrimental to desirable moral qualities and work habits. Police still arrested a few people for begging, but as long as mendicants stayed out of more serious trouble, the police and judicial system took a permissive attitude toward them after midcentury.

The data in Table 10, however, suggest that the same was not true for what was defined as vagrancy, which the police used to move against just about anybody they wanted off the streets. In 1866 the chief of police criticized the practice of sending vagrants to the one month at labor prescribed in the criminal code, suggesting that it did more harm than good: "Serving his sentence, the vagrant or vagabond acquires neither skills nor habits of work, but it is enough time to extinguish the last flicker of self-respect." After a term in prison the vagrant "returns to his cohorts more daring, having lost the fear of punishment." The chief preferred to oblige vagrants to sign promises to seek honest employment, the violation of which led to a jail term of three months and sometimes longer. While just 15 people were arrested for begging during 1865, sub-

TABLE 10

Arrests in Rio Police Jail, 1862 and 1865: Public Order Offenses

Offense	1862		1865	
	No.	%	No.	%
Curfew violation	1,148	26.7	1,132	25.1
Vagrancy	493	11.5	1,081	23.9
Disorder	835	19.4	611	13.5
Drunkenness	555	12.9	727	16.1
Capoeira	404	9.4	93	2.1
Verbal insult	127	3.0	215	4.8
Disobedience	197	4.6	107	2.4
Illegal weapons	115	2.7	85	1.9
Desertion (military)	66	1.5	122	2.7
Gambling	87	2.0	77	1.7
Insubordination	111	2.6	18	0.4
Riot	30	0.7	48	1.1
Found in brothel	60	1.4	15	0.3
Resisting arrest	4	0.1	44	1.0
Offense to morals	22	0.5	20	0.4
Obscenities	0	0.0	32	0.7
Resistance	13	0.3	16	0.4
Harboring escaped slave	4	0.1	24	0.5
Threats	8	0.2	19	0.4
Illegal assembly	24	0.6	0	0.0
Begging	0	0.0	15	0.3
Disrespect	0	0.0	13	0.3
Total	4,303	100.0	4,514	100.0

SOURCE: Same as Table 9.

TABLE 11

Arrests in Rio Police Jail, 1862 and 1865:
Offenses Against Person, Property, and "Neutral"

Offense	No. in 1862	No. in 1865
Offenses against person		
Physical injury	497	252
Murder	5	10
Attempted murder	0	4
Kidnapping	2	9
Defloration	2	4
Bigamy	1	0
Subtotal	507	279
Offenses against property		
Theft	790	246
Trespassing	271	67
Robbery	45	0
Fraud	4	5
Property damage	13	23
Counterfeiting	8	8
Contraband	6	0
Subtotal	1,137	44
"Neutral" offenses		
Investigation	851	1,778
Ordinance violation	246	350
Request of consul	138	123
Mentally deranged	40	68
Request of owner (slave)	65	13
Other (unspecified)	3	17
Subtotal	1,343	2,349
Total of all offenses	7,290	7,491

SOURCE: Same as Table 9.

TABLE 12

Arrests in Rio Police Jail, 1862 and 1865: Types of Offense

Offense	1862		1865	
	No.	%	No.	%
Public order	5,538	76.0	6,765	90.3
Against person	507	7.0	279	3.7
Against property	1,137	15.6	349	4.7
Neutral	108	1.5	98	1.3
Total	7,290	100.0	7,491	100.0

SOURCE: Same as Table 9.

delegados had obtained such promises from 64 arrested for vagrancy, of whom 23 were Brazilian and 41 foreigners. Of the latter, 34 were Portuguese, 3 English, 2 Spanish, 1 Belgian, and 1 was from the United States.[50] During the same year more than a thousand people were arrested and hauled into the central police station jail for vagrancy.

Other types of offenses for which people were arrested in 1862 and 1865 are shown in Table 11. Wide discrepancies in the numbers of arrests for the more important specific offenses again suggest variations in police practice and record keeping (particularly the precipitous decline in offenses against property), but there is a consistent pattern for the larger categories. Theft, trespassing, and robbery were the principal crimes against property, and physical injury was by far the most important crime against a person. Arrests for investigation and unspecified ordinance violations have been included here as neutral. From descriptive material on police operations, however, it is clear that most of these cases qualify as public order arrests. For 1865 the clerks kept track of specific types of investigation included in the aggregate figure in Table 11. Of the 1,778 total, 142 were investigations of theft, 42 of robbery, 169 people were brought in to verify whether they were slave or free, and 6 on murder investigations, leaving 1,414 as unspecified police investigations (*averiguações policiais*). In other words, even when more specific records were kept there remained a large catchall category. Whatever the ordinance violations left unspecified in Table 11, they were not against person or property. Also, those arrested "at request of consul" were primarily foreign sailors for being drunk, disorderly, insulting authorities, or similar public order offenses. The arrest was attributed to the representative of the detainee's home government for reasons of protocol and to reduce the incidence of cases like that involving the officers of HMS *Southampton*. Table 12 groups the subtotals for the four types of offenses, including arrests for investigation, ordinance violation, and "request of consul" in the public order category.

Of the thousands arrested many were released after a short time in the police station jail (2,233 in 1862 and 2,379 in 1865), and many more were sent on to the House of Detention to serve the sentence determined in internal police judicial decisions (4,001 in 1862 and 3,130 in 1865, as shown in Appendix 5). Others were sent to military arsenals to be conscripted, to hospitals, and remanded to foreign consular authorities.

TABLE 13

Reported Crime in Rio, 1862 and 1865

Offense	1862		1865	
	No.	%	No.	%
Public order	0	0.0	19	4.3
Against person	325	48.1	225	50.7
Against property	346	51.2	188	42.3
Not specified	5	0.7	12	2.7
Total	676	100.0	444	100.0

SOURCE: Same as Table 9.

These arrest data stand in sharp contrast to the number of crimes reported to the police in these two years, shown in Table 13.[51] The chief of police, referring to the most numerous specific types of reported crimes, explained that the personal injuries (306 in 1862 and 199 in 1865) were "for the most part very insignificant, no more than simple scratches and light bruises." As for the cases of theft (285 in 1862 and 156 in 1865), "the great majority involved small objects of almost no value," and among the reported cases of property damage (26 in 1862 and 12 in 1865) there were "some caused by vehicles."[52]

While police authorities and the press talked about the few hundred reported thefts and assaults in the course of a year, the police chief did what he could to downplay the importance of the cases that reached his attention. In the meantime, civilian police authorities, pedestres, and military police soldiers were rounding up thousands of people every year, primarily for victimless public order violations or unspecified investigations. Traditional patterns of repression were made more effective and efficient by the midcentury reforms. New prisons and a dramatic decline in the officially sanctioned whipping of slaves meant that punishments had been modernized. Policing, however, despite the newly streamlined record-keeping system and larger force, had not fundamentally changed. Nor had the people of Rio's resistance, which was reflected in countless acts of quiet circumvention and defiant confrontation.

Physical Resistance

No one should imagine that the subjugated people of Rio de Janeiro resigned themselves to the physical restrictions and the burdens they suffered for disciplinary purposes or to punishments imposed by administrative fiat or through judicial proceedings. A sampling of reported cases illustrates a range of efforts to resist their condition or to escape their lot.

In January 1845 an incident in the Calabouço started with an apparently minor rule infraction and became a major confrontation. Joaquim Lucas Ribeiro, the overseer (*feitor*) in charge of the "free" Africans held there pending assignment to work in government departments or for private individuals, took an African named Jacinto to task for speaking to him without removing his hat. Jacinto then insulted Ribeiro, saying "he would not doff his hat to the emperor himself, much less to an overseer." The next day Ribeiro reported the incident to the director of the House of Correction of which the Calabouço was part, who in turn ordered the head guard to assemble all the "free" Africans in the place and in their presence to punish Jacinto with a few strokes of the *palmatória*. Ribeiro was also present. When Jacinto was brought forth he adamantly refused to submit to the prescribed punishment. Instead he pulled a knife and attacked Ribeiro with apparent intent to kill. Luckily for Ribeiro, he fell to one side as Jacinto lunged toward him, and the knife struck a wall. Three military police soldiers on guard duty came to the rescue and joined the head guard and another prisoner in subduing Jacinto "after a great struggle and strong resistance." Jacinto had retrieved his weapon, and so furious was the fight that the guards broke the knife in the effort to remove it from Jacinto's grip.

Alluding to the necessity of making an example of him for the other "free" Africans in the House of Correction "who must be kept under all discipline and respect," the director of the prison charged Jacinto with attempted murder. Like other prisoners awaiting trial he was sent to be held in the Aljube jail, where authorities expressed concern that he would be corrupted by contact with common criminals. In a cruel bit of bureaucratic irony, he was issued a letter of emancipation by the judge in charge of "free" Africans to clear the way for his trial and punishment as a free man rather than as a legal ward of the state.[53] His original offense—refusing to doff his hat—was a purely symbolic act of resistance to being imprisoned simply for having been caught in Africa, surviving the middle passage, and being brought into Brazil contrary to the country's own laws. Yet the government that kept him in that condition did not want to take responsibility for him in court.

Police records are replete with examples of acts of resistance and of the close collaboration between those who owned or controlled slaves and the repressive apparatus of the state. In February 1850, for example, Eugenio, a Congo slave of a Frenchman named Madei, a resident in Sacramento parish, was taken into custody for injuring his owner when the latter attempted to tie up Eugenio before sending him to the Calabouço. "In the struggle a corporal of the military police who came to assist in the arrest was also injured."[54] In October 1850 Pedro, a Mina slave owned by José Vicente Lisboa, a resident of the Prainha district, was arrested for injuring his owner's wife, Constança Maria de Sant'Anna. The woman had been stabbed several times and had wounds on her right chest and left side, but none were life-threatening. Upon interrogation, Pedro, who worked as a cook and house cleaner, said his owner's wife had entered the kitchen in a distraught condition and asked him if he knew that his master was maintaining an "illicit friendship" with two slave women in the house. When she came at Pedro saying she was going to kill him "because killing a black is no crime," Pedro grabbed a knife and struck back in self-defense. He further claimed that he had been tempted to do something like this before but held back and that he had asked his owner to sell him "before he threw himself out the window" so that he would be free of Constança's arbitrary harassment.[55] In her frustration over the liaison between her husband and his slave women, Constança had lashed out at Pedro, the cook, whose reaction brought his arrest on charges of physical injury to another person.

In the early morning hours of 13 April 1855, Agostinho, a pardo slave, was waiting in the Aljube jail to be hanged for the murder of his owner, José Muniz Feijó, a coffee merchant Agostinho had stabbed to death for mistreating him. The prisoner managed in a fit of fury to pry open and squeeze out of the stocks holding him and attacked anyone who came near. The jailer, with the help of five other blacks and three soldiers of the military police, was able to subdue the prisoner and put him in irons "at considerable trouble and risk." Agostinho had spent the night "shouting in great agitation," so doctors were called in to check him for possible madness. They concluded that he was not insane but that his actions were caused by "the despair of his morale." In the course of the examination the doctors noted that "the wrist irons are so tight that the prisoner's arms are swollen," and they were "convinced that his life is in danger." Because the medical report attributed Agostinho's "furious outbursts" to despair and not to an extenuating circumstance like mental illness, the police chief's proposed solution to the problem was to get the hanging over with as quickly as possible.[56] Agostinho was caught, convicted, and hanged for his ultimate act of resistance to enslavement. It took nine men to restrain him when he burst his bounds, but his rage persisted to the end.

Other slaves died unintentionally in their efforts to resist. Police routinely reported in January 1852 that black João, a slave belonging to the Santo Antonio monastery and subjected to disciplinary punishment inside that establishment looming above Carioca Square, "died as a result of injuries he suffered while trying to escape from stocks in which he was being kept prisoner." Others chose suicide as a way of escape from their legal condition or from attempts to bring them under tighter control. Drowning and hanging were common methods, but many others used the technique employed by Domingos, a pardo slave sent to the Calabouço by his master in 1844. Upon being taken into the Calabouço, he took a small knife from his pocket, cut himself deeply at the neck, and bled to death within a few minutes.[57]

In early July 1854 Caetano, a pardo slave of Fuão Leite and a carpenter by trade, was standing in the doorway of a general store on Imperatriz Street (now Camerino) in Santa Rita parish, chatting with two men and a woman, slaves of Mina ethnic stock. An unidentified white man in a frock coat appeared on the other side of the street. Unseen by Caetano the man beckoned to one of the Minas, and said that if he would help capture Caetano, who was wanted for escape, the white man would pay for the assistance. The Mina then called Caetano aside, but the latter suspected something was up and took off running. The two slaves he had been talking to ran after him shouting "Stop, thief!" and the inevitable crowd was drawn into pursuit. When Caetano reached the corner of Principe Street (now Senador Pompeu), onlookers saw him put his hand to his neck then fall to the ground. When his pursuers reached him, they saw that Caetano was dead from a great gash at his throat apparently made by the straight razor they found on the ground beside him. The subdelegado who reported this extraordinary chain of events had no further explanations to provide, but because Caetano's owner Leite was traveling in Portugal at the time, the stranger in the frock coat may well have been a professional slave thief who planned to sell Caetano in another province after his capture. Later that month Pacífica, slave of Dona Clementina de Paula Oliveira, fell from an upstairs window of her owner's residence on Alcântara Street, but it was not a suicide attempt. By her own statement she had fallen by accident in a frantic effort to escape a whipping from her owner. The investigating subdelegado confirmed that while there were "no serious injuries on the slave, she seems quite mistreated, with her face quite inflamed and barely able to walk."[58]

In periodic reports of "notable incidents" at the middle of the century, police routinely recorded slave suicides at a rate of two to four per month, often in addition to several cases of attempted suicide. From March through May 1850, for example, seven suicides were reported, of which six were slaves. In April 1851 police investigated the case of "a black slave who tried to kill himself by cutting his own throat with a knife. Also Joana, slave of Manoel Ferreira Rosa, tried to hang herself with a cord." In the next month a slave named Maria was sent to the charity hospital after trying to cut her own throat with a knife. In July 1851 a slave named Lino "tried to commit suicide by cutting himself several times on the neck." And in October of that year "an old black who was mentally deranged and lived by begging for alms threw himself into the sea on Glória beach, and drowned." It was not clear if this was suicide or an accident, but one might speculate on what would have led the old man to end his life. In April 1859 Felipe, 60 years old, slave of Manoel Alvares de Azevedo, resident of São Pedro Street, "attempted suicide, in a state of complete drunkenness, cutting himself on the left side of the throat, which does not appear to be serious."[59] It may have been that Felipe drank to fortify his courage, and became too incapacitated to finish the job. In his annual report for 1860 the chief of police listed 23 suicides, including 22 men and 1 woman, 9 free people and 14 slaves. In addition there were 17 attempted suicides, including 11 men and 6 women, 7 free and 10 slaves. In his assessment of these incidents, the chief provided a telling commentary on his own mind-set: "The origin of these suicides lies mainly in insanity and drunkenness, and perhaps one or another in poverty. The slaves, for their part, did not show signs of beatings or bad treatment that might have compelled them to end their existence."[60] For this representative of the system of control established by the slave-owning class, destitution might drive a free person to suicide, but enslavement itself seemed an inadequate motivation. Many blacks thought otherwise.

An incident similar to the 1833 revolt of the kettle makers took place in 1858, when Manoel Ferreira Guimarães, a merchant in Rio's port area, decided to close down his business as a coffee middleman and sell the seven slaves who worked in the place. Calixto and his colleagues in 1833 had begun by refusing to submit to routine but arbitrary punishment. For the slaves of Guimarães in 1858, sale on the open market probably meant they would end up as field hands on a plantation in the Paraíba valley, where coffee groves were advancing across the hills and slave labor was in short supply.[61] They barricaded themselves inside the shop in protest, armed with knives. When the first delegado of the police along with the commander of the military police and a detachment of army soldiers arrived on the scene, the rebels began to throw bottles, bricks, and stones down on the assembled authorities. As the chief of police later reported,

As the situation deteriorated an additional force of military police and [army] riflemen arrived, and still the insurgents persisted in their criminal purpose, becoming increasingly fierce and wounding some of the soldiers. It thus became necessary to break down the door and effect their arrest, which after considerable trouble was accomplished. One of the rebels was seriously wounded and was sent to the hospital of the Santa Casa de Misericórdia, the others being sent to the House of Detention.[62]

It was common for owners and overseers to oblige some slaves to control or punish others, but occasionally the practice backfired. In January 1845 a merchant sent his cashier and one of his slaves, Francisco, to retrieve another slave, José, of Cabinda stock, from the Calabouço. When the cashier ordered Francisco to put shackles on José, the latter pulled a knife and seriously wounded Francisco. José went back to jail, and Francisco went to the infirmary. In January 1859 Antonio Fernandes Jr., foreman of a tannery on Pescadores Street, ordered a Creole slave in the shop, also named Francisco, to punish one of his fellow captives. Francisco attacked the foreman instead, wounding him with a compass he had been using for marking cuts on hides. The subdelegado reporting the incident added that "this slave is poorly behaved, having once before attacked Fernandes with a razor, being restrained by other slaves. The foreman did not insist that Francisco be punished for that incident." This time, however, with Fernandes wounded, Francisco fled. He was captured six days later and held for attempted murder and escape.[63]

In April 1862 police and prison officials were faced with temporary overload of the state-supplied system of repression, when

Vicente Pereira da Silva Porto had a "disagreeable incident" with his slaves. Porto sent 259 of them to the Calabouço in one group and paid to have the lash applied to 47 of the "most arrogant," the leaders of what was characterized as mass insubordination. The matter was unusual enough for the chief of police to ask the minister of justice for guidelines on how to proceed, noting that although there was no law limiting the number of slaves a single owner could have in the city, "prudence and public utility" required some upper limit because so many slaves together could "complicate" order and public tranquility. The minister of justice agreed.[64]

Cultural Resistance

About 10 P.M. on the night of 12 June 1849, the subdelegado of suburban Engenho Velho parish, Roberto Jorge Haddock Lobo, found his repose disturbed by the loud and incessant throbbing of drums from a large gathering off in the direction of the Maracanã River on the outskirts of his jurisdiction. He sent three police pedestres accompanied by five of his own slaves, whom he supplied with weapons, to investigate. When they returned at 2 A.M. one of Lobo's slaves was wounded on the head, and they had a tale to tell. When the squad reached the source of the uproar, they saw that it was at the country place of Antonio Alves da Silva Pinto. The gates to the yard were closed, and in any case the pedestres and their slave assistants could tell from the noise of the crowd that they were vastly outnumbered. Reluctant to report back to Lobo empty handed, they decided to wait outside and arrest individuals as they entered or left the premises. They had captured four men by this ill-advised tactic when one got away and ran to inform the others the police were outside. In response about a hundred men armed with clubs, scythes, and other tools from the farm emerged from the enclosed yard, attacked the pedestres, and freed their captured comrades, wounding one of the slaves the subdelegado had sent along as he was defending himself. A passerby, Manoel Maria, joined in to assist the pedestres, but in the ensuing melee he was killed by a blow from a scythe. When the attackers saw Maria fall dead, they quickly dispersed, and the squad returned to report to the subdelegado. The next morning Lobo ordered the arrest of some slaves in the area who were implicated in the affair and conducted a formal medical inspection before burying the body of

Manoel Maria, which he could do because the subdelegado was also a medical doctor.

Upon receiving Lobo's report the chief of police brusquely demanded to know why the subdelegado had armed and sent his own slaves on such a mission, rather than requesting that the nearby Mataporcos military police cavalry barracks provide a force adequate to carry out the task at hand. Such a force, the chief suggested, assisted by the inspector of the ward where the gathering took place, might have managed to arrest the blacks involved and avoid the tragic death of Manoel Maria. Lobo's equally curt justification was that he had no advance notice of the gathering nor even its precise location. The information he did have came from the pounding of the drums, and "not supposing there was any man who would consent to a gathering of more than two hundred of his neighbors' slaves at his house," he had sent the small squad of pedestres and his own slaves to "prohibit the continuation of the batuque" not to attack the armed blacks who eventually got the best of the encounter.

As to the suggestion that he should have requested a detachment of military police cavalry, Lobo sounded the familiar refrain of lower civilian police authorities, saying that "whenever I make such a request, they only give me two men, according to their standing orders." Even after the tumult at the batuque, when on the following night Lobo made a special request for armed escort while patrolling the area as a precautionary measure, the military police provided only four men to assist him. "Without a force to make myself respected," he complained, "it is impossible to maintain public calm, as much effort and vigilance as I might apply."[65] He had apparently gained enough respect from the slaves who were his own property that he could trust them to back up the pedestres he sent to close down the batuque. Despite his status as slave owner, medical doctor, and police subdelegado, however, Lobo could demand the deference and submission of the inhabitants of his district only when his place in the hierarchy was confirmed by an armed force.[66]

Such nighttime batuques, with pounding drums, expressive dancing, and African songs unintelligible to the whites, were a means for slaves and free blacks to socialize in ways that they found culturally congenial but which were alien and therefore threatening to the slave-owning class. They often took place in suburban backyards and in isolated spots in the wooded hills among which the city spread. Police authorities seemed to tolerate a certain level of such activity until the gatherings became too large, too boisterous, or too close. Even when a batuque reached a decibel level that would carry several city blocks, as at the *chácara* in Engenho Velho on 12 June 1849, the original intent of the local police authority was, in effect, to require the landlord to quiet down a party that was disturbing the neighborhood. When the unsupervised squad of pedestres and loyal slaves decided that the better part of valor was to lurk outside and capture batuqueiros one by one, confrontation and tragedy followed.

Other forms of cultural expression among the dominated population were also tolerated within certain limits, as long as they were kept under surveillance and did not pose a direct and immediate challenge to the hierarchy of order and public tranquility. In late 1849 Minister of Justice Eusébio de Queiroz received one of the few reports of African or Afro-Brazilian religious practices that became a matter for police intervention. Beyond providing hints as to the nature of the practices themselves and who was involved, the report reflects a curiously permissive attitude on the part of the authorities.

For some time before by Police Chief Antonio Simões da Silva's account, his men had been aware that blacks of Mina ethnic stock met "in secret associations, where under impenetrable mystery they performed suspicious rituals." More threatening to public order than the ceremonies themselves, however, was the practice of "communicating among themselves with enciphered writings," especially because groups of the same Mina "nation" in Bahia, São Paulo, and Minas Gerais also used such written documents among themselves. As an investigative precaution, Silva ordered the second delegado and the subdelegado in São José parish to search the houses where these rituals were performed, arrest those involved, and confiscate any material that could provide more information.

A predawn raid on 29 November yielded "an infinity of papers written in different inks and in unknown characters, along with some books filled with handwritten text." The experts called in to decipher and translate the writings declared that they were "nothing but prayers, mostly taken from the Koran, written in spurious Arabic, with words of Malê, the Mina language, mixed in." Upon interrogating those arrested in the raid, Silva "discovered that, in fact, their rituals and meetings were concerned with religious things. I therefore returned the papers and books to them and ordered them set free, because as the authority concerned with crime I found no grounds for detention and prosecution." The constitution of the empire established Roman Catholicism as the official religion of the state, but Brazilian law also declared freedom of worship as long as non-Catholic ceremonies were held in private residences or in buildings that bore no outward sign or symbol of religion. Belying his apparent leniency and adherence to the relatively liberal norms of the constitution, Silva decided to keep the Minas under surveillance as "they are without a doubt suspect, because although the ostensive purpose of their practices, meetings, and rites might be the simple exercise of religion, which no law prohibits as long as it is done privately, it is still quite natural that the spirit of religious association might carry them further, and that the converts that they might make, fanaticized by their beliefs, might take advantage of that religion to confirm and promote ideas against slavery." Referring to a notorious example of a premeditated effort by slaves of the same Malê ethnic group to rebel fifteen years earlier, the chief pointed out that "everything found in these searches is just like the material found in Bahia, at the time of the slave insurrection of 1835." [67]

Organized Resistance—Capoeira

One form of cultural expression common among Rio's lower-class men was the practice of capoeira. Today capoeira is well known in Brazil as a stylized form of martial art of Afro-Brazilian origin, rhythmically performed to the music of percussion and the *berimbau*, a bow-shaped instrument using a gourd as a resonating chamber to amplify the low tones produced by tapping its single string with a stick. With graceful and powerful movements resembling gymnastic floor exercise, the *capoeirista* strikes intricate blows (or would-be blows) primarily with the feet and head, which the partner/opponent parries, evades, and returns. This activity developed from an earlier form of deadly foot fighting, which was often assisted by daggers, razors, stones, and clubs and practiced by groups organized into gangs known as *maltas* or *badernas*. [68]

Popular tradition records the names of some of the maltas, organized by the church parish that usually gave each district of Rio its common name: Cadeira da Senhora (the Lady's Chair) in Santa Ana, as Saint Anne (mother of the Virgin Mary) is usually depicted seated; Três Cachos (Three Bunches) and Flor da Uva (Flower of the Grape) in Santa Rita, referring to the grapes associated with that saint; Franciscanos in São Francisco de Paula; Flor da Gente (Flower of the People) in Glória; Espada (Sword) in Lapa; Lança (Lance) in São Jorge, referring to the weapon used to slay the dragon; Luzianos in Santa Lúzia; Ossos (Bones) in Bom Jesus do Calvário; and Santo Inácio in the Castelo, where the Jesuit church was located. Notorious individual adepts acquired such nicknames as Quebra-Côco (Skull Buster), Clave de Sol (Treble Clef), Chico Africano (Frankie the African), Zé Maluco (Crazy Joe), Desdentado (Toothless), Trinca-Espinha (Spine Splitter), Carrepeta (Ironwood), Boca-Negra (Black Mouth), Manduca (Chomper), and Corta-Orelha (Ear Cutter).[69]

Capoeira emerged in the late eighteenth century, and it was recognized in form and name by the early nineteenth century, when Vidigal's troops in the Guarda Real de Polícia directed concerted attacks against it. It became something of a generic epithet police authorities used to label street rowdies, especially when they operated in groups, whether or not they engaged in the particular gymnastic fighting techniques associated with the term today. Capoeira remained a police problem in Rio until the 1890's.[70] The primary concern for Rio police in the nineteenth century was not specifically the form of foot fighting, which was then as now a distinguishing characteristic. The problem was the physical assault, bloodshed, disturbance, and general mayhem the maltas engaged in. Capoeira was never mentioned in the 1830 criminal code nor in the 1838 compilation of Rio's municipal ordinances or later revisions. Nevertheless, police authorities often took measures aimed at ending or at least reducing the incidence of a phenomenon that they considered dangerous and a constant threat to "public tranquility."

From another point of view, the recurrent attempts to repress those engaged in capoeira indicate the continuity of the phenomenon and suggest its importance as a response, on the part of slaves and their allies in the lower strata of urban society, to the system of control the emerging state imposed on them. The gangs, led by those most skilled in capoeira fighting, operated in territories that they defended from both rival groups and police incursions. The activities of the gangs and their specific fighting technique make capoeira the most persistent and perhaps the most successful effort by urban Afro-Brazilians to establish a social "space," an area of activity that they controlled, used for their advantage largely on their own terms, and from which they could exclude outsiders. The world of the capoeira was ruled by violence that was often internecine, such as that reflected in a July 1852 report from São José parish that mentioned the black capoeira Firmino had been injured by other capoeira and the Cabinda slave João was murdered by capoeiras.[71] But the world of the police and of the slave system more generally was also violent. In a social hierarchy maintained fundamentally by the threat and reality of physical harm, engaging in capoeira gave those on the bottom the opportunity to meet force with force. It should not be surprising that the internal hierarchy of the gangs and the competition among them should have a similar basis.

In April 1845 a chief of police sent a circular memo to all the subdelegados urging harsher treatment of capoeiras, "who in recent days have become most daring," committing physical attacks on peaceful citizens and generally disturbing the peace. The new policy, which the minister of justice approved, looked much like the old one of the 1820's, before the promulgation of the criminal code. Immediately after arrest for capoeira, slaves were to be sent to the House of Correction and summarily given a hundred lashes, after which they were to serve one month at hard labor on public works "to see if with this measure we manage to bring them to order."[72] In August of the same year, however, following complaints from owners deprived of the services of their slaves, these orders were changed to increase the number of lashes to 150 and eliminate the additional sentence of a month at hard labor. The result of this ongoing tension between the state's demand for order and the slave owners' demand for labor was 50 more strokes of the lash for every slave brought in for capoeira. An inspector of the prison system noted in October 1852 that these orders continued in effect, and "presently when a slave is arrested for capoeira, with no further formality whatever he is sent to the House of Correction, where he immediately suffers the 150 lashes." The inspector, a criminal court judge, considered such punishment excessive.[73]

Those arrested for capoeira continued to receive severe punishment, despite the lack of any law prohibiting capoeira activity per se, and local police officials continued to struggle against a problem that at times required special measures. In April 1849 the subdelegado in the downtown Sacramento parish requested a special detachment of military police to pursue the several capoeira gangs operating in the area. They had "committed acts of great disrespect" and had seriously injured four persons. "This type of ruffian," the subdelegado noted, was "one of the scourges peculiar to our fair city," and he had seen the "rage of these wrongdoers increase" despite the efforts of the ward inspectors of his district, police duty officers, and the one pedestre assigned to him. Denying the request, the commander of the military police, observing the traditional autonomy of his institution, replied that staffing shortages made it impossible to supply a special detachment for anti-capoeira duty. He did, however, offer to increase the number of regular patrols in the district. The problems persisted until the subdelegado prevailed on the chief of police to use his authority to provide a military police detachment. Two months later there were further reports of capoeira activity in Sacramento parish, and Minister of Justice Eusébio de Queiroz demanded an explanation. The subdelegado reported that thanks to the recently redoubled efforts, aided by the increased force at his disposal, the capoeiras had been chased out of Capim Square, their favorite gathering point, and that "if any capoeiras now appear in this parish, they are just passing through to other points in the city, as my inspectors have observed."[74]

In 1849 police made one of their periodic efforts to rid the city of groups whose crimes against personal security were "becoming notable for their frequency if not for their seriousness." The police chief claimed that armed capoeira gangs committed beatings and personal injury "intentionally to provoke the authorities into using extreme measures, which in turn are always criticized and often rebuked." Given the difficulties of making criminal charges stick in such cases, the police resorted to alternative measures for getting such "vagrant and disorderly elements" off the street. In this campaign, 60 men were obliged to sign promises to behave well and seek honest employment. Unlike vague charges such as engaging in capoeira, breaking the conditions of such a probationary bond was a clear violation of the law and usually brought a swift jail sentence. In addition, 40 men were conscripted into military service in this sweep. These and related measures against such a large number of people, the chief claimed, "relieved the city of the shadow cast by the clouds of capoeiras and troublemakers that for some time had alarmed the population."[75] The arrest records for 1850, immediately following the anti-capoeira campaign of 1849, confirm that among slaves capoeira by far exceeded those reasons for arrest related more directly to slave status (as shown in Table 4).

Twelve years later more than four times as many people were brought into the jail of the central police station as in 1850, and there were 404 arrests for capoeira (as shown in Table 10).

Although police authorities often claimed to be mystified by what they saw as irrational outbursts of violence, they did little to penetrate the world of the capoeira gangs. In his annual report to the minister of justice for 1853, the chief of police provided an indication of how poorly the white elite understood the gang warfare and territorial defense and aggression that was behind much capoeira activity:

One of the most frequent crimes in this city is homicide and more or less serious injury. It is singular that neither revenge nor the desire to commit theft is the cause of these offenses. It is the pleasure of seeing blood flow or, in the terms used by this type of criminal, the "desire to try out the steel," that brings them to commit such serious attacks. The perpetrators are known by the common name of "capoeiras." In just one afternoon in the month of February these knaves committed seven murders in Santa Ana parish.[76]

As in other assessments over the years, the chief found it noteworthy that capoeira gangs seemed little interested in theft and that their aggressive behavior could not be explained by the usual assumptions regarding motives for interpersonal crimes, such as response to insult or desire for revenge. These observations do, however, reiterate the fear capoeiras instilled in their social opponents and the need both sides felt to meet violent force with a similar response.

Authorities were hard pressed to explain the rationale behind what appeared to be random attacks on innocent bystanders. When capoeiras did battle with police patrols, the basis for the conflict was clear enough. When gangs fought one another, it was often interpreted as evidence of a running feud, in which each new offense demanded retribution in a continuing cycle. Police recognized that such conflicts often involved territorial rivalries, as intrusion into one group's "turf" by another was in itself a major cause of periodic confrontations. Attacks on tavern or shop owners or their cashiers may well have been precipitated by the efforts of such merchants to prevent capoeiras from using their establishments as meeting points, which in turn might bring police surveillance. And it is possible that not only extortion but also racial antagonism and antiforeign sentiment were involved in attacks on businesses because many proprietors in petty commerce, and even more typically their trusted employees, were Portuguese immigrants. Less easily explained were cases of injury, usually vicious razor attacks that sometimes resulted in the death of the victim, which were suffered by people with no apparent connection to capoeira and no obvious reason to be targets. Given the deliberate secrecy and autonomy of the gangs, however, there is the possibility that such apparently random attacks were carefully planned and disguised to punish those who violated the internal discipline of the group, to avenge offenses defined as such by capoeira but unknown to police, or were commissioned for personal, economic, or political reasons by people outside the capoeira structure itself.

In the early decades of the nineteenth century, capoeira was closely identified with slaves along with some former slaves and a few free people of color, later including such semislaves as the "free" Africans. Although slaves continued to be involved, capoeira became an activity for increasing numbers of free persons as well after the middle of the nineteenth century, as slavery in the city went into relative and then absolute decline. Increasingly, membership in the maltas connected those on the bottom of society, slave and free, with resistance to the forces of order and state power. Despite institutional developments that reinforced the traditional control of the dominators over the dominated, the extent and persistence of capoeira suggest that there were aspects of life in Rio de Janeiro that those in charge could not control.

Not only were interpersonal relations beyond the normal purview of police, but public places and social networks involving both slave and free people, what we might call social space, were as well. Capoeira can be seen as a problem of order and public security or as successful resistance used to establish relative autonomy, depending on one's point of view. It stands out as common and recurrent among the various methods of resistance used by the slaves of Rio de Janeiro, which ranged from work slowdowns and sabotage, the most available and direct ways of resisting forced labor, to escape and the formation of runaway slave communities on the outskirts of the city, to outright armed rebellion, even if on a small scale and always quickly stamped out by security forces.[77] Especially as slavery declined after the middle of the nineteenth century, capoeira became increasingly an activity of the nonslave lower classes, the functional successors to slaves both by their techniques of resistance and as the targets of police repression.

SIX

Continuity, 1866-89

In the last two decades of the empire, the police of Rio de Janeiro continued to develop more specialized bureaucracies for patrolling the streets and for the judicial processing of those who broke the rules. In 1871 civilian police officials lost their authority to judge and sentence people for minor offenses in the first major change in the judicial system after 1841. Along with traditional forms of resistance through myriad individual challenges and the persistence of capoeira gangs another form of popular action returned—collective rioting by street mobs the likes of which Rio had not seen since the disturbances of the early 1830's gave rise to the police institutions themselves. The Paraguayan War, the decline and abolition of slavery, and the proclamation of the republic in November 1889 took place during continued urban expansion and the emergence of residential specialization on class lines, as the new middle sectors escaped to the suburbs. Intimidation and physical injury to suspects and short-term detention for minor offenses, however, persisted as informal police practice. Hostility, antagonism, and reciprocal violence between the police and the public continued to be the deeply ingrained and expected norm. Most police activity on patrol and the vast majority of arrests still aimed at preventing or punishing victimless violations of public order.

As slavery continued to fade economically, demographically, and socially, the phasing out of the Calabouço in the decade prior to its closing in 1874 reflected the general change toward modern institutions, even as traditional social relations were preserved under new guises. The slave jail continued to serve as a state-sponsored site of detention and discipline, but its reason for existence declined along with slavery itself in the third quarter of the century. Although some slaves continued to be sent by their owners for correctional punishments, court-ordered whipping declined dramatically. In 1869, for example, when a total of 632 slaves passed through the Calabouço, just three were sent there by judges to suffer corporal punishment. Through the next year 640 slaves entered the establishment, of whom seven were sent for judicially ordered whipping.[1]

In 1873 there was a spate of complaints from slave owners accusing the staff of the Calabouço of treating slaves lightly, not shaving their heads upon entry as had been the standard practice, and using their labor for private purposes while they were detained. The chief administrative officer of the ministry of justice, called in to review its operations, concluded the Calabouço was an anachronism, "one of the few institutions remaining from colonial times which has resisted the civilizing reforms of the present century." He recalled the former practice of "tieing slaves to posts in public squares, where their backsides were lashed in the presence of great numbers of spectators who stood by impassively watching the moans and contortions of the victims" but pointed out that "such spectacles ended some 40 years ago" (i.e., about 1833).[2] After that time whippings were administered only with the permission of police authorities, and they took place inside the jail grounds out of public view.

As of 1873 even their owners were not allowed to witness the punishment of slaves, giving rise to suspicions that the Calabouço staff was lax in its duty. Some slaves were not punished as severely as their owners had requested because the resident physician, who examined each slave before punishment, sometimes interceded to reduce or eliminate the whipping, leaving the slave simply to spend time in jail instead. In other cases the owners themselves ordered just enough punishment to break what they considered willfulness. Such was the fate of the mulatta slave Clara, whose owner asked the *feitor* who administered punishments "to avoid bruising her excessively and to stop as soon as she humbles herself." Clara's torture was reduced from 48 strokes with the palmatória to 36.[3]

During the last year of its operation, from June 1873 through May 1874, there were 554 slaves sent to the Calabouço, including 399 born in Brazil and 155 born in Africa, 395 men and 159 women. On the day it closed, 28 May 1874, 31 slaves were there at their owners' request, and 46 were held for simple detention on the orders of judicial authorities. Included in the inventory of its property were "16 whips, total value 14$850," and "200 neck irons, total value 500$000." Sixteen years before slavery's final demise, when there were still some 35,000 slaves in the city of Rio, civilization caught up with the Calabouço, and its residual functions were absorbed into the House of Detention.[4]

Clear distinctions need to be made between slavery and freedom, but as slavery faded the institutions that supported it blended into their counterparts that emerged in the course of the nineteenth century. In the economic, legal, and judicial realms there was no sharp break with the past. Early in the century the police functioned as a state-sponsored extension of the control of the owner class over people who were property. The police grew accustomed to treating slaves and the free lower classes in similar ways, and as the proportion of slaves in the population declined after midcentury, attitudes and practices of the system of repression were transferred smoothly to the nonslave lower classes and persisted.

The Urban Guard

In January 1866 a new police force called the urban guard (Guarda Urbana) was created for Rio de Janeiro, the first qualitative change in police structures since the marginalization of the justices of the peace in 1841. In July 1865 a group of 501 military police infantry soldiers had left Rio to join Brazilian forces in the conflict pitting Argentina, Uruguay, and Brazil against Paraguay. In the preceding year that conflict had gone from diplomatic challenge to armed confrontation, and the war of the Triple Alliance dominated national politics for the next five years. The ready response of Rio's military police to the call to arms reflected the close association of the police corps with the regular army, from which some officers in the police corps continued to be drawn. In Paraguay they were designated the 31st volunteer battalion and served as a front-line infantry unit until hostilities wound down in 1870.

As of early 1865, before the disruption of the war, the military police had reached its largest size to that time: a total force of 686, including 555 infantry soldiers. By late 1866, after the departure of the 31st volunteers and hurried recruiting to try to make up the shortfall, the total was down to 469, with 333 infantry. By 1870 the military police was at its lowest level since 1832: a total of 351 men. A year later with the return of the veterans of Paraguay, the total was back up to 493, reaching 502 as of 1878.[5]

To help make up the shortage of military police during the war, some units of the national guard were temporarily assigned to auxiliary police duty, but in 1873 the guard was relieved of police functions entirely.[6] Although not completely abolished until the third decade of the twentieth century, after 1873 the national guard was reduced to the status of an honorific institution. In a less definitive way, the civilian ward inspectors, who like the national guard were unpaid and part-time members of the police apparatus, also declined in relative importance after the 1860's. As the professional bureaucracies continued to grow, the ward inspectors—one of the last remnants of premodern citizen-police institutions—were increasingly relegated to an auxiliary or support role.[7]

More important in the long run than the last effort to make use of the "volunteer" national guard during the Paraguayan War was the creation of the urban guard, a force of paid policemen authorized at 560 men, the same level as the authorized strength of the military police. By October 1866 there were 389 urban guards in service, increasing to 432 by March 1875, and pushing the authorized limit at 558 in March 1879. By the mid-1870's, then, the national guard was out of the picture, and the combined strength of the military police and urban guard was over a thousand men.

Also marginalized in this institutional change was the old pedestre corps, which had been built up during the 1850's from 30 to 100 men. For some time before the creation of the urban guard, vacancies in the ranks of pedestres had been left unfilled, so that by early 1866 there were just 63 pedestres in service. The urban guard was to have replaced the pedestres entirely, but about 30 of them continued to serve through the rest of the empire, attached to outlying districts of the municipality of Rio like Santa Cruz, Inhaúma, and Governors' and Paquetá islands, assisting the local subdelegados and ward inspectors with the relatively minor problems of petty crime and public order that sporadically arose in those semirural parishes. Officials were reluctant to station military police soldiers at such isolated posts, far from the regimen of their barracks, because "small detachments of soldiers, off by themselves, lose the habits of military discipline."[8]

Ironically, criticism of military discipline was one of the main justifications for establishing the uniformed but nonmilitarized urban guard. The police soldiers, the minister of justice said, "subject to the heavy regimen of the barracks, constantly distracted by showy parade drills, disparage those functions to which they should pay direct attention."[9] Unlike the military corps that were under separate command, the urban guards were directly controlled by the civilian chief of police, as the pedestres had been. They were formed into detachments ranging from 30 to 55 men per unit in each of the downtown police districts. Thus each subdelegado in the central part of Rio would have a sizable force at his direct command. Guards were required to reside in the district to which they were assigned, and their patrols were restricted to the same territorial limits, based in newly established guard posts in each district. They were to be recruited from men aged 21 to 50 who were in good health and of "recognized morality," with a preference for veterans of military service or other government employment. Their pay was to be 40$000 per month, considerably higher than the 24$000 per month military police soldiers made at the time. But police soldiers continued to receive room and board as well as medical care, none of which was provided to the urban guards.

In justifying the urban guard proposal as early as 1861, the minister of justice made no mention of the failed 1836 initiative of the same name, despite some similarities in principle between them. The explicit inspiration this time was "nothing less than an imitation of the acclaimed police of the city of London, also adopted in Paris in September 1854." Invoking the English policeman as the model, he hoped for the same "good results that some of the most populous cities of Europe have obtained from morally correct agents, charged with continually patrolling a specific and limited territory." The military police, according to the original plan, would be held in readiness in case of public emergency or other extra duty or to be engaged in large-scale police operations that the urban guards would not be available for because they would stay with their assigned beat.[10]

According to its advocates, a uniformed but nonmilitarized force of patrolmen would "help prevent many crimes and prevent activities which, while not crimes as such, are nevertheless the preliminary steps toward criminal acts." Accordingly, operating instructions ordered urban guards to arrest people for behavior that was neither a crime nor infraction of ordinances, such as "individuals found carrying objects or packages which by reason of the quality or condition of such individuals makes them suspect." It was not a crime to carry a package in public, but if it appeared to a patrolling guard that a certain type of person should not be carrying a certain type of package, the "culprit" would be subject to arrest. Guards were further ordered to repress without making arrests if possible other unacceptable behavior, including shouting or excessive noise and "singing and musical performances [*cantatas e tocatas*] by slaves in taverns or *botequims*." Any person "standing near a door, wall, or fence in a suspicious way" was to be watched, interrogated, and arrested if suspicions were confirmed. Victimless threats against public order, whether real or potential, were to be the urban guards' main focus.

Included in the operating instructions of the new organization were several pointed admonitions. In dealing with the public, a guard was to "show himself to be polite and courteous to all, very carefully avoiding disputes or altercations with anyone, always conducting himself with the utmost prudence even with those who are rude or provocative." While making arrests it was "absolutely prohibited for guards to mistreat prisoners in any manner, either by word or gesture, much less physically. If, however, a suspect does not obey and attempts to escape, guards will use the degree of force necessary to carry out the arrest." Although urban guards were not subject to military discipline nor housed in barracks, the chief of police could punish those who violated regulations with reprimands, by docking their pay for up to fifteen days, with detention for up to five days, or dismissal. One infraction subject to such penalties was "the occurrence of a robbery or disorder which is not repressed by the urban guard on duty at the time." If such failure to exercise preemptive control could not be satisfactorily explained, the guard in question was to be punished and then "delivered to the competent authority for any formal charges the case may warrant."[11]

By 1869 the minister of justice was ready to give a pessimistic

assessment of the experiment with policemen. Reluctant to pro-
claim the urban guard a complete failure, he admitted that "there
is no way to hide what is demonstrated in practice every minute of
every day: since the creation of the guard some three years ago,
public surveillance has not improved." He attributed the problem
to a lack of discipline and regimentation, which would make the
guards "essentially obedient. Otherwise I cannot conceive of the
possibility of providing those in authority with the necessary instrument for the faithful execution of orders."[12] Without a rigid command structure and an unquestioning compliance with orders ingrained by military regimentation, control broke down. Urban
guards more often acted like armed renegades than the tropical
version of London bobbies the political authorities had hoped for.

In 1873 the pay of men in the guard was increased to 60$000
per month, but three years after that the minister of justice echoed
a refrain that police chiefs and his own predecessors had repeated
for years with regard to the urban guard since its founding, the
pedestres before them, and soldiers of the military police throughout their history. He claimed that the guard could be of considerable service, if it could attract the right kind of personnel. Unfortunately, "any artisan, even doing the most menial work, can earn
a wage higher than the 2$000 per day the state pays for service in
the urban guard." It was therefore not surprising that men "who
offer guarantees of intelligence and morality prefer other occupations, more remunerative and less burdensome." The result was
that the men in the urban guard were of a "moral and intellectual
quality" lower than might be desired. In 1882 the minister of justice lamented that the urban guard, "because it is so poorly paid, is
made up almost exclusively of individuals with no skills or apti-
tudes who are forced to subject themselves to such burdensome
employment because they cannot find other work that is less risky
and more advantageous." The implication of such circumspect language was that by not attracting the right kind of men the guard
attracted the wrong kind. The chief of police made that assessment
explicit in 1884 as he recommended the extinction of the urban
guard. Several years earlier he had been in favor of a nonmilitarized police force but admitted that the experiment had been a
failure. He became convinced that "without a barracks regimen,
without discipline, without military command, no public force is
possible."[13]

Compounding the lack of military regimentation was another fundamental distinction between the guards and the military police soldiers whose home was in the barracks and who were assigned wherever the needs of service demanded, given little chance to establish personal familiarity with the people they policed. For the soldier the relevant constellation of personal relationships was his unit, among his comrades in arms. He received support and favors in the reciprocally supportive hierarchy there as well as rewards and punishments. The barriers dividing the police soldiers from society were deliberately instilled and maintained.

The civilians who advocated the urban guards, in contrast, explicitly hoped that by living and patrolling within a circumscribed beat, the guards would get to know the residents and their habits, give help where needed, and inhibit criminal activity by their presence and their eventual familiarity with the normal routine of the area. Men were taken from among the underemployed lowest stratum of the free population, given a uniform and a sword, and placed back in a neighborhood where they soon developed relationships with the people they were assigned to watch and over whom they had considerable de facto authority. Rather than representing the institutional presence of the state, many of these neighborhood policemen operated on the basis of the personal linkages in the reciprocal hierarchy so basic to Brazilian social relations. For the urban guard the relevant constellation of personal relationships grew among his civilian neighbors in his permanent beat. By the logic of the social network, he expected to receive support and favors there by exercising the power his position gave him to reward and punish.[14] In practice this led to what the liberal reformers defined as abuse of authority and corruption, as some guards demanded or accepted payoffs in money or other favors from their friends and neighbors in return for leniency in applying the laws of an impersonal state they were supposed to represent. The minister of justice delicately assessed the problem in 1878, once again suggesting that better salaries would attract more recruits, which in turn would make it possible to be more selective in the hiring process. Screening out the lowest of the free lower class would, he hoped, "be a guarantee against the worries and weaknesses to which poverty makes them susceptible."[15] Those in charge saw corruption as bad in itself, but they were also concerned about the secondary consequence of such collusion between the police and the people. Laws and regulations would be violated with impunity, and once the cycle began it could lead to an unacceptable breakdown of the apparatus of control.

To say that the guards established relationships with the people they policed is not to suggest that the relationship was always amicable and positive. The military police had acquired a reputation as a strict and ruthless, often arbitrary and violent instrument of repression. But the urban guard soon exceeded the police soldiers in brutality, which was exacerbated by their lack of discipline. There were constant problems of staffing turnover and shortfalls, as guards were dismissed for failing to report for work, physical assault on the people they encountered in the line of duty, corruption, and confrontations with members of the other police organizations with which they were supposed to coordinate their activity. In the first half of July 1880, for example, the police chief expelled 26 urban guards for "drunkenness, neglect of duty, abuse of prisoners, and indecent conduct." During the five months from November 1883 through March 1884, when the total strength of the guard was still 560 men, there was a total turnover of 270, including 86 who quit voluntarily, 6 who died, and 178 who were expelled for being "of bad conduct and incapable of service."[16] In yet another contrast with the military police corps, the latter often had trouble keeping its ranks filled to authorized strength through voluntary enlistment, but it had a much lower rate of turnover among the rank-and-file troops than did the urban guard.

Excessive use of weapons was also a problem with the urban guard, as it had been with pedestres and continued to be with military police soldiers. In September 1869, for example, John Christ, an Englishman, was being brought in for public drunkenness when he tried to flee from the arresting guard, who then drew his sword and injured Christ. The minister of justice instructed the chief of police that "it is necessary to prevent the abuse, committed by members of the urban guard, of using their weapons to overcome any sort of minor resistance . . . punishing severely those who do so in clear violation of regulations." In October of that year military police soldiers routinely reported the arrest of an urban guard "for beating an individual on Invalidos Street." In 1872 the chief of police resorted to mild euphemism when he admitted that police members of the guard had "become accustomed to certain rough manners and habits absolutely incompatible with the character of the institution." Two years later the police chief stopped short of exonerating the guard, while laying the blame for police brutality on the resistance they faced in the line of duty: [17]

Urban guards have been severely punished when investigations have shown the complaints of harshness and bad treatment of prisoners to be valid. It is nevertheless necessary to point out that in many cases a mitigating circumstance is the violent provocation on the part of the prisoners themselves against the guards, who do not always have the courteous manners and the appropriate integrity to disregard such excesses.

Two examples from many such incidents illustrate the variable attitude of those in charge of the police, depending on where brutality was directed. At 1 A.M. on 27 November 1870, a squad of urban guards and military police together broke into the offices of the *Jornal do Comércio* newspaper in pursuit of a suspect. During the search they beat several employees as well as the man they were looking for, José Correia de Vasconcelos. When the publisher of the newspaper complained directly to the minister of justice, the latter ordered the chief of police to investigate the "criminal act" on the part of the soldiers and guards, "whose punishment must be all the more severe because the crime was committed by agents of the public force." In August of the following year a reporter for the newspaper *A Reforma* approached a squad of urban guards who were beating a prisoner in the downtown palace square in full public view at 3:30 in the afternoon. Rather than justify their actions, the guards insulted the journalist in obscene language by his account. When the complaint of this incident worked its way back through the system, the chief of police claimed that the reporter had merely been asked to leave the scene, as it was not his affair. As for the prisoner whose beating was the source of the problem, "he is a vagrant half-breed (*caboclo*) who with many others hangs out in the dock area, is in the habit of getting drunk," who had been arrested many times and often had to be subdued.[18] Policemen who beat newspaper employees who were under the protection of an influential publisher were to be brought up short, but a drunken half-breed was fair game.

Two minor incidents a decade later show that police practices were more concerned with repression and arbitrary use of authority than with regulating and protecting society. On 4 July 1880 three urban guards arrested a black man for disorderly conduct on

Riachuelo Street and "started for the station with him, beating him unmercifully all the way." When passersby remonstrated them for such behavior, the head of the police squad said he was only follow-ing orders. On the same day "three urban guards with drawn swords pursued a man into the interior of a house on Senhor dos Passos street, and when the proprietor protested they threatened him with their swords." As the newspaper report pointed out, "po-lice authorities forget that such an invasion is a gross violation of law."[19] A more notorious case was the death of João Alves de Castro Malta in November 1884 after his arrest by urban guards on Sete de Setembro Street in downtown Rio. Malta was held for three days in police custody before he was turned over to the House of Deten-tion in such bad shape that he could not give his name to the clerk. He expired moments later and was quickly buried after police doc-tors declared the cause of death was "hepatic congestion." Accord-ing to widespread word on the street and newspaper reports, the arresting urban guards had beaten Malta so severely at the time of his arrest that he died of his wounds, but after a forensic team appointed by the chief of police exhumed the body and confirmed the earlier official cause of death, the case was officially closed.[20]

As complaints and problems built up over the years, officials had more misgivings about the possibility of rehabilitating the urban guard, and it was finally abolished by new police regulations of 7 March 1885.[21] Reviewing its troubled history, the minister of jus-tice recalled that the neighborhood-based force had seemed like a good idea in 1866, "taking as a model similar institutions in more advanced nations." But achievements did not match expectations.

The advantages offered to the urban guard were not sufficient to attract men of a certain ability, who might replace with circumspection and a sense of duty, the absence of severe military discipline from their operat-ing procedures. . . . With the passage of time the urban guard lost pres-tige, and this fact, reflected in constant complaints about frequent aggres-sion by and resistance to the guards, led to the decision to abolish the institution.[22]

In September of the same year the military police was reorganized and expanded from an authorized strength of 560 to 1,008 to fill the space the urban guard had occupied for nineteen years. Like the justice of the peace and the national guard before it, the urban guard was directly inspired by European models. Also like those foreign imports, it was given a serious and extended trial and found lacking. The policing of Rio reverted to the military corps which, despite name changes and varying relations with other parts of the police structure, remained very similar to the unit Caxias had forged in the 1830's.

Secret Police

Though by its nature more difficult to document than the urban guard, the secret police persisted through the late empire despite recurrent efforts to rid the service of criminal elements and start with a fresh group of agents. From a few investigators and informers in the 1850's, the secret police existed at varying levels of activity in the next three decades. It was not a formal institution with publicly recognized staffing levels, operating guidelines, or regulations, but was made up of secret agents of two related types. A small cadre of undercover agents was on regular retainer, and the police chief and delegados called upon them in special circumstances to spy on suspected criminal activity, make the rounds of the gambling houses and brothels that proliferated as the city grew, or assist in mounting surprise attacks during police operations. Other men were hired on a temporary basis in numbers considered necessary to meet specific threats or assist in crowd control and paid a fee for services rendered.

Circulating in shady activities and among criminal elements, secret agents were not above using their position for their personal advantage. As with the community-based urban guards, one problem was tenuous regulation and control. For the secret agents the relevant social environment became the criminal and marginal underworld in which they operated, and the imperatives of that environment were not necessarily compatible with the goal of the civilian political elite in reducing activity the latter found threatening or objectionable. When in October 1880 the police chief ordered the discharge of all secret agents, one newspaper praised the order "in view of the abuses committed by the secret police and their improper use by unscrupulous officials."[23] Police chiefs and ministers of justice recognized that although these men were difficult to control, they were useful, and the secret force was soon built up again. In 1883 the chief of police said the secret agents "were not investigators of crime, but rather the protectors of criminals," and that those who were not themselves outlaws justified their jobs by provoking desperate people to commit crimes, then turning them in for the reward. Others used the cover of their connections to run prostitution rings or gambling houses. Despairing of remedial action, he dissolved the secret police.[24] That order also had only temporary effect, and when a new minister of justice took office in 1887 and took stock of police personnel, he expelled from service several "incorrigible" military police soldiers, and "many secret agents." Finally in 1890 the first minister of justice of the republic ordered that the police chief would no longer have at his disposal a discretionary secret fund. Instead, 35 secret agents were put on a regular salary considered adequate to facilitate selective hiring and reduce the temptations of payoffs and bribes.[25] This was another step toward standardizing and specifying staffing and procedures for the police bureaucracy, whether or not it reduced the abuses for which the secret police became notorious.

The Military Police to the End of the Empire

After the extinction of the urban guard, the soldiers of the military police were again the main front-line force, and they expanded their ruthless procedures into the public space the urban guard had failed to control to the satisfaction of the people in charge. Much of what the residents of Rio de Janeiro considered commonplace by this time was still shocking to foreigners, even those from countries with a tradition of militarized police themselves. An Italian visitor in 1885, for example, minced no words in his assessment: "The police of Rio de Janeiro is the most despotic, the most arbitrary and brutal police in the world, made up for the most part of the lowest social stratum of the city, lax and violent at the same time, and which acts in a manner completely the opposite of guarding and protecting the life and security of the citizens."[26] The police soldier on the street was caught between the elite's need for control and the difficulty of dealing with a recalcitrant and hostile population, people who never accepted the intrusion of the state into their lives as legitimate and who resisted that imposition in many small ways. When police soldiers decided to assert themselves to dominate a situation or when provoked by insult, they invoked the authority of their uniform or slashed out with their weapons, thus adding to the problem of public order rather than reducing it. What foreigners considered arbitrary brutality had become the expectable norm, even as commanding officers and civilian officials continued their sporadic efforts to keep police practice within what they considered acceptable bounds.

The disciplinary problems that plagued the military police in the last years of the empire illustrate the persistence of patterns developed decades before. Not long after the military police had expanded and taken over the duties of the extinct urban guard, the commander felt the need to issue a new general order, "in view of the cases of beatings of persons arrested for crimes or infractions, which increase each day on the part of police soldiers." He laid the blame on the squad commanders and corporals in charge of street patrols who failed to enforce repeated orders to prevent such abuses. Henceforth, those in command were to be held strictly accountable for the behavior of their subordinates, whose actions "affect the discipline and dignity of this corps."[27]

Controlling the behavior of soldiers through their superior officers is a clear example of military discipline and esprit de corps. The urban guard had not been organized along such rigid hierarchical lines and had no officer corps to take responsibility for the policeman's transgressions or to suffer dishonor by extension, then to take action to reduce the brutal and arbitrary police action on the streets. Each member of the urban guard had become a power unto himself, and from the perspective of those in charge, too many guards abused their de facto authority. Secret police agents were as arbitrary and uncontrolled. Compared to those institutional approaches, the advantages of the militarized police became clear. To defend their honor and the reputation of their corporate home, the officer corps could be called upon to impose internal discipline that worked as a check on the actions of the soldiers on patrol. The soldiers, for their part, shared in this corporate solidarity at least to a degree, and their compliance continued to be enforced through the positive incentive of esprit de corps and the negative sanctions of harsh punishment for transgressions.

The directives reminding officers they were responsible for the actions of their subordinates were soon put into effect. In October 1887, for example, military police Corporal Luiz José Pereira, on duty as an orderly at the police substation in Glória parish, arrested a Portuguese man without cause and in the process grabbed him by the throat, beat him, insulted, and threatened him. Pereira was demoted to simple soldier and jailed for fifteen days in Santa Cruz fort, where he suffered the further ignominy of being assigned to a cleaning detail. The officer of the day on whose shift this incident took place, and who initially tried to claim that the arrested Portuguese was drunk and that he suffered no beating, was issued a severe written reprimand that was entered into his file.[28]

In January 1887 two police soldiers arrested a drunk and put him in the holding cell at the police post where they were on duty. The man they had arrested persisted in shouting insults, so they entered the squad leader's office in his absence, took the key ring, went into the cell where the arrestee was being held, and beat him with a sabre and a broom handle. Two other soldiers came in response to the man's cries for help and saw that he was seriously injured on the head. The military police commander severely reprimanded the officer in charge of the detail for dereliction. A few days later another officer was called before a board of investigation when soldiers under his command, intervening in an altercation between a group of sailors and people in the street, beat those on both sides of the dispute with their swords. The officer was accused of urging his men to this excessive behavior. As the police commander stated the problem, such acts not only were detrimental to the dignity of the officer involved but also "to the discipline and morale of this corps."[29]

Commanders continued to enforce discipline and punish infractions of a range of rules, revealing patterns of behavior that had become chronic but also showing the importance of corporate identity in inhibiting such actions. In September 1881, for example, two police soldiers were accused of extortion from Laurentino Severino dos Santos, whom they had arrested and released when he paid them 22$000. The military police commander, reminding his men that such a "revolting" crime "brought shame on this entire corps," ordered the soldiers to repay the sum in question, serve fifteen days in the guardhouse, and then be "expelled from the corps because they do not deserve to belong in it." In March 1888 a police soldier was expelled for what the commander called the "repugnant crime" of taking a watch and gold chain from a drunk Frenchman he had arrested. In early 1888 a group of 25 police soldiers were expelled from the corps, sent to serve in the regular army in exchange for army troops chosen for their desirable qualities. Eleven were expelled for being chronically drunk and disorderly, nine for repeated failure to report for duty, two for insubordination, two for stealing, and one for dereliction.[30]

The record was not all one-sided, and commanders extended the positive incentive of commendation to show approval for a job well done. In November 1886 a merchant near the Passéio Público tried to pay a police soldier in order to avoid being turned in for an ordinance violation. The soldier was praised for refusing the bribe. In December 1887 the commander praised soldier José Gonsalves for his arrest of three thieves who tried to bribe Gonsalves with 50$000 from their hoard of loot. The soldier refused and brought the culprits to jail. But also in 1887 an order was issued "expressly forbidding officers and soldiers of the corps from receiving fines imposed for any reason." Such "instant" fines were simple payoffs, and the troops were reminded that only competent judicial authority could assess legal fines.[31]

In 1888 the colonel in command of the military police perceptively assessed the social context within which his unit operated in terms appropriate to the liberal principles of the modern state. The right of the citizen to protection, he noted, is one that all governments try to guarantee, "but it is a difficult problem, involving the morality, intelligence, and customs of the people, as well as the financial resources of the government." Referring to the relationship between the military police and society, he said: "It does not take much to perceive that elements taken out of a whole to constitute a separate body will bring to the latter the properties of the former. It is no surprise, therefore, that a nation's police will exhibit the characteristics of the morality, customs, and intelligence of its people." In again justifying the military regimentation of the corps, he nevertheless recognized a problem that made police work different from the role of the soldier in regular army operations. A soldier needed to follow orders without question, and any independent action was detrimental to the unified chain of command. The military police, in contrast, needed to institute an "intelligent discipline, so that each police soldier would exercise his own initiative, as appropriate for the special circumstances he might encounter."[32]

Achieving a workable balance between discipline and initiative was a recurring issue for Rio's police forces. The experience of the nonmilitarized police units, principally the pedestres and the urban guard, as well as the recurring problems within the military police itself led those in charge to favor discipline over independent action. The commander also recognized the difficulty of drawing a clear line between protection of arrestees from excessive physical coercion and the standing orders of the military police to bring violators into submission. As one delegado stated the quandary in 1888, "An arrested person has a right to be protected from the authority in whose custody he finds himself. But that does not mean that [the police] should not put into effect all due energy when respect for the law is not obtained by other means."[33] The precise definition of what would constitute all due energy in the heat of the moment, in action against a hostile adversary on the streets, remained elusive. The military police corps was never the finely tuned, smoothly operating, and neutral instrument of state power that some political leaders might have liked. But failed experiments over the years, along with lessons learned during periods when the military regimen itself became relatively slack, showed that the military police was as good as the civilian elite was going to get.

At the time of the military coup d'etat that ended the monarchy on November 15, 1889, there were 1,539 men in the military police, more than double the size of the force 25 years before. Their commander extended praise for maintaining calm in the city during "the most important of sociological phenomena . . . the explosion of democratic sentiments that resulted in the elimination of a form of government that could no longer continue in America." In recognition of the political change and to claim lineage with the French Revolution of a century earlier, military police officers began to use the title "citizen" between their rank and their name. In January 1890 a new set of regulations was issued renaming the military police the Police Brigade of the Federal Capital, authorized at a strength of 1,705 men. The corps that Caxias had shaped during the 1830's entered the era of the republic with more men and a new name and was strengthened for having weathered the shifting circumstances of the late empire. Some things, however, had not changed much from the days of Major Vidigal and the long years when inflicting physical punishment on the slaves at the point of arrest was part of a police soldier's expected duty. In one of the first general orders of the new era, the commander noted that "beatings carried out by members of this corps against arrested individuals have become more frequent lately." He ordered company commanders and station chiefs to instruct their troops in modern procedures, "making them understand that they must use the weapons they carry only for legitimate defense and not to beat helpless individuals, who are often inebriated, with whom they must use even greater moderation."[34]

The Judicial Reform of 1871

During the time the experiment with urban guards as neighborhood policemen was being tried and found wanting, changes in the legal framework and institutional structure altered the judicial system and the civilian police hierarchy, which continued to exercise operational control over military police soldiers and which administered the urban guards directly. As one of a package of reforms in the early 1870's, parliament approved a law again significantly altering the code of criminal procedure.

Since December 1841 the chiefs of police and their delegates had supervised the operation of the police system and investigated cases of criminality by gathering evidence. In addition they exercised the authority to put together a judicial case against the accused (*formação da culpa*, analogous to bringing indictment in the United States judicial system) as well as to pass judgment and sentence those found guilty of a wide range of lesser offenses against person, property, and public order. From the first few months after the 1841 reform, liberals had objected to its centralizing and authoritarian concentration of powers. Several bills were introduced to alter the system, starting in 1846 and 1848, then again in 1854, 1862, and 1866. These proposals usually focused on the need to separate police functions from judicial authority. José Thomaz Nabuco de Araújo, one of the major figures of the liberal faction in parliament, stated the case succinctly during debates on the 1854 bill: Brazil's judicial system was exceptional in its "confusion or overlap of the power to arrest with the power to judge. Certainly it is repugnant that in a well-organized country the police would be enmeshed with the courts. Elsewhere, where the action of the court begins, the action of the police ends, but here everyone can arrest and at the same time pass judgment."[35] Long a pet project of the liberal ideologues, the reform was put through by the conservative cabinet headed by the visconde do Rio Branco in September 1871.

Ending the anomalous confusion of police and judicial authority was the principal feature of the 1871 reform, along with expanding the judicial system to assume the duties previously handled by police chiefs, delegados, and subdelegados. Violations of the criminal code in Rio de Janeiro and the most important provincial capitals could henceforth only be tried by district judges (*juizes de direito*) or judges of the court of appeal (*relação*). Furthermore, the offices of police chief, delegado, and subdelegado were declared incompatible with the exercise of any judicial functions. If a district judge were appointed police chief, for example, he could no longer carry out his duties as judge while he held the police post.

To handle the anticipated increased caseload that this change entailed, the number of judgeships was expanded severalfold. There had been three district judges in Rio de Janeiro under the law of 3 December 1841, one of whom served as chief of police. (The two delegados and sixteen subdelegados, of course, also acted as judges in misdemeanor cases.) The regulations putting the reform of September 1871 into effect called for eleven district judges, plus nine substitutes "to help the district judges in the preparation of cases and fill in for them during absences." To handle appeals, there were 25 judges (*desembargadores*) of the Rio de Janeiro Relação. At the same time, the number of substitutes (*suplentes*) backing up each police delegado and subdelegado was reduced from six to three. By the new law police chiefs were still charged with the gathering of evidence that would form the legal case against the accused, but the results of this *inquérito* (inquest, investigation) were delivered to public prosecutors or judges for evaluation and final disposition. Thus neither the police chief nor his delegates could make the final decision on guilt or innocence, but he retained considerable de facto power in criminal cases through the diligence or delay with which he conducted an inquérito and the final recommendations such reports conveyed to judicial officials.[36]

The practical effects of the 1871 reform were several. By adding to the number of judicial positions, it increased the patronage available to the government which, like the judicial hierarchy, was run and staffed by an elite corps of law school graduates linked by class ties, regional origins, family connections, and patronage networks.[37] Some of these new judges had to be on duty or on call at all times to handle cases as they arose, but their position was now distinct from that of police authorities. This was a major step toward the professionalization of Brazil's police and judicial system, by which those who held distinct positions in the hierarchy exercised functions that were more discrete and specialized. Similarly, the qualifications necessary for holding the newly circumscribed positions were hierarchically ordered. District judges, who were to be law school graduates and have four years of professional experience to qualify for appointment, now presided over frequent court sessions and judged minor offenses but would not debase their status by risking direct confrontations with street rabble. Delegados and subdelegados, who had never been required to have formal legal training, were now dedicated exclusively to strictly police functions in addition to the supervision of personnel and office administration.

The prestige of the delegados and subdelegados and the social standing of people who filled such posts suffered a decline after the 1871 reform from which they never recovered. Formerly frontline or lower-level members of the structure of judicial authority, after 1871 they became agents serving that structure but not members of it. They continued to derive power from their position, but the formal authority to pass judgment on the acts of others devolved to members of the judicial elite, and administrative police activities were left in the hands of people who became lesser functionaries in the expanding bureaucracy of control.[38]

One previous condition of delegados and subdelegados remained, however, through the end of the empire: they were still not paid a regular salary. Emoluments and gratuities—some paid from the chief of police's discretionary, secret fund—provided sporadic relief from the financial burden of taking on the job, but only people who had some other source of income could afford to take such a position. At an intermediate stage in the historical transition of government bureaucracies from qualification by inherited status to qualification by education and specialized training, leaving an important position with no regular stipend or salary helped ensure that only the "right" sort of person occupied such posts. The operative principle—explicit in the rationale for the short-lived municipal guard of the 1830's and implicit in the formation of the national guard—was that those with an economic stake in the system could be expected to defend the hierarchy that gave them their status. But by the late empire the demands of a professional police structure overrode those traditional criteria. As the minister of justice explained in 1887, without salaried police officials it was impossible to maintain a staff of "proven aptitude, full dedication to the job, and efficient responsibility—three conditions essential to any regularized system." Finally, as one of a series of modernizing administrative changes in 1890 after the proclamation of the republic, all officials of the police system became salaried, full-time professionals.[39]

Patterns of Arrest

In the years following the 1871 judicial reform, police officials frequently criticized the newly tightened requirement that they obtain a written warrant from a judge for any arrest not in flagrante. Lacking the authority to order the preventive detention of suspects before obtaining a warrant, the chief of police or his delegates occasionally had to set people free who they were convinced should be held and charged.[40] But there was no grumbling that the loss of judicial authority per se lessened surveillance and punishment of the minor public order offenses that continued to make up the bulk of police operations. The apparatus of repression continued to function smoothly and to expand as it became more complex. The 1871 reform is usually interpreted as a liberalization of the conservative regime established in December 1841, but its practical effect was to facilitate more effective and extensive surveillance and control.

Consider the data on the numbers of arrestees brought into the police jail over the years, as shown for the last two decades of the empire in Figure 7.

In 1850 a total of 1,676 persons had been brought into the police jail (as analyzed in Chapter 5), and by 1858 the figure had nearly doubled to 3,240. During 1858 the police system was reorganized and expanded, and by 1860 the number of arrestees jumped to 7,772, more than double that of two years before. That general level was maintained through the early 1870's, when there was another rapid increase, hitting a high in 1876 of 12,762 arrestees. Whereas in 1850 there had been an average of four people per day brought into the police jail, 26 years later the average was 35 per day.

An apparent decline and then leveling off in the rate of arrests

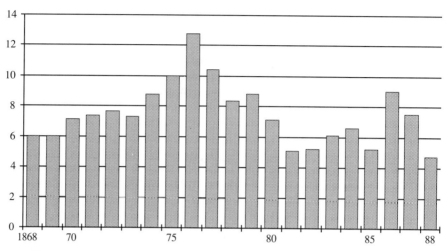

Fig. 7. Persons Detained in Rio Police Jail, 1868–88 (in thousands). Based on Appendix 5.

in the 1880's is explained by a shift of increasing numbers of arrestees to the House of Detention and not through the central police station jail. In 1880, for example, 7,107 people were detained in the police jail, and 3,801 of them were sent on to the House of Detention (which in 1856 had replaced the Aljube jail as the main center of short-term imprisonment for minor crimes). But House of Detention records show 7,375 entries for 1880, nearly twice as many as were sent there from the police jail. In 1881 only 5,115 people were processed through the police jail, and 2,278 of them were sent to the House of Detention. It, however, recorded 8,223 entries in 1881, more than three and a half times the number sent there from the central police jail.[41] During the last decade of the empire the police jail declined in relative importance, while the House of Detention became the first stop for many people police took off the streets, and the total number of arrests continued to climb.

The 1871 judicial reform restricting the autonomous authority of the delegados and subdelegados had little limiting effect on the exercise of the power of the state against the people of Rio de Janeiro whose behavior was considered undesirable, disruptive, or threatening. On the contrary, creating more employment opportunities for judges, while at the same time freeing delegados and subdelegados to devote themselves to police administration and front-line vigilance, made repression more specialized and efficient. Criticizing the system put into effect in 1841, liberal jurist Tavares Bastos wrote in 1870 that "posterity will ask in wonder how it is that during a long period now exceeding a quarter of a century . . . Brazil could descend into such an odious, irritating, and humiliating judicial organization! Revising the law of 3 December 1841 is doubtless one of the most urgent reforms, the first one liberals call for."[42] From the bottom up the new system seemed hardly less humiliating than the old.

1875 as Case Study

The year 1875, with the Calabouço closed, the judicial system modernized, the urban guard in operation, and the anomaly of the Paraguayan War no longer distorting the staffing levels of the military police, provides a portrait of the institutions of repression and their operations in the late empire.[43] At the top of the pyramid of punishment was the criminal division of the House of Correction, the rigid cellular regime in which 141 people were held at the beginning of the year to be joined by 38 more in the course of 1875. These people were sentenced to long terms for murder, serious injury to another person, or large-scale robbery and similar major crimes. Next was the correctional division of the same establishment where 12 at the start of the year were joined by 89 more, of whom 78 completed their relatively short sentences for lesser crimes during the year. Both these categories of prisoners labored in workshops established inside the House of Correction as part of the routine of punishment, according to the Auburn system. Thirty-eight were sentenced for short terms of "simple" prison without a labor requirement.

There were still 52 prisoners who had been sentenced to the old punishment of "galleys" (galés), which involved forced labor on public works, but no new prisoners sentenced to that ancient penalty were added during 1875.[44] Many of the galé prisoners were slaves, and in 1878 the minister of justice pointed to the anomaly by which such punishment "applied to slaves is totally ineffective, that is, it does not have the effect of *intimidation*. The slave sentenced to galés changes his residence but not his condition. Forced labor? He suffered it in his former life. Moral suffering? His status excludes it." His suggestion was that galé sentences should be changed to solitary confinement at labor in absolute silence, according to the Pennsylvania system. Such a sentence "does not have the barbarous character of galés, but in the opinion of practical men it is more difficult to endure."[45] According to the ideology of prison reform of which Brazilian specialists were well aware, the minister of justice pointed out a year before the end of the empire that the galé chain gang was "incompatible with the liberal spirit of our constitution, and is the last vestige of the tortures and stigmas long since proscribed. The person in correction should learn to love work and not suffer it under the pressure of the shackles of ignominy."[46]

The four categories in the House of Correction prison, then, received just 165 new entries in 1875. During the same year more than 23 times as many people, a total of 3,876, entered the House of Detention. Of those, 24 had been sentenced during court proceedings, and formal charges had been filed against 158 more who were awaiting trial. The remaining 3,685 were sent there for "simple detention," to be held for short jail terms on the authority of police or lower judicial officials. This practice did not violate the strictures on the exercise of judicial authority on the part of the police because these detainees were not formally charged, tried, nor convicted of any offense requiring court action. Following practices that predated the 1871 reform by decades, they were simply put in jail for "corrective" punishment. While the 1841 judicial system was in effect, police were explicitly given the judicial authority to order jail terms, and after 1871 such action continued because the new law did not expressly forbid "preventive or disciplinary imprisonment" for "infractions of municipal ordinances or police regulations." Whatever the specific legal basis, as a method of police operations such detention dated from the founding of the police intendancy in 1808, when the new official was expressly charged with punishing people for "crimes that require no punishment other than some correction," as discussed in Chapter 2. Reporting on 1885, when 8,377 people entered the House of Detention, the minister of justice noted that as many as six hundred inmates at a time were packed into an area built for two hundred, and urged that a separate building be constructed that would be "compatible with our state of civilization." Only rarely did anyone in authority suggest, as did the minister of justice in 1888, that the

TABLE 14

Prisoners in Rio de Janeiro House of Detention,
1875: Type of Detainee

Detainee	No.	%
Free Brazilian	708	19.2
Self-supporting	25	0.7
Men	25	0.7
Women	0	0.0
Indigent	683	18.5
Men	602	16.3
Women	81	2.2
Free Foreign	744	20.2
Self-supporting	56	1.5
Men	56	1.5
Women	0	0.0
Indigent	688	18.7
Men	672	18.2
Women	16	0.4
Slave	2,233	60.6
Men	1,708	46.4
Women	525	14.2
Total	3,685	100.0

SOURCE: Relatório do Ministro da Justiça, 1876, appendix tables.

many people held for simple detention should either be formally charged with a crime or released.[47] Subdivisions among the people held in simple detention during 1875 are shown in Table 14.

The "self supporting" and "indigent" categories (*abastado* and *proletário*, respectively) distinguish those who were able to pay for having their own food brought in from those who needed to be fed at government expense. It is not surprising that few of the men and none of the women who found themselves in the House of Detention were of an economic status that would enable them to obtain outside meals to replace the meager and monotonous jail rations. Other aspects of these data are better appreciated in the context of the composition of the total population for the same subgroups, as shown from the 1872 census in Table 15. Foreigners were about half the number of free Brazilians in the 1872 population, yet they accounted for roughly equal proportions of the 1875 inmates in the House of Detention. This pattern supports the recurrent refrain from police authorities in the last decades of the empire that indigent immigrants were causing much more than their share of the trouble on the streets.[48]

Slaves, who by 1872 were only 16.4 percent of the city's population, accounted for 60 percent of the 1875 House of Detention inmates. While the immigrant population was overwhelmingly male,
both free Brazilians and slaves (by 1872) were fairly evenly balanced by sex. Yet only slave women found themselves in detention
in fairly large numbers. Some of the slaves who before 1874 would
have gone to the Calabouço were in the House of Detention at their
owners' request, but most were there for punishment after arrest
by police. Whether their punishment was private or public, however, a large proportion of the people feeling the brunt of repression were slaves, and at this late date slaves were present in the jail
population far out of proportion to their presence in the general
population. But beyond that, thirteen years before final abolition
the slaves were in the same jail as indigent immigrants and free Brazilians for similar rule violations under similar treatment. This is
one aspect of the multifaceted and step-by-step transition by which
the dwindling numbers and proportions of slaves in the city's population became in many ways little different from the nonslave lower
classes. That evolutionary process facilitated the continuation of
operational practices and attitudes of Rio de Janeiro's police from
a society of masters and slaves to one of employers and workers.

Patterns similar to those from the House of Detention show up
in the records of people detained during 1875 in the central police
jail, the next step down the broadening pyramid of punishment, as
shown in Table 16. At this level, reflecting day-to-day police opera-

TABLE 15

Population of Rio de Janeiro, Urban Parishes,
1872: Slave or Free

Population	No.	%
Free Brazilian	121,708	53.2
Men	62,596	27.4
Women	59,112	25.8
Free Foreign	69,468	30.4
Men	53,216	23.3
Women	16,252	7.1
Slave	37,567	16.4
Men	18,837	8.2
Women	18,730	8.2
Total	228,743	100.0

SOURCE: Brazil, Directoria Geral de Estastística, *Recensea-*
mento . . . 1872, Municipio Neutro.

TABLE 16

Arrests in Rio Police Jail, 1875: Slave or Free

Detainee	No.	%
Free	7,371	73.8
Men	6,880	68.8
Women	491	4.9
Brazilian	3,244	32.5
Foreign	4,127	41.3
Slave	2,623	26.2
Men	2,008	20.1
Women	615	6.2
Total	9,994	100.0

SOURCE: Relatório do Ministro da Justiça, 1877, annex table 4.

tions closer to the street, the proportion of slaves affected was closer to their proportion of the population. Immigrants, however, are even more overrepresented than in the House of Detention, accounting for considerably more arrests than of either free Brazilians or slaves as of 1875. From 1870 through 1887, the last full year for which data on slave arrests are relevant (final abolition occurred in May 1888), only about one-third of the people detained in the central police jail were free Brazilians. Slaves declined in that period from more than one-third in the early 1870's to just 9 per cent in 1887, as a higher proportion of free foreigners were arrested (see Appendix 6).

Knowing what types of people the police brought in during 1875, we can better appreciate the reasons for their arrests, as shown in Table 17. As with the data for 1862 and 1865 discussed in Chapter 5, the categories need to be adjusted to reflect more accurately the preponderance of victimless public order violations. It is impossible to describe with certainty the 10.7 percent of all arrests that clerks considered so insignificant or for which there was such tenuous legal basis that they were grouped as an unspecified category. Nevertheless, if those left unspecified, along with the arrests for investigation, ordinance violation, and "complaint" had been offenses against person or property, they would have been so classified in the annual summary report. Because only 11 percent of arrests were for offenses to person or property, then, we may conclude that something over 85 percent of the nearly ten thousand people processed through the Rio police jail in 1875 were there for public order offenses.

TABLE 17
Arrests in Rio Police Jail, 1875: Type of Offense

Offense	No.	%
Against public order		
Drunkenness	2,950	29.5
Disorderly conduct	1,827	18.3
Illegal weapons	840	8.4
Vagrancy	391	3.9
Desertion (military)	293	2.9
Gambling	264	2.6
Capoeira	259	2.6
Begging	137	1.4
Riot	84	0.8
Offense to morals	57	0.6
Breaking good conduct promise	55	0.6
Insubordination	51	0.5
Resistance	31	0.3
Verbal insult	21	0.2
Curfew violation	6	0.1
Subtotal	7,266	72.7
Against person		
Physical injury	423	4.2
Murder	12	0.1
Rape	8	0.1
Attempted murder	6	0.1
Kidnapping	5	0.1
Subtotal	454	4.5
Against property		
Theft (*furto*)	282	2.8
Sneak thief (*ratoneiro*)	190	1.9
Robbery (*roubo*)	81	0.8
Trespassing	69	0.7
Fraud	8	0.1
Counterfeiting	8	0.1
Subtotal	638	6.4
"Neutral" offenses		
Mentally deranged	237	2.4
Conscription (military)	129	1.3
Complaint (unspecified)	44	0.4
Investigation	41	0.4
Request of consul	34	0.3
Other (unspecified)	1,065	10.7
Subtotal	1,636	16.4
Total	9,994	100.0

SOURCE: Same as Table 16.

While begging returned in 1875 as a significant reason for arrest (in contrast to the data in Table 11 for 1862 and 1865), curfew violation—another minor offense that accounted for significant proportions of arrests in previous years—declined dramatically. For the half-century after it was instituted in 1825, the "curfew of Aragão" had been signaled by church bells at 10 P.M. After that the streets had belonged to the police, who only begrudgingly or due to staffing shortages suffered others to occupy the public space of the city. If the others were black, brown, foreign, poor, or engaged in suspicious or threatening behavior in the presence of a police agent or official, they were caught in the nightly dragnet. The many thousands of arrests for violation of curfew and the persistence of the people's refusal to submit constitute one of the most widespread if less extreme examples of resistance to arbitrary authority in nineteenth-century Rio.

In July 1873 the military police commander reminded his patrols that "all business establishments of whatever nature, as well as workshops, offices, and tents [from which items were sold]" were required to close at 10 P.M. New enforcement efforts brought a flurry of reaction, and in November of that year a clarification was issued mitigating the sweep of the curfew. The 10 P.M. closing time still applied to "taverns, houses where alcoholic beverages or beer are sold, the boarding houses known as *táscas*, and similar establishments that might serve as meeting places of drunks, vagrants, and ruffians (*desordeiros*)." Other businesses, specifically the kiosks set up in many open areas downtown selling snacks, drinks, and tobacco products as well as sweet shops (*confeitarias*) and hotels were allowed to remain open until 1 A.M.[49] The problem was not retail business catering to the public, but those businesses that attracted the wrong element. Boarding houses and taverns catered to the lower classes; hotels and confeitarias catered to the newly emerging middle sectors. The new curfew exceptions implied that the patrons of the exempt establishments would be allowed to be on the streets after 10 P.M. as well. As long as a person in public stayed out of trouble, within the bounds of public behavior that police practice had long since established, an arrest for curfew violation became less likely between 10 P.M. and 1 A.M. Finally in June 1878, recognizing that trying to enforce the earlier closing time was more trouble than it was worth, the city council resolved to allow any legitimate business to remain open until 1 A.M., and in September of that year the chief of police formally lifted the 10 P.M. curfew. The bells of Aragão's decree were heard for the last time on 19 September 1878.[50]

The fate of the 9,994 people brought into the police jail during 1875 provides further information about the operation of the system, as shown in Table 18. The largest single category was of people released after an unspecified time in the police lockup. As in the simple detention in the House of Detention, police did not need the permission of any higher authority to hold these people. They were doing what the political elite expected of them: get the vagrants, troublemakers, capoeiras, drunks and similar undesirables off the street, and the fewer questions asked about court procedure and legal basis the better. Many others were sent on to the House of Detention for a longer "non-judicial" jail term, and a few were sent there to await trial for serious offenses. (Of the 3,876 entering the House of Detention in 1875, nearly all—98 percent— were sent from the police lockup.) A significant number of those arrested were sent to the military, many more, in fact, than the 293 deserters and 129 men brought into the jail for no offense other than being eligible for service (as shown in Table 17). Thus by 1875, long after the Paraguayan War had ended, military conscription was still used to remove undesirables from the streets for extended periods. Also, although only 41 foreigners were arrested using "request of consul" as the authority, more than six times that many, 261, were turned over to foreign consuls after arrest.

Patterns of arrest and imprisonment should be compared to the

TABLE 18

Arrests in Rio Police Jail, 1875: Destination upon Exit

Destination	No.	%
Released	4,587	45.9
House of Detention	3,791	37.9
Conscripted	754	7.6
Army	366	3.7
Navy	388	3.9
Beggars' shelter	434	4.3
Foreign consuls	261	2.6
Insane asylum	5	0.1
Other (unspecified)	162	1.6
Total	9,994	100.0

SOURCE: Same as Table 16.

TABLE 19

Crimes Reported in Rio de Janeiro, 1875

Offense	No.	Offense	No.
Light injury	301	Resisting arrest	6
Theft	269	Threats	6
Robbery	97	Rape	5
Illegal weapons	86	Attempted murder	4
Manslaughter	56	Counterfeiting	3
Serious injury	43	Burglary tools	2
Murder	24	Moral offense	2
Bankruptcy	20	Contraband	2
Fraud	17	Illegal enslavement	2
Verbal insult	15	Prisoner escape	1
Perjury	13	Kidnapping	1
Property damage	12	Total	987

SOURCE: Relatório do Chefe de Polícia do Rio de Janeiro, 1876, statistical appendix.

incidence of crime recorded by the same police system. Table 19 lists the crimes reported to have occurred in Rio during 1875. As with the total numbers and reported reasons for arrests, these data are not necessarily closely related to the real numbers and types of illegal acts actually committed. As measures of the incidents that police institutions discovered or received reports of, however, they provide a revealing contrast to the number and types of arrests and of the people imprisoned for serious crime.[51] Ten times as many people were arrested as crimes were reported, and while 72 percent of reported crimes were for some form of theft or personal injury, only 11 percent of arrests were for offenses against person or property. The majority of arrests (more than 72 percent, as shown in Table 17) were for public order violations. Rio's police system did deal with crimes against person or property, and it had the prisons to punish those few people convicted of such serious offenses. But as had been the case since the 1820's under the police intendant, the vast majority of manpower, resources, energy, administrative focus, and activity was devoted to preventing, repressing, and punishing victimless violations of the public order.[52]

Economic Riot, Political Murder

At the beginning of 1880 a major disturbance rocked Rio de Janeiro on a scale not seen since the political upheavals of 1831. Unlike those earlier crises precipitated by the final stages of politi-

cal independence, the abdication of Pedro I, and the ensuing political vacuum, the riots of 1880 represented the political manifes-
tation of social and economic pressures in a city that had grown
and changed considerably in the intervening half century. By 1880
mule-drawn streetcar lines connected the downtown area with several suburbs, including São Cristóvão, Tijuca, Botafogo, and Jardim Botânico, and city residents were increasingly dependent on
this early form of mass transit. Strapped for funds, the national
government decided to introduce a tax of one *vintém* (twenty réis)
to be collected as a separate surcharge on regular streetcar fares,
which ranged from 100 to 400 réis. The tax would thus represent
a 5–20 percent increase in the cost of each trip. It was approved in
October 1879, and in mid-December specific instructions were issued for its collection to begin 1 January 1880. Passengers were to
obtain a receipt each time they paid the tax and show the receipt
to tax inspectors on demand. For the well-to-do the tax involved
little more than the irritating necessity of using small change, but
the cumulative result on the poor, according to one Rio newspaper,
would be to "weigh heavily on small salaries."[53] What the political
elite considered a minor extra charge for cheap transportation was
a major burden for working people.

On 28 December 1879 a crowd estimated at five thousand
gathered near the Emperor Pedro II's suburban São Cristóvão
palace to listen to a stirring call to resistance from José Lopes
Trovão, a well-known journalist, orator, and advocate of republican government. When a delegation from the crowd tried to advance toward the palace to petition the emperor, it was met by military police cavalry and a line of the plainclothes agents of the secret
police armed with clubs. After a tense confrontation the crowd dispersed. When a delegation of political leaders tried to get Afonso
Celso, the minister of finance, to suspend the tax, he gave the classic response of those in power when challenged by people in the
street, dismissing the São Cristóvão demonstrators as "animals"
(*bestas*).[54]

Lopes Trovão and his supporters spread handbills over the city
calling for another rally in the downtown Palace Square (now
XV de Novembro) on 1 January, the first day the tax was to be
imposed. This time the crowd was estimated at four thousand, and
like the gathering in São Cristóvão the rally itself was peaceful.
Following the meeting, however, groups of people surged through

the narrow streets toward São Francisco Square, the terminus of several trolley lines. As cars arrived from outlying areas the crowd attacked, beating conductors, killing mules, and overturning and burning cars. Army troops and navy riflemen had been called to reinforce the military police, as the crowd ripped up tram rails and paving stones for barricades. Critics of the government charged that secret police agents provocateurs threw the first stones at the military, who then responded with cavalry charges with sabres flashing and rifle volleys with ball ammunition (the usual ammunition for riot control was less lethal but wider-reaching buckshot). At least three people were killed and more than 30 wounded. Among the injured were nine army soldiers and three officers, and fifteen members of the urban guard.[55] The government declared a state of siege, declaring an emergency curfew and calling on military reinforcements to patrol the streets, and the confrontations diminished within a few days. In the aftermath most passengers simply refused to pay the surtax, and the government made only desultory efforts to enforce it. The cabinet that put the tax through Parliament was shaken, fell to the opposition in March, and the new government quietly repealed the tax the following September.

The vintém riots ushered in a new era of mass rallies, demonstrations, and violent actions by unpredictable crowds.[56] Despite the high visibility of a few journalists and ideologues from the ranks of the upper social strata, these demonstrations clearly pitted masses against elites—or against the police as agents of elite power. The oratory of Lopes Trovão was a catalyst, but the tax itself was the issue that brought thousands of people into the streets to risk life and limb, and no single agitator's appeal can account for the huge rallies and the outburst of destruction and violence. That violence, moreover, was selectively directed at those streetcar lines that tried to enforce the tax and at the police and army troops sent to subdue the crowds. The managers of the Jardim Botânico line had announced they would pay the tax to the government without raising fares, and its lines and equipment were not harmed.[57] Dangerous and damaging though it was, the mob action gave the common people a channel of political expression, one of the few available to them that those in power could not ignore. It broke through the shield of "order and public tranquility" the police system had so assiduously built up and maintained. The riots revealed to the government and to the social elite that was its constituency that despite all the efforts to keep the population under control, they were sitting on a potential powder keg. Those at the top put aside their factional differences in the face of such outbursts from below, rallying to deal with the potential for social upheaval.

By its nature the social war between the police and the people was never won. At best it was a holding action that had been maintained and strengthened through the police bureaucracies that evolved as Rio de Janeiro grew and changed. For those in charge the adversary was not to be vanquished but contained. Regular policing was adequate to keep the myriad acts of resistance by individuals and small groups within acceptable bounds, but when angry crowds numbering in the hundreds or thousands stormed through the streets, more force and different tactics were necessary. The military police had long tried to maintain a reserve force to respond to emergencies, but they were often distributed to routine service aimed primarily at keeping the urban rabble from disturbing the civil and religious rituals that confirmed the social hierarchy or the social functions the elite enjoyed. The threat of such outbursts as the vintém riots led to the formation of special units within the military police, always on ready alert through shifting ideological winds and political crises, to meet unstructured mob action with an armed and disciplined "shock battalion."[58]

Nearly four years after the vintém riots changed the rules of engagement between the police and the people, a notorious assassination showed the persistence of elite attitudes toward the selective enforcement of the law when the special circumstances of political rivalries and powerful adversaries were involved. Riots in the aftermath gave further evidence that the problem of controlling the lower classes had qualitatively changed from the days when resistance was mainly diffuse and individual, punctuated by occasional outbursts from small groups of slaves and the recurring depredations of capoeira gangs.

Apulcro de Castro was by 1883 a well-known public figure, a mulatto who from his beginnings as a typographer had risen to be the publisher of the newspaper O Corsário, through which he criticized his political enemies and government officials for what he considered arbitrary exercise of authority. He often criticized the character and personal honor of his opponents. An English-language newspaper catering to the foreign business community characterized Castro's paper as "a virtual corsair in politics, a libertine in morals. . . . It attacked private characters without scruple, it denounced public officials without fear, and it pandered to the debased and prurient desires of men without shame." *O Corsário* reportedly had a circulation of some 20,000, suggesting that its critical style and political position had a certain appeal among a broad sector of the city's literate population. Among the targets of Castro's vitriolic pen were sectors of the military engaged at the time in a series of disputes with the government over institutional prerogatives and the political abuse of army service through conscription.[59] Castro soon found out why few other public figures or the press dared criticize the army. On 9 October 1883 a group of officers and men of the first cavalry regiment, in uniform, broke into the printing office of *O Corsário* and left it in ruins. They also broke into an adjacent residence, beat an occupant, and destroyed the furniture. Police made no move to pursue the perpetrators of the attack.[60]

In the early afternoon of 25 October 1883, Castro entered the secretariat of the civilian police on Lavradio Street, saying his life was in danger and requesting police protection. While he was in the station conferring with Police Chief Belarmino Peregrino da Gama e Melo, suspicious groups totaling perhaps a hundred rough-looking men gathered in and around adjacent buildings. Police Chief Melo did not have a force at hand to face such a crowd, but he knew that several officers of the first cavalry regiment were involved, crudely disguised to hide their identity. The cabinet of the imperial government happened to be meeting in the nearby headquarters of the ministry of the interior, so Melo sent one of his delegados for instructions from the minister of justice. The latter conferred with the minister of war, and they sent word back to Melo advising him to avoid a confrontation with the army. Melo felt that the only possibility for averting bloodshed was to appeal to the army high command to bring the junior officers outside his office under control. The police chief sent a messenger to army headquarters on the Campo de Santana, and Captain João Antônio de Avila, aide to the army adjutant general, reported to the police station in response.

After conferring with several of the men lingering outside the police offices, Avila took responsibility for guarding Castro, who left the station at 4:45 P.M. in the company of the army captain. Their carriage had barely started off when it was stopped and attacked by a group of armed men in civilian clothes whose faces were covered with large artificial beards. Castro received seven stab wounds and two gunshot wounds in the assault. He was taken from the carriage into the lobby of the police secretariat where he had gone to seek protection and within a few minutes died of his wounds. His attackers escaped unhindered among the crowd that had gathered in the hours that had passed since the journalist had first sought protection and rumors spread that something was up. Captain Avila, according to official statements, suddenly came down with an illness that kept him confined to his quarters incommunicado for several weeks. Police Chief Melo was dismissed two days after the murder. A formal investigation of this case concluded that eleven army officers had committed the crime, but more than a year after the attack the public prosecutor submitted a formal report that there was insufficient evidence for a trial, and a judge dismissed the charges. None of those implicated was ever arrested or brought to trial, but several were transferred to what was considered the temporary exile of an outpost on the isolated Mato Grosso frontier.[61]

The murder of Apulcro de Castro evokes several parallels with the murder of journalist Clemente José de Oliveira by Lieutenant Carlos Miguel de Lima e Silva half a century earlier. In 1833 Caxias's younger brother avenged personal attacks on his powerful family by killing the offending journalist in broad daylight in Carioca Square. He was brought to trial but the charges were dismissed when no one appeared to testify against him, and he was sent to Belgium as military attaché. In 1883 an anonymous group of army officers avenged insults to their corporate honor by killing the offending journalist in broad daylight in front of the central police station. This time there was not even an attempt to hold a trial, although the identity of the culprits became well known.[62] In the Brazilian version of the transition from traditionalism and personalism to the impersonal institutions of modernity, urban political violence also became more impersonal. But the underlying pattern of impunity in cases of violence by those of a protected status against opponents of the regime persisted.

There was a major difference in the effects of these two murders. Apulcro de Castro had a popular following that took to the streets. For several nights after the assassination, crowds roamed the downtown area engaging in various forms of violent protest. According to a German visiting Rio at the time, demonstrators destroyed street lamps to shouts of "Long live the revolution" and were met by "detachments of urban guards armed, not very urbanely, with rifles," while "military police cavalry cleared the streets at a gallop, with sabres drawn," and plainclothes secret police agents beat demonstrators back with their clubs. One group of protesters found two large barrels in São Francisco Square and rolled them noisily down Ouvidor Street, the main location for middle class shopping and socializing, shouting for businesses to close. "Vagrants and capoeiras joined the street urchins, and when the urban guard appeared they faced a hail of stones from the crowd." Late on 29 October, four days after Castro's assassination, a group attempted to set fire to the building housing the ministry of justice on Lapa Square. When the mob attacked the building where the imperial cabinet was meeting, the ministers of state had to make their escape by the back doors, and some reportedly took refuge on ships in the bay.[63]

From what the authorities could conclude, the protesters blamed the police for not preventing Castro's death and for not arresting the perpetrators—not an unreasonable position in view of notoriously public circumstances surrounding the affair. The government finally got the upper hand by 29 October, according to the newly installed police chief, as the holding cells of the downtown urban guard stations were "stuffed to overflowing with those arrested." Police tenaciously pursued other ringleaders who slipped through the net, and they were captured within the next few days. Matos knew that a sustained police dragnet was necessary to restore calm to the city, but he was harder pressed to explain the connection between Castro's murder and the subsequent disturbances. In his estimation the rioters were no more than ruffians engaging in disorder for its own sake, looking for an excuse to "sow terror in the population." For several years prior to the Castro affair, Matos had noticed "vices latent in a certain social stratum, predisposed to explosions whenever an opportunity arises."[64] The possibility that the demonstrators might have been frustrated over the public and unpunished murder of a man they admired did not enter into Matos's public position on the matter. Whether the crowds of protestors were citizens demanding justice or evil people looking for an excuse to make trouble, they created a situation that police authorities could not ignore. Understandably, given the destructive nature of the popular outburst, the response was repression.

The Persistence of Capoeira

Among the crowds in the streets protesting the murder of Apulcro de Castro were known members of capoeira groups identifiable
by their coordinated activities, characteristic dress (including broad-
brimmed hats with ribbons attached with the colors of their gang),
and their distinctive acrobatic fighting techniques. Rio police had
engaged in running battles with capoeiras since early in the century, and capoeira was one of the offenses still prominent in the
1875 arrest statistics. Through the last years of the empire the
number of slaves in the city dwindled—to about seven thousand at
the time of final abolition in May 1888—and the downtown area
was increasingly taken over by squalid tenements and rooming
houses as those with money retreated to residential suburbs.[65]
Judging from its public notoriety and the police records of the period, capoeira increased in the last years of the empire despite repeated efforts to suppress it and even as slavery declined.

In 1872 the chief of police noted the difficulty of dealing with
capoeira, since it was "not a crime according to the criminal code"
and members of the gangs had to be dealt with according to specific
offenses, such as physical injury or murder. Echoing his predecessors since Eusébio de Queiroz, the chief claimed that through the
"most active vigilance and constant persecution" he had managed
to "repress the audacity of the capoeiras, who were the terror of
the peaceful population, and they no longer dare to gather openly
in the streets and squares as they once did." He recognized that
"they form a sort of association, divided by neighborhood, with
specific leaders. They not only do battle among themselves, but also
injure and murder innocent passersby."[66] A typical example
of injury to bystanders came once again on 7 December 1874,
when capoeiras running through downtown streets slashed a slave
boy named Gervásio in the stomach then stabbed a slave named
Bernardo nearby. While claiming again that concerted repressive
measures had dissolved the organized maltas, the chief of police
recognized that "there are still troublemakers who, armed with
knives and razors, occasionally fight among themselves, with tragic
consequences."[67]

In 1878, reporting on yet another campaign to rid the streets of
Rio of what he called "one of the strangest moral diseases of this
great and civilized city," the chief of police again urged that ca-

poeira be formally declared a crime. He advocated that foreigners arrested for the offense be deported and Brazilians sent to rigorous penal colonies, such as the one recently established on isolated Fernando de Noronha island in the South Atlantic. The chief likened capoeiras to "the bloody sect of those who worship Siva, or the homicidal Druses" and characterized them as "a regularly organized association, subdivided into gangs with their own special signs and slang terms." The gangs, supposedly dissolved years earlier, took advantage of the cover provided by crowds during popular gatherings and public festivals to fight over their own rivalries. "That is the time that some, the most cruel, disperse themselves among the people, razor in hand, wounding at random those whom they encounter, sometimes committing murder, with no reason for complaint against them, and without even knowing them." Arrested in the 1878 sweep were 645 capoeiras, including 507 free men and 138 slaves.[68]

Alfonso Lomonaco, the Italian visitor who in 1885 called Rio's police "the most arbitrary and brutal in the world," also left a detailed assessment of the capoeira gangs, divided by that time into two great rival factions called the Nagoas, whose distinctive color was white, and the Guayamus, whose color was red. Armed with razors and clubs, they not only fought one another for control over sections of the city but delighted in injuring innocent bystanders.[69] After decades of repressive efforts by Rio police, the situation still seemed little changed when in May 1886, "a group of more than fifteen armed capoeiras attacked a tavern on Visconde de Sapucai Street and beat the owner. Escaping down the street they continued their mischief, clubbing passersby and leaving wounded the Portuguese Francisco Gonçalves Saloca, who later died."[70]

About this same time, the French visitor Émile Allain wrote that the capoeiras

are a stain on the civilization of a great city. . . . [A]lmost all people of color, they are organized in "maltas," and divide themselves into two or more rival groups. The weapon of the capoeiras is the knife, and often the razor, which they use in fights among themselves, against their enemies, or against those at whom they direct their revenge. It sometimes happens that their victims are innocent passersby, against whom they have no reason for animosity.

Allain also provided one of the few early descriptions of capoeira as public performance when, echoing police reports, he noted that "they are present at all large gatherings. One sees them especially in the front of parades at popular festivities, engaged in a gymnastic performance or special dance, also called capoeira."[71] While their presence on such occasions may indicate popular acceptance of capoeiras, the police considered this another example of the gangs' use of the cover of the crowd to engage in mischief or worse. The observations of an English botanist passing through Rio, apparently intended to convey the picturesque habits of the natives, suggest the deadly nature of the game played out during carnival festivities in the 1880's: "Every kind of horse-play is exercised. Numerous mulattos, called *Capoeiros*, dance about and run 'amok' with open razors strapped to their hands, with which they rip people up in a playful manner. The police are always on the look-out for these gentlemen and rush out on them with drawn swords!" Public events sometimes involved a martial presence that was more than symbolic, as when troops marching in the Santa Rita procession in June 1880 encountered a gang at the corner of Ouvidor with Ourives streets, and "the soldiers charged upon the capoeiras with drawn bayonets and several wounds were inflicted."[72]

A charge by Lomonaco and other critics that members of the police force were recruited from among capoeiras is borne out by internal records of disciplinary punishment. In 1887, for example, military police Lieutenant Argemiro Pereira de Araujo Cortez was arrested as a member "of the well-known and incorrigible gang of capoeiras that . . . caused the disorders in Constitution Square." This case, reported in the *Jornal do Comércio*, reminded the commander of another incident on Senhor dos Passos Street, in which the same lieutenant "beat up an individual, and roamed through the bars and taverns in the company of capoeiras and troublemakers." For these infractions of regulations, which gave "the most deplorable example of indiscipline . . . keeping company with individuals of the lowest class, with whom he equalled himself in committing indecorous acts," Cortez was severely reprimanded and imprisoned for fifteen days in the internal jail of the military police headquarters.[73] This case, like the sporadic evidence that some members of the police, national guard, and army soldiers were involved in capoeira, indicates that at the level of the street the social division between the forces of order and the forces of disruption sometimes seemed more like a permeable membrane than a solid barrier.

Without alluding to such complicity by some of his own men, the military police commander argued in March 1888 that his force of 966 soldiers was insufficient for policing "this large city, the tranquility of which, unfortunately, is constantly disturbed by an element of disorder, called '*capoeiragem.*' It persists, despite the efforts in various periods to annihilate it and despite public condemnation."[74] It is apparent from the free run capoeira gangs had of many parts of the city in broad daylight as well as under cover of darkness and from their ostensive presence at festivals where they performed feats of agility at the head of street processions and for large audiences that public condemnation of them was less than universal.

Between the abolition of slavery in May 1888 and the overthrow of the empire in November 1889, an organization known as the Black Guard emerged out of the capoeira gangs, with the purpose of countering the growing pro-republican political movement. Taking as their own the cause of Princess Isabel, the heiress apparent to the imperial throne who had signed the abolition law, members of the Black Guard broke up republican rallies and harassed opponents of the monarchy.[75] Finally, soon after the proclamation of the republic, João Batista Sampaio Ferraz, police chief of the provisional government, launched a sustained effort against the capoeira gangs. Given discretionary powers to deal with the problem by Provisional President Deodoro da Fonseca himself, Ferraz summarily deported many of those arrested in several dragnets to the prison colony on Fernando de Noronha Island, effectively breaking the strength of the maltas.[76] Moreover, the new penal code of the republic, decreed in October 1890 to replace the 1830 criminal code, for the first time included a provision that specifically prohibited "practicing in the streets and public squares the exercise of agility and corporal dexterity known by the term capoeiragem, running through the streets with weapons or instruments capable of bodily injury, provoking tumult or disorder, making threats against specific persons or in general, or arousing fear of some evil act." The penalty was to be 2–6 months in prison for the first offense, and 1–3 years in a remote prison colony for repeat offenders. Acting in concert with others was an aggravating circumstance, and leaders would receive double sentences. Although capoeira criminality in Rio did not end swiftly and completely, it was greatly reduced as a threat to public order by the 1890's, only to be subsequently maintained and eventually revived primarily as a form of martial art skill and public performance.[77]

Conclusion

To assess the broader significance of capoeira and other less sensational but more pervasive forms of resistance in nineteenth-century Rio de Janeiro and of police efforts to control them, we might return to the theme of institutional transition and consolidation during the independence era from 1808 through the 1820's and particularly following the abdication of Emperor Pedro I in 1831. These police operations provide important guideposts for better understanding the development of Brazil's institutions and the evolving relationship of the state to urban society through the nineteenth century. A fundamental aspect of that process is the penetration of the state not only into the streets and public spaces of the city but also into the relations of master with slave, so basic in the social development of Brazil.

Police and their practices in Rio de Janeiro after independence were the product of the introduction of modern institutional forms, as the state assumed some functions of social control formerly left in the hands of the property owners and their private agents. The liberal reforms of the 1830's, intended to ensure due process and limit arbitrary and excessive punishment, were not enforced in practice nor maintained in police regulations when authorities decided that more forceful means of repression were necessary. Not legally defined as a crime until 1890, capoeira continued to be dealt with in the nonjudicial realm of correction established in the 1808 order given to the newly created office of intendant, which specified and codified the customary role of the police as disciplinary agent. The liberal restrictions were honored mainly in the breach, and the punitive power of the police was formally restored in 1841 and informally expanded after 1871. Slave owners retained considerable responsibility for and discretion over their human property, even as slavery—and the state-sponsored repressive apparatus aimed directly at slaves—declined in the last two decades before May 1888. Only with abolition itself did the state assume full authority and responsibility for disciplining those who violated acceptable norms of public behavior.[78] Thus, beyond its specific effects the formal criminalization of capoeira in the 1890 penal code and the effective application of the new law under Sampaio Ferraz marked an important step in the more general process of expanding state authority into urban space. As long as some people owned others as property, the state shared its authority with private slave owners. To the extent that capoeira gangs exercised control over physical and social space in the city, only their virtual extermination could allow the state to make good on its claim to monopolize the use of coercive force.

The last decades of the empire saw further evolution of repressive institutions, as the formal judicial powers of the civilian police were curtailed by the reform of 1871, the national guard was definitively removed from police service in 1873, the slave jail Calabouço was closed in 1874, the urban guard was created in 1866 and then abolished in 1885, and the civilian police structure was at last fully professionalized in the first few months of the republican regime in 1890. At the same time, the preventive role of ostensively patrolling police soldiers was increased, physical abuse of suspects and detainees remained commonplace, and the numbers of people imprisoned without judicial process increased severalfold over midcentury levels.

Despite such bows to social change as the lifting of the old curfew in 1878 and the decline and disappearance of offenses specific to slaves, patterns of arrest in the late empire show clear continuities from earlier times. To be sure the police and judicial apparatus was charged with capturing and punishing those who stole or damaged property and injured or killed other people. But in addition to preventive patrolling as the first line of control, the overwhelming majority of police activity was devoted to the arrest and summary punishment of people who, by their victimless public behavior, violated norms of order and hierarchy as defined by those who created and maintained the increasingly elaborate and efficient police response.

SEVEN

Conclusion

The traditional social hierarchy in Brazil was regulated by the direct subjugation of slaves and by vertical ties of patronage and obligation for many free people. Those forms of control became increasingly attenuated in urban nineteenth-century Rio de Janeiro. More than did their rural counterparts in plantation work gangs, some urban slaves had opportunities to avoid the direct supervision of master or overseer, and growing numbers of slaves who hired out for a variety of tasks had a relative and sporadic independence forced by their condition. For many of the free poor, who were as numerous as slaves by midcentury and grew both proportionally and absolutely thereafter, life in Rio was a cruel perversion of the medieval aphorism that the urban environment gave one independence. It was far too late in the history of capitalism for that group to constitute the seed from which the bourgeoisie could sprout. The free poor of nineteenth-century Rio lived in a social world ruled by the commercial bourgeoisie and political elite who had inherited the colonial project on the periphery of the capitalist world economy. In their eager embrace of the neocolonial order, the elite needed to deal with the social consequence of that order as cities like Rio de Janeiro grew and changed.

The exclusionary hierarchy was already well in place, forged during the Portuguese intrusion into Brazil and tempered by three centuries of colonial rule. During the coffee boom and the state building of the nineteenth century, the political elite developed a level of internal security they thought was a reasonable compromise between smothering control and the flexibility necessary for agrarian and commercial capitalism to prosper. That underlying system needed certain freedoms in which to operate. People with money to invest and spend wanted the freedom to use their resources as they saw fit, without fear that an arbitrary and absolutist state would unduly limit their options or confiscate their capital. At the same time, that class of people wanted a secure environment in which their activities would not be disrupted, their profit margins compromised, or their lives and property endangered. So they created a government based on the liberal principles of benefit to their class. But unlike their bourgeois counterparts in modernizing Europe, they had little interest in forcing upon the lower class the freedom to starve, drift, and sell their labor to survive. The neocolonial elite of independent Brazil maintained slavery for the productive base of export agriculture and continued to control the free rural lower classes through exclusion or through coopting clientelism. But in commercial and administrative urban centers slavery was different from the plantation variety, and the nonslaves of the lower classes presented special problems of control.[1]

Because Rio was administered directly by the central government, authorities thinking nationally created institutions and established practices that took effect most quickly and completely in the capital city where they lived and worked. Despite some conditions in common with those in other urban centers of the time, Rio's police developed special attributes because of the city's position as the national capital, major port, and obligatory point of entry for foreign businessmen, diplomats, and tourists. Through the nineteenth century the minister of justice of the national government remained personally involved in administering the police of Rio, and both the civilian police chief and commander of the military police reported directly to him. This made Rio at times a laboratory for institutional experimentation and its police a reflection of the ideas and goals of the group dominant in national politics. Rio was the stage for national political discourse, both in the halls of government and in the streets and squares, so policing it was at once a political and a social task. This was especially so during the institutional transition attending political independence from 1821 to 1832, as street demonstrations became an important mechanism for articulating grievances and making demands on the constituted authorities. The lower classes began to engage in collective actions against the system again in the 1880's, and the police were ready.

Rio's special position as the capital city also meant that its inhabitants were expected to be on their best behavior, because the need for public tranquility went beyond the requirements of the local business community and the sensibilities of "good" people. If the political elite of Brazil felt the need for a showcase for their successful administration of the state, it was in Rio. And if there was a city they should have been able to affect, it was Rio. The state builders in Parliament and the ministry of justice could see the institutions they created parading on holidays, on duty in the theater where they heard an itinerant bel canto troupe, patrolling the streets as their carriages rattled home after the performance, or standing by the door as they entered their offices the next day. They received citizens' complaints about excessive police brutality or lax protection and read the diatribes of the opposition press. They heard from their majordomo or wife about the assault the slave girl suffered on the way to the public market or about the boy in the household who was sent on an errand and failed to return to his quarters the previous evening and was caught by police in the company of other slaves. Members of the elite had their own direct experience and that of their circle of family and clients with the successes and shortcomings of police activity and were familiar with public opinion from political debate and press reports. And they had the collective power to act on their impressions through their control of the political process and access to the resources of the national government.[2]

Rio de Janeiro was not a city-state with the rest of the country as irrelevant periphery, but several considerations justify the focus on Rio and on the relationship between the highest levels of the national government and life on the streets. For one thing there was institutional and physical proximity. The ministers of justice of the empire took an interest in the policing of Rio de Janeiro because it was an important part of their mandate. Willingly or not, they were drawn into jurisdictional disputes among competing police and judicial authorities or had to make decisions in unanticipated circumstances. At several important junctures, the officials of the national government took over what amounted to operational command of the forces of repression in the city.[3]

As a more complex, fluid, and impersonal society grew, new techniques were needed to supplement the control of owners over slaves and to extend that control over the growing numbers of free people of the lower social orders. The new state moved to fill the need, and the police system inherited from the late colonial era evolved to repress and exclude that segment of the urban population that received few or none of the benefits that liberalism protected for the ruling minority. The system of control built up and streamlined to deal with the threat of political rebellion and from urban slaves was maintained and expanded even as it lost much of its original rationale, through political consolidation and slavery's long demise. It then became available for new tasks in a changing socioeconomic environment, which were handled with considerable continuity in structure, attitude, and procedure.

Forced to fend for themselves, the poor were free to hire themselves out, sell small items on the street, or market what they made in home workshops or had traded for. They could also beg, steal, and go without. They had to make do as best they could in an economy in which most organized labor was done by slaves and where there were few opportunities for free people who were destitute, illiterate, unskilled, and usually black or brown or foreign. The elite considered much of what such people did to sustain and entertain themselves to be parasitical, disruptive, and immoral. Their simple efforts to live off the urban land and to socialize with others of their kind in street or square, tavern or botequim or backyard batuque, often accompanied by drinking, loud talking and music, public displays of affection, and confrontations among adversaries and competitors, violated patterns of decorum dear to those in charge.[4] Beyond being scandalous, such spontaneous behavior provided an environment in which, in the eyes of the agents of control, theft, property damage, assault, and riot could spawn, especially in the dark of night. The public behavior of people who were likely to violate the rules written by the elite had to be watched, the boundaries on behavior set, and transgressions repressed.

The personal authority of those of high status was inadequate for the task, as what they considered to be the problem reached dangerous and threatening dimensions. Deference and submission was rational for those on the bottom end of each link in the personalistic chain of hierarchical dyads because such behavior served to obtain a free person protection and sustenance or to help a slave avoid whipping and other punishments. Personalistic hierarchies were never abandoned nor completely superseded by an impersonal universalism, but they no longer ensured adequate control. In the impersonal environment of the city many people's attempts at deference would bring little or no reward. Most had little to lose, and little option in any case, by leading an independent life in the transitional area between the positive incentive of respite and reward and the negative sanction of police action, imprisonment, and physical pain and deprivation. As the nineteenth century progressed, a general mission of Rio's professional police, civil and military, was to fill that growing gap.

The evidence for this is in the effort of the state to mount a credible threat in the streets through ostensive patrolling and in the tens of thousands of arrests and disciplinary actions, from beating to imprisonment, for victimless violations of the public order. Police forces generally like to be known for preventing or punishing crimes against person and theft. The police of Rio de Janeiro made attempts in that direction and congratulated themselves on their success. But the pursuit and capture of the relatively few murderers and thieves were like a flashy façade covering the mundane, persistent, unedifying effort to clean up the streets. Ideologically related but secondary to their main mission was enforcing a code of public behavior to ensure that the elite's moral sensibility was not violated egregiously and with impunity. The slaves and free lower class of Rio de Janeiro resisted surveillance and control by continuing to act in ways that the elite found distasteful or threatening. When those on the bottom sometimes struck back out of desperation or bravado, the immediate reaction was usually swift and brutal. The longer-term response was the creation, expansion, and fine tuning of the interlocking institutions of police, courts, and prisons. Further resistance brought more repression in an ongoing struggle. It would be blaming the victim to suggest that the street people of Rio by their unruly and threatening behavior "caused" the police system to be developed—yet that is the logic of the dialectical relationship of repression and resistance.

The study of society and politics in the modern world often seems to be predicated on the notion that the relevant locus of power is the state, and that members of any interest group (faction, party, class) engaging in purposeful political behavior seek actively either to reduce the control of the state over them (supposedly the objective of laissez-faire liberalism) or to overthrow, radically alter, or replace the state with something the group likes better. In this paradigm, groups are expected to act in a collective and organized way in the rational pursuit of clear objectives. Such assumptions project onto historical actors what the observer assumes to be the rational course of action, but it also assumes that the group under examination shares a broad range of assumptions with both the observer and those who control the state apparatus in question. The problem is if members of the group under study do not seem to act in ways the observer assumes are rational or logical or legitimate, then the observer is hard pressed to assess and understand their actions.

These considerations are relevant to the interpretation of resistance that those in charge regarded as criminal and disruptive, either in fact or in potential. Is it reasonable to expect members of the lower-class majority of nineteenth-century Rio de Janeiro, slave and free, to have conceived of overthrowing or replacing the state or even fundamentally altering the system of domination? More likely, the lower classes thought of the state apparatus—the police being the main front-line force—as part of their environment, something that they had to live and cope with, adapt to, or resist. Resistance, then, does not necessarily imply conscious action against the state or its representatives, nor a deliberate, collective, and sustained challenge to the system of domination. For the people it largely meant just getting by, trying to avoid getting caught in the net that they had no active part in creating. But those who established and regulated the state apparatus did consider much of the behavior of the lower classes as resistance, in the sense that they did not submit but continued to engage in activity the elite considered unacceptable. Those who controlled the state responded with a repressive apparatus.

Repression was organized, regulated (i.e., it could be increased or relaxed as circumstances dictated) through institutionalized mechanisms with historic precedent, legal foundations, legitimacy among the elite, and an explicit ideological rationale. It was ostensive, preemptive (in sense of anticipating and heading off trouble or nipping it in the bud), and physical (in sense of its being a visibly uniformed and armed presence as well as in its techniques of control: intimidation, beating, whipping, imprisonment). The structures and processes of repression left voluminous documentation. Resistance in contrast was amorphous, sporadic, illegitimate, illegal, immoral, antisocial, disruptive, intrusive, unpredictable, dangerous, threatening. And the evidence of it is primarily to be found in the information its adversary collected—in police records.[5] The two sides interacted necessarily. Through a progressive concentration of force and a long series of strikes against the enemy, sometimes reactive but more often preemptive, the state more than held its own in a social war that it could not in any permanent and definitive sense win.

In generalizing about Brazilian history it is common to refer to the appeal of outside sources of inspiration, whether for technology, patterns of dress and architecture, business practices, or political ideologies and institutional forms.[6] Examples of this habit are evident in police and judicial institutions, including specific imports like the French-inspired intendancy and national guard, the British-inspired justice of the peace, the U.S.-inspired debates over penitentiary regimes, and more generally in constitutional monarchy, republicanism, and liberal ideology.

Rio's police originated with the transfer of the mechanisms of enlightened despotism along with the Portuguese court in 1808, adopting the police intendancy for administrative oversight and judicial processing and the Guarda Real for street patrol. With political independence and when the opportunity to replace the Guarda Real was forced by its mutiny and subsequent dissolution in July 1831, the Brazilian elites had the opportunity to establish their own version of such institutions. Their first impulse was to import from Europe those models they thought worthy of emulation, as if society could be made to emulate an idealized European model. Some institutional experiments in the first years after independence, notably the justice of the peace and the national guard, did not survive. They were intended by their advocates to be the mainstay of the local judicial and police spheres respectively, but both yielded to the specialized, professionalized, and centralized system deemed necessary for efficient policing, which was put in place definitively by the judicial reform of late 1841.

A distinctive characteristic of the history of policing Rio de Janeiro has been the evolution of institutions and practices in loco and sui generis. The justice of the peace, national guard, urbanos initiative of 1836, and urban guard from 1866 to 1885 were not marginalized or abandoned because of shifts in some abstract ideological wind, nor because they fell out of fashion in Europe, but because they did not work, given the resources available to those in charge and their objectives. Other offices, such as the district subdelegados and local ward inspectors, continued to be filled by unpaid citizen-police, remnants of the era when those with a stake in the system were expected to maintain it through direct service. Only at the end of the empire did ward inspectors cease to be relevant officials, and delegados, stripped of their judicial functions by the reform of 1871, finally became paid professionals.

By that time, street patrolling had been in the charge of paid professionals for 40 years, since the creation of the military police. When members of the political elite resolved to hire members of the free lower classes as their repressive agents, the recurring problem was how to ensure that the men thus armed, uniformed, and sent back into the streets contributed more than they detracted from the general objective of order and public tranquility. One way discipline was enforced was through economic means. Underemployed and unskilled members of the lower classes would submit to rigid discipline, as well as public hostility, for the minimal income of a police soldier. But financial rewards had their limits, given societal expectations regarding what such an employee was worth in view of his low social origins and minimal expected standard of living.

The lower classes did not take an active and positive part in creating the police, nor did they benefit much from its existence. It is likely that attacks and theft by poor people against others of a similar station were common in Rio de Janeiro, but poor-on-poor crime was not a central concern of the police. Many poor and marginal people, in fact, suffered from police activity, and their resistance constituted the very reason for the development of a repressive apparatus, which they were asked to serve in. By signing on a military police soldier had to agree to submit to the rigid military discipline of the corps, but more broadly, while on duty and off, he had to adhere to a level of honorable and respectful behavior demanded by the property-owning classes and the state they created. The recurrent problems of enforcing control and discipline among pedestres and national guardsmen in the early period and in the urban guard from 1866 to 1885 provided a continuing rationale for the continuity of the militarized police force in which discipline, hierarchy, and unquestioned following of orders were deeply ingrained. Through long trial and error those in charge concluded that military discipline, including corporate solidarity, esprit de corps, and rigid norms of internal enforcement, provided the best mechanism they could devise for extending their authority onto the streets and shielding their repressive agents from the hostile resistance of the public.

The military police emerged as the mainstay armed force of the Rio de Janeiro police system and the eventual model for similar organizations throughout the country. It underwent minor reorganizations and name changes in 1842, 1858, 1866, and 1889, but the military police has maintained remarkable continuity in composition and mission since October 1831. The military police was the functional successor to the Guarda Real, and it shares some historical similarities to other militarized police forces such as the gendarmes of France, carabinieri of Italy, and the Spanish civil guards. It was formed in explicit rejection of the Guarda Real, however, and the similarities with European analogs in the nineteenth century were mostly coincidental. The military police was a local response to local conditions, building on local resources and the precedents available in 1831. It was originally conceived as a branch of the army on permanent internal guard duty, and it remained fully militarized in its internal organization and disciplinary regimen. The origin and history of the military police of Rio de Janeiro (and by extension of Brazil) thus contradicts the notion that Brazilian institutions have been neocolonial adaptations of imported models.

Men in the rank and file have been in a generalized and institutionalized way clients in a patron-client dyad. They received the protection of and incurred obligations to their patron—the state. But like those on the bottom end of private hierarchical links regulated by personalism, they did not move up in social status by becoming police soldiers nor did they get more respect from their social superiors for having agreed to serve. Gratitude and honor came only from adhering to the norms of discipline and unquestioningly carrying out assigned tasks or performing above and beyond the call of duty. Intangible psychological rewards became the mechanisms for ensuring the efficient operation of a system that remained strictly and explicitly hierarchical. On the other side of the incentive system were rigid norms of internal control with a variety of disciplinary punishments available to ensure compliance, from a few hours of forced march with heavy pack to lengthy internal imprisonment and then expulsion. Expulsion from the corps or transfer to the regular army was considered an extreme step, taken only after efforts at corrective punishment failed to produce the desired results.

As an all-purpose armed force, the military police has always been subordinate to civilian control. Although the institutional autonomy that Caxias insisted on establishing in the 1830's set the military unit apart, after 1841 the civilian police chief, with close supervision by the minister of justice, exercised operational control in principle and in practice. The power of arrest, central to the police function in the modern world, was never formally delegated to the military police. Police soldiers made many arrests to be sure, but like the pedestres and urban guards under more direct civilian control they could only take such action in the name of civilian authorities. From 1831 to 1841 that authority was usually the justice of the peace, and after 1841 it was the subdelegado, delegado, or chief of police—all of whom exercised judicial as well as police function until the reform of 1871 stripped them of the former. Only the lowly ward inspector did not clearly outrank police soldiers on patrol, but neither was he subordinate to them—a situation that gave rise to numerous revealing disputes over the years.

Whether they were military police soldiers, pedestre and urban guard patrolmen or duty officers under the civilian structure, or auxiliaries like the national guard, regular army, or municipal guards, the police served several functions. They were the muscle behind the judicial, fiscal or regulatory power of the state, keeping order in courtrooms and giving physical backing to the authority of tax collectors and market inspectors. They pursued those who committed theft, physical injury to others, or murder, and they sometimes succeeded in capturing the culprits. They served as prison guards to enforce judicially ordered punishment, and as riot police when crises broke through the normal barriers of domination. Their very presence in the public space of the city helped to maintain order. But much of what members of the police system did falls under the rubric of disciplinary agent, whose actions were intended not only to be the eyes of the state watching for those who broke the state's laws, or to facilitate the application of judicially ordered punishment, but to discipline transgressors directly.[7]

Foucault suggests that European reformers wanted to abandon public torture and brutality because it stirred up rebellious instincts and was thus counterproductive.[8] In Rio de Janeiro physical injury continued to be part of an arsenal of techniques used to keep the behavior of the population within bounds and to instill fear. Police violence was not simply a holdover from an earlier era but was incorporated into the regulated structures of repression. The new era, however, required and made possible certain refinements. No longer were ruthless brutes like Vidigal to be given a free hand to bludgeon insubordinate slaves, vagrants, and miscreants. Immediate and public whipping of slaves was moderated, controlled, yet long maintained. After public brutality was no longer formally approved, police continued to beat detainees into submission on the spot, at the point of arrest. The threat and often the reality of violence and humiliation became an expected part of a hostile encounter with police. Brazilians find such an assertion unremarkable, even though many also find the state of affairs lamentable. Its origins and persistence require further consideration.

An important reason for establishing the police was to supplement the coercive discipline slave owners traditionally supplied, given the difficulties of maintaining vigilance over slaves in an increasingly complex and impersonal urban environment. Once the police system came into operation it began to encroach on the traditional right of the slave owner to do with his property as he saw fit, when slaves exceeded the bounds of behavior the new order demanded. If slave owners were unable or unwilling to keep their human property under control went the reasoning of state authorities, the police were ordered to fill the breach and keep slaves from carrying weapons, frequenting taverns, and gambling dens or the streets at night, creating disturbances around the fountains providing public water supplies, or hanging out in capoeira gangs.

As the century wore on and slaves dwindled proportionally in the population, they became less and less the object of special attention. By the time slavery's final abolition came in 1888, the police were long since accustomed to dealing with slaves, free blacks and browns, indigent immigrants, sailors on shore leave, and other members of the city's lower classes as a largely undifferentiated group. The early role of the police as a disciplinary agent directed against slaves left a persistent legacy in police techniques and in the mutually hostile attitudes between police and those sectors of society that felt the brunt of their action.

Unacceptable acts that today are called criminal or that call for formal regulation by the state were then too commonplace or petty to warrant the cumbersome application of liberal principles like the rule of law and due process. This practice is similar to the nonjudicial punishment of soldiers within the corporate environment of military institutions (including the internal regulations of the Brazilian military police itself). An owner, for example, had the right—and as a representative of the dominant class the obligation—to keep slaves in line. The employer had a similar right to punish apprentices and subordinates who were not slaves. In the liberal era the employer could dismiss offending employees or dock their pay but not beat or incarcerate them. Between the points at which private citizens were to be either left alone or charged with breaking the law there remained a wide gray area of disciplinary correction.

When the police system was created, its agents were expected to correct those whose faults lay within that gray area, and that tradition was not easily or completely eliminated. Authoritarian liberals like Feijó in the 1830's replaced Vidigal's indiscriminate "shrimp dinners" with the measured application of the whip, the broad side of the sabre, or the truncheon. Beating in the act of arrest continued to be routine, as punishment for assumed transgressions and also—importantly—to instill respect for authority, or fear on the part of the potential rule breakers, which was eventually accompanied by loathing. The history of what is today called police brutality is not the unintended result of attracting amoral sadists into an unsavory branch of public service. The police expected to play that role as disciplinary agent over minor transgressions and especially over people who did not matter to those at the top of this highly segmented and stratified society except as a problem to be controlled. A disciplinary function, with punishment meted out by the police themselves, was for a long time explicitly incorporated into operating procedures. From 1808 to 1831 it was still part of the broader definition of police, necessary for keeping things working, along with provisioning, providing water, and paving streets. There followed a decade-long experiment at delegating first-line authority over petty crime to the elected justices of the peace, who were quickly absorbed into lower levels of the police system. After 1841 the punishment function was assigned to the delegados and subdelegados, as duly set forth in the conservative reform of the procedural code, and to centralized bureaucracies. When judicial authority was removed from local police officials in 1871, correctional detention without formal charge continued to be the lot of thousands of people every year, slave and free.

The 1841–71 judicial authority of the police chief and his delegates was a modernized version of the comprehensive authority of the intendancy of 1808–32, with the criminal code of 1830, the procedural code of 1832, and the judicial reform of December 1841 specifying and standardizing the structure and process. The successive changes, by specifying the guidelines by which the system was to operate, made it easier for those in charge to manage and adapt to change. But in many ways this concept of authority was an updated version of the institutions and procedures established in Lisbon in 1760 and transplanted to Rio in 1808. Although the labels, the titles, and the rhetoric of ideological cover changed through time, there was fundamental continuity in the disciplinary function of the police from colonial times to the republic. It should not be surprising that the informal repressive function exercised by police on the streets through intimidation and physical assault should also persist.

There were analogous continuities in the patterns of resistance, despite such apparently fundamental transformations as the abolition of slavery. The extent of capoeira activity in Rio de Janeiro, for example, through the extended period of slavery's decline and extinction suggests the need to reconsider some commonly held notions regarding urban slavery, slaves as part of the larger society, and the relevance of legal abolition for social relations more broadly defined. If today we can think of slave capoeiras as freedom fighters resisting oppression, what are we to make of their comrades and successors who were not slaves? The urban underclass of nineteenth-century Brazil was a social category that extended across the legal boundary of slave and free, the racial spectrum of black to white, and the ethnic divisions of Africans, Brazilians of primarily Portuguese stock, and recent European immigrants. Recognizing that slavery was a uniquely limiting and marking condition that only those in bondage could know, we might also suggest that in their common experience urban slaves shared much with their cohorts who could not legally be sold or whipped, but who were considered by the coercive arm of the state to be in a similarly hostile relationship with the dominant class. As slavery gradually gave way to a nonslave working class, the adversarial relationship between the police and the people continued.

To understand the continuities of the Brazilian class structure, the incomplete or uneven transition from traditional to modern, the persistent domination of the many by the few, it is necessary to explore the myriad and interrelated ways the system of domination has been maintained. Those mechanisms of control have been neither stagnant nor brittle, and one of the keys to the continuity has been flexibility in adapting to changing conditions. In political history it is common to point to independence from Portugal (achieved in stages from 1808 to 1831), the abolition of slavery (achieved in stages from 1850 to 1888), and the replacement of the monarchy by a republic (in a bloodless coup in 1889, after some twenty years of open and legitimate political activity by advocates of republicanism) as evidence of the propensity of the Brazilian elites for compromise and change. (More recent examples are the "revolutions" of 1930 and 1964, and the transition from military to civilian rule of 1979–85, all of which took place without major institutional breakdown or widespread violence and destruction.)

This evolutionary trajectory of compromise and negotiation at the top, punctuated by apparently dramatic watershed events, has been made possible because of the pervasive and efficient mechanisms of domination exercised by the few above over the many below. These mechanisms have constituted barriers to serious disruption, much less revolutionary change. They are economic, as the many are exploited by the few, and the few use their wealth to acquire symbols of status and instruments of power along with the expected physical comforts. They are political, as horizontal elite consensus and vertical networks of power and patronage have adapted to changing times, and the vast majority of Brazilians have been excluded from active participation in the decisions that affect their lives. And they are racial, as the spectrum of white through shades of brown to black "fortuitously" has continued to parallel the social, economic, and political hierarchy through the past century, following 350 years of slavery. An important intermediate filter has been variable access to education, through which children of the elite have been socialized into their historical role and children of the majority on the bottom have been systematically denied the skills that might allow them to pass through barriers that are as obvious as they are informal.

For all the rhetoric of liberal ideology, modern administrative systems, modern police forces, the elimination of the public whipping post, the replacement of dungeons with penitentiaries, the purpose and the effect of the entire complex of repression have been continuity—responding to economic and social change in order to prevent fundamental disruption of the hierarchy of dominance and subordination. Police, courts, and the impersonal law have functioned not as safeguards of civil or human rights but as instruments of repression.

One of the illusions of liberalism and modernism in Brazil is that the removal of most legal divisions among social categories, which began for free people during the independence era and culminated with the abolition of slavery in 1888, served to break down the horizontal barriers of class. The principle of equality before the law, intended in its northern European point of origin to break down the vertical barriers insulating corporate segments of society, has had quite different effects in Brazil. It is the major contribution of nineteenth-century liberalism to the long-term stability of the system of control. Liberalism helped break down the advantages some sectors or factions of the elite had over others, mitigating sources of tension and facilitating compromise at the top. In effect, liberalism standardized the rules by which subgroups of the elite played their own game to their collective advantage and to the continued domination, exploitation, or marginalization of the majority of society. The genius of the complex of horizontal barriers separating classes, part of the flexibility of the system as a whole, is that they are not fixed by law. This means they have been permeable in principle, and the occasional examples of passage have been used by apologists for the system as evidence that the barriers do not exist. Since the barriers are not legal, it also means that legal means are not much help in attacking a system that is informal, subtle, and shifting.[9]

In fact, equality before the law is hardly a universal concept in the Brazilian judicial system even today. Military officers (including officers of the military police), for example, retain corporate privileges and obligations that distinguish them from the rest of society. These modern analogs of the colonial *foro* predate and succeed the military dictatorship of 1964–85. Holders of college degrees are eligible for special jail facilities separating them from prisoners who lack such marks of distinction. This privilege has nothing to do with the nature of the offense but is based on the social status of the offender. More informally, given the subtleties of distinguishing social rank when one person's clothes might look much like another's, there is the common and humorous use of the phrase "Do you know who you're talking to?" when the speaker feels the need to invoke a status superiority.[10]

The mechanisms maintaining the horizontal barriers, both formal and informal, have not usually been brutal and violent for most people. The advantage of a hierarchy of domination based on patron-client ties and asymmetrical reciprocity is that physical coercion is necessary only as a last resort, a reserve weapon available to the powerful when personalism and clientelism become dysfunctional or unavailable. But the Brazilian elites have resorted to brutality and violence when necessary, however "unfortunate" that necessity has been for those members of the elite or their agents charged with carrying it out, or for those who have assumed the role of guardians of moral cover for the system. Physical coercion was central and pervasive under slavery, and the long transition out of slavery permitted a gradual extension of such mechanisms on an informal basis to the functional successors of slaves (many of whom are, of course, the biological descendants of slaves). In the rural environment private armies and hired thugs continued as the coercive backup for the authority of the powerful. The urban society of Rio de Janeiro early became so large, complex, and transitory that personal hierarchies were inadequate as mechanisms of control. Control was therefore extended through the interlocking and evolving network of police organizations in association with the judicial system and penal institutions.

In the vast and scattered rural zones of Brazil after independence, the area of negotiation or shared authority was between the private patrons and the representatives of state power. Local private authority assumed or accommodated the power of the state, reinforcing and legitimizing existing power relations.[11] In the cities the master-slave and patron-client hierarchies were long maintained, but they were increasingly supplemented and supplanted by more impersonal and more complex patterns of social interaction. The state developed a standardized, professional, consistently applied system to represent and exercise the coercive authority of those in power over the people who did not feel bound by direct lines of personal authority and obligation and who violated rules of behavior that the powerful deemed necessary to impose and maintain.

The police constituted an institutionalized and self-perpetuating instrument of repression, the armed force making coercion possible and effective. It was usually enough merely to exhibit uniforms, guns, swords, and clubs in order to obtain the desired effect—as long as the implied willingness to exert physical coercion was confirmed by direct action as circumstances required. It required a steady allocation of resources and occasional updating and adjustment, but it continued to function in the interest of the dominant class. The universalizing concepts of modernism—the principles of neutrality and evenhanded enforcement of the rules of behavior—were subverted in the realm of social control as they were in politics, race relations, access to educational opportunity, and economic resources.

Police activity was generally limited to a well-defined public sphere that included downtown streets, squares, docks, and market areas, as well as the interiors of theaters, taverns, lodging houses, and retail stores. This was the risky, impersonal, potentially dangerous world of the street, occupied primarily by the urban poor, many of whom were outside the personalistic system of control and protection. Members of the upper orders of society, in contrast, whether old elite or new middle class, were not likely to engage in activities or be present in locations where police repression was applied. Such people continued to enjoy the protection of the household, the support networks of family, friends, patrons, and clients to meet their needs. If members of the upper levels of society did happen to be caught in the net of surveillance and repression, they could appeal to their status ("Do you know who you're talking to?"), their wealth (through payoffs and bribes), or their power (through interlocking networks of influence and mutual support among members of the elite) to extricate themselves from the clutches of the system their forefathers established to protect themselves and their descendants.[12]

In nineteenth-century Rio de Janeiro there was a step-by-step development resulting in a bureaucracy of repression that was increasingly larger, more differentiated, coordinated, and rational (i.e., engaged in the efficient performance of discrete functions, operating through a clear hierarchy of authority)—a process Max Weber identified as characteristic of the age.[13] It was modernization in the strict descriptive sense of a process involving the growth of bureaucratic structures and instruments of state regulation, increased efficiency of operation, and a clearer delimitation of the public and private spheres. But the underlying rationale was not only to enable the ruling class to maintain control. It was to increase control through state structures, filling in the gap in the mechanisms of domination and subordination left by the relative decline of personalized hierarchies of patronage and power that had served through earlier times. The private relationships of domination and subordination, or put more gently, of patrons and clients never faded away. The development of impersonal state institutions to fill the gap in the public sphere, in fact, relieved strain on the personalistic system of control, allowing it to thrive. In this sense there was no confrontation between the institutions of modernity and the traditional social hierarchy. One complemented the other.

Brazil's partial or inconclusive transition to modernity, then, was a way of coping with growth and change and managing it in the interest of the small group of people who were the functional heirs (and in some cases the biological heirs) of the colonial elite. Without violating cause and effect, it would not be exaggerated to suggest that the establishment and development of the urban police system were a necessary precondition for the transition from slavery to the free labor regime. That transition, in turn, posed no serious or fundamental challenge to the successful operation of police institutions. The police had become adept at maintaining the level of repression deemed necessary to keep the myriad small and personal acts of resistance from becoming disruptive or generative.

Only a tiny fraction of the total population, those few caught and punished for the most egregious violations of behavioral norms, ended up in long-term prison. Although the prison might function as a useful metaphor for the regimentation and discipline of modern society, as Foucault suggests, it is an extreme institutional form and its inhabitants constitute a small, skewed, and exaggerated sample. There may be some shock value in portraying the all-encompassing surveillance and control of the panopticon, the depravity of inmates and their travail, and then suggesting that what we see there is the regimentation of the modern world in stark clarity.[14] Police activities, on the other hand, produce a much broader sample of institutional operation and public response, for the most part involving less sensational violations of behavioral norms and less severe retribution. Moving out of the penitentiary and into the streets, we must move from a fascination with the grotesque to a more mundane consideration of the banalities of daily life.

Such a perspective on nineteenth-century Rio de Janeiro reveals the extension of surveillance and repression into the public realm and the resistance of the people. Some resistance was passive and elusive, such as avoiding contact with the police. Other forms involved the stubborn persistence in behavior that brought repression. The institutional presence of police authority in the street was never total, but it became a network covering the city with the agents representing lines of the grid of control that were never very far from one another for very long. And they were backed up by the lash, the sword, the club, layers of reserve force, the law, the courts, the jail, detention center and prison. Rio de Janeiro's lower classes were not brought into the modern era through the diffusion of impersonal and consensual mechanisms of control. They were left out, they resisted, and traditional forms of disciplinary surveillance and punishment continued to be applied through increasingly institutionalized and efficient police repression. In Gramscian terms, a hegemonic consensus about what was necessary emerged in the upper levels of society, but the lower classes were kept in line through coercive domination.[15]

By the criteria of elite political history, there might seem to be little linking emperor Pedro I, who imposed the liberal constitution, Father Diogo Antônio Feijó, who helped found both the liberal party and the police system of Rio de Janeiro, and liberal ideologues like Tavares Bastos and Thomaz Nabuco de Araujo, who advocated the reform of the judicial system later in the century. Yet each in his own way advanced the cause of liberalism. There is even less obvious affinity between those men and three major figures in the conservative faction of the political elite: Caxias, who set Rio's military police firmly on its persistent historical path; Eusébio de Queiroz, who played a similar role in the history of the civilian police system; and the Viscount Rio Branco, who saw the liberal judicial reform of 1871 to passage in parliament. From independence through the nineteenth century the authoritarian liberals and the moderate conservatives helped bring to parts of Brazil some of the institutional forms of the modern era.[16]

The cumulative result was more than merely to facilitate the preservation of the old hierarchical order. The imperatives of participating in the growth and change of the capitalist world economy (called progress at the time) were such that fundamental and far-reaching changes took place in nineteenth-century Rio de Janeiro. Modern institutions of control were necessary not simply to preserve the status quo, which would have been impossible in any case, but to cope with the social effects of the breakdown of the old order. In this sense the development of the apparatus of repression was also progressive and farsighted. It allowed the political and economic elite to maintain the upper hand in the social war, to keep the slaves and their functional successors in line, and the rabble at bay. Brazil lives with the results to this day.

Appendixes

Appendixes

APPENDIX 1

Population of Rio de Janeiro by Legal Status, 1799–1890

Year	Total	Free		Slave	
		No.	%	No.	%
1799	43,376	28,390	66	14,986	34
1821	79,321	43,139	54	36,182	46
1838	97,162	60,025	62	37,137	38
1849	205,906	127,051	62	78,855	38
1872	228,743	191,176	84	37,567	16
1890	429,754	429,745	100	0	0

APPENDIX 2

Population of Rio de Janeiro by Selected Social Categories, 1838–72

Year	Free Brazilian		Free foreign		Women	
	No.	%	No.	%	No.	%
1838	50,779	52	9,246	10	42,551	44
1849	90,731	44	36,320	18	85,176	41
1872	121,708	53	69,468	30	94,094	41

SOURCES: Abreu, *Evolução urbana*, pp. 39, 54; Karasch, *Slave Life*, pp. 61–66; *Relatório do Ministro do Império*, 1839, Annex, and 1875, Annex; "Mapa da população da Côrte e província do Rio de Janeiro em 1821," RIHGB, 33 (1870), p. 137; *Recenseamento do Rio de Janeiro . . . de 1906*, pp. 4–117; Linhares and Levy, "Aspectos da história demográfica."

Tables include data only for the urban parishes, which as of 1821 were Candelária, São José, Santa Rita, Sacramento, Santa Ana, Engenho Velho, and Lagoa. Glória, Santo Antonio, Espírito Santo, São Cristóvão, Gávea, and Engenho Novo were added by 1890. There were partial censuses of the city in 1834 and 1856. A more complete census in 1870 is not included here because of its proximity to the 1872 national census.

APPENDIX 3

Cases Judged by Intendant of Police in Rio de Janeiro, 1810–21

Reason	No.	%
Public order offenses:		
Capoeira	438	9.6
Group disorders	283	6.2
Weapons possession	270	5.9
Suspicion	207	4.5
Disorderly conduct	160	3.5
Curfew violation	123	2.7
Throwing stones	84	1.8
Drunkenness	71	1.5
Gambling	63	1.4
Insulting a policeman	59	1.3
Vagrancy	51	1.1
Unidentified person	18	0.4
Leading persons astray	14	0.3
No fixed residence	10	0.2
Gathering of slaves	10	0.2
Lacking passport	8	0.2
Whistling like capoeira	7	0.2
Insulting owner	4	0.1
Possession of musical instrument	4	0.1
Witchcraft	1	0.0
(Subtotal, category "public order")	(1,885)	(41.2)
Slave escape and related offenses:		
Escape	751	16.4
Found in *quilombo*	55	1.2
Suspicion of escape	27	0.6
Conspiracy against owner	9	0.2
Having a hideout	6	0.1
Harboring escaped slave	5	0.1
Communication with quilombo	3	0.1
Operating a quilombo house	3	0.1
(Subtotal, category "escape")	(859)	(18.8)
Offenses against property:		
Theft (unspecified)	225	4.9
Theft of clothing	223	4.9
Theft of objects	153	3.3
Theft of animals	144	3.1
Theft of food	113	2.5
Theft of money	86	1.9
Theft of slave	31	0.7
Theft from owner	9	0.2
Suspicion of theft	69	1.5
(All theft combined)	(1,053)	(23.0)
Breaking and entering	18	0.4
Attempted breaking and entering	4	0.1

APPENDIX 3 *continued*

Reason	No.	%
Eat and drink without paying	8	0.2
Delivering slave to *capitão do mato*	2	0.0
(Subtotal, category "property")	(1,085)	(23.7)
Offenses against person:		
Fighting	215	4.7
Assault	137	3.0
Beating another person	73	1.6
Injuring another person with a knife	40	0.9
Aggression	21	0.5
Attempted aggression	20	0.4
Attempted murder	16	0.3
Attack on owner	15	0.3
Butting (with head)	14	0.3
Attempted rape	2	0.0
Rape	1	0.0
(Subtotal, category "person")	(554)	(12.1)
Neutral offenses:		
At master's request	134	2.9
At request of third party	39	0.9
Escape from jail	15	0.3
Escape from chain gang	11	0.2
Making false statement	2	0.0
Suspicion of complicity in a crime	2	0.0
Attempted suicide	1	0.0
(Subtotal, category "neutral")	(204)	(4.4)
Subtotal, known reasons	4,587	100.0
Other offenses, impossible to categorize	270	
Unknown (offense not listed or illegible)	221	
Total	5,078	

SOURCE: Algranti, *O feitor ausente*, pp. 211–12, from AN, Códice 403, vols. 1 and 2, Relação das prisões feitas pela polícia (1810–21). These data are also discussed with minor variations in tabulations by subcategories and in the translation of the categories of offenses in Algranti, "Slave Crimes."

These data include cases that came before the police intendant for disposition in his capacity as judge of minor offenses from June 1810 to June 1816 and from June 1817 to May 1821. More serious offenses such as murder were in the jurisdiction of higher courts and do not appear here. The aggregate period covered is close to ten years, so for rough annual averages one may move the decimal one place to the left. Labels for the specific offenses shown are those determined by Algranti from descriptive information in the original source with some minor alterations (e.g., her "found in quilombo house" and "sent from quilombo" are combined here as "found in quilombo"). The groupings by type of offense and the resulting subtotals are determined by the criteria of the present study. Criteria for the "neutral" category include those cases for which the original offense or the reason for the judicial action is vague or cannot be determined. For example, "escape from jail" is an offense in itself, but it leaves the original reason for imprisonment unspecified.

Arrests Recorded at Central Police Station of Rio de Janeiro, 1850

4.1: Region of Origin of Arrestee

Free	No.	% of total	Slave	No.	% of total
Brazil	606	36.2	Brazil (crioulo)	286	17.1
Portugal	288	17.2	African (unspecified)	25	1.5
Spain	23	1.4	Mina	53	3.2
United States	14	0.8	Angola	47	2.8
France	10	0.6	Cabinda	43	2.6
Germany	6	0.4	Moçambique	34	2.0
Italy	4	0.2	Benguela	33	2.0
Uruguay	4	0.2	Congo	25	1.5
England	3	0.2	Monjolo	13	0.8
Africa (free)	3	0.2	Caçanje	9	0.5
Sweden	2	0.1	Rebollo	8	0.5
Belgium	1	0.1	Inhambane	6	0.4
Greece	1	0.1	Moange	4	0.2
Russia	1	0.1	Mocena	2	0.1
Unknown	110	6.6	Quilimane	2	0.1
Total	1,076	64.2	Baca	1	0.1
			Mihumbe	1	0.1
			Monilo	1	0.1
			Quiçiman	1	0.1
			Unknown	6	0.4
			Total	600	36.1

4.2: Arrests for Public Order Violations

Offense	No.	% of known offenses	Offense	No.	% of known offenses
Disorder	86	11.2	Neglect of police duty	4	0.5
Drunkenness	73	9.5	Failure to present document	4	0.5
Capoeira	69	9.0			
Insults	55	7.2	Unlawful imprisonment	4	0.5
Curfew violation	26	3.4	Immoral acts	3	0.4
Weapons possession	22	2.9	Resisting arrest	3	0.4
Vagrancy	20	2.6	Necessities of nature	3	0.4
Gambling	20	2.6	Speeding vehicle	3	0.4
Fighting	18	2.4	Stamping in theater	3	0.4
Absent from work	13	1.7	Leaving streetlamps unlit	3	0.4
Carriage unattended	11	1.4	Suspicion of desertion	2	0.3
Illegal carriage stop	9	1.2	Refusing passengers	2	0.3
Violating police order	8	1.0	Resistance	1	0.1
Indecent language	8	1.0	Impersonating coachman	1	0.1
Desertion (military)	7	0.9	Illegal use of sedan chair	1	0.1
Sleeping in street	6	0.8	False statement	1	0.1
Disrespect	5	0.7	Total	499	65.2
Disobedience	5	0.7			

APPENDIX 4 *continued*

4.3: Person Making Arrest

Arrester	No.	% of all arrests	Arrester	No.	% of all arrests
Pedestre	642	38.3	Watchman	5	0.3
Military police	225	13.4	Slave	2	0.1
Duty officer (oficial)	172	10.3	Ship captain	2	0.1
Ward inspector	104	6.2	Judge	2	0.1
Bailiff (Alcaíde)	76	4.5	Inspector (municipal)	1	0.1
Municipal Guard	47	2.8	Customs inspector	1	0.1
National guardsman	41	2.4	Port inspector	1	0.1
Army personnel	35	2.1	Total known	1,421	84.8
Subdelegado	25	1.5	Unknown	255	15.2
Private individual	21	1.3	Total	1,676	100.0
Owner (of slave)	19	1.1			

4.4: Disposition of Case

Destination of arrestee	No.	% of all arrests	Destination of arrestee	No.	% of all arrests
Released	1,024	61.1	Conscripted into police	7	0.4
Sent to other authority	152	9.1	Held for deposit	6	0.4
Aljube jail	126	7.5	Charity hospital	5	0.3
House of Correction	119	7.1	Public works	4	0.2
Army headquarters	67	4.0	Custodian of free Africans	3	0.1
Navy arsenal	55	3.3			
Foreign consul	24	1.4	Total known	1,622	96.8
Owner (of slave)	20	1.2	Unknown	54	3.2
Punished and released	10	0.6	Total	1,676	100.0

SOURCE: Arquivo Nacional do Rio de Janeiro, Códice 398, Prisões no Rio, 1849–50.

APPENDIX 5

Arrests and Detentions in Rio de Janeiro, 1850–88

Year	Total arrests in police jail	Sent from police jail to House of Detention	Total entries into House of Detention
1850	1,617	na	na
1853	1,740	na	na
1854	2,642	na	na
1858	3,240	na	na
1860	7,772	4,026	na
1862	7,290	4,001	na
1865	7,491	3,130	na
1868	6,010	2,523	2,559
1869	5,927	na	na
1870	7,105	2,516	2,758
1871	7,380	2,572	2,576
1872	7,652	1,915	na
1873	7,341	1,863	na
1874	8,778	3,163	3,352
1875	9,994	3,791	3,867
1876	12,762	3,566	na
1877	10,376	5,115	na
1878	8,367	4,829	na
1879	8,815	5,521	6,832
1880	7,107	3,701	7,518
1881	5,114	2,278	8,380
1882	5,223	2,519	8,077
1883	6,149	5,490	8,469
1884	6,565	na	7,862
1885	5,221	na	8,377
1886	9,041	na	9,435
1887	7,491	na	10,476
1888	4,751	na	5,841

SOURCE: Annual reports of chief of police of Rio de Janeiro and minister of justice, various years.

APPENDIX 6

Arrests in Rio de Janeiro Police Jail by Legal Category, 1870–87

Year	Total arrests	Brazilians		Slaves		Foreigners	
		No.	%	No.	%	No.	%
1870	7,105	1,623	23	2,375	33	3,107	44
1871	7,380	1,983	27	2,868	39	2,529	34
1872	7,652	2,106	28	2,919	38	2,627	34
1873	7,341	1,803	25	3,026	41	2,512	34
1874	8,778	2,785	32	2,441	28	3,552	40
1875	9,994	3,244	32	2,623	26	4,127	41
1876	12,762	4,386	34	2,436	19	5,940	47
1877	10,376	4,736	46	2,459	24	3,181	31
1878	8,367	1,567	19	2,142	26	4,660	56
1879	8,815	na		na		na	
1880	7,107	3,675	52	1,475	21	1,957	28
1881	5,114	2,785	54	1,033	20	1,296	25
1882	5,223	na		na		na	
1883	6,149	2,533	41	1,103	18	2,513	41
1884	6,565	na		1,091	17	na	
1885	5,221	na		1,023	20	na	
1886	9,041	na		866	10	na	
1887	7,491	na		653	9	na	
Average for known years			34		24		39

SOURCE: Annual reports of chief of police of Rio de Janeiro and minister of justice, various years. Percentages may not total 100 due to rounding.

Reference Matter

Notes

Complete authors' names, titles, and publication data are given in the Bibliography, pp. 339–62.

Abbreviations

ACD	Anais da Câmara dos Deputados
AGCRJ	Arquivo Geral da Cidade do Rio de Janeiro
AG PMERJ	Arquivo Geral da Polícia Militar do Estado do Rio de Janeiro
AN	Arquivo Nacional do Rio de Janeiro
CCPC	Comandante do Corpo Policial da Corte
CMP	Corpo Militar de Polícia
CP	Chefe de Polícia
CLB-APL	Coleção das Leis do Brasil—Atas do Poder Legislativo
CLB-APE	Coleção das Leis do Brasil—Atas do Poder Executivo
CR	Correspondência Recebida
GIFI	Grupo de Identificação de Fundos Internos (a collection of uncataloged documents in the Arquivo Nacional, retrievable by the bundle designation listed in notes)
OCP-C	Ofícios do Chefe de Polícia da Corte (do Rio de Janeiro)
OD	Ordens do Dia
ODet	Ordens de Detalhe
RCP-RJ	Relatório do Chefe de Polícia do Rio de Janeiro
RIHGB	Revista do Instituto Histórico e Geográfico Brasileiro
RMJ	Relatório do Ministro da Justiça
SPC	Serviço Policial da Corte

ONE ▲ Introduction

1. The documentary record reflects primarily what James Scott calls the "official transcript," which interprets the behavior of the subordinate groups from the perspective of the dominant elites; Scott, *Domination*, p. 87. See also Goody, *Logic*, pp. 127–32.

2. Foucault, *Discipline and Punish*. See the early critique of the original French version of Foucault's essay by O'Brian, "Crime and Punishment"; the critical reading by Lentricchia, *Ariel and the Police*, pp. 29–102; and its extension to the United States by Dumm, *Democracy and Punishment*. Complementary works include Rothman, *The Discovery of the Asylum*, and Ignatieff, *A Just Measure of Pain*. An important compilation of review essays and case studies is Cohen and Scull, eds., *Social Control and the State*. On related themes in French history see R. Schwartz, *Policing the Poor*; Forster and Ranum, eds., *Deviants and the Abandoned*; Chevalier, *Laboring Classes*; Cobb, *The Police and the People*; Tilly, *The Contentious French*; and Reinhardt, "Crime and Royal Justice." On England, see Hay et al., *Albion's Fatal Tree*, and Cockburn, ed., *Crime in England*.

3. Such an inquiry would also lead to a consideration of the concept of hegemony associated with the work of Antonio Gramsci, which essentially involves control through consent rather than primarily through coercive force. Gramsci called the latter "domination," and it is given little attention by those who study and interpret his ideas. For an introduction see Femia, *Gramsci's Political Thought*, pp. 24–25, 47–49.

4. Allan Silver, "The Demand for Order"; Spitzer and Scull, "Social Control."

5. Foucault, *Discipline and Punish*, p. 96. In the published translation of *Surveiller et Punir*, the French term *justice* is rendered directly in the English homograph. Given the connotations in English relating justice to fairness and equity, I believe the cognate is false. Foucault often uses justice as a shorthand term to refer to judicial institutions and procedures, which may or may not involve fairness. The equivalent English term is court, as in "take the case to court," i.e., pass it through the institutions and procedures referred to in French as *la justice* (and in Portuguese as *a justiça*).

6. As used in this book, modernization and the contrast between traditional and modern refer to the multifaceted changes affecting western Europe and historically related areas roughly from the mid-1700's to the mid-1800's, which were marked by the maturation of capitalism and the emergence of the nation-state—not to the more narrowly conceived approach to development policies current in the 1950's and 1960's. By calling the process incomplete in Brazil, I do not mean to imply a value judgment, or that the historical outcome should have been or might have been different. An essay exploring such issues is Morse, *New World Soundings*, pp. 169–200.

7. See, inter alia, Miller, *Cops and Bobbies*; Thompson, *Whigs and Hunters*; Hobsbawm, "Distinctions Between Socio-Political and Other Forms of Crime"; Bailey, ed., *Policing and Punishment*; Gatrell, Lenman, and Parker, eds., *Crime and the Law*; Hall, ed., *Police, Prison, and Punishment*; Monkkonen, *Police in Urban America*; Lane, *Policing the City*; Richardson, *Urban Police in the United States*. While some students of English social history unselfconsciously use Marxian categories and concepts, that approach in U.S. historiography is less subtle, and struggles as much against the "consensus" school as it is informed by the class struggle itself; see, e.g., Harring, *Policing a Class Society*.

8. Emsley, *Policing and Its Context*; Fosdick, *European Police Systems*; Davis, *Conflict and Control*; Stead, *The Police of France*; Hindus, *Prison and Plantation*.

9. See, e.g., Donnici, *A criminalidade no Brasil*. The notion that Brazilian history has been characterized by the conciliatory style of the "cordial man" has suffered major revision since it was enunciated by Sérgio Buarque de Holanda in *Raizes do Brasil*, pp. 93–110. For an analysis of the cordial man theme in Brazilian school texts, see Cerqueira Filho and Neder, "Conciliação e violência"; in the popular press, Magda de Almeida, "O brasileiro, cada vez menos cordial," *O Estado de São Paulo*, 11 October 1981, p. 30. Reinterpretations of slavery led another author to reject "the claim that Brazilian society resulted from an integrative process, almost always peaceful and harmonious, [characterized by] nonviolent solutions to social conflicts" (Albuquerque, "A propósito," p. 88).

10. Da Matta, "The Quest for Citizenship," p. 312. An expanded version of Da Matta's essay is chapter 3 of his *A casa e a rua*. See also his "Do liberalismo no Brasil: ou a teoria na prática é outra coisa," *Explorações*, pp. 37–51; *O que faz o brasil, Brasil?*; and *Carnavais, malandros e heróis*.

11. A study of Rio's modern police, analyzing the gap between legal principles and action on the streets, is Kant de Lima, "Legal Theory."

12. Examples include Flory, *Judge and Jury*; Macaulay, *Dom Pedro*; Barman, *Brazil*; Mattos, *O tempo Saquarema*; two studies by J. M. de Carvalho, *A construção da ordem* and *Teatro de sombras*; and R. Graham, *Patronage and Politics*.

13. J. H. Rodrigues, *Conciliação e reforma*, pp. 50–53, lists some 26 armed clashes from 1831 to 1848. The revolts are considered in the context of national politics in Prado Júnior, *Evolução política*, pp. 135–64; Bethell and Carvalho, "Brazil from Independence to the Middle of the Nineteenth Century," in Bethell, ed., *Cambridge History*, 3: 679–746. Individual episodes are studied in Leitman, *Raízes socio-econômicas*; M. Carvalho, "Hegemony and Rebellion"; Filler, "Liberalism in Imperial Brazil"; and Naro, "The 1848 Praieira Revolt."

14. A compilation of anecdotes, with a preface by Filinto Müller, Rio

police chief under Getúlio Vargas, is Barreto Filho and Lima, *História da polícia*. Some aspects of institutional history, with little consideration of police activity, are in Neder, Naro, and Da Silva, *A polícia na Corte*. Institutional histories of the police in São Paulo include Fernandes, *Política e segurança*; and Vieira and Silva, *História da polícia civil*. The study of police and policing in Latin American history is an underdeveloped field, despite the central role of such institutions in maintaining the dominance of a small elite over subordinated and marginalized majorities. See Vanderwood, *Disorder and Progress*; Fagerstrom, *Apuntes y transcripciones*; and Rodríguez, *Cuatrocientos años*. A collection on aspects of social control and police activity in the history of Argentina is Johnson, ed., *The Problem of Order*.

15. A general essay is Mattoso, *Ser escravo*. Examples for the city of Rio include Karasch, *Slave Life*; Algranti, *O feitor ausente*; M. R. N. da Silva, *Negro na rua*; Soares, "Urban Slavery"; and Chalhoub, *Visões da Liberdade*. For rural São Paulo see Machado, *Crime e escravidão*. Much of this literature is reviewed in Robert Levine, "Turning on the Lights." The starting point is Freyre, *Casa Grande e Senzala*, translated as *The Masters and the Slaves*. Also relevant for the urban focus of the present study is Freyre's *Sobrados e mucambos*, translated as *The Mansions and the Shanties*.

16. This apt phrase is from Aufderheide, "Order and Violence."

17. See two works by Robert Conrad, *The Destruction*, and *Brazilian Slavery*; Toplin, *The Abolition*; E. V. da Costa, *Da senzala à colônia*; and Gebara, *O mercado de trabalho livre*.

18. Works that have begun to change this historiographical dichotomy of elite studies vs. slave studies include S. L. Graham, *House and Street* and A. M. da S. Moura, *Cocheiros e carroceiros*. On the period following that covered in this book see Hahner, *Poverty and Politics*; Chalhoub, *Trabalho, lar e botequim*; Esteves, *Meninas perdidas*; J. M. de Carvalho, *Os bestializados*; and Adamo, "The Broken Promise." A pioneering study of the São Paulo town of Guaratinguetá is Franco, *Homens livres*. The situation of market women in São Paulo city in the first half of the nineteenth century is examined in Dias, *Quotidiano e poder*, and an assessment of police activity in São Paulo in the later period is Fausto, *Crime e cotidiano*.

19. See, e.g., Johnson, *American Law Enforcement*.

20. What Rio police defined as *capoeira*—gang violence in which the martial arts techniques associated with the term today played an important part—is discussed later in this book and in Holloway, "A Healthy Terror." The massive illegal slave importations after 7 November 1831 were openly discussed in parliamentary debates, e.g., in the Chamber session of 20 July 1841, ACD 1841, vol. 2 (Rio de Janeiro, 1884), p. 264. See also Bethell, *The Abolition*.

21. Stanley Diamond objects to reducing morality to a technical question of legal interpretation in "The Rule of Law versus the Order of Cus-

tom," in *In Search of the Primitive*, pp. 257, 280; and as Howard Zinn says in discussing the history of civil disobedience in the United States, "the test of justification for an act is not its legality but its morality" (*Declarations*, p. 128).

22. One wide-ranging review of literature and debates over social banditry and related forms of rural protest and resistance grapples at length with distinctions between protest crime (implicitly understood to be acceptable and legitimate) and normal crime—without recognizing that the boundaries between such categories are artificial creations stemming from the ideology and moral code of the observer (Joseph, "On the Trail"). Another attempt to deal with such definitional issues is Rudé, *Criminal and Victim*, pp. 78–88.

23. Foucault, *Discipline and Punish*, pp. 26–27.

24. Weber, *Economy and Society* 1: 37, emphasis added. See also Rheinstein, ed., *Max Weber on Law*, pp. 322–37 ("Domination"), and pp. 349–55 ("Rational and Irrational Administration of Justice").

25. Foucault, *Discipline and Punish*, p. 49. As Mark Poster observes in discussing *Discipline and Punish*, Foucault "might have chosen a Weberian frame for his work" (*Critical Theory*, p. 121). Foucault himself made several mentions late in his life to a Weberian point of reference in his thinking; see, e.g., Hoy, ed., *Foucault*, p. 22.

26. This is to locate the present study with regard to the "modes of production" debate, rather than enter into it. Marx declared that "political economy does not recognize the idler, the member of the working class outside the labor relationship. The cheat-thief, swindler, beggar, the unemployed, the starving, wretched, the criminal in forced labor—these are figures that do not exist for political economy, existing only for the eyes of the physician, the judge, the grave digger, and the jailer—ghosts outside its realm" (*Economic and Philosophic Manuscripts of 1844*, pp. 120–21). In other words such social categories did not fit his model. In other writings, particularly "Class Struggles in France" and "The 18th Brumaire of Louis Bonaparte," Marx sharply criticized the "lumpenproletariat" not on moral grounds but for their reactionary political role. For a discussion of these issues see Hirst, "Marx and Engels."

27. Scott, *Domination*, makes a persuasive case that slaves, serfs, peasants, and untouchable castes have long managed to carve out "social space" in which they develop structured and modestly successful techniques for resisting the impositions of dominant elites. For a case study based on research among Malaysian villagers, see Scott, *Weapons of the Weak*.

28. This underlying continuity is a general thesis of one of the classics of Brazilian political history, Faoro, *Os donos do poder*.

29. Emília Viotti da Costa makes a similar point regarding the conscious agency of Brazilian elites of the nineteenth century in shaping their

world in *The Brazilian Empire*, p. xiv. On the imperative of the actor-observer distinction see Berkhofer, *A Behavioral Approach*, pp. 40–50.

30. As a distinguished practitioner of social history has said regarding research strategies, the objective "is not simply to discover the past but *to explain it*, and in doing so to provide a link with the present" (Hobsbawm "History from Below," p. 72, emphasis in original).

31. Organizations and activity associated with social control defined broadly, often those with no or only quasi-governmental support and that focus on education, welfare, the protection of children and women to instill moral rectitude among the lower classes, have had only rudimentary development in Brazil, and few have been studied historically. For examples of such phenomena from English history, see Behlmer, *Child Abuse*; and Laqueur, *Religion and Respectability*.

32. Da Costa, *The Brazilian Empire*, p. xvii. A review of these themes in the historiography of Spanish America is Taylor, "Between Global Process," pp. 140–54. A general discussion of such methodological issues is Stearns, "Social and Political History."

33. Foucault, *Discipline and Punish*, p. 27.

34. For other tours of nineteenth-century Rio de Janeiro, each shaped by the author's purpose and time focus, see Karasch, *Slave Life*, pp. 55–60; S. L. Graham, *House and Street*, pp. 23–27; Hahner, *Poverty and Politics*, pp. 11–15; and Needell, *A Tropical Belle Epoque*, pp. 22–28. An overview of the physical and demographic development of the city is Abreu, *Evolução urbana*. Among several compendia of local history anecdotes are Azevedo, *O Rio de Janeiro*, and Brasil Gerson, *História das ruas*.

35. Useful map collections include Barreiros, *Atlas*; and Da Cunha, ed., *Álbum cartográfico*. A 1713 map showing the defensive wall at the approximate location of the present Uruguaiana street is in L. C. de M. Coelho, "Aspectos da evolução," 1: 282.

36. On the economic development of the city see Lobo, *História*.

37. Sweigart, *Coffee Factorage*; Holloway, *Immigrants*, pp. 3–34.

38. *Rocio* is an ancient Portuguese word for a plot of land used for common grazing. After Prince Regent Pedro in this square declared allegiance to the liberal Portuguese constitution in April 1821, the name became Praça da Constituição, and in the 1860's an equestrian statue of Pedro I was raised in the center. After the fall of the empire the name was changed to Tiradentes. A smaller square called Rocio Pequeno was located two blocks further inland from old Santa Ana Church. Its name was later changed to Onze de Junho (11 June, date of the 1865 Paraguayan War victory at Riachuelo), and it was obliterated by the construction of President Vargas Avenue in the 1940's, along with Capim and São Domingos squares.

39. Bunbury, "Narrativa de viagem," p. 18; Kidder and Fletcher, *Brazil*

and the Brazilians, pp. 124–26. Kidder and Fletcher were mistaken in assuming that the 10 P.M. curfew applied only to slaves, accounting for their surprise that almost no one was on the streets after that hour.

40. Hahner, *Poverty and Politics*, p. 26. An evocative novel set in the 1880's, originally published in 1890, is Azevedo, *O cortiço*. On the pleasures of life in the *palacetes* of Botafogo as of 1864, see Scully, *Brazil*, pp. 177–78.

41. Leslie Bethell, ed., *Cambridge History*, 3: 169–71.

42. These demographic data are from the manuscript report of the results of the 1849 census of Rio de Janeiro, discovered during research for this book in April 1988 in an uncatalogued manuscript collection in the Arquivo Nacional, Rio de Janeiro. The location was GIFI 5B 447, but the census documents were then held separately in the Archive for eventual publication. Summary data from earlier published versions of the census are in Karasch, *Slave Life*, p. 66.

T W O ▲ Foundations, 1808–30

1. A good point of entry into the extensive literature on the history of European and North American police systems is Emsley, *Policing and Its Context*.

2. S. Schwartz, *Sovereignty and Society*, pp. 45–54; C. Almeida, ed., *Código Philippino*; Kant de Lima, "Cultura jurídica."

3. Rezende, "Polícia administrativa," p. 402.

4. Gonçalves, "Instituições"; Pereira, "Os códigos criminal," 4: 172.

5. Faoro, *Os donos do poder*, 1: 191; see also Prado Júnior, *The Colonial Background*, pp. 378–83. The formal designations of the military categories reflected the levels of hierarchy and readiness. The regular army was the "first line," militias the "second line," and the literal translation of *ordenança* is "orderly," the military term for aide or assistant.

6. On the independence era, see Russell-Wood, ed., *From Colony to Nation*; Barman, *Brazil*; Mota, ed., *1822: Dimensões*; J. H. Rodrigues, *Independência*; and Macaulay, *Dom Pedro*.

7. Manchester, *British Preëminence*.

8. An informed and insightful collection of essays, in which the contradictions of Brazilian liberalism are a recurring theme, is E. V. da Costa, *The Brazilian Empire*, pp. 53–77. On the ideological debates and institutional experimentation in the judicial realm, see Flory, *Judge and Jury*.

9. Araujo, *Estudo histórico*, pp. 10–27. An 1868 dictionary of the Portuguese language, while noting derivation from Latin *polis* (city), recognized the emergence of a narrower conception of *polícia* with the following definition: "Government and good administration of the state, of the security of citizens, public health, subsistence, etc. Today refers particularly to cleanliness, lighting, security, and all matters with respect to vigilance

over vagrants, beggars, thieves, criminals, and seditious persons, etc." The same source defines a second usage of *polícia*, derived from Latin *polire* (to polish), as "culture, polish, the perfecting of a nation, the process of civilization" and warns that the two meanings, each with its own origin and connotation, should not be confused (Almeida and Lacerda, *Diccionario*, 2: 743). In thinking about what their role in society should be, Rio's police authorities did consider these two areas of activity or connotations of the term—repressing criminality and civilizing the urban lower classes—to be extensions of one another.

For a discussion of the broader use of the term *police* in old regime France, see R. Schwartz, *Policing the Poor*, p. 3.

10. Quoted in Leal, "História Judiciária," p. 1119.

11. Sanctos, *Memórias,* 1: 73, 93–94.

12. M. B. N. da Silva, "A Intendência-Geral," pp. 187–204; "Centenário da polícia," pp. 2–13; J. C. F. Pinheiro, "Paulo Fernandes," pp. 65–76. On the oath to the planned constitution, see Macaulay, *Dom Pedro,* pp. 78–80.

13. A. J. de M. Moraes, *História da trasladação,* pp. 95–96.

14. Luccock, *Notes on Rio de Janeiro,* pp. 136–37, 548–49.

15. "Abreviada demonstração," RIHGB 55: 1 (1892) 374; Barreto Filho and Lima, *História da Polícia,* 1 : 261–63.

16. A summary of these reforms is in A. M. Silva, "Imperial Reorganization."

17. Sanctos, *Memórias,* 1: 133–34.

18. A soldier's salary was 2$400 per month, a corporal made 3$600, and a top sergeant's monthly pay was 8$400, at a time when a free artisan's wage might approximate 12$000 to 18$000 per month. Staffing and salaries are from AN IJ6 891, Guarda Real de Polícia (the personnel registry book for 1817–29). Units were stationed on the Campo de Santana, on Mataporcos Street (now Haddock Lobo) next to Espirito Santo Church, at the Ajuda convent (the present site of Cinelândia), and near the Prainha docks, now called Praça Mauá (E. M. de Carvalho, "A P.M. carioca," 6: 294).

19. Barreto Filho and Lima, *História da Polícia,* 1: 207–8; Araujo, *Estudo histórico,* pp. 55–56; J. C. F. Pinheiro, "Paulo Fernandes," p. 74. Vidigal is immortalized in *Memórias de um sargento de milícias,* by Manuel Antônio de Almeida, chapters V, XIII–XIV, and passim. This literary classic, first published in 1852–54, has been read by generations of students as one of Brazil's first novels. The central character, the ne'er-do-well Leonardo, served as a grenadier in the Guarda Real de Polícia under Vidigal's command. Modern assessments include Candido, "Dialética da malandragem"; and Schwarz, *Que horas são?*, pp. 129–55.

20. Luccock, *Notes on Rio de Janeiro,* pp. 548–49.

21. Walsh, a chaplain with the British diplomatic mission, also claimed that police soldiers were "the only natives I ever saw drunk," suggesting he had fairly limited exposure to nightlife in the streets of Rio (*Notices of Brazil*, 1: 489–90).

22. He lived to a ripe old age and died in Rio in 1843 (Fazenda, *Antiqualhas e memórias*, 4: 87–90).

23. Luccock, *Notes on Rio de Janeiro*, p. 137.

24. Algranti, *O feitor ausente*, pp. 157–201, 209–11.

25. A fuller discussion of *capoeira*, including the uncertain etymology of the term, is in Chapter 5.

26. For a detailed discussion of the geographical source of these names and their representation in Rio's slave population, see Karasch, *Slave Life*, pp. 3–28, 371–83.

27. AN Códice 403, vol. 2, dates cited, all in 1820.

28. AN, Códice 323, vol. 6, folha 35, cited in Algranti, *O feitor ausente*, pp. 165 n. 20, and p. 171.

29. Wade, *Slavery in the Cities*, pp. 187–88. Wade also reports the case of a man who witnessed a public whipping in Georgia in 1826, and who was shocked and horrified to calculate that the victim might have received "nearly one hundred lashes," p. 94.

30. These comparisons contradict the hypothesis concerning milder treatment of slaves in the colonies of Iberian cultures versus harsher treatment in English America posited by Tannenbaum, *Slave and Citizen*. For a discussion of and contribution to the debates on comparative slavery in the United States and Brazil see Degler, *Neither Black nor White*.

31. Macaulay, *Dom Pedro*, pp. 96, 251; Barman, *Brazil*, p. 159. Personal animosity between Paulo Fernandes Viana and prince regent Pedro exacerbated their political differences. Pedro personally accepted and conveyed to his father the crowd's demand that Viana be dismissed, on 26 February 1821. In the last days of April one of Pedro's first acts as regent was spitefully to send cavalry troops riding over a formal garden Viana had established in a corner of the Campo de Santana opposite his residence to destroy it. Viana had a fit of apoplexy and died soon after, on 1 May 1821. Barreto Filho and Lima, *História da Polícia*, 1: 191; Araujo, *Estudo histórico*, p. 59.

32. Rezende, "Polícia administrativa," 3: 403–7.

33. The text of the 1824 constitution is in Torres, *A democracia coroada*, pp. 479–96.

34. Portaria of 29 November 1821 from Comissão Militar to Carlos Frederico de Caula, minister of war, cited in Araujo, *Estudo histórico*, pp. 59–62, 90.

35. Cited in Algranti, *O feitor ausente*, pp. 170–71.

36. "A verdade da repressão," in Candido, *Teresina etc.*, p. 113.

37. Goulart, *Da palmatória*, p. 195.

38. The commander was to receive 16$000 extra, the assistant commander 12$000, captains 8$000, and lieutenants 4$000. Araujo, *Estudo histórico*, pp. 126–31; "Centenário da polícia," p. 7; Barreto Filho and Lima, *História da Polícia*, 1: 281.

39. *Regulamento para os comissários*. A printed copy of this pamphlet containing the edict, regulations, and instructions is located in AN, Caixa 777, pacote 1.

40. In 1823 the intendant charged 1$600 for a passport for foreign travel, a permit to go to the mining region of Minas Gerais cost $160, and the fee for a permit to go to Parati or São Sebastião on the coast between Rio and Santos was increased from $500 to $840 (Barreto Filho and Lima, *História da Polícia*, 1: 262).

41. It was also apparently modeled on the French *Commissaire de Police*, a precinct-level official with a similar range of duties. See Cobb, *The Police and the People*, pp. 14–17.

42. A study of the ideological debates and political maneuvering surrounding the justice of the peace proposal is Flory, *Judge and Jury*.

43. ACD, 28 June 1827, p. 176.

44. Ibid.

45. Russell-Wood, "Local Government," p. 195; Leithold and von Rango, *O Rio de Janeiro visto por dois prussianos*, p. 44. For details on the role of the *capitão do mato* in the sugar zone of Rio de Janeiro province in the late eighteenth century, see Lara, *Campos de violência*, pp. 295–322. Rugendas, who visited Brazil in the early 1820's, produced an engraving of a wide-eyed mulatto *capitão do mato*, mounted and armed with a musket and bringing in a bound captive, that has become emblematic of the domination exercised over slaves. See his *Viagem pitoresca*, plate 2/11, and the reproduction in Costa, *The Brazilian Empire*, p. 142.

46. AN, Códice 330, Correspondência da polícia, 18 Dec. 1822 and 3 Feb. 1823.

47. Luccock, *Notes on Rio de Janeiro*, p. 548.

48. AN, Códice 385, Receita de bilhetes de correção de escravos, Intendente Geral de Polícia, 1826. See Karasch, *Slave Life*, table 5.1, p. 125 for a tabulation of these data by sex and number of lashes.

49. Wade, *Slavery in the Cities*, p. 96.

50. RJM, 1831, p. 6.

51. After independence the *cadeia velha* adjacent to the Paço da Cidade became the meeting site of the chamber of deputies of the national government and was replaced in the 1920's by a new building on the same site, the Palácio Tiradentes, now occupied by the legislative assembly of the state of Rio de Janeiro (Fazenda, "O Aljube").

52. RJM, 1831, p. 6. The room dimensions are from an 1835 report,

included in yet another from 1838; AN IJ6 186 (OCP-C), 26 April 1838.

53. AN IJ6 166 (OCP-C), 23 April 1833. Of the 68 prisoners held in the fort on Santa Barbara island at the same time, 13 had no records (RJM, 1833, p. 35).

54. CLB-APL, 16 Dec. 1830, pp. 142–99.

55. Three penalties held over from the old regime, seldom subsequently applied in practice, were *banimento*, exile from Brazil; *desterro*, internal exile to any part of Brazil except a specific territory, usually the province in which the crime was committed; and *degredo*, internal exile to a specifically restricted territory. An annotated edition of the criminal code, with commentary on subsequent interpretations and alterations, is Tinôco, *Código criminal*. A study of the 1835 revolt is Reis, *Rebelião escrava*.

THREE ▲ Crisis, 1831–32

1. This pendulum periodization dates at least as far back as the influential interpretive essay by conservative journalist Justiniano José da Rocha, "Ação; reação; transação," which appeared in 1856. See Magalhães Júnior, *Três panfletários*, pp. 127–218. It has been passed on with some modifications and refinements by generations of Brazilian historians and provides the basis of the periodization of two major studies of the era in English—Flory, *Judge and Jury*, pp. 45–128; and Barman, *Brazil*, pp. 160–88; as well as a study of the Rio police by a team at the Pontífica Universidade Católica of Rio, Neder, Naro, and Silva, *A polícia na corte*, pp. 16–181.

2. RMJ, 1831, p. 3. The street battles of mid-March, 1831 are known as the "nights of the bottle-throwing" (*noites das garrafadas*).

3. Macaulay, *Dom Pedro*, pp. 248–53; Barman, *Brazil*, p. 159.

4. CLB-APE, 4 May 1831, pp. 7–12.

5. McBeth, "The Brazilian Recruit," pp. 71–86. See the discussions of the bills in parliament on the whipping of soldiers in 1828 and forced conscription in 1835 in J. H. Rodrigues, *O parlamento*, 2: 215–17, 223–25.

6. The text of the law, on which the following discussion is based, is in CLB-APL, 6 June 1831, part 1, pp. 1–4.

7. CLB-APE, part 1, 14 June 1831, p. 15.

8. Castro, *A milícia cidadã*, p. 22.

9. CLB-APE, 14 June 1831, pp. 16–18.

10. Feijó, a major figure in the politics of the independence and regency periods, who himself became single regent from 1835 to 1837, has been the subject of much debate and several biographies, the best of which is Sousa, *Diogo Antônio Feijó*. Events of his career set forth by an anonymous confidant are in A. J. de M. Moraes, ed., *Necrologia*.

11. "A organisação do exército brasileiro," in Holanda, ed., *História geral*, tomo 2, 1: 275.

12. M. de Azevedo, "Sedição militar de julho de 1831," pp. 182–83.

13. J. H. Rodrigues, *O parlamento*, vol. 2, tomo 2: 221.

14. J. M. P. da Silva, *História do Brazil*, p. 24.

15. J. H. Rodrigues, *O parlamento*, vol. 2, tomo 2: 220.

16. CLB-APE, 1831, pp. 22–23.

17. This included Luis Alves de Lima e Silva, whose former unit, the emperor's personal guard, was disbanded after the abdication of Pedro I. See Pilar, *Os patronos*, p. 25; and Campos, *Vida do grande cidadão*, p. 41.

18. CLB-APL 17 July 1831 pt. 1, pp. 83–84.

19. M. de Azevedo, "Sedição militar de julho de 1831," p. 189. Another detailed account of this episode is in Sousa, *Diogo Antônio Feijó*, pp. 127–43.

20. CLB-APL 17 July 1831 pt. 1, p. 34.

21. J. M. P. da Silva, *História do Brazil*, p. 28.

22. Quoted in A. J. de M. Moraes, ed., *Necrologia*, p. 15.

23. RMJ, 1831, p. 5.

24. RMJ, 1832, p. 5.

25. *O Raio de Júpiter*, 14 April 1836, cited in Sousa, *Diogo Antônio Feijó*, p. 138.

26. In discussing police activity in the nineteenth-century United States, Monkkonen notes that intimidation and abuse short of arrest, "although an important and feared tool of social control, still goes unmeasured today" (*Police in Urban America*, p. 84).

27. In a telling omission, França mentions in his detailed and revealing *Relatório* to parliament, dated 7 May 1831 (p. 3), that he ordered the sundown curfew for sailors but does not mention extending it to slaves. The internal police memo from which the data in Table 3.1 are drawn clearly indicates slaves were included. The reconfirmation of the curfew for sailors is in AG PMERJ-CR, 16 Nov. 1832.

28. All these reports are in AN IJ6 166, OCP-C 1831, for the dates mentioned in the text.

29. J. M. P. da Silva, *História do Brazil*, p. 45.

30. A sociological study of the national guard, with a heavy overlay of Weberian theorizing, is Uricoechea, *Patrimonial Foundations*. On the guard's relationship to the army, see Sodré, *História militar*, pp. 116–35. The guard is one of the central institutions Richard Graham weaves into his analysis of *Patronage and Politics*.

31. CLB-APL 18 Aug. 1831 pt. 1, pp. 49–73.

32. Castro, *A milícia cidadã*, pp. 24–25. See also Rodrigues, Falcón, and Neves, *A Guarda Nacional*, pp. 33–47.

33. A detailed assessment of the problems of staffing the guard is in RMJ, 1834, pp. 11–12.

34. RMJ, 1836, p. 22.

35. CLB-APE, 23 Dec. 1831, part 1, pp. 88–89.

36. RMJ, 1832, p. 4.

37. RMJ, 1834, p. 10.

38. Rambo, "The Role of the Carioca Press," p. 99.

39. An account of this incident, involving lingering anti-Portuguese sentiment and army officers confronting civilian authorities, is M. de Azevedo, "Os tiros no theatro," pp. 349–58. The site is now occupied by the João Caetano theater, where Avenida Passos enters the Praça Tiradentes.

40. CLB-APE 29 Apr. 1831, part 1, p. 6.

41. M. de Azevedo, "Sedição militar na Ilha das Cobras." The origins of the martyred municipal guard are mentioned in "Cartas de João Loureiro," p. 378.

42. A. J. de M. Moraes, ed., *Necrologia*, pp. 17–18.

43. Sousa, *Diogo Antônio Feijó*, pp. 152–53.

44. AN IJ6 166, OCP-C, 27 July 1831; AN IJ6 165, OCP-C, 27 Dec. 1831.

45. Feijó quoted in M. de Azevedo, "Motim político de 3 de abril de 1832," p. 374. The law authorizing the military police is in CLB-APL, 10 Oct. 1831, part 1, pp. 129–30

46. As a measure of the gap between soldiers and officers, each of the four company commanders with the rank of captain received 70$000, and the commander of the corps, a lieutenant colonel at the time of the founding, received 120$000 per month. The regulations governing the military police, including disciplinary measures and pay, are in CLB-APE, 22 October 1831, part 1, pp. 48–51.

47. AN IJ6 165 (OCP-C), 28 Nov. 1831; AG PMERJ-OD, 29 Nov. 1831.

48. AG PMERJ-CR, 13 Feb. 1832.

49. AG PMERJ-CR, 7 May 1832.

50. RMJ, 1832, p. 3.

51. CLB-APE, 1831, annex, p. 17.

52. Later Brazilian reformers sometimes used the English term "policeman" to characterize the restrained, nonmilitarized, citizen-police ideal they would like to achieve in Brazil, in contrast to soldiers under military organization and discipline. The usual model was the Metropolitan Police of London created in 1829, just two years before the military police of Rio de Janeiro. New York's modern police system was formed only in 1845, and its patrolmen were not uniformed until 1853; see Miller, *Cops and Bobbies*, pp. 2, 36.

53. He was called baron of Caxias, the first level of the honorific title by which he is commonly known in history, in July 1841, after his term as military police commander and after pacifying the northern province of Maranhão, including a successful campaign against rebels in the town of

Caxias. His title of nobility also entered the vernacular, as a *caxias* in modern Brazilian slang refers to a rigid authoritarian. His wife, Ana Luiza Viana, was the daughter of Paulo Fernandes Viana, Rio's first police intendant. A useful curriculum vitae is in Pilar, *Os patronos*, pp. 15–27. Two of many hagiographic versions of his life are Joaquim Pinto de Campos, *Vida do grande cidadão* and A. de Carvalho, *Caxias*.

54. M. de Azevedo, "Motim político de 3 de abril de 1832," p. 370.

55. AG PMERJ-CR, 4 April 1832; Campos, *Vida do grande cidadão*, pp. 43–44. An overview of the theme is Hayes, *The Armed Nation*.

56. AG PMERJ-CR, 5 June 1832.

57. AG PMERJ-CR, 22 Sept. 1832.

58. AG PMERJ-CR, 2 July, 6 July 1832.

59. The procedural code is in CLB-APL, 29 Nov. 1832, pp. 155–99. Among the specific items reflecting slavery and patriarchy were the provisions that a slave could not bring criminal complaint against his or her owner—but neither could father against son or vice versa, spouse against spouse, or sibling against sibling. A slave could not testify in court—but neither could next of kin, spouses, relatives "to the second degree," or children under 14. The presiding judge could take formal depositions from any of these persons, however, and enter the statement as evidence as he saw fit. The needs of generations of Brazilian law students have been met by a series of studies of the judicial system and its history, including annotations and commentary. Among the most useful for historical purposes are J. I. Ramalho, *Elementos*; Bueno, *Apontamentos*; Filgueiras Júnior, *Código do processo*; Pessoa, *Código do processo criminal*; Almeida Júnior, *O processo criminal*.

60. RMJ, 1833, pp. 21–22.

61. Biographical details on Eusébio and his father are from M. de Q. M. Ribeiro, *Apontamentos*. At the time of his appointment to district judge he had not attained the minimum age nor had he been out of law school for the one year required by the procedural code, but the code had not yet been formally put into effect and he slipped by those restrictions.

62. During this period the demand for slaves in the rapidly expanding coffee industry overcame international pressure, primarily from Great Britain, to end the importation of new slaves from Africa to Brazil. On the "Queiroz Law" see Bethell, *The Abolition*, pp. 339–41.

63. RMJ, 1836, p. 26. On his father's influence, see Palha, *Dez estadistas*, p. 43.

64. An example of this approach is Barman, *Brazil*, pp. 160–74.

FOUR ▲ Transition, 1833–41

1. Sir Charles J. F. Bunbury, who was visiting Rio at the time, describes this incident in "Narrativa de viagem," p. 39. Carlos Miguel joined the

army in 1824 at age 11, serving as an orderly to his father, general and later regent Francisco de Lima e Silva. Following the fatal encounter with Oliveira, Carlos Miguel was posted as military attaché in Belgium. After traveling in Europe and the United States, he returned to Brazil in 1842, whereupon he served under his brother Caxias in the campaign against rebels in Minas Gerais and then against the separatists in Rio Grande do Sul, where he died of fever in 1845 at age 32, having attained the rank of major. H. Vianna, *Contribuição*, pp. 192–95.

2. In this administrative transition the ministry of the empire assumed the public works functions of the old intendancy, and the city council took over regulation of markets and public accommodations.

3. AN IJ6 209 (SPC-Contabilidade) 2 Jan. 1838; IJ6 171 (OCP-C) 18 Aug. 1835. To put these income levels in the context of the require- ments for voting and membership in the national guard, military police soldiers met the 200$000 per year required of electors, and *pedestres* were above the 100$000 income required to vote in primary level.

4. AG PMERJ-CR, 14 Nov. 1833.

5. AN IJ6 177 (OCP-C), 28 July 1837.

6. AN GIFI 5B 517, 16 May 1833.

7. Mary Karasch discusses the apparent absence of violent slave rebel- lion in Rio in *Slave Life*, pp. 323–31, including the explanation that control was tight. On rural revolts see C. Moura, *Rebeliões de senzala*; and L. L. da G. Lima, *Rebeldia negra*.

8. RMJ, 1833, p. 24. The flexibility of urban slavery relative to the regi- mentation of the plantation is assessed in E. V. da Costa, *Da senzala*, pp. 227–40; and Mattoso, *Ser Escravo*, pp. 141–43, 147–48.

9. This is not to reduce the incident to the simplistic criteria of func- tionalist "rational choice" game theory, but to suggest that rationality is relative. For a comment on this issue see Scott, "Resistance without Pro- test," p. 450.

10. *Os escravos são homens, e as leis os compreendem*, RMJ, 1832, p. 11. The regulations of the Calabouço are in AN IJ6 165 (OCP-C), 15 Oct. 1831 and AN IJ6 173 (OCP-C), 2 Aug. 1836.

11. Richard Graham's assessment of the "family paradigm" governing both personal and political hierarchies helps explain the apparent con- tradictions of Feijó's "humanitarianism": "No dichotomy existed between force and benevolence: Each drew its meaning from the other. They simply represented two aspects of the same technique for controlling oth- ers" (*Patronage and Politics*, p. 24).

12. This is a Brazilian variation of Foucault's interpretation of the tran- sition to the modern world (*Discipline and Punish*, p. 55), and of Weber's ideas on the emergence of impersonal bureaucracies (*The Theory of Social and Economic Organization*, pp. 337–40). It also builds on Roberto Da Mat-

ta's characterization of the contrasting worlds of the house vs. the street in Brazilian culture (*A casa e a rua*, pp. 25–54) but sees both domains as governed by authoritarian hierarchies, one personal and patriarchal and the other impersonal and bureaucratic, which together combine to form the possibilities and limitations of life.

13. Three memos discussing the case of Rosa and Agapito are in AN IJ6 173 (OCP-C), 5, 8, and 16 Nov. 1836. The law making the slave traffic illegal was the specific measure that gave rise to the Brazilian phrase *para inglês ver*, "for the Englishman to see," meaning "for appearances' sake." Brazilian abolitionists later claimed that more than one million slaves were illegally imported after 1831, and by conservative estimates of the British government the number was 485,726; only about 11,000 became "free" Africans. See Bethell, *The Abolition*, pp. 388–93. The origin and fate of the "free" Africans is discussed in Robert Conrad, "Neither Slave nor Free."

14. As of 1836 there were 130 "free" Africans working on the prison project, and by 1840 there were 173 Calabouço prisoners on the job, along with 162 "free" Africans, who received a daily gratuity of 10 to 20 réis per day; RMJ, 1836, p. 28; 1840, p. 25.

15. AN IJ6 193 (CMP–Contabilidade), 22 Dec. 1835.

16. Four documents discussing this incident (the letter of transmission, the interrogation of Jacomo Rombo, the physicians' examination report, and the term of obligation Rombo was required to agree to) are in AN, GIFI 5B 425, 3 Jan. 1837. The original language of the phrase preceding the footnote number is *Também dizia algumas vezes que havia de tirar as teimas dos brancos.*

17. [*N*]*ada poderá conter senão o saudável terror.* Luis da Costa Franco e Almeida to Gustavo Adolfo d'Aguilar Pantoja, 3 Jan. 1837; AN, GIFI 5B 425. Several documents discussing the suspected January 1836 slave uprising in Niterói and Jacotinga, Rio Province, are in AN, Caixa 773, pacote 3. One of the murders Almeida referred to appears in the routine weekly report of police activity, as follows: "José, Angola slave of Bento José do Rego, arrested for the stabbing death of Antonio Simões Pereira, cashier at Rosário Street No. 198"; AN IJ6 173, (OCP-C), 3 Dec. 1836. A similar note on the case at hand is in a later weekly report: "Examination was conducted on the contusions and inflammations resulting from the whipping Jacome [sic] Rombo gave his slave Graciano, Mina"; AN IJ6 174 (OCP-C), 5 Jan. 1837.

18. AN GIFI 5B 425, 3 Jan. 1837.

19. A seminal essay on the contradictions between liberal ideology and hierarchical, segmented society in Brazilian history is Schwarz, "As idéias fora do lugar." See also E.V. da Costa, *The Brazilian Empire*, pp. 53–77.

20. AN IJ6, 177 (OCP-C), 12 June 1837.

21. AN IJ6 166 (OCP-C), 30 Jan. 1833.

22. RMJ, 1833, pp. 9–14, 22.

23. RMJ, 1834, p. 12.

24. RMJ, 1835, p. 31.

25. AN IJ6 173 (OCP-C), 26 Nov. 1836.

26. The 1838 census counted a total population for the município of Rio of 137,078 people, including 97,162 in the "urban" parishes, of which Lagoa was the smallest by far. The downtown Sacramento parish, divided into three judicial districts, had a total population of 24,256, in 3,843 families; *Relatório* do Ministro do Império, 1839, appendix.

27. AN GIFI 5B-452, 23 May, 27 May 1837.

28. AN GIFI 5B-452, 19 Apr., 2 May 1837. The low-cost housing district was along Alcântara Street [now Benedito Hipólito], present site of the Sambadrome built for carnival processions, in the neighborhood recognized as the birthplace of modern samba musical form.

29. AN IJ6 177 (OCP-C), 7 Aug., 1 Sept. 1837.

30. AN IJ6 186 (OCP-C), 12 Feb. 1838.

31. AN GIFI 5B-452 (Instituições policiais) 12 Apr. 1832.

32. *Galego* has long been derogatory Rio slang for Portuguese, which was also the nationality of the others in this small sample. AN IJ6 173 (OCP-C), 17 Nov. 1836; AN IJ6 187 (OCP-C), 18 June 1838; AN IJ6 190 (OCP-C), 22 Oct., 12 Nov. 1838.

33. AN IJ6 177 (OCP-C), 14, 15, 19 June 1837.

34. AN GIFI 6D-57, 18 Aug. 1837. *Botequim* was the name for the traditional tavern of Rio de Janeiro, site of much drinking and socializing over the decades—and an object of constant police surveillance.

35. RMJ, 1833, p. 25; AN IJ6 187 (OCP-C), 24 Sept. 1838.

36. AN IJ6 187 (OCP-C), 27 Sept. 1838; 190 (OCP-C), 2 Oct. 1838.

37. AN IJ6 187 (OCP-C), 28 Sept. 1838. Kidder and Fletcher reported that 171 beggars were rounded up in this 1838 sweep, and that over 40 were delivered to the navy (*Brazil and the Brazilians*, p. 128).

38. AN IJ6 190 (OCP-C), 5 Oct., 9 Nov. 1838.

39. AN IJ6 186 (OCP-C), 28 Apr. 1838.

40. Despite the literal translation of the name, the *Polícia Militar* should not be confused with the internal police of the army, called military police in the armies of the United States and other countries, which in Brazil is called the *Polícia do Exército*. Details on staffing levels, organization, and duty assignments are from AN IJ6 179, (CMP, Ofícios), 1831–48.

41. AN IJ6 193 (CMP-Contabilidade), 7 Nov. 1835.

42. AG PMERJ-CR, 1 Feb., 18 May, 7 July, 23 Aug., 13 Nov. 1833; 14 Nov. 1835.

43. AG PMERJ-CR, 19 Jan. 1835; AN GIFI 6D-57, 25 Sept. 1837. The Rocio Pequeno, later called Praça Onze de Junho, was long the site of such executions. It was obliterated by the construction of Avenida Presidente

Vargas in the 1940's, and now occupying the location is a monumental bust of Zumbi, martyred leader of the seventeenth-century fugitive slave community, the *quilombo* of Palmares.

44. AG PMERJ-CR, 2 Aug. 1836; AN GIFI 5B 452, 11 May 1837; AG PMERJ-CR, 23 Jan. 1840.

45. AG PMERJ-CR, 7, 14 Dec. 1840, 21 Jan. 1841.

46. AN IJ6 179, (CMP, Ofícios), 2 Oct. 1832.

47. AN IJ6 179, (CMP, Ofícios), 2 Oct. 1832; AG PMERJ-CR, 29 May, 18 June, 11 July 1835.

48. AG PMERJ-CR, 8, 9 Oct. 1833.

49. AN GIFI 5B-517, 22 Dec. 1834.

50. AG PMERJ-CR, 12 Jan. 1836, 13 Aug. 1836.

51. AG PMERJ-CR, 10 Feb. 1836.

52. A discussion of the concept of *condição*, in the context of the hierarchy of patron-client relations, is in R. Graham, *Patronage and Politics*, p. 30.

53. AN GIFI 6D-57, 15 Dec. 1837.

54. AN GIFI 5B-285 (Polícia da Corte), 6 May 1839.

55. RMJ, 1846, annex, includes a detailed list of the fountains, their sources of water, and the number of spigots at each. The number of households is from the 1838 census, cited in note 19. Not until the 1850's was piped water made available at public spigots numbering eventually in the hundreds throughout the city before indoor plumbing became widely available. On the importance of public fountains as centers of work and socializing see S. L. Graham, *House and Street*, pp. 24, 52–57.

56. AN GIFI 5B-285, 16 Apr. 1833.

57. AN GIFI 5F-241, 21 June, 25 June 1836.

58. AN GIFI 5F-241, 28 Aug. 1840. Caxias, who allowed Frias to escape in April 1832, had by 1840 been sent to pacify the province of Maranhão.

59. In 1835 Debret described the making and selling of the wax balls, called *limões de cheiro* ("smelly lemons"), as an important cottage industry for poor people in the weeks prior to Ash Wednesday and illustrates various aspects of the *entrudo* in *Viagem Pitoresca*, 1: 298–99. A description from 1846, including middle-class revelry indoors, is in Ewbank, *Life in Brazil*, pp. 96–103.

60. AG PMERJ-CR, 24 Feb. 1836.

61. For a modern statement attributing the longevity of the military police to its esprit de corps and internal discipline, see E. M. de Carvalho, "Criar novas polícias," pp. 12–14. The modern institution, in fact, claims to date its history from the establishment of the Guarda Real de Polícia in 1809, ignoring the dissolution of the Guarda after its troops mutinied and went on a rampage in July 1831.

62. AN GIFI 5B-285, 30 Sept. 1833.

63. AN GIFI 5B-285, 30 Oct. 1833. *Chimango* was slang for "varmint," i.e., an animal that it would be a waste of bullets to kill while hunting; Paulo Pereira Castro, "A 'experiência republicana,' 1831–1840," in Holanda, ed., *História geral*, tomo II, 2: 25.

64. AN GIFI 6H-17, 23 Jan. 1836. The continuing and general relevance of the challenge "Do you know who you're talking to?" (*Você sabe com quem está falando?*) in reinforcing the status hierarchy in Brazilian society is discussed in R. Da Matta, *O que faz o brasil, Brasil?*, p. 101.

65. AG PMERJ-CR, 9 June 1837. The thesis that some sectors of Brazilian society have seen militarization as a historical project is set forth in Hayes, *The Armed Nation*. Like most other treatments of the history of the Brazilian army and national guard, Hayes ignores the military police as a relevant focus of analysis.

66. AN Códice 773, pacote 3, 15 Jan. 1836; AN IJ6 187 (OCP-C), 11 July 1838. The national guard as a patronage network is a central theme of Uricoechea, *The Patrimonial Foundations*. On the same theme, and the military draft as instrument of control, see R. Graham, *Patronage and Politics*, pp. 27–30, 92–94, 225–26.

67. RMJ, 1835, p. 32; 1841, p. 36. The opposition press and politicians voiced similar complaints during these years that police patrol duty was unduly burdensome for national guardsmen; see Castro, *A milícia cidadã*, pp. 40–42.

68. The decree was dated 4 Feb. 1836. A printed copy is in AN IJ6 177 (OCP-C), 7 Mar. 1836.

69. RMJ, 1836, pp. 224–25.

70. AN IJ6 173 (OCP-C), 13 Feb. 1836.

71. AN IJ6 177 (OCP-C), 5 Feb. 1836.

72. *O Guarda Nacional* (Rio), 26 Feb. 1836, quoted in Castro, *A milícia cidadã*, p. 43.

73. RMJ, 1837, p. 27.

74. For a discussion of the "theater of elections," see R. Graham, *Patronage and Politics*, pp. 101–21.

75. AN GIFI 5B-285, 14 Mar. 1833. A contemporary illustration depicting the chaotic scene inside a church during a nineteenth-century election is in Flory, *Judge and Jury*, p. 47.

76. AG PMERJ-CR, 4 Apr. 1835. The political role of the *Sociedade Defensora* is discussed in Barman, *Brazil*, p. 165.

77. AN GIFI 5B-285, 14 Sept. 1833.

78. AG PMERJ-CR, 26 Sept. 1836.

79. AN GIFI 6D-57, 5 Nov. 1840; AG PMERJ-CR, 7, 8, 10 Sept. 1840. The violent politics of the period, particularly the notorious elections of September and October 1840, are discussed in Flory, *Judge and Jury*, pp. 169–70, and Barman, *Brazil*, pp. 208–9.

80. AG PMERJ-CR, 29 Oct. 1840.

81. M. de Q. M. Ribeiro, *Apontamentos*, pp. 29–32.

82. *Beleguim* is one of several printable pejorative or derogatory nicknames by which police soldiers and civilian police agents have been known in Rio, along with such epithets as *miganha, meirinho, milico, tira,* and *guarda.*

83. Aufderheide, "Order and Violence," p. 101.

84. ACD 1841, vol. 2 (Rio de Janeiro 1884), session of 20 July 1841, p. 264.

FIVE ▲ Maturity, 1842–65

1. ACD, 1841, vol. 3, pp. 627, 664, 725; Barman, *Brazil*, pp. 200–201, 207, 213; R. Graham, *Patronage and Politics*, p. 53.

2. RMJ, 1840, p. 15.

3. Justices of the peace continued to preside on the boards supervising local elections and were still charged with helping reduce the incidence of drunks and beggars on the streets. They could also adjudicate minor civil disputes, something like a small claims court (CLB-APL, 1841, pp. 75–95 [law of 3 Dec. 1841]). One reason the office of justice of the peace was not completely abolished was that it was established in principle by the constitution of 1824, and its extinction would have required a constitutional change (ACD 1841, vol. 3, p. 705). An annotated compendium of the major laws and regulations on police and judicial matters, from the code of criminal procedure of 1832 through the reform of 3 December 1841 and the next reform in September 1871, is Filgueiras Júnior, *Codigo do Processo.* Flory provides a litany of complaints about the justice of the peace in practice in *Judge and Jury*, pp. 131–36.

4. A. C. T. Bastos, *A Província*, p. 110.

5. Crimes over which the police had full jurisdiction, from investigation of the incident to sentencing and supervising punishment, included violations of municipal ordinances, which commonly included a curfew and prohibitions on vagrancy, loitering, public drunkenness, disturbing the peace, and gambling; and all crimes punished by fines up to 100 milréis, prison, banishment, or exile of up to six months, with the fine corresponding to up to half that time or without additional fine, or by three months in jail or public workshops where they existed. CLB-APL, 1832, pp. 156–57 (Article 12 of the Procedural Code); 1841, pp. 75–76, (Articles 4 and 5 of the judicial reform law).

6. Bueno, *Apontamentos*, pp. 4, 18–19, 186–89.

7. AN IJ6 199 (OCP-C), 11 May, 23 May 1842. As an example of the precedent set by such rulings originally issued locally for Rio de Janeiro, the explicit prohibition on justices of the peace assigning jail terms, in the exact wording of the internal memo of 23 May, was subsequently issued as

an *Aviso* with nationwide application; see Filgueiras Júnior, *Codigo do Processo*, 1: 444.

8. AN IJ6 212 (OCP-C), 13 Nov. 1849.

9. AN IJ6 293 (OCP-C), 10 May 1858; 483 (OCP-C), 12 Dec. 1858; 224 (Polícia-Contabilidade) 1 Mar. 1856. Considerable information is available about the activities and working conditions of hired slaves, but little on wage rates or on how much of their pay they were required to pass on to their owners; see M. R. N. da Silva, *Negro na rua*, pp. 143–46; and Karasch, *Slave Life*, pp. 185–213.

10. Each of the eight suburban hamlets of the municipality of Rio de Janeiro scattered beyond the central city—Inhaúma, Irajá, Jacarepaguá, Guaratiba, Campo Grande, Santa Cruz, Ilha do Governador, and Ilha de Paquetá—also became a police district with a subdelegado and minimal staff. Most reports of police staffing and activities focus on the central city, and unless explicitly noted the data presented here refer to the eight urban parishes, which became nine in 1854 when Santo Antonio was created out of sections of Sacramento, São José, and Santa Ana.

11. Demographic data to the ward level are from the manuscript census of 1849, discussed in Chapter 1, note 42.

12. ACD 1841 (21 July 1841), vol. 2, pp. 283–84.

13. AN IJ6 224 (Polícia-Contabilidade), 13 Feb. 1850.

14. AN IJ6 168 (Polícia-Contabilidade), 31 Dec. 1858; 205 (Polícia-Contabilidade), 9 Mar. 1858; 217 (OCP-C), 22 Jan. 1854; 224 (Polícia-Contabilidade), 13 Feb. 1850, 24 Dec. 1851.

15. RMJ, 11 Jan. 1850, annex, 1851, p. 19. Staffing and wages for 1865 are in AN IJ6 192 (CMP-Ofícios), 1 Jan. 1865. Police soldiers' pay was considerably better than that of regular army conscripts, who after a raise in 1842 received just $120 per day.

16. AN IJ6 192 (CMP-Ofícios), 1 Jan. 1865. In both 1849 and 1872 (the nearest censuses to 1865), 42 percent of the free male population of Rio was foreign born, and of those Portuguese were the overwhelming majority. New military police regulations in 1866 limited non-Brazilians to a maximum of one-third of the total corps membership.

17. AN GIFI 5B 285 (Polícia da Corte), 9 Mar. 1853; GIFI 6D 122 (Polícia da Corte), 6 June 1856. As in similar personnel cases and related documentation from police records, there is seldom mention of the skin color or other racial characteristics of soldiers, pedestres, or other staff. The casual observation of North American visitor Thomas Ewbank in 1846, that Rio's military police were "mostly colored," must be seen in relation to the virtual absence of African Americans in U.S. police forces of his time (*Life in Brazil*, p. 434).

18. AG PMERJ-OD, 12 Apr. 1866; Correspondência, 11 Apr. 1848.

19. AN IJ6 179 (CMP-Ofícios), 12 May 1847. The soldier's original offense was not specified in the petition.

20. AN IJ6 202 (OCP-C), 21, 22 Nov. 1844.

21. Kidder and Fletcher, *Brazil and the Brazilians*, p. 125; AN IJ6 211 (OCP-C), 7 July 1848.

22. AG PMERJ-CR, 5 May 1845.

23. One history of police institutions (Neder, Naro, and Silva, *A polícia na corte*) focuses unduly on the park watchmen, market inspectors, and other employees of the city administration in the 1831–71 period, thus missing much of the development of the civilian police and military police forces, which were subordinated directly to the national government.

24. ACD 1841 vol. 2 (Rio de Janeiro, 1884), session of 21 July 1841, p. 280; AN Caixa 777, pacote 1, 24 Mar. 1841; Caixa 780, pacote 1, 27 Jan. 1859. Data on the guard are in RMJ, 1850, appendix. See also Rodrigues, Falcón, and Neves, *A guarda nacional*.

25. AN IJ6 211 (OCP-C), 7 Aug. 1848.

26. AN IJ6 212 (OCP-C), 24, 27 Nov. 1849.

27. AN IJ6 214 (OCP-C), 22 Dec. 1851; 217 (OCP-C), 11 Feb. 1854.

28. Memos on this affair, dated as in text, are in AN IJ6 202 (OCP-C), Oct. 1844.

29. AG PMERJ-CR, 18 Jan. 1865.

30. RCP-RJ, 1838, annex to RMJ 1839, p. 27.

31. AG PMERJ-OD, 17 Dec. 1858.

32. AN IJ6 212 (OCP-C), 14 Sept. 1849.

33. ACD 1841, vol. 2 (21 July 1841), p. 276.

34. AN IJ6 202 (OCP-C), 11 Dec. 1844.

35. AN IJ6 212 (OCP-C), 13 Nov. 1849.

36. Twelve documents resulting from this case, including a statement from virtually every official directly involved, the minister of justice and minister of foreign affairs, who called the arrests "unjustifiable" and felt fortunate to avoid a formal diplomatic protest from Britain, as well as detailed statements from both arrestees, are in AN IJ6 214 (OCP-C), 4–17 Sept. 1850. At the time the British fleet was chasing slave-trading vessels into Brazilian ports, applying the Aberdeen Act, and threatening even more direct action to end the slave trade. On 12 July Queiroz had introduced into the Brazilian parliament the bill for which he is known in history, declaring the slave trade to be piracy, and it was approved on 4 September as this incident was unfolding. See Bethell, *Abolition*, pp. 327–41.

37. AN IJ6 215 (OCP-C), 10 Sept. 1851.

38. There were 58 such trials in Rio in 1850 involving 71 people, among them 17 Brazilians and 54 foreigners. Along with the 48 mentioned, 10 were tried for robbery, 6 for illegal weapons possession, 2 for fraud, 2 for illegal enslavement, 2 for vagrancy, and 1 for resisting arrest. Forty-four were acquitted (RMJ, 1852, annex). Flory discusses political and ideological aspects of the jury system in this period in *Judge and Jury*, esp. pp. 109–28, but there is no adequate study of the functioning of juries in

criminal cases and their social implications. Compared to the many arrests during day-to-day police operations, the few jury trials were reserved primarily for serious crimes.

39. AN IIIJ7, (Ofícios do Calabouço), 19 May 1845.

40. The ledger book is filed in the Arquivo Nacional in Rio de Janeiro as Códice 398, "Prisões no Rio, 1849–1850." It actually covers the period from 15 December 1849 to 15 December 1850, so for quantitative analysis I have taken the liberty of recording the last two weeks of 1849 as if they were in 1850 in order to make a complete calendar year. As a document internal to the police Secretariat, the ledger was not originally intended for eventual deposit in the National Archive, and it probably went there at some point by chance with other files. There is no record in the Archive of similar books for other years, nor is it known if other ledgers in the series are preserved elsewhere. Inquiries at the Museum of the Civil Police of Rio de Janeiro (successor to the nineteenth-century Secretariat) during 1987–88 yielded no results.

One reason for the gaps in the quantified version is that each original ledger entry is a brief text paragraph containing some standardized information and other details specific to each case, but not all categories of information for each entry. The disposition of each case, for all but 49 of the 1,676 total, was later recorded in the ledger margin next to the original entry, and tabulated in Appendix 4.4.

41. AN IJ6 211 (OCP-C), 27 Nov. 1848. The two designated pickup spots continue to be important points where public transportation routes make contact with pedestrian traffic in the old part of the city. The regulations also include a table of rates by zone. Near the downtown area cabs were to charge 1$000 per hour, 1$500 if it was raining—more than a full day's pay for a police soldier or free laborer. Beyond that area the rate rose to 2$000 per hour, and after 9 P.M. drivers were to reach a mutually acceptable agreement with their fare on the cost of the trip.

42. It is also possible that such conscription, grouped in a specific period, reflected the use of the draft as an instrument of political coercion during election time. For examples of such abuse of military conscription, see R. Graham, *Patronage and Politics*, pp. 92–93.

43. AN IJ6 217 (OCP-C), 20 Jan. 1854; 219 (OCP-C), 20 Jan. 1855.

44. AN IJ6 222 (OCP-C), 23 Feb. 1856.

45. On the general transition, see Foucault, *Discipline and Punish*. On the Auburn system (contrasted to the Pennsylvania system of permanent solitary confinement), see Rothman, *Discovery*, and Dumm, *Democracy and Punishment*. Progress reports on the prison construction appear in most minister of justice annual reports during the 1840's. On *libambos* earlier in the century, see Karasch, *Slave Life*, pp. 118–19, and on their elimination AN IIIJ7 42 (Ofícios do Calabouço), 26 Sept. 1844.

46. Karasch, *Slave Life*, p. 125 (and mentioned in Chapter 2).

47. AN III7 42, (Ofícios do Calabouço), 3 April 1845; IV7 2 (Calabouço-Matricula de Presos), 22 Mar. 1858. Claudina's original offense was not given.

48. RCP-RJ, 1863, annex to RMJ, 1863, p. 6; J. T. Bastos, *História da organização.*

49. These data are used here as a representative sample of the immense amount of data generated by Rio's police system after the 1850's, not all of which was regularly published or even preserved.

50. RCP-RJ, 1866, Annex to RMJ, p. 2.

51. RCP-RJ, 1863, p. 1; 1866, p. 2.

52. RCP-RJ, 1863, Annex to RMJ, p. 2.

53. AN IIIJ7, (Calabouço-Ofícios), 13 Jan., 20 Jan. 1845.

54. AN IJ6 214 (OCP-C), 6 Aug. 1850.

55. AN IJ6 214 (OCP-C), 14 Oct. 1850.

56. AN IJ6 219 (OCP-C), 13 Apr. 1855. This murder is mentioned in Gerson, *História das ruas*, p. 103.

57. AN IJ6 215 (OCP-C), 8 Mar. 1852; IIIJ7 42 (Calabouço, ofícios), 2 Sept. 1844.

58. AN IJ6 217 (OCP-C), 8 July, 29 July 1854.

59. AN IJ6 214 (OCP-C), 6 Aug. 1850; IJ6 215 (OCP-C), 25 Aug., 22 Oct. 1851; IJ6 485 (OCP-C), 27 Apr. 1859. According to Afro-Brazilian folk beliefs, by dying in the water that connected their homeland and their place of captivity, the souls of Africans could return home after death. For more on slave suicides see Karasch, *Slave Life*, pp. 316–20.

60. RCP-RJ, 1860 (annex to RMJ, 1861), p. 3.

61. The classic monograph on the Paraíba valley coffee era is Stein, *Vassouras.*

62. AN IJ6 483 (OCP-C), 19 July 1858. The French traveler F. Biard, who was passing through Rio when this incident took place, reported there were 60 soldiers involved in subduing the seven slaves (*Dois anos no Brasil*, p. 51).

63. AN IIIJ7 42 (Calabouço, Ofícios), 30 Jan. 1845; IJ6 484 (OCP-C), 1 Feb. 1859.

64. AN IJ6 516 (OCP-C), 14 Apr. 1862.

65. AN IJ6 212 (OCP-C), 13–15 June 1849.

66. In 1849 Haddock Lobo was in the early stages of a distinguished career in Rio de Janeiro politics and public health institutions. He was born in Portugal in February 1817 and emigrated to Rio as a young man, graduating from the medical college in 1842. While maintaining his medical practice for the rest of his life, he registered as a merchant, and served in a variety of public positions. In January 1848 he was appointed first alternate to the subdelegado of Engenho Velho and was later promoted to subdelegado. At the time of the batuque incident reported here, he was about to begin supervision of the first real census of the city, conducted in the

last half of 1849. Haddock Lobo later served several times on the city council of Rio between 1853 and 1864 and was a member of the commission charged with erecting the equestrian statue of Emperor Pedro I, Rio's first major monumental sculpture, in the Praça da Constituição, today the Praça Tiradentes. He died in Rio de Janeiro on 30 December 1869 at age 52. Today the main avenue through the neighborhood where he spent most of his life and career, formerly the caminho do Engenho Velho, is named Rua Haddock Lobo in his honor. See F. A. de N. Santos, "Haddock Lobo."

67. AN IJ6 212 (OCP-C), 2 Dec. 1849. A study of the Bahia revolt, which was betrayed by creole slaves who apparently feared police persecution in its aftermath and therefore suppressed within a few hours, is Reis, *Rebelião escrava*. For more on the various connotations of the Mina ethnic label, see Karasch, *Slave Life*, pp. 25–27, 284–85.

68. The etymology of these terms is uncertain, but *capoeira* is probably related to the standard Brazilian Portuguese name for second-growth brushland, derived from the Tupi linguistic elements *caá* (vegetation, forest) and *puêra* (that which has disappeared)—a place of hiding for fugitive slaves. A partridgelike bird typically inhabiting scrubland, the male of which aggressively resists intrusions into its territory by attacking and clawing rivals, is also called capoeira. While most discussions of capoeira suggest it is a uniquely Brazilian phenomenon, some modern sources, particularly those focusing on the Afro-Brazilian culture of Salvador, surmise it may have Angolan origins; see Kubik, *Angolan Traits*, pp. 29–31. An extended discussion of the etymological debates, including many bibliographical notes, is Rego, *Capoeira angola*, pp. 16–29.

Malta may be related to old Lisbon slang for itinerant laborers and street rowdies, who stereotypically were migrants from the island of Malta, or may denote the members' sticking together like the wax and tar sealing mixture of the same name. *Baderna* is still used in Brazil to refer to urban gangs or groups of people acting more or less in concert in public. Its origin is probably in the term for light ratlines used to secure the rigging of sailing ships and is used to denote a connecting and reinforcing link.

69. A. J. de M. Moraes Filho, *Festas e tradições*, pp. 459–60; A. M. de los Rios Filho, *O Rio de Janeiro Imperial*, pp. 53–54.

70. The German artist Rugendas, who visited Brazil in the 1820's, included an engraving of "Jogo de Capoeira" (reproduced in Karasch, *Slave Life*, 246) in his 1835 portfolio. Luiz Edmundo da Costa provides a fictionalized version of the image of the capoeira in the city in the late eighteenth century in *O Rio de Janeiro*, pp. 37–40. Since the 1940's it has reemerged as a major focus of folklore studies, as a system of physical training, and Brazil's contribution to the range of martial arts traditions from various parts of the world, and as public performance. Essays focusing on capoeira as athletic performance and folkloric tradition include Carneiro, *Capoeira*;

Cascudo, *Folclore*, pp. 179–89; B. Almeida, *Capoeira*; and Lewis, "Semiotic and Social Discourse."

71. AN IJ6 215 (OCP-C), 25 Aug. 1852.
72. AN IJ6 203 (OCP-C), 8 Apr. 1845.
73. AN IJ6 215 (OCP-C), 9 Oct. 1852.
74. AN IJ6 212 (OCP-C), 25 Apr. and 16 June 1849. Capim Square, obliterated by the construction of Avenida Presidente Vargas in the early 1940's, was located on Rua dos Andradas between Rua São Pedro and Rua General Câmara (formerly Sabão).
75. AN IJ6 212 (OCP-C), 13 Nov. 1849.
76. AN IJ6 217 (OCP-C), 20 Jan. 1854.
77. For wider-ranging discussions of slave resistance, see C. Moura, *Rebeliões da senzala*; Freitas, *Insurreições escravas*; L. L. da G. Lima, *Rebeldia negra*; and Silva and Reis, *Negociação e conflito*.

SIX ▲ Continuity, 1866–89

1. RMJ, 1870, annex, p. 91; 1871, annex, p. 78.
2. AN IIIJ7 94 (Ofícios do Calabouço), 5 Feb. 1873.
3. AN IIIJ7 94 (Ofícios do Calabouço), 9 Apr., 12 May 1873.
4. AN IIIJ7 91 (Ofícios do Calabouço), 28 May, 3 June 1874. As shown in Table 15, the 1872 census counted 37,567 slaves in the eleven urban parishes of the city, 16 percent of a total population of 228,734.
5. Azevedo, *O Rio de Janeiro*, p. 388. Staffing levels are in RMJ, various years.
6. The national guard was reorganized by law 2,395 of 20 Sept. 1873, by which it was "relieved of all service, except in the provinces of Mato Grosso and Rio Grande do Sul" (RMJ, 1877, p. 39).
7. See, e.g., the order by the chief of police for ward inspectors in Sacramento parish to desist from intervention in the regulation of business activities on Sundays (AN IJ6 (OCP-C), 3 Nov. 1869).
8. RCP-RJ, 1866, annex to RMJ, 1866, p. 6; AN IJ6 19 (Polícia-Avisos), 27 Sept. 1870.
9. RMJ, 1866, p. 1.
10. RMJ, 1861, p. 5; 1866, p. 28.
11. The regulations are in AN IJ6 195 (Polícia Militar-Contabilidade), 27 Jan. 1866, and in Decree 3,609 of 17 Feb. 1866. Staffing levels are from RMJ, various years.
12. RMJ, 1869, pp. 1, 48.
13. RMJ, 1877, p. 35; 1882, p. 39; RCP-RJ, 1884, annex to RMJ, 1884, pp. 6–7.
14. Modern reflections on this theme are in Da Matta, "Quest for Citizenship," pp. 307–35.
15. RMJ, 1878, p. 108.

16. *The Rio News*, 15 July 1880, p. 2; RCP-RJ, 1884, (annex to RMJ), p. 44.

17. AN IJ6 19 (Polícia-Avisos), 29 Sept. 1869; AG PMERJ-CR, 8 Oct. 1869; RCP-RJ, 1872, (annex to RMJ), p. 194; RCP-RJ, 1874, (annex to RMJ), p. 198.

18. AN IJ6 19 (Polícia-Avisos), 27 Nov. 1870; 518 (OCP-C), 24 Aug. 1871.

19. *The Rio News*, 15 July 1880, p. 2.

20. RMJ, 1885, pp. 5–6; Barreto Filho and Lima, *História* 3: 128–30. Public indignation over this incident helped push the police chief to resign in December 1884 and led to the extinction of the urban guard three months later.

21. Carvalho, "Criar novas polícias?" p. 13.

22. RMJ, 1886, p. 184, annex pp. 95–115.

23. *The Rio News*, 24 Oct. 1880, p. 2; RMJ 1877, p. 33.

24. RCP-RJ, 1884 (annex to RMJ), p. 19. "Secret expenses" consistently appear as a category in the accounts of the secretariat of police, but with few hints at what was accomplished by the monthly allocations of funds to secret agents at the discretion of the chief of police; AN IJ6 178 (Polícia-Contabilidade), 1868–76.

25. RMJ, 1888, p. 2. The annual salary for the newly institutionalized secret agents was to be 2:400$000; RMJ, 1890, pp. 7, 96.

26. Lomonaco, *Al Brasile*, p. 47

27. AG PMERJ-OD, 3 Nov. 1886.

28. AG PMERJ-OD, 19 Oct. 1886.

29. AG PMERJ-OD, 4 Jan., 22 Jan. 1887.

30. AG PMERJ-OD, 17 Sept. 1881; AN IJ6 264 (Polícia Militar-Ofícios), 26 Mar., 24 Apr. 1888.

31. AG PMERJ-OD, 28 Nov. 1886; 22 Aug. 1887; 4 Dec. 1887.

32. AN IJ6 264 (OCP-C), 24 Mar. 1888.

33. AN IJ6 264 (OCP-C), 27 Mar. 1888. See also the detailed new regulations of the corps issued 5 Apr. 1889, in RMJ, 1889, annex, pp. 41–92.

34. AG PMERJ-OD, 21 Nov. 1889; 6 Jan. 1890; 23 Jan. 1890.

35. The parliamentary history of these efforts is in Mello, "O poder judiciário," pp. 141–48. See also Rezende, "Polícia administrativa," p. 412.

36. The annotated text of the reform law and its enabling regulations are in Filgueiras Júnior, *Código do processo*, 3: 722–812. Outside Rio and major provincial capitals, the first level of judicial authority was the *juiz municipal*, one level below the *juiz de direito*.

37. See Barman and Barman, "Role of the Law Graduate," and Pang and Seckinger, "Mandarins." On the importance of judgeships in the patronage network, R. Graham, *Patronage and Politics*, p. 219.

38. Roberto Kant de Lima analyzes the continuing importance of the

inquérito and the persistence of an informal adjudicative and punitive role for Rio's modern police, in "Legal Theory," pp. 79–84, 164–72, 209–45.

39. RMJ 1887, pp. 138–39. Decree 463 and 464, of 7 June 1890, are in RMJ 1890, pp. 71–96. In the same reforms, the old cloth sashes of office were replaced by modern metal badges. By another change in 1892, the office of subdelegado was abolished, and subsequently only the title of delegado was used for district-level police administrators; "Centenário da Polícia," p. 12.

40. See, e.g., the extended discussion of this problem in the RCP-RJ, 1874, annex to RMJ, 1874, pp. 184–91.

41. Police jail and House of Detention data are collected in Appendix 5.

42. A. C. T. Bastos, *A província*, p. 161.

43. Other reasons to choose 1875 for this synchronic survey are that there is a reasonably complete set of data available for that year on the various parts of the system, and the proximity to the 1872 census facilitates comparisons to the total population. The data in this section come from the statistical appendices of the annual reports of the minister of justice, chief of police, director of the house of correction, and military police commander, and percentages may not total 100 due to rounding. Similar quantitative information was collected and published for these and many other aspects of police, court, and prison activity from the 1860's on but seldom in consistent time series. A more detailed presentation of various fragmentary and interrupted data series would lead to digital overload and would not fundamentally change the argument that the vast majority of police actions were directed at controlling minor violations of public order.

44. Although *galés* was not formally abolished until the new republican penal code was issued in 1890, less than half a dozen people per year sentenced to *galés* entered the Rio House of Correction during the last decades of the empire on average, and like many others in that prison for major crimes, they came from surrounding provinces as well as the city proper.

45. RMJ, 1878, p. 89, emphasis in original. On the Pennsylvania versus Auburn prison regimes, see Rothman, *Discovery*, pp. 79–108.

46. RMJ, 1888, p. 126.

47. RMJ, 1886, pp. 125–26; 1888, p. 2.

48. Support for that impression also comes from data on all people sentenced for major crime to serve time in the Rio House of Correction from its formal opening in 1850 through 1869. In those two decades 1,099 people entered the prison, an average of 55 per year (including some from the provinces surrounding the city of Rio). Of the total, only 506 (46 percent) were Brazilians, and of the foreigners, 437 (40 percent) were Portuguese nationals; RMJ, 1870, statistical appendix.

49. AG PMERJ-ODet, 31 July, 24 Nov. 1873.

50. AG PMERJ-ODet, 21 Mar., 26 June 1878; Barreto Filho and Lima, *História*, 3: 103.

51. One unexplained anomaly in the reported crimes for 1875 is the 56 cases of manslaughter (*homicídio involuntário*). In thirteen other years for which the police chief listed reported crimes in his annual report, including complete series for 1836–40 and 1862–65, no other cases of manslaughter appear. The 1875 figure may include all unexplained deaths in the city, many of which were reported in other years, but not necessarily listed as suspected involuntary homicide.

52. For the city of São Paulo minor infractions made up 78 percent of arrests in 1892–96, increasing to 86 percent in 1912–16. This led Boris Fausto to conclude that São Paulo police "showed an intense concern for public order" over crimes against person or property; *Crime e cotidiano*, pp. 33–34. Tracing aggregate data in major United States cities from 1860 to 1920, Monkonnen found that victimless public order offenses accounted for a high proportion of arrests earlier in the period (63 percent in 1880), but that such police activity eventually declined on a per capita basis in favor of concern for crimes against person and property; *Police in Urban America*, pp. 84–85, 103.

53. *Jornal do Comércio*, 9 Jan. 1880, p. 3. The full text of the tax regulations, which imposed similar taxes on railway and steamship fares over the entire country but on city tramways only in Rio de Janeiro, is in *The Rio News*, 24 Dec. 1879, p. 2.

54. For a discussion of such epithets with the recognition that there was more to pre-modern rebellions than atavistic outbursts, see Huppert, *After the Black Death*, pp. 80–100.

55. *The Rio News*, 5 Jan. 1880, p. 2; RMJ, 1880, p. 4

56. This is also the thesis of the most complete modern analysis of the affair, S. L. Graham, "The Vintem Riot."

57. *The Rio News*, 5 Jan. 1880, p. 2; 24 Apr. 1880, p. 1. In percentage terms, the fixed-sum tax would be least burdensome for Jardim Botânico passengers, who already paid $400 per ride from downtown to the southern suburbs, compared to $100 and $200 fares on the Vila Isabel, São Cristóvão, and Carris Urbanos lines. Likewise the company, owned by North American capitalists, could better afford to absorb the tax rather than charge its riders for it.

58. This is the literal name of the military police *batalhão de choque*, which also might be translated "confrontation battalion." For an analysis of nonstandard forms of mass political participation in the early republic, focusing on the popular revolt against compulsory smallpox vaccination in 1904, see Carvalho, *Os bestializados*.

59. The complex of army resentments and disputes, known collectively

as the "military question," is often cited as contributing to the decline of the monarchy during the 1880's. See Costa, *The Brazilian Empire*, pp. 212–14; and Torres, *A democracia coroada*, pp. 454–59.

60. *The Rio News*, 5 Nov. 1883, p. 2. This issue reproduces lengthy reports on the incident from the Rio newspapers *Gazeta de Notícias*, *Jornal do Comércio*, and *Folha Nova*.

61. Melo's statement of his version is reproduced in *The Rio News*, 15 Nov. 1883, pp. 3–4. The closing of the case is reported in *The Rio News*, 3 Dec. 1884, p. 5, and 5 Jan. 1885, p. 5.

62. According to Euclides da Cunha, who was a student about to enter the military academy in Rio when this incident took place, the leader of the assassination squad was Captain Moreira César, who gained notoriety and martyrdom in the campaign against the backlanders at Canudos in 1897 (*Os Sertões*, p. 263). Other details are in Hahner, *Poverty and Politics*, pp. 55–56; and Barreto Filho and Lima, *História da polícia*, 3: 120–24.

63. Koseritz, *Imagens*, pp. 233–35, 238–39; Dent, *A Year*, p. 190. Some of the government authorities' predecessors had used the same refuge during the uprising of July 1832 discussed in Chapter 3.

64. RCP-RJ, 1883, annex to RMJ, 1883.

65. The estimate of the number of slaves at the time of abolition is from Soares, "Urban Slavery," p. 449. The increase and composition of the *cortiço* population is discussed in Hahner, *Poverty and Politics*, pp. 25–29.

66. RCP-RJ, 1872, pp. 22–23, annex to RMJ, 1872.

67. RCP-RJ, 1875, p. 184, annex to RMJ, 1875.

68. Like his predecessors following similar efforts, the chief declared capoeira "nearly extinct, except for an isolated act here and there." RCP-RJ, 1878, pp. 31–32, annex to RMJ, 1878.

69. Lomonaco, *Al Brasile*, pp. 47–48. Reporting on a battle between gangs in Carioca Square, an English-language newspaper speculated on the etymology of capoeira, "a most comprehensive word. It includes jungle or the aftergrowth of the virgin forest, a bird, a species of cage for fowls, and finally the gentlemen of Rio who try whether their knives are well sharpened on the stomachs of passersby" (*The Rio News*, 15 Mar. 1885, pp. 2, 5).

70. RMJ, 1887, p. 7.

71. Allain, *Rio de Janeiro*, pp. 271–72.

72. Dent, *A Year*, p. 239; *The Rio News*, 25 June 1880, p. 2.

73. AG PMERJ-OD, no. 188, 5 Aug. 1887.

74. AN IJ6 264 (Polícia Militar-Ofícios), 27 Mar. 1888.

75. On the Black Guard, see Silva, *Queixas*, pp. 68–69; Freyre, *Ordem e Progresso*, 1: 13; and Needell, "The *Revolta*," p. 259.

76. For his toughness, Ferraz acquired the nickname "the steel goatee" (*o cavanhaque de aço*). The acquisition of capoeira skills was the fashion

among young dandies of the elite, including "Juca" Reis, son of the count of Matosinhos, owner of *O País* newspaper; José Maria da Silva Paranhos, future minister of foreign affairs and baron of Rio Branco; republican conspirator and future Provisional President Floriano Peixoto, during his days as a military cadet; and Sampaio Ferraz himself. See Ribeiro, *Crónicas*, pp. 29–33; Rego, *Capoeira*, pp. 301–8; Neder, Naro, and da Silva, *A polícia*, pp. 238–40; Hahner, *Poverty and Politics*, pp. 57–60; Carvalho, *Os bestializados*, pp. 23, 41.

77. The relevant articles 402–404 of the 1890 code are in RMJ, 1890, pp. 252–53. The thesis that the elite reduced the threat of capoeira in this period through cooptation rather than primarily by repression is set forth in Adamo, "The Broken Promise," pp. 247–51. Formal criminalization is probably why capoeira appears as a specific reason for imprisonment in Recife only after the enactment of the 1890 code; see Huggins, *From Slavery*, p. 124. On the continuation of capoeira activity in the early years of the republic, see Silva, *As queixas*, pp. 116–18. An essay on the change in the public image of capoeira, concluding that as it became better known in the 1950's it "could become, in fact, our national game," is Galvão, "Reabilitação."

78. For further consideration of the intrusion of the state into master-slave relations, see Chalhoub, *Visões*, pp. 192, 271 n. 58.

SEVEN ▲ Conclusion

1. On urban slavery generally, see Mattoso, *Ser escravo*, pp. 130, 141–42. For Rio, see Karasch, *Slave Life*.

2. Rio was a large city for Brazil at the time, and important in economic, administrative, and political terms, so it is an appropriate place to investigate the mechanisms of repression and their application. Some generalizations about Rio would hold true for other large cities, but some would not—even less so for smaller interior towns, and less than that for the countryside. There is much room for comparative investigation, and if future research reveals the degree to which this assessment of Rio de Janeiro is generalizable (or how much it must be altered or redrawn for Rio itself), one of my objectives will be realized. I have collected detailed material for one provincial capital, analyzed in "The Brazilian 'Judicial Police.'" Although Florianópolis, Santa Catarina was a town of some 12,000 inhabitants, its police institutions resembled a miniature version of those in Rio de Janeiro, and victimless public order offenses were the focus of their attention.

On early institutional developments in Recife, see Carvalho, "Hegemony and Rebellion," pp. 75–105. A study of patterns of imprisonment in Recife from 1860 through the 1920's also shows that public order violations predominated and argues, though without direct evidence, that arrestees were used to meet periodic increases in labor demand by the sugar economy of the region (Huggins, *From Slavery*, pp. 77–108). Despite the continued use of convicts and slaves under disciplinary detention for labor on public works in Rio de Janeiro, there is no hint that policing and rates of arrest were directly related to labor demand in the regional economy.

A history of police institutions in São Paulo from the 1820's to the 1920's, stressing the repressive mission and the internal discipline of the militarized forces but not exploring the activity of police on patrol or patterns of arrest, is Fernandes, *Política e segurança*. In a major study of São Paulo from the 1880's through the 1910's, Boris Fausto shows that the police instigated pre-trial proceedings (*inquéritos*) only for some 10 percent of arrestees, leading him to conclude that most police activity was directed at social control rather than at apprehending those who committed criminal acts (*Crime e cotidiano*, pp. 31–33).

3. What happened in Rio often set a precedent for the rest of the country, but the reverse was seldom true. One exception was the law prescribing death for slaves who killed or seriously injured their owner or the owner's immediate family or overseers—a direct response to the Malê slave uprising in Bahia in 1835, analyzed in Reis, *Rebelião escrava*.

4. For a characterization of the lower-class majority population of Rio at the beginning of the twentieth century, see Carvalho, *Os Bestializados*, pp. 38–39.

5. In terms James Scott has analyzed with reference to peasants, slaves, and members of subordinate castes, the system of domination produced the "official transcript," both the historical record and the ideology of appropriate versus unacceptable behavior, and "on those occasions when subordinate groups do put in an appearance, their presence, motives, and behavior are mediated by the interpretation of dominant elites" (*Domination*, p. 87). The objective of what Scott aptly terms the "arts of resistance" was "not to overthrow or transform a system of domination but rather to survive" ("Resistance without Protest," pp. 417, 424).

6. For an exploration of this theme, see R. Graham, *Britain*.

7. For a study of the way Rio de Janeiro's civilian police structure functions today as disciplinary agent, centered on the precinct-level delegados, see Kant de Lima, "Legal Theory."

8. Foucault, *Discipline and Punish*, pp. 73–74.

9. It has become a commonplace in the historiography of race relations to point to such "spongyness" to help explain the continuation of pervasive but informal racism in Brazil. See Degler, *Neither Black nor White*; and Hasenbalg, *Discriminação*.

10. For interpretations of these cultural mechanisms, see Da Matta, *O que faz*, p. 101.

11. A richly nuanced study of this process is R. Graham, *Patronage and Politics*.

12. The contrast between the personalized, supportive hierarchy of the house and the hostile and impersonal world of the street in Brazilian urban culture is developed by Freyre, *Sobrados e Mucambos*, pp. 57–86 and analyzed for domestic servants in nineteenth-century Rio de Janeiro by S. L. Graham, *House and Street*. It is also the theme of Da Matta, *A casa e a rua*, pp. 25–54. While I recognize the distinction is important, Da Matta's generalizing language obscures the specificity of his perspective: that of the middle-class white male. In nineteenth-century Rio de Janeiro, the vast majority of the population was people who were not middle-class white males, and for many of them Da Matta's calm, protective, and nurturing world of the house could have been no more than an elusive ideal.

13. Weber, *The Theory*, pp. 329–41.

14. A full consideration of Foucault's litany of the institutional horrors emblematic of the modern world would move beyond the prison of *Discipline and Punish* to the mental asylum of *Madness*, and on to the hospital of *The Birth*.

15. Discussing Italian unification in the late nineteenth century (which provides some parallels with nineteenth- and early twentieth-century Brazil), Gramsci explains: "The supremacy of a social group is manifested in two ways: through 'domination' [*dominio*], and through 'intellectual and moral leadership' [*direzione intellettuale e morale*, usually translated as 'hegemony']. A social group which strives to 'liquidate' or to subjugate adversary groups, even by armed force, exercises domination; it exercises hegemony over similar or allied groups" (*Il Risorgimento*, p. 70). For an assessment of how Weber's views on these questions converge with those of Gramsci, see Bocock, *Hegemony*, pp. 83–93. See also Femia, *Gramsci's Political Thought*, pp. 47–49; and Williams, "The Concept of 'Egemonia,'" pp. 590–91.

16. R. Graham, in *Patronage and Politics*, has demonstrated that a search for programmatic consistency or ideological coherence in the nineteenth-century political groupings is illusory. Fundamentally, the two parties were elaborate and competing, but occasionally intertwined, patronage networks. On liberalism in theory and practice in the period, see Costa, *The Brazilian Empire*, pp. 53–77; and Santos, "Liberalism in Brazil."

Bibliography

From the establishment of the intendancy of police in 1808 through the end of the empire in 1889, the police system of the city of Rio de Janeiro was administered directly by the national government, and from 1831 by the ministry of justice. A municipal council for Rio was established in 1834, and it subsequently took administrative and regulatory responsibility for public works, transportation, markets, building regulations, and public health measures. The city council hired guards to watch over public parks and to protect and enforce the orders of tax collectors and market inspectors. (The collections of the archive of the city of Rio de Janeiro—AGCRJ—thus contain some information relevant to this study.) Policing, however, along with the court and prison system, remained under central government control. The justices of the peace in the 1830's reported to the minister of justice through the chief of police. From its establishment in 1831 the commander of the military police in Rio reported directly to the minister of justice. And with the judicial reform of 1841 the much-strengthened chief of police of Rio reported directly to the minister of justice. This meant that the administrative offices of the ministry, and often the minister himself, received frequent and detailed correspondence and summary reports from the two main branches of the city's police system.

These internal memoranda (*ofícios*) include a wide range of information on personnel matters, territorial jurisdiction, institutional rivalries within the police system as well as incidents police dealt with on the streets, from political riots and slave revolts to begging, vagrancy, and curfew violation. By provisions of the 1841 judicial reform, tightened in 1865, the chief of police was required to submit periodic reports of activities within his administrative jurisdiction, including patterns of arrest and judicial actions, "notable incidents" like fire, murder, and major theft, and information on the prison population and conditions. When the memoranda requested an interpretation of regulations or instructions on how to proceed in a case at hand, the filed copies often include notations of the response from the chief administrative officer of the ministry of justice or from the minister himself. These documents thus provide information on particular events and chronic conditions the police considered noteworthy, as well as the interpretations various officials gave to such matters and the response of the highest authorities.

As it happens, from the time of its establishment in 1838, the national archive of Brazil, located in Rio de Janeiro, has also been an administrative dependency of the ministry of justice. At the time of its creation it began to gather the records already piling up in government offices, particularly in the judicial system of which the police were considered an extension. After 1838 the national archive became the eventual destination of immense files of memoranda and reports on the internal workings and day-to-day activities of Rio's police. That rich and varied collection of documents, including internal memoranda, instructions (*avisos*), interagency correspondence (*correspondência*), budgets and financial accounts (*contabilidade*), and periodic reports (*relatórios*) is a main source of primary information for this study.

The minister of justice, like other members of the imperial cabinet, was expected to submit a formal accounting of his activities at the opening of each session of the parliament. Those printed reports, which become more elaborate and detailed in the course of the century, are extant for most years since 1831. Because members of parliament were personally concerned with security and public order in Rio de Janeiro, and because the minister of justice was responsible for the police system of the city, his reports contain considerable information and commentary relevant to this study. The minister of justice also supervised the activities of the national guard, so his reports also include data on that institution while it was involved in policing Rio de Janeiro.

The annual reports of the chief of police and commander of the military police were intended to provide information on which the minister could base his own general report, and they often include details which the minister later summarized or left out of his own version. Before mid-century most of the annual reports of the chief and the commander that have been preserved exist only in the manuscript form submitted to the ministry of justice. Later such reports were often (but not always) appended to the printed version of the minister's report to parliament. The same is true for reports on jails and prisons, the activities of criminal courts, and other activities falling generally within the purview of the ministry of justice.

Another important documentary collection for this study is the internal archive of Rio de Janeiro's military police (AG PMERJ), which includes considerable but not complete chronological files dating from 1831. In addition to memoranda and instructions received from the ministry of justice (the other end of the exchange received by the ministry and preserved in the national archive), there are general orders and statements of policy issued periodically (in military parlance, the order of the day, *ordem do dia*) and more specific instructions to patrols and detachments (order of detail, *ordem de detalhe*), as well as information on personnel matters, posting, and disciplinary actions in the corps.

To these archival materials and printed annual reports have been added the debates in parliament related to issues of concern to this study, published collections of laws and decrees, and press reports. Material that also might be considered primary is the published library of annotated versions of the criminal code, the code of criminal procedure, the reform laws of 1841 and 1871 and their implementing legislation, related decrees and regulations. Some of these were intended as teaching material for the two law schools established in 1827 (in Recife and São Paulo), and others were intended as procedural guides and reference works for authorities from the lower court judge and the chief of police to the ward inspector. They are included in the following list of published materials, unpublished theses, and serial publications consulted.

Years given in brackets after some entries are original dates of publication. See p. 305 for abbreviations used below.

A.P.D.G. *Sketches of Portuguese Life, Manners, Costume and Character.* London, 1826.

Abreu, Maurício de A. *Evolução urbana do Rio de Janeiro.* Rio de Janeiro, 1987.

"Abreviada demonstração dos trabalhos da polícia em todo o tempo que a serviu o Desembargador do Paço Paulo Fernandes Viana." *RIHGB*, 55:1 (1892), 373–80.

Abu-Luighold, Lila. "The Romance of Resistance: Tracing Transformations of Power Through Bedouin Women." *American Ethnologist* (1989), 41–55.

Adamo, Sam. "The Broken Promise: Race, Health, and Justice in Rio de Janeiro, 1890–1940." Ph.D. diss., Univ. of New Mexico, 1983.

Agassiz, Luis, and Elizabeth Agassiz. *A Journey in Brazil.* Boston, 1868.

Albuquerque, Francisco de Paula d'Almeida. *Breves reflexões retrospectivas, políticas, moraes e sociaes sobre o Império de Brazil.* Paris, 1854.

Albuquerque, Manoel Maurício de. "A propósito da rebelião e trabalho escravo," *Encontros com a civilisação brasileira*, 5 (Nov. 1978), 79–90.

Alencastro, Luiz-Felipe de. "Prolétaires et Esclaves: Immigrés Portugais et

Captifs Africains a Rio de Janeiro, 1850–1872." *Cahiers du CRIAR*, 4 (1984), 119–56.

Alford, Robert, and Roger Friedland. *Powers of Theory: Capitalism, the State, and Democracy.* Cambridge, Eng., 1985.

Algranti, Leila Mezan. *O feitor ausente: Estudos sobre a escravidão urbana no Rio de Janeiro, 1808–1822.* Petropólis, 1988.

———. "Slave Crimes: The Use of Police Power to Control the Slave Population of Rio de Janeiro." *Luso-Brazilian Review*, 25:1 (1988), 27–48.

Allain, Emile. *Rio de Janeiro, quelques données sur la capital et sur l'administration du Brésil.* Rio de Janeiro, 1886.

Almeida, Bira. *Capoeira, a Brazilian Art Form.* Richmond, Calif., 1982.

Almeida, Candido Mendes de, ed. *Codigo philippino; ou, ordenações e leis do reino de Portugal . . . décima quarta edição segundo a primeira de 1603 e a nona de Coimbra de 1824 . . . .* Rio de Janeiro, 1870.

Almeida, José Maria d', and Araujo Corrêa Lacerda. *Diccionario Encyclopedico ou novo diccionario da lingua portugueza.* 3d ed., 2 vols. Lisbon, 1868.

Almeida, Manuel Antônio de. *Memórias de um sargento de milícias.* São Paulo, 1987 [1853].

Almeida Júnior, João Mendes de. *O processo criminal brazileiro.* 2d ed., 2 vols. Rio de Janeiro, 1911.

Alonso, Anibal Martins. *Poder de polícia.* Rio de Janeiro, 1954.

Andrade, Octacílio de Oliveira. "A embriaguez no direito penal brasileiro," *Revista do IMESC* (São Paulo), 4:1 (1981), 35–41.

Andrews, Christopher Columbus. *Brazil, its Conditions and Prospects.* New York, 1887.

Araujo, Elysio de. *Estudo histórico sobre a polícia da capital federal.* Rio de Janeiro, 1898.

Assis, Joaquim Maria Machado de. *Esaú e Jacó.* Brasília, 1973 [1904].

Aufderheide, Patricia Ann. "Order and Violence: Social Deviance and Social Control in Brazil, 1780–1840." Ph.D. diss., Univ. of Minnesota, 1975.

Autran, Manoel Godofredo de Alencastro. *Código do processo criminal.* Rio de Janeiro, 1881.

Azevedo, Aluísio. *O cortiço.* 9th ed. Rio de Janeiro, 1943 [1890].

Azevedo, Celia Maria Marinho de. *Onda negra, medo brando; O negro do imaginário das elites—século XIX.* Rio de Janeiro, 1987.

Azevedo, Moreira de. "Motim político de 3 de abril de 1832 no Rio de Janeiro," *RIHGB*, 37:2 (1874), 367–81.

———. *O Rio de Janeiro, sua história, monumentos, homens notaveis, usos e curiosidades.* Rio de Janeiro, 1877.

———. "Os tiros no theatro: Motim popular no Rio de Janeiro." *RIHGB*, 36 (1873), 349–58.

———. "Sedição militar de julho de 1831 no Rio de Janeiro." *RIHGB*, 37:2 (1874), 179–90.
———. "Sedição militar na Ilha das Cobras em 1831." *RIHGB*, 34 (1871), 276–92.
Azevedo, Vincente de Paula. "O centenário do código criminal." *Revista dos Tribunais*, 77 (1931), 441–61.
Bailey, Victor, ed. *Policing and Punishment in Nineteenth Century Britain*. New Brunswick, N.J., 1981.
Barman, Roderick J. *Brazil, The Forging of a Nation, 1798–1852*. Stanford, Calif., 1988.
Barman, Roderick and Jean Barman. "The Role of the Law Graduate in the Political Elite of Imperial Brazil." *Journal of Inter-American Studies and World Affairs*, 18:4 (Nov. 1976), 423–50.
Barreiros, Eduardo Canabrava. *Atlas da evolução urbana da cidade do Rio de Janeiro*. Rio de Janeiro, 1965.
Barreto Filho, Mello and Hermeto Lima. *História da polícia do Rio de Janeiro*. 3 vols. Rio de Janeiro, 1939–43.
Barroso, Gustavo. *História militar do Brasil*. 2d ed. São Paulo, 1938.
Bastos, Aureliano Cândido Tavares. *A província*. 2d ed. São Paulo, 1937 [1870].
Bastos, Cassiano Cândido Tavares. *Guia dos delegados e subdelegados de polícia*. Rio de Janeiro, 1886.
———. *Guia dos inspectores de quarteirão*. Rio de Janeiro, 1886.
Bastos, Cassiano Machado Tavares. *Estatistica criminal na República*. Rio de Janeiro, 1910.
Bastos, José Tavares. *História da organização da estatistica criminal no Brazil*. Rio de Janeiro, 1930.
Bayley, David H. *Patterns of Policing: A Comparative International Analysis*. New Brunswick, N.J., 1985.
———, ed. *Police and Society*. Beverly Hills, Calif., 1977.
Beattie, J. M. *Crime and the Courts in England, 1660–1800*. Princeton, N.J., 1986.
———. "The Criminality of Women in Eighteenth-Century England." *Journal of Social History*, 8:4 (Summer 1975), 80–116.
Beaurepaire-Rohan, Henrique de. *Diccionário de vocábulos brazileiros*. Rio de Janeiro, 1889.
Behlmer, George K. *Child Abuse and Moral Reform in England, 1870–1908*. Stanford, Calif., 1982.
Benevides, Maria Victoria. *Violência, povo e polícia*. São Paulo, 1983.
Berger, Paulo. *Bibliografia do Rio de Janeiro de viajantes e autores estrangeiros, 1531–1980*. Rio de Janeiro, 1980.
———. *As freguesias do Rio antigo, vistas por Noronha Santos*. Rio de Janeiro, 1965.

———. *Dicionário histórico das ruas do Rio de Janeiro.* Rio de Janeiro, 1974.

Bergstresser, Rebecca B. "The Movement for the Abolition of Slavery in Rio de Janeiro, Brazil, 1880–1885." Ph.D. diss., Stanford Univ., 1985.

Berkhofer, Robert F. *A Behavioral Approach to Historical Analysis.* New York, 1969.

Bethell, Leslie. *The Abolition of the Brazilian Slave Trade.* Cambridge, Eng., 1970.

———, ed. *The Cambridge History of Latin America.* 5 vols., vol. 3, *From Independence to c. 1870.* Cambridge, Eng., 1985.

Biard, Francois Auguste. *Dois anos no Brasil.* São Paulo, 1945 [1862].

Black, Donald. *The Behavior of Law.* New York, 1976.

Blackwelder, Julia K. "Urbanization, Crime, and Policing: Buenos Aires, 1880–1914." In Johnson, ed., *The Problem of Order in Changing Societies,* pp. 65–88.

Blake, Augusto Vitorino Alves do Sacramento. *Diccionário bibliográfico brasileiro.* 7 vols. Rio de Janeiro, 1883–1902.

Bocock, Robert. *Hegemony.* Chichester, Eng., 1986.

Bordua, David, ed. *The Police: Six Sociological Essays.* New York, 1967.

Boschi, Renato Raul, ed. *Violência e cidade.* Rio de Janeiro, 1982.

Boyer, Paul S. *Urban Masses and Moral Order in America, 1820–1920.* Cambridge, Mass., 1978.

Brandão, Berenice Cavalcante, Ilmar Rohloff de Mattos, and Maria Alice Rezende de Carvalho. *A polícia e a força policial no Rio de Janeiro.* Série Estudos–PUC/RJ no. 4. Rio de Janeiro, 1981.

Brazil, Congresso, Câmara dos Deputados. *Anais do parlamento brasileiro, 1826–1889.* Rio de Janeiro, annual publication.

Brazil, Congresso. *Coleção da leis do Brasil, 1826–1889.* Rio de Janeiro, annual publication.

Brazil, Directoria Geral de Estastística. *Recenseamento da população do Imperio do Brazil a que se prodeceu no dia 1º de agosto de 1872.* Rio de Janeiro, 1873–76.

Brazil, Ministério da Justiça. *Relatório.* 1831–90

Brazil, Serviço Nacional de Recenseamento. *Resumo histórico dos inquéritos censitários realizados no Brasil.* Documentos Censitários, série B, no. 4. Rio de Janeiro, 1951.

Briggs, Frederico Guilherme. *The Brasilian Souvenir: a Selection of the Most Peculiar Costumes of the Brazils.* Rio de Janeiro, n.d. (c. 1849).

Bueno, José Antonio Pimenta. *Apontamentos sobre o processo criminal brasileiro.* 2d ed., Rio de Janeiro, 1857.

Bunbury, Charles J. F. "Narrativa de viagem de um naturalista inglês ao Rio de Janeiro e Minas Gerais (1833–1835)." *Anais da Biblioteca Nacional do Rio de Janeiro,* 62 (1940), 15–135.

Burmeister, Herman. *Viagem ao Brasil através das provincias do Rio de Janeiro e Minas Gerais.* São Paulo, 1952.

Calmon, Pedro. *História do ministério da justiça, 1822–1922.* Brasília, 1972.

Câmara, Alfredo Arruda. *As polícias militares.* Rio de Janeiro, 1935.

Câmara, José Gomes B. *Subsídios para a história do direito pátrio.* 4 vols. Rio de Janeiro, 1954–1965.

Cameron, Jain A. *Crime and Repression in the Ouvergne and the Guyenne, 1720–1790.* Cambridge, Eng., 1981.

Campos, Joaquim Pinto de. *Vida do grande cidadão brasileiro Luiz Alves de Lima e Silva.* Lisbon, 1878.

Candido, Antônio. "Dialética da malandragem." *Revista do Instituto de Estudos Brasileiros,* 8 (1970), 67–89.

———. *Teresina, etc.* Rio de Janeiro, 1980.

Cardim, Elmano. *Justiniano José da Rocha.* São Paulo, 1964.

Carneiro, Edison. *Capoeira.* Rio de Janeiro, 1975.

———. *A sabedoria popular.* Rio de Janeiro, 1975.

———. *Ladinos e crioulos.* Rio de Janeiro, 1964.

Carrara, Sérgio Luis. "Os mistérios de Clarice: etnografia de um crime na avenida." *Papéis Avulsos da Fundação Casa de Rui Barbosa,* 2 (Aug. 1986), 39–63.

"Cartas de Jõao Loureiro, escriptas do Rio de Janeiro ao Conselheiro Manuel José Maria da Costa e Sá." *RIHGB,* 76:2 (1913), 273–468.

Carvalho, Affonso de. *Caxias.* Rio de Janeiro, 1942.

Carvalho, Carlos Delgado de. *História da cidade do Rio de Janeiro.* Rio de Janeiro, 1926.

Carvalho, Elisio de. *A polícia carioca e a criminalidade contemporânea.* Rio de Janeiro, 1910.

Carvalho, Erasto Miranda de. "Criar novas polícias: repetir um velho erro?" *Revista da Polícia Militar do Rio de Janeiro,* 1:4 (Oct. 1984), 12–14.

———. "A P.M. carioca no processo da independência," *Anais do congresso de história da independência do Brasil,* 6 vols., vol. 6, (1975), 293–99.

Carvalho, José Murilo de. *Os bestializados: O Rio de Janeiro e a república que não foi.* São Paulo, 1987.

———. *A construção da ordem.* Rio de Janeiro, 1980.

———. *A formação das almas.* São Paulo, 1990.

———. "Political Elites and State Building: The Case of Nineteenth-Century Brazil." *Comparative Studies in Society and History,* 24:3 (July 1982), 378–99.

———. *Teatro de sombras: a política imperial.* São Paulo, 1988.

Carvalho, Marcus J. "Hegemony and Rebellion in Pernambuco (Brazil), 1821–1825." Ph.D. diss., Univ. of Illinois, 1989.

Cascudo, Luis da Câmara. *Dicionário do folclore brasileiro.* 2 vols. Rio de Janeiro, 1972.

———. *Folclore do Brasil.* Rio de Janeiro, 1967.

Castro, Jeanne Berrance de. *A milícia cidadã: a Guarda Nacional de 1831 a 1850.* São Paulo, 1977.

"Centenário da polícia, 1808–1908." *Boletim Policial* (Rio de Janeiro), 2:1 (1908), 2–13.

Cerqueira Filho, Gisálio. *A questão social no Brasil*. Rio de Janeiro, 1982.

Cerqueira Filho, Gisálio, and Gizlene Neder. "Conciliação e violência na história do Brasil." *Encontros com a civilisação brasileira*, 8 (Feb. 1979), 189–227.

Chalhoub, Sidney. "Medo branco de almas negras: escravos, libertos e republicanos na cidade do Rio." *Papéis Avulsos da Fundação Casa de Rui Barbosa*, 2 (Aug. 1986), 64–89.

———. *Trabalho, lar e botequim: O cotidiano dos trabalhadores no Rio de Janeiro da belle époque*. São Paulo, 1986.

———. *Visões da liberdade: Uma história das últimas décadas da escravidão na corte*. São Paulo, 1990.

Chevalier, Louis. *Laboring Classes and Dangerous Classes in Paris During the First Half of the Nineteenth Century*. New York, 1972.

Chiavenato, Julio José. *O negro no Brasil: Da senzala à guerra do Paraguai*. 4th ed. São Paulo, 1987.

Cobb, R. C. *The Police and the People: French Popular Protest, 1789–1820*. Oxford, 1970.

Cockburn, J. S., ed. *Crime in England, 1550–1800*. Princeton, N.J., 1977.

Código de posturas da Ilma Câmara municipal do Rio de Janeiro e editaes da mesma Câmara. Rio de Janeiro, 1870.

Coelho, Edmundo Campos. *A oficina do diabo: Crise e conflitos no sistema penitenciário do Rio de Janeiro*. Rio de Janeiro, 1987.

Coelho, Lucinda Coutinho de Mello. "Aspectos da evolução de uma cidade-estado." In Euripedes Simões de Paula, ed., *A cidade e a história*. 2 vols., vol. 1, 267–303. São Paulo, 1974.

Cohen, Stanley, and Andrew Scull, eds. *Social Control and the State*. New York, 1983.

Conrad, Robert. *Brazilian Slavery: An Annotated Research Bibliography*. Boston, 1977.

———. *The Destruction of Brazilian Slavery, 1850–1888*. Berkeley, Calif., 1972.

———. "Neither Slave nor Free: the *Emancipados* of Brazil, 1818–1868." *Hispanic American Historical Review*, 53:1 (Feb. 1973), 50–70.

Cordeiro, Carlos Antonio. *Código criminal do império do Brasil*. Rio de Janeiro, 1861.

Corrêa, Viriato. *Páginas cariocas*. 3d ed., Rio de Janeiro, 1927.

Costa, Emília Viotti da. *The Brazilian Empire: Myths and Histories*. Chicago, 1985.

———. *Da senzala à colônia*. São Paulo, 1966.

Costa, Luiz Edmundo da. *O Rio de Janeiro no tempo dos vice-reis (1763–1808)*. 2d ed. Rio de Janeiro, 1932.

Couty, Louis. *O Brasil em 1884: Esboços sociológicos*. Brasília, 1984 [1884].

Cultura brasileira, tradição/contradição. Rio de Janeiro, 1987.

Dabadie, F. *A travers L'Amerique du Sud: Rio de Janeiro et environs, Les esclaves au Brésil*. Paris, 1859.

Da Cunha, Euclides. *Os Sertões*. 5th ed. Rio de Janeiro, 1914.

Da Cunha, Joaquim Bernardes. *Primeiras linhas sobre o processo criminal*. Rio de Janeiro, 1863.

Da Cunha, Lygia da Fonseca, ed. *Album cartográfico do Rio de Janeiro, séculos XVIII e XIX*. Rio de Janeiro, 1971.

Da Matta, Roberto. *Carnavais, malandros e heróis*. Rio de Janerio, 1979.

———. *A casa e a rua*. São Paulo, 1985.

———. *Explorações*. Rio de Janeiro, 1986.

———. *O que faz o brasil, Brasil?* 2d ed. Rio de Janeiro, 1986.

———. "Raizes da violência no Brasil." In *A violência brasileira*. São Paulo, 1982.

———. "The Quest for Citizenship in a Relational Universe." In Wirth et al., eds., *State and Society in Brazil*, pp. 307–35.

Davis, John Anthony. *Conflict and Control: Law and Order in Nineteenth Century Italy*. Atlantic Heights, N.J., 1988.

Debret, Jean Baptiste. *Viagem Pitoresca e Histórica ao Brasil*. 2 vols. São Paulo, 1978.

Degler, Carl. *Neither Black nor White: Slavery and Race Relations in Brazil and the United States*. New York, 1971.

Dent, Charles Hastings. *A Year in Brazil*. London, 1886.

Diamond, Stanley. *In Search of the Primitive: A Critique of Civilization*. New Brunswick, 1974.

Dias, Luiz Sérgio. "Escravo urbano e repressão na corte imperial." *Boletim Informativo do AGCRJ*, 2:6–8 (1981), 15–21.

Dias, Maria Odila Leite da Silva. "Nas fímbrias da escravidão urbana: negras de tabuleiro e de ganho." *Estudos Econômicos*, 15 (1985), 89–110.

———. *Quotidiano e poder em São Paulo no século XIX*. São Paulo, 1984.

Direito que tem as assembleas provinciaes de legislar decretando penas para as praças dos corpos policiaes. Rio de Janeiro, 1857.

Donajgrodzki, A. P., ed. *Social Control in Nineteenth Century Britain*. Totowa, N.J., 1977.

Donnici, Virgílio Luiz. *A criminalidade no Brasil (meio milênio de repressão)*. Rio de Janeiro, 1984.

Dumm, Thomas L. *Democracy and Punishment: Disciplinary Origins of the United States*. Madison, Wis., 1987.

Duncan, Julian Smith. *Public and Private Operation of Railways in Brazil*. New York, 1932.

Dunlop, Charles J. *Subsídios para a história do Rio de Janeiro*. Rio de Janeiro, 1957.

Eckstein, Susan, ed. *Power and Popular Protest: Latin American Social Movements*. Berkeley, 1989.

Egas, Eugenio. "Regencia trina e una, perfil político de Feijó." *Anais do Congresso Internacional de História da América*, 3 (1922), 123–45.

Ellis Júnior, Alfredo. *Feijó e a primeira metade do século XIX*. 2d ed. São Paulo, 1980.

Emsley, Clive. *Crime and Society in England, 1750–1900*. London, 1987.

———. *Policing and its Context, 1750–1870*. New York, 1984.

Esteves, Martha de Abreu. *Meninas perdidas: os populares e o cotidiano do amor no Rio de Janeiro da Belle Epoque*. Rio de Janeiro, 1989.

———. "Em nome da moral e dos bons costumes: discursos jurídicos e controle social." *Papéis Avulsos da Fundação Casa de Rui Barbosa*, 2 (Aug. 1986), 1–20.

Ewbank, Thomas. *Life in Brazil*. New York, 1856.

Faoro, Raymundo. *Os donos do poder*. 7th ed., 2 vols. Rio de Janeiro, 1987.

Fausto, Boris. *Crime e cotidiano: a criminalidade em São Paulo (1880–1924)*. São Paulo, 1984.

Fazenda, José Vieira. "O Aljube." *RIHGB*, 86:1 (1919), 358–62.

———. *Antiqualhas e memórias do Rio de Janeiro*. 5 vols. Rio de Janeiro, 1923–28.

———. "Aspectos do período regencial." *RIHGB*, 77:1 (1914), 41–65.

Femia, Joseph V. *Gramsci's Political Thought*. Oxford, 1981.

Fernandes, Heloisa Rodrigues. *Política e segurança*. São Paulo, 1973.

Filgueiras Júnior, Araujo. *Codigo do Processo do Império do Brazil*. 3 vols. Rio de Janeiro, 1874.

Filler, Victor M. "Liberalism in Imperial Brazil: The Regional Rebellions of 1842." Ph.D. diss., Stanford Univ., 1976.

Flory, Thomas. *Judge and Jury in Imperial Brazil, 1808–1871*. Austin, Tex., 1981.

———. "Race and Social Control in Independent Brazil." *Journal of Latin American Studies*, 9:2 (Nov. 1977), 199–224.

Fonseca, Hermes R. da. *Polícia da Capital Federal—Instrucções das rondas e patrulhas*. Rio de Janeiro, 1902.

Forster, Robert, and Orest Ranum, eds. *Deviants and the Abandoned in French Society*. Baltimore, 1978.

Fosdick, Raymond B. *European Police Systems*. New York, 1915.

Foucault, Michel. *The Birth of the Clinic: An Archaeology of Medical Perception*. New York, 1973.

———. *Discipline and Punish: The Birth of the Prison*. New York, 1979.

———. *Madness and Civilization*. New York, 1965.

———. *Power/Knowledge*. New York, 1980.

Franco, Ary Azevedo. *Aspectos legaes e sociaes da contravenção de vadiagem.* Rio de Janeiro, 1930.

Franco, Maria Sylvia de Carvalho. *Homens livres na ordem escravocrata.* São Paulo, 1969.

Freitas, Décio. *Insurreições escravas.* Porto Alegre, 1976.

Freyre, Gilberto. *Casa Grande e Senzala.* Rio de Janeiro, 1933.

———. *Ordem e progresso.* 2 vols. Rio de Janeiro, 1959.

———. *Sobrados e mucambos.* São Paulo, 1936.

Galvão, Flávio. "Reabilitação da capoeira." *O Estado de São Paulo,* 2 Nov. 1956, p. 8.

Gatrell, V. A. C. "The Decline of Theft and Violence in Victorian and Edwardian England." In V. A. C. Gatrell et al., eds., *Crime and the Law,* pp. 238–338.

Gatrell, V. A. C., Bruce Lenman, and Geoffrey Parker, eds., *Crime and the Law: The Social History of Crime in Western Europe Since 1500.* London, 1980.

Gebara, Ademir. *O mercado de trabalho livre no Brasil (1871–1888).* São Paulo, 1986.

Gerson, Brasil. *História das ruas do Rio.* 4th ed. Rio de Janeiro, 1965.

Gonçalves, Lopes. "Instituições do Rio de Janeiro colonial: os quadrilheiros." *RIHGB,* 205 (1949), 401–11.

Goody, Jack. *The Logic of Writing and the Organization of Society.* Cambridge, Eng., 1986.

Goulart, José Alípio. *Da fuga ao suicídio (aspectos da rebeldia de escravos no Brasil).* Rio de Janeiro, 1972.

———. *Da palmatória ao patíbulo (castigos de escravos no Brasil).* Rio de Janeiro, 1971.

Graff, Harvey J. "'Pauperism, Misery, and Vice': Illiteracy and Criminality in the Nineteenth Century." *Journal of Social History,* 11:2 (Winter 1977), 245–68.

Graham, Richard. *Britain and the Onset of Modernization in Brazil, 1850–1914.* Cambridge, Eng., 1968.

———. *Patronage and Politics in Nineteenth-Century Brazil.* Stanford, Calif., 1990.

Graham, Sandra Lauderdale. *House and Street: The Domestic World of Servants and Masters in Nineteenth-Century Rio de Janeiro.* Cambridge, Eng., 1988.

———. "The Vintem Riot and Political Culture: Rio de Janeiro, 1880." *Hispanic American Historical Review,* 60:3 (Aug. 1980), 431–49.

Gramsci, Antonio. *Il Risorgimento.* Turin, Italy, 1949.

Greenberg, David F., ed. *Corrections and Punishment.* Beverly Hills, 1977.

Guia para os Inspectores de Quarteirão da Província de S. Paulo. São Paulo, 1868.

Hahner, June E. *Poverty and Politics: The Urban Poor in Brazil, 1870–1920.* Albuquerque, N.M., 1986.

Hall, Kermit L., ed. *Police, Prison, and Punishment: Major Historical Interpretations.* New York, 1987.

Harring, Sidney L. *Policing a Class Society: The Experience of American Cities, 1865–1915.* New Brunswick, N.J., 1983.

Hasenbalg, Carlos. *Discriminação e desigualdades raciais no Brasil.* Rio de Janeiro, 1979.

Hay, Douglas, et al. *Albion's Fatal Tree: Crime and Society in Eighteenth-Century England.* New York, 1975.

Hay, Douglas, and Francis Snyder, eds. *Policing and Prosecution in Britain 1750–1850.* Oxford, 1989.

Hayes, Robert. *The Armed Nation: The Brazilian Corporate Mystique.* Tempe, Ariz., 1989.

Hearn, Francis. *Domination, Legitimation, and Resistance: The Incorporation of the Nineteenth-Century English Working Class.* Westport, Conn., 1978.

Heath, James. *Eighteenth-Century Penal Theory.* London, 1963.

Hindus, Michael. "Black Justice Under White Law: Criminal Prosecutions of Blacks in Antebellum South Carolina." *Journal of American History,* 62 (1976), 575–96.

———. *Prison and Plantation: Crime, Justice and Authority in Massachusetts and South Carolina, 1767–1868.* Chapel Hill, 1980.

Hirst, Paul Q. "Marx and Engels on Law, Crime, and Morality." *Economy and Society,* 1:1 (Feb. 1972), 28–56.

Hobsbawm, E. J. *Bandits.* New York, 1969.

———. "Distinctions between Socio-Political and Other Forms of Crime." *Society for the Study of Labor History Bulletin,* 25 (Fall 1972), 5–6.

———. "History from Below—Some Reflections." In Krantz, ed., *History from Below,* pp. 63–73.

———. *Primitive Rebels: Studies in Archaic Forms of Social Movements in the Nineteenth and Twentieth Centuries.* New York, 1959.

Holanda, Sérgio Buarque de. *Raizes do Brasil.* Rio de Janeiro, 1936.

Holanda, Sérgio Buarque de, ed. *História geral da civilização brasileira.* Tomo II, vols. 1 and 2, *O Brasil Monárquico.* São Paulo, 1962, 1964.

Holloway, Thomas H. "The Brazilian 'Judicial Police' in Florianópolis, Santa Catarina, 1841–1871." *Journal of Social History,* 20:4 (Summer 1987), 733–56.

———. "'A Healthy Terror': Police Repression of *Capoeiras* in Nineteenth-Century Rio de Janeiro." *Hispanic American Historical Review,* 69:4 (Nov. 1989), 637–76.

———. *Immigrants on the Land: Coffee and Society in São Paulo, 1886–1934.* Chapel Hill, N.C., 1980.

Hoy, David Couzens, ed. *Foucault: A Critical Reader.* Oxford, 1986.

Huggins, Martha. *From Slavery to Vagrancy in Brazil*. New Brunswick, N.J., 1985.
Huppert, George. *After the Black Death: A Social History of Early Modern Europe*. Bloomington, Ind., 1986.
Ignatieff, Michael. *A Just Measure of Pain: The Penitentiary in the Industrial Revolution, 1750–1850*. New York, 1978.
Instrucções para o serviço das rondas e patrulhas, em execução do art. 22 do regulamento annexo ao decreto n. 9395 de 7 de março de 1885. Rio de Janeiro, 1886.
Itier, Jules. *Journal d'un Voyage en Chine en 1843, 1844, 1845, 1846*. 3 vols. Paris, 1849–53.
Jakubs, Deborah. "Police Violence in Times of Political Tension: The Case of Brazil, 1968–1971." In Bayley, ed., *Police and Society*, pp. 85–106.
Johnson, David R. *American Law Enforcement: A History*. St. Louis, Mo., 1981.
Johnson, Lyman, ed. *The Problem of Order in Changing Societies: Essays on Crime and Policing in Argentina and Uruguay*. Albuquerque, N.M., 1990.
Jones, David. *Crime, Protest, Community and Police in Nineteenth-Century Britain*. London, 1982.
Joseph, Gilbert M. "On the Trail of Latin American Bandits: A Reexamination of Peasant Resistance." *Latin American Research Review*, 25:3 (1990), 7–54.
Kant de Lima, Roberto. "Cultura jurídica e práticas policiais: A tradição inquisitorial no Brasil." *Revista Brasileira de Ciências Sociais*, 4:10 (June 1989), 37–52.
———. "Legal Theory and Judicial Practice: Paradoxes of Police Work in Rio de Janeiro City." Ph.D. diss., Harvard Univ., 1986.
Karasch, Mary C. "Rio de Janeiro: From Colonial Town to Imperial Capital." In Robert Ross and Gerard Telkamp, eds., *Colonial Cities*, pp. 123–51. Dordrecht, 1985.
———. *Slave Life in Rio de Janeiro, 1808–1850*. Princeton, N.J., 1987.
Kidder, Daniel P. *Sketches of Residence and Travels in Brazil*. 2 vols. Philadelphia, 1845.
Kidder, Daniel P., and J. C. Fletcher. *Brazil and the Brazilians*. Philadelphia, 1857.
Koseritz, Carl von. *Imagens do Brasil*. São Paulo, 1943.
Kowarick, Lúcio. *Trabalho e vadiagem: A Origem do trabalho livre no Brasil*. São Paulo, 1987.
Kowarick, Lúcio, and Clara Ant. "Violência: reflexões sobre a banalidade do cotidiano em São Paulo." In Renato R. Boschi, ed., *Violência e cidade*, pp. 29–74. Rio de Janeiro, 1982.
Krantz, Frederick, ed. *History from Below: Studies in Popular Protest and Popular Ideology in Honour of George Rudé*. Montreal, 1985.

Kubik, Gerhard. *Angolan Traits in Black Music, Games and Dances of Brazil.* Lisbon, 1979.

Laemmert, Eduardo von. *Almanak administrativo mercantil e industrial do Rio de Janeiro.* Rio de Janeiro, 1843–89.

Lane, Roger. "Crime and the Industrial Revolution: British and American Views." *Journal of Social History,* 7:3 (Spring 1974), 287–303.

———. *Policing the City: Boston, 1822–1885.* Cambridge, Mass., 1967.

Lanna, Ana Lúcia Duarte. *A transformação do trabalho.* Campinas, 1988.

Laqueur, Thomas W. *Religion and Respectability: Sunday Schools and Working Class Culture, 1780–1850.* New Haven, Conn., 1976.

Lara, Sílvia Hunold. *Campos da violência: Escravos e senhores na capitania do Rio de Janeiro, 1750–1808.* Rio de Janeiro, 1988.

Leal, Aurelino. "História judiciária do Brasil." In *Diccionário histórico Geográphico e Ethnográphico do Brasil.* Vol. 1, pp. 1107–87. Rio de Janeiro, 1922.

———. *Polícia e poder de polícia.* Rio de Janeiro, 1918.

Leithold, Theodor von, and L. von Rango. *O Rio de Janeiro visto por dois prussianos em 1819.* São Paulo, 1966.

Leitman, Spencer. *Raízes socio-econômicas da Guerra dos Farrapos: Um capítulo de história do Brasil no século xix.* Rio de Janeiro, 1979.

Lemgruber, Julita. "Polícia, direitos humanos e cidadania: notas para um estudo." *Papéis Avulsos da Fundação Casa de Rui Barbosa,* 2 (Aug. 1986), 21–38.

Lenman, Bruce, and Geoffrey Parker. "The State, the Community and the Criminal Law in Early Modern Europe." In V. A. C. Gatrell et al., eds., *Crime and the Law,* pp. 11–48.

Lentricchia, Frank. *Ariel and the Police: Michel Foucault, William James, Wallace Stevens.* Madison, Wis., 1988.

Levine, Robert. *Brazil, 1822–1930: An Annotated Bibliography for Social Historians.* New York, 1983.

———. "Turning on the Lights: Brazilian Slavery Reconsidered One Hundred Years after Abolition." *Latin American Research Review,* 24:2 (1989), 201–17.

Lewis, John L. "Semiotic and Social Discourse in Brazilian Capoeira." Ph.D. diss., Univ. of Washington, 1986.

Lichtenstein, Alex. "'That Disposition to Theft, With Which They Have Become Branded': Moral Economy, Slave Management, and the Law." *Journal of Social History,* 21:3 (Spring 1988), 413–40.

———. "Vigilante and the Police: The Creation of a Professional Police Bureaucracy in San Francisco, 1847–1900." *Journal of Social History,* 21:2 (Winter 1988), 197–227.

Lima, Lana Lage da Gama. *Rebeldia negra e abolicionismo.* Rio de Janeiro, 1981.

Lima, Manuel de Oliveira. *O império brazileiro*. São Paulo, 1927.

Linhares, Maria Yedda, and Maria Bárbara Levy. "Aspectos da história demográfica e social do Rio de Janeiro (1808–1889)." In *L'Histoire quantitative du Brésil de 1800 à 1930*, pp. 123–38. Paris, 1973.

Lobo, Eulália Maria Lahmayer. "Evolução dos preços e do padrão de vida no Rio de Janeiro, 1820–1930." *Revista Brasileira de Economia*, 26 (Oct.–Dec. 1971), 36–49.

———. *História do Rio de Janeiro (do capital comercial ao capital industrial e financeiro)*. 2 vols. Rio de Janeiro, 1978.

Lobo, Eulália Maria Lahmayer and Eduardo Navarro Stotz. "Formação do operariado e movimento operário no Rio de Janeiro." *Estudos Econômicos*, 15 (1985), 49–88.

Lomonaco, Alfonso. *Al Brasile*. Milan, 1889.

Lopes, Helena Theodoro, José Jorge Siqueira and Maria Beatriz Nascimento. *Negro e cultura no Brasil*. Rio de Janeiro, 1987.

Lopes, Luis Carlos. *O espelho e a imagem: O escravo na historiografia brasileira (1808–1920)*. Rio de Janeiro, 1987.

Lopes, Levindo Ferreira. *Promptuario policial*. Ouro Preto, 1888.

Luccock, John. *Notes on Rio de Janeiro and the Southern Parts of Brazil; Taken during a Residence of Ten Years in That Country, from 1808 to 1818*. London, 1820.

Lyra, Roberto. *Introdução ao estudo do direito criminal*. Rio de Janeiro, 1946.

Macaulay, Neill. *Dom Pedro: The Struggle for Liberty in Brazil and Portugal, 1798–1834*. Durham, N.C., 1986.

Macedo, Roberto. *Apontamentos para uma bibliografia carioca*. Rio de Janeiro, 1943.

———. *Paulo Fernandes Viana, administração do primeiro intendente geral da polícia*. Rio de Janeiro, 1956.

Macedo, Roberto, ed. *Aspectos do Distrito Federal*. Rio de Janeiro, 1943.

Machado, Maria Helena P. T. *Crime e escravidão: Trabalho, luta e resistência nas lavouras paulistas, 1830–1888*. São Paulo, 1987.

Machado Neto, A. L. *História das idéias jurídicas no Brasil*. São Paulo, 1969.

Maestri, Mário. *A servidão negra*. Porto Alegre, 1988.

Magalhães, João Batista. "História da evolução militar do Brasil." *Anais do IV Congresso de História Nacional*, 4 (1950), 347–607.

Magalhães Júnior, Raimundo. *Tres panfletários do segundo reinado*. São Paulo, 1956.

Maggie, Yvonne. "Medo do feitiço: relações entre magia e poder no Brasil." Doctoral diss., Federal Univ. of Rio de Janeiro, 1988.

Manchester, Alan K. *British Preëminence in Brazil; Its Rise and Decline: A Study in European Expansion*. Chapel Hill, N.C., 1933.

Marx, Karl. *Economic and Philosophic Manuscripts of 1844*. New York, 1964.

Mattos, Ilmar Rohloff. *O tempo saquarema*. São Paulo, 1987.

Mattoso, Kátia de Queirós. *Família e sociedade na Bahia do século XIX*. São Paulo, 1988.

————. *Ser escravo no Brasil*. 2d ed. São Paulo, 1988.

McBeth, Michael C. "The Brazilian Recruit During the First Empire: Slave or Soldier." In Dauril Alden and Warren Dean, eds., *Essays Concerning the Socioeconomic History of Brazil and Portuguese India*, pp. 71–87. Gainesville, Fla., 1977.

McCann, Frank D. "The Nation in Arms: Obligatory Military Service During the Old Republic." In Dauril Alden and Warren Dean, eds., *Essays*, pp. 211–43.

Meade, Teresa. "'Civilizing Rio de Janerio': The Public Health Campaign and the Riot of 1904." *Journal of Social History*, 20:2 (Winter 1986), 301–22.

————. "'Living Worse and Costing More': Resistance and Riot in Rio de Janeiro, 1890–1917." *Journal of Latin American Studies*, 21 (May 1989), 241–66.

Mello, Alfredo Pinto Vieira de. "O poder judiciário do Brasil, 1532–1871." Instituto Histórico e Geográfico Brasileiro, *Primeiro Congresso de História Nacional*, 4 vols., vol. 4, 99–148. Rio de Janeiro, 1916.

Mello, Gustavo Moncorvo Bandeira de. *História da polícia militar do Distrito Federal desde a época de sua fundação*. 3 vols. Rio de Janeiro, 1925–1953.

Miller, Wilbur R. *Cops and Bobbies: Police Authority in New York and London, 1830–1870*. Chicago, 1977.

————. "Police Authority in London and New York City, 1830–1870." *Journal of Social History*, 8:2 (Winter 1975), 81–101.

Mizruchi, Ephraim H. *Regulating Society: Marginality and Social Control in Historical Perspective*. New York, 1983.

Monkkonen, Eric H. "From Cop History to Social History: The Significance of the Police in American History." *Journal of Social History*, 15:4 (Summer 1982), 575–91.

————. "A Disorderly People? Urban Order in the Nineteenth and Twentieth Centuries." *Journal of American History*, 68:3 (Dec. 1981), 539–59.

————. *Police in Urban America, 1860–1920*. Cambridge, Eng., 1981.

————. *The Dangerous Class: Crime and Poverty in Columbus, Ohio, 1860–1885*. Cambridge, Mass, 1975.

Monteiro, Albino. *Polícia militar do Distrito Federal*. Rio de Janeiro, 1924.

Moraes, A. J. de Mello. *História da trasladação da corte portugueza para o Brasil em 1807–1808*. Rio de Janeiro, 1872.

Moraes, A. J. de Mello, ed. *Necrologia do senador Diogo Antônio Feijó, escripta por * * * [attributed to Fr. Geraldo Leite Bastos]*. Rio de Janeiro, 1861.

Moraes, Eneida de. *História do carnaval carioca*. Rio de Janeiro, 1958.

Moraes, Evaristo de. *A escravidão africana no Brasil (das origens à extinção)*. Rio de Janeiro, 1933.

Moraes Filho, A. J. de Mello. *Festas e tradições populares do Brasil.* 4th ed. Rio de Janeiro, 1967 [1889].

Morales de los Rios Filho, Adolfo. *O Rio de Janeiro imperial.* Rio de Janeiro, 1946.

Morse, Richard M. "Cities and Society in Nineteenth-Century Latin America: The Illustrative Case of Brazil." In R. P. Schaedel, J. E. Hardoy, and N. S. Kinzer, eds., *Urbanization in the Americas from Its Beginnings to the Present,* pp. 283–302. The Hague, 1978.

————. *New World Soundings.* Baltimore, 1989.

Mosse, George, ed. *Police Forces in History.* London, 1975.

Mota, Carlos Guilherme, ed. *1822: Dimensões.* São Paulo, 1972.

Mota, Carlos Guilherme, and Fernando Novais. *A independência política do Brasil.* São Paulo, 1986.

Moura, Ana Maria da Silva. *Cocheiros e carroceiros: Homens livres no Rio de Janeiro de senhores e escravos.* São Paulo, 1988.

Moura, Clóvis. *O negro: de bom escravo a mau cidadão?* Rio de Janeiro, 1977.

————. *Rebeliões da senzala.* 4th ed. Porto Alegre, 1988.

Nabuco, Joaquim. *Um estadista do Império.* São Paulo, 1936.

Naro, Nancy. "The 1848 Praieira Revolt in Brazil." Ph.D. diss., Univ. of Chicago, 1981.

Neder, Gizlene, Nancy Naro, and José Luiz Werneck da Silva. *A polícia na Corte e no Distrito Federal, 1831–1930.* Série Estudos-PUC/RJ no. 3. Rio de Janeiro, 1981.

Needell, Jeffrey D. *A Tropical Belle Epoque: Elite Culture and Society in Turn-of-the-Century Rio de Janeiro.* Cambridge, Eng., 1987.

————. "The *Revolta Contra Vacina* of 1904: The Revolt Against 'Modernization' in *Belle-Epoque* Rio de Janeiro." *Hispanic American Historical Review,* 67:2 (May 1987), 233–69.

Nequete, Lenine. *Poder judiciário no Brasil.* Porto Alegre, 1973.

Novais, Fernando A. *Estrutura e dinâmica do antigo sistema colonial.* 4th ed. São Paulo, 1987.

Nye, Robert. "Crime in Modern Societies: Some Research Strategies for Historians." *Journal of Social History,* 11:4 (Summer 1978), 490–507.

O'Brian, Patricia. "Crime and Punishment as Historical Problem." *Journal of Social History,* 11:4 (Summer 1978), 508–20.

Oliveira, D. Martins de. "A polícia no Distrito Federal e sua evolução." In Macedo, ed., *Aspectos do Distrito Federal,* pp. 91–129.

Oliven, George Ruben. *Violência e cultura no Brasil.* Petrópolis, 1982.

Palha, Américo. *Dez estadistas do Império.* Rio de Janeiro, 1961.

Palmer, Thomas W. "A Momentous Decade in Brazilian Administrative History, 1831–1840." *Hispanic American Historical Review,* 30:2 (May 1950), 209–17.

Pang, Eul-Soo. "Modernization and Slavery in Nineteenth-Century Brazil." *Journal of Interdisciplinary History*, 9:4 (Spring 1979), 667–88.

Pang, Eul-Soo and Ron L. Seckinger. "The Mandarins of Imperial Brazil." *Comparative Studies in Society and History*, 14:2 (Mar. 1972), 215–44.

Pereira, Virgilio de Sá. "Os codigos criminal, de processo e commercial, formação de nosso direito civil. A reforma judiciária de 1871." Instituto Histórico e Geográfico Brasileiro, *Primeiro Congresso de História Nacional*, 4 vols., vol. 4, 151–81. Rio de Janeiro, 1916.

Peri Fagerstrom, René. *Apuntes y transcripciones para una historia de la función policial en Chile*. Santiago, 1982.

Perry, Mary Elizabeth. *Crime and Society in Early Modern Seville*. Hanover, N.H., 1980.

Pessoa, Vicente Alves Paula. *Codigo do processo criminal de primeira instância do Império do Brazil*. Rio de Janeiro, 1880.

Philips, David. *Crime and Authority in Victorian England: The Black Country, 1835–1860*. London, 1977.

————. "'A New Engine of Power and Authority': The Institutionalization of Law-Enforcement in England, 1780–1830." In V. A. C. Gatrell et al., eds., *Crime and the Law*, pp. 155–89.

Pilar, Olyntho. *Os patronos das forças armadas*. Rio de Janeiro, 1981.

Pinaud, João Luiz Duboc, et al. *Insurreição negra e justiça: Paty do Alferes, 1838*. Rio de Janeiro, 1987.

Pinheiro, J. C. Fernandes. "Paulo Fernandes e a polícia de seu tempo." *RIHGB*, 39 (1876), 65–76.

Pinheiro, Paulo Sérgio de M. S., ed. *Crime, violência e poder*. São Paulo, 1983.

Pinho, Ruy Rebello. *História do direito brasileiro, período colonial*. São Paulo, 1973.

Pinto, Antonio Pereira. "Memória [sobre prisões no Rio de Janeiro]." *RIHGB*, 21 (1858), 441–55.

Pinto, Luis A. Costa. *O negro no Rio de Janeiro*. São Paulo, 1952.

Planitz, Carlos Roberto. *O Rio de Janerio na maioridade*. Rio de Janeiro, 1958.

Poster, Mark. *Critical Theory and Poststructuralism: In Search of a Context*. Ithaca, N.Y., 1989.

Prado, Francisco Silveira do. *A polícia militar fluminense no tempo do império (1835–1889)*. Rio de Janeiro, 1969.

Prado, J. F. de Almeida. *Thomas Ender: Pintor austríaco na córte de D. João VI no Rio de Janeiro*. São Paulo, 1955.

Prado Júnior, Caio. *The Colonial Background of Modern Brazil*. Berkeley, Calif., 1967.

————. *Evolução política do Brasil*. 2d ed. São Paulo, 1947.

Providências lembradas ao Conselheiro Intendente Geral de Polícia. Rio de Janeiro, 1825.

Quinney, Richard. *Critique of Legal Order: Crime Control in Capitalist Society.* Boston, 1973.
————. *The Social Reality of Crime.* Boston, 1970.
Rago, Margareth. *Do cabaré ao lar: a utopia da cidade disciplinar, Brasil, 1890–1930.* Rio de Janeiro, 1985.
Ramalho, Joaquim Ignacio. *Elementos do processo criminal.* São Paulo, 1856.
————. *Praxe brasileira.* São Paulo, 1869.
Ramalho, José Ricardo. *Mundo do crime: a ordem pelo avesso.* Rio de Janeiro, 1979.
Rambo, Marion. "The Role of the Carioca Press During the Triune Regencies." Ph.D. diss., Univ. of Virginia, 1973.
Recenseamento do Rio de Janeiro (distrito federal) realisado em 20 de setembro de 1906. Rio de Janeiro, 1907.
Reformas do codigo do processo criminal, lei no. 261 de 3 de dezembro de 1841, e regulamentos nos. 120 de 31 de janeiro e 122 de 2 de fevereiro de 1842. Ouro Preto, 1842.
Rego, Waldeloir. *Capoeira angola: ensaio socio-etnográfico.* Rio de Janeiro, 1968.
Regulamento do Corpo Militar de Polícia da Corte. Rio de Janeiro, 1889.
Regulamento para o corpo municipal permanente na província de São Paulo. São Paulo, 1844.
Regulamento para os commissários de polícia do império do Brasil. Rio de Janeiro, 1825.
Reinhardt, Steven G. "Crime and Royal Justice in Ancien Regime France: Modes of Analysis." *Journal of Interdisciplinary History,* 13:3 (Winter 1983), 437–60.
Reis, João José. *Rebelião escrava no Brasil: A história do levante dos malês (1835).* 2d ed. São Paulo, 1987.
Relatório do exame das prisões, carceres, hospitaes, e estabelecimentos de caridade apresentado à ilustríssima Câmara Municipal da Corte. Rio de Janeiro, 1837.
Renault, Delso. *O dia-a-dia no Rio de Janeiro segundo os jornais, 1870–1889.* Rio de Janeiro, 1982.
————. *Rio de Janeiro: A vida da cidade refletida nos jornais, 1850–1870.* Rio de Janeiro, 1978.
Rezende, Astolpho. "Polícia administrativa, polícia judiciária, o código do processo de 1832, a lei de 3 de dezembro de 1841, a lei de 20 de setembro de 1871." Instituto Histórico e Geográfico Brasileiro, *Primeiro Congresso de História Nacional,* 4 vols., vol. 3, 401–22. Rio de Janeiro, 1916.
Rheinstein, Max, ed. *Max Weber on Law in Economy and Society.* Cambridge, Mass., 1954.
Ribeiro, Fernando Bastos. *Crónicas da polícia e da vida do Rio de Janeiro.* Rio de Janeiro, 1958.
Ribeiro, Manoel de Queirós Mattoso. *Apontamentos sobre a vida dos conselhei-*

ros Eusébio de Queirós Coitinho da Silva e Eusébio de Queirós Coitinho Mattoso Camara. Rio de Janeiro, 1885.

Richardson, James F. *The New York Police: Colonial Times to 1901.* New York, 1970.

———. *Urban Police in the United States.* New York, 1974.

Rodrigues, Antonio Edmilson Martins, Francisco José Calazans Falcón, and Margarida de Souza Neves. *A Guarda Nacional no Rio de Janeiro, 1831–1918.* Série Estudos-PUC/RJ no. 5. Rio de Janeiro, 1981.

Rodrigues, José Honório. *Conciliação e reforma no Brasil.* 2d ed. Rio de Janeiro, 1982.

———. *Independência: revolução e contra-revolução.* 5 vols. Rio de Janeiro, 1975.

———. *O parlamento e a evolução nacional.* 2 vols. Brasília, 1972.

Rodríguez, Adolfo Enrique. *Cuatrocientos años de policía de Buenos Aires.* Buenos Aires, 1981.

Rothman, David J. *The Discovery of the Asylum: Social Order and Disorder in the New Republic.* Boston, 1971.

Rudé, George. *Criminal and Victim: Crime and Society in Early Nineteenth-Century England.* Oxford, 1985.

Rugendas, Johann Moritz. *Viagem pitoresca através do Brasil.* São Paulo, c. 1967 [1835].

Rusche, Georg, and Otto Kirchheimer. *Punishment and Social Structure.* New York, 1939.

Russell-Wood, A. J. R. "Local Government in Portuguese America: A Study in Cultural Divergence." *Comparative Studies in Society and History,* 16:2 (Mar. 1974), 187–231.

———, ed. *From Colony to Nation: Essays on the Independence of Brazil.* Baltimore, 1975.

Salgado, Graça, ed. *Fiscais e meirinhos: a administração do Brasil colonial.* Rio de Janeiro, 1985.

Sanctos, Luiz Gonçalves dos. *Memórias para servir à história do reino do Brazil.* 2 vols. Lisbon, 1825.

Santos, Boaventura de Sousa. "The Law of the Oppressed: The Construction and Reproduction of Legality in Pasargada." *Law and Society Review,* 12:1 (Fall 1977), 5–126.

Santos, Francisco Agenor de Noronha. *As freguesias do Rio antigo.* Rio de Janeiro, 1965.

———. "Haddock Lobo." *RIHGB,* 76:1 (1913), 275–83.

Santos, Wanderley Guilherme dos. *Cidadania e justiça.* Rio de Janeiro, 1979.

———. "Liberalism in Brazil: Ideology and Praxis." In Morris Blackman and Ronald Hellman, eds., *Terms of Conflict: Ideology in Latin American Politics,* pp. 1–38. Philadelphia, 1977.

Schlichthorst, C. *O Rio de Janeiro como é, 1824–1826.* Rio de Janeiro, 1943.

Schluchter, Wolfgang. *The Rise of Western Rationalism: Max Weber's Developmental History.* Berkeley, Calif., 1981.

Schneider, John C. *Detroit and the Problem of Order, 1830–1880: A Geography of Crime, Riot, and Policing.* Lincoln, Neb., 1980.

Schwartz, Robert M. *Policing the Poor in Eighteenth-Century France.* Chapel Hill, N.C., 1988.

Schwartz, Stuart. *Sovereignty and Society in Colonial Bahia: The High Court of Bahia and Its Judges, 1609–1751.* Berkeley, Calif., 1973.

Schwarz, Roberto. "As idéias fora do lugar." *Estudos CEBRAP*, 3 (1973), 151–61.

———. *Ao vencedor as batatas.* São Paulo, 1977.

———. "Misplaced Ideas: Literature and Society in Late Nineteenth-Century Brazil." *Comparative Civilizations Review*, 5 (1980), 33–51.

———. "Nacional por substração." In *Cultura brasileira, tradição/contradição*, pp. 91–110. Rio de Janeiro, 1987.

———. *Que horas são?* São Paulo, 1987.

Scott, James C. *Domination and the Arts of Resistance: Hidden Transcripts.* New Haven, Conn., 1990.

———. "Resistance Without Protest and Without Organization: Peasant Opposition to the Islamic *Zacat* and the Christian Tithe." *Comparative Studies in Society and History*, 29:3 (July 1987), 417–52.

———. *Weapons of the Weak: Everyday Forms of Peasant Resistance.* New Haven, Conn., 1985.

Scully, William. *Brazil, Its Provinces and Chief Cities.* London, 1866.

Seidler, Carlos. *História das guerras e revoluções do Brasil de 1825 a 1835.* São Paulo, 1939.

Senna, Ernesto. *Rascunhos e perfis: Notas de um reporter.* Rio de Janeiro, 1909.

Sevcenco, Nicolau. *Literatura como missão: Tensões sociais e criação cultural na Primeira República.* São Paulo, 1983.

Sharpe, J. A. *Crime in Early Modern England, 1550–1750.* London, 1984.

Shirley, Robert W. "Legal Institutions and Early Industrial Growth." In Wirth and Jones, eds., *Manchester and São Paulo*, pp. 157–76.

Silva, Andrée Mansuy-Diniz. "Imperial Reorganization, 1750–1808." In Leslie Bethell, ed., *Colonial Brazil*, pp. 253–61. Cambridge, Eng., 1987.

Silva, Eduardo. *As queixas do povo.* Rio de Janeiro, 1988.

Silva, Eduardo, and João José Reis. *Negociação e conflito: A resistência negra no Brasil escravista.* São Paulo, 1989.

Silva, Fernando Nascimento, ed. *Rio de Janeiro em seus quatrocentos anos.* Rio de Janeiro, 1965.

Silva, J. M. Pereira de. *História do Brasil de 1831 a 1840.* Rio de Janeiro, 1878.

Silva, Joaquim Norberto de Souza e. *Investigações sobre os recenseamentos da população do Império.* Rio de Janeiro, 1870.

Silva, Josino do Nascimento. *Código criminal do império do Brazil.* Rio de Janeiro, 1859.
———. *Código do processo criminal.* Rio de Janeiro, 1864.
Silva, Maria Beatriz Nizza da. *Cultura e sociedade no Rio de Janeiro (1808–1821).* São Paulo, 1977.
———. "A Intendência-Geral da Polícia, 1808–1821." *Acervo* (Rio de Janeiro), 1:2 (July–Dec. 1986), 187–204.
Silva, Marilene Rosa Nogueira da. *Negro na rua: A nova face da escravidão.* São Paulo, 1988.
Silver, Allan. "The Demand for Order in Civil Society: A Review of Some Themes in the History of Urban Crime, Police, and Riot." In Bordua, ed., *The Police,* pp. 1–24.
Sites, Paul. *Control: The Basis of Social Order.* New York, 1973.
Slatta, Richard W. "Rural Criminality and Social Conflict in Nineteenth-Century Buenos Aires Province." *Hispanic American Historical Review,* 60:3 (Aug. 1980), 450–72.
———, ed. *Bandidos: The Varieties of Latin American Banditry.* New York, 1987.
Slatta, Richard W., and Karla Robinson. "Continuities in Crime and Punishment: Buenos Aires, 1820–50." In Johnson, ed., *The Problem of Order,* pp. 19–46.
Smart, Barry. "The Politics of Truth and the Problem of Hegemony." In Hoy, ed., *Foucault,* pp. 157–73.
Snyder, Francis, and Douglas Hay, eds. *Labour, Law, and Crime: An Historical Perspective.* London, 1987.
Soares, Luis Carlos. "Urban Slavery in Nineteenth Century Rio de Janeiro." Ph.D. diss., Univ. of London, 1988.
Socolow, Susan M. "Women and Crime: Buenos Aires, 1757–97." *Journal of Latin American Studies,* 12 (1980), 39–54.
Sodré, Nelson Werneck. *História Militar do Brasil.* Rio de Janeiro, 1965.
Sousa, Octávio Tarquínio de. *Diogo Antônio Feijó.* Rio de Janeiro, 1942.
———. *História dos fundadores do Império do Brasil.* 2d ed., 10 vols. Rio de Janeiro, 1957–58.
Souza, Francisco Belisário Soares de. *O sistema eleitoral no Império.* Brasília, 1979.
Souza, João Francisco de. *Memória sobre as medidas a adoptar contra a prostituição no paiz.* Rio de Janeiro, 1876.
Spencer, Elaine G. "Police-Military Relations in Prussia, 1848–1914." *Journal of Social History,* 19:2 (Winter 1985), 305–17.
Spittler, Gerd. "Peasants and the State in Niger (West Africa)." *Peasant Studies,* 18:1 (Winter 1979), 30–47.
Spitzer, Steven, and Andrew T. Scull. "Social Control in Historical Perspective: From Private to Public Responses to Crime." In Greenberg, ed., *Corrections and Punishment,* pp. 265–86.

Stead, John Philip. *The Police of France*. New York, 1983.

Stearns, Peter. "Social and Political History." *Journal of Social History*, 16:1 (Spring 1983), 3–5.

Stein, Stanley. *Vassouras, a Brazilian Coffee County*. Cambridge, Mass., 1957.

Storch, Robert D. "The Policeman as Domestic Missionary: Urban Discipline and Popular Culture in Northern England, 1850–1880." *Journal of Social History*, 9:4 (Summer 1976), 481–508.

Sumner, Colin. "Crime, Justice and Underdevelopment: Beyond Modernisation Theory." In Colin Sumner, ed., *Crime, Justice and Underdevelopment*, pp. 1–39. London, 1982.

Susano, Luis da Silva. *Guia do processo policial e criminal*. Rio de Janeiro, 1859.

Sweigart, Joseph. *Coffee Factorage and the Emergence of a Brazilian Capital Market, 1850–1888*. New York, 1987.

Szuchman, Mark D. "Continuity and Conflict in Buenos Aires: Comments on the Historical City." In Stanley Ross and Thomas F. McGann, eds., *Buenos Aires: 400 Years*, pp. 53–67. Austin, Tex., 1982.

———. "Disorder and Social Control in Buenos Aires, 1810–1860." *Journal of Interdisciplinary History*, 15:1 (Summer 1984), 83–110.

Tannenbaum, Frank. *Slave and Citizen*. New York, 1947.

Tapajós, Vicente. *História administrativa do Brasil*. Brasília, 1984.

Tavares, Luís Henrique Dias. *Comércio proibido de escravos*. São Paulo, 1988.

Taylor, William B. "Between Global Process and Local Knowledge: An Inquiry into Early Latin American Social History, 1500–1900." In Zunz, ed., *Reliving the Past*, pp. 115–90.

Thompson, E. P. "Eighteenth-Century Crime, Popular Movements, and Social Control." *Society for the Study of Labor History Bulletin*, 25 (Fall 1972), 9–11.

———. "Patrician Society, Plebeian Culture." *Journal of Social History*, 7:4 (Summer 1974), 382–405.

———. "The Moral Economy of the English Crowd in the Eighteenth Century." *Past and Present*, 50 (Feb. 1971), 76–136.

———. *Whigs and Hunters: The Origin of the Black Act*. New York, 1975.

Tilly, Charles. *The Contentious French*. Cambridge, Mass., 1986.

Tinôco, Antonio Luiz Ferreira. *Codigo Criminal do Império do Brazil, annotado*. Rio de Janeiro, 1886.

Tombs, Robert. "Crime and the Security of the State: The 'Dangerous Classes' and Insurrection in Nineteenth-Century Paris." In V. A. C. Gatrell et al., eds., *Crime and the Law*, pp. 214–37.

Toplin, Robert. *The Abolition of Slavery in Brazil*. New York, 1972.

Torres, João Camilo de Oliveira. *A democracia coroada: Teoria política do império do Brasil*. Rio de Janeiro, 1957.

Uricoechea, Fernando. *The Patrimonial Foundations of the Brazilian Bureaucratic State*. Berkeley, Calif., 1980.

Vanderwood, Paul J. *Disorder and Progress: Bandits, Police, and Mexican Development.* Lincoln, Neb., 1981.

Vasconcellos, José Marcelino Pereira de. *Actos, Attribuições, deveres e obrigações dos juizes de paz.* Rio de Janeiro, 1862.

——. *Código criminal do Império do Brasil.* Rio de Janeiro, 1878.

——. *Consultor jurídico, ou manual de apontamentos, em forma de diccionário, sobre variados pontos de direito prático.* Rio de Janeiro, 1862.

——. *Roteiro dos delegados e subdelegados de polícia.* Rio de Janeiro, 1857.

Vianna, Hélio. *Contribuição à historia da imprensa brasileira, 1812–1869.* Rio de Janeiro, 1945.

——. *Vultos do império.* São Paulo, 1968.

Vianna, Pedro Antonio Ferreira. *Consolidação das disposições legislativas e regulamentares do processo criminal.* Rio de Janeiro, 1876.

Vieira, Hermes, and Oswaldo Silva. *História da polícia civil de São Paulo.* São Paulo, 1955.

Wade, Richard. *Slavery in the Cities: The South, 1820–1860.* New York, 1964.

Walsh, Robert. *Notices of Brazil in 1828 and 1829.* 2 vols. London, 1830.

Weber, Max. *Economy and Society.* Ed. Guenther Roth and Claus Wittich. 3 vols. New York, 1968.

——. *The Theory of Social and Economic Organization.* New York, 1947.

Weisser, Michael R. *Crime and Punishment in Early Modern Europe.* Atlantic Highlands, N.J., 1979.

Williams, Gwyn A. "The Concept of 'Egemonia' in the Thought of Antonio Gramsci: Some Notes on Interpretation." *Journal of the History of Ideas*, 21:4 (Oct.–Dec. 1960), 586–99.

Wirth, John D., and Robert L. Jones, eds. *Manchester and São Paulo: Problems of Rapid Urban Growth.* Stanford, Calif., 1978.

Wirth, John D., Edson de Oliveira Nunes, and Thomas Bogenschild, eds. *State and Society in Brazil.* Boulder, Colo., 1987.

Wolf, Eric. *Europe and the People Without History.* Berkeley, Calif., 1982.

Zaluar, Alba. *A maquina e a revolta: As organizações populares e o significado da pobreza.* São Paulo, 1985.

Zehr, Howard. *Crime and the Development of Modern Society: Patterns of Criminality in Nineteenth-Century Germany and France.* London, 1976.

——. "The Modernization of Crime in Germany and France, 1830–1913." *Journal of Social History*, 8:4 (Summer 1975), 117–41.

Zinn, Howard. *Declarations of Independence: Cross-Examining American Ideology.* New York, 1990.

Zunz, Olivier, ed. *Reliving the Past: The Worlds of Social History.* Chapel Hill, N.C., 1985.

Index

In this index an "f" after a number indicates a separate reference on the next page, and an "ff" indicates separate references on the next two pages. A continuous discussion over two or more pages is indicated by a span of page numbers, e.g., "57–59." *Passim* is used for a cluster of references in close but not consecutive sequence.

Abandoned children, 133–34
Abolition, *see* Slavery
Abrilada, 97–98, 147, 150
Absolutism, 31–32, 34, 44, 49, 64, 92, 105f, 157f, 168, 273, 278
Actor-observer distinction, 13, 277
Afonsine Code, 29
African-born slaves, 121, 284; in arrest data, 39–41, 192, 197f, 202, 207, 231. *See also* "Free" Africans
Alcaíde, 29, 109
Alferes, 29
Algranti, Leila, 38
Aljube jail, 22, 56–58, 62, 89, 114, 135–41 *passim*, 175f, 188–92 *passim*, 203f, 215, 250
Allain, Émile, 267
Almotacél, 29
Anti-Portuguese sentiment, 33, 65, 72
Arabic script used by Moslem slaves, 222

Aragão, Francisco Alberto Teixeira de, 46–47, 49, 58, 79, 109
Araújo, José Thomaz Nabuco de, 246
Army, 30, 66, 71, 74, 83, 94, 96, 154, 174–75, 231, 243, 263–64, 311n5; acting as police, 34, 36, 52, 66, 158, 177–78, 194, 219, 261, 268, 280
Arrest patterns, 38–42, 77–78, 191–203, 208, 210–14, 249–50, 251–59
Assault, *see* Person, crimes against
Auburn system, 204, 251
Aufderheide, Patricia, 164
Avila, João Antonio de, 263–64

Badge, *see* Sash of office
Bahia, 336n3
Bailiff, 170–71
Banditry, 309n22
Barata, Cipriano, 86f
Barreto, João Paulo dos Santos, 74
Bastos, Aureliano Cândido Tavares, 167, 251, 290

Batuque, 35, 41, 161, 220–22, 275
Beating, see Brutality; Person, crimes against
Beggars, 20, 48, 127, 131–33, 178, 210–11, 257, 321n37
Beleguim, 163, 234
Berimbau, 223
Black Guard, 269
Botafogo, 97, 125, 189
Botanical Garden, 125, 260
Botequim, 130, 161, 184, 275, 321n34
Brandão, Theobaldo Sanches, 95
Brasil Aflito (newspaper), 108
Bribery, see Corruption
Brutality, 229, 274, 282ff; by Guarda Real, 34–35; by military police, 91, 138, 142–47 passim, 162, 180, 182, 184, 241–42, 243, 245–47, 271; by pedestres, 110, 190, 200; by urban guard, 234, 237–39

Cabeça de porco, 24
Calabouço, 21f, 45ff, 54, 55–56, 62, 112–17 passim, 146, 192, 194, 203, 204–8, 215f, 219f, 229–31, 251, 254, 271
Calixto, slave rebel, 112–16, 219
Câmara, Eusébio de Queiroz Coutinho Matoso, see Queiroz, Eusébio de
Campo de Santana, 22, 66f, 71f, 74, 81, 96f, 129–30, 137, 161, 263, 313n31
Cândido, Antônio, 44
Capital punishment, 58–59, 137, 216–17
Capitão do mato, 49, 51–54, 314n45
Capoeira, 8–9, 37, 39–40, 44f, 81, 120, 133, 137, 175, 193, 197, 209, 223–29, 256, 258, 266–71, 284, 329nn68, 70, 334n69, 335n77
Carceral society, 4, 45
Carioca square, 21, 110, 135, 146f, 151
Carnival, 148, 178–79, 181, 195, 268
Castro, Apulcro de, 262–65
Caxias, see Lima e Silva, Luis Alves de
Celso, Afonso, 260
César, Captain Moreira, 334n62
Charity hospital, 20, 139
Chief of police, 156, 163, 273; under

1832 procedural code, 102–3, 107, 128; under 1841 reform, 167f, 171, 179–89 passim, 233f, 238, 281; under 1871 reform, 247, 263
Children, 133–34
Chimango, 150
Cisplatine war, 66, 95
Civil Police, 109, 169–71, 263, 271, 336n7. See also Chief of police
Class structure, 285–89
Cobras island, 21, 86–87, 96
Coffee industry, 20, 107, 128, 163, 270, 318n62
Colonial institutions, 29–31, 272
Comissário proposal, 48–49, 154
Conscription, 21, 35, 39, 67, 74, 84, 132–33, 136, 153, 185, 195, 201, 213, 226, 258, 321n37, 327n42
Conservative party, 104, 162f, 290–91
Constitution of 1824, 43, 46, 49, 58, 101, 223, 324n3
Constitution Square, 22, 71f, 310n38
Consular officials, 128f, 258
Copacabana, 125
"Cordial man" theme, 307n9
Corporate identity, see Military, corporate solidarity of
Correctional punishment, 32, 38, 113–14, 167, 205, 207, 215, 230, 252, 270, 276, 282f, 290. See also Detention; Whipping
Corruption, 53–54, 143–45, 236f, 240f, 244
Corsário (newspaper), 262–63
Cortiço, 23f, 266
Costa, Emilia Viotti da, 15, 309n29
Coutinho, Aureliano de Souza de Oliveira, 123, 139
Crime rate as methodological problem, 10, 78, 203, 210, 259
Crimes reported, 77, 214, 259
Criminal code of 1830, 9, 58–62, 100, 106, 115, 133, 269. See also Penal code of 1890; Procedural code
Criminal judge, 32, 68, 90
Criminal procedure code, see Procedural code
Cunha, João Ignacio da, 43, 64
Curador, 117ff

Curfew, 23, 46–47, 79f, 161, 184, 186, 191, 193, 198, 210, 257–58, 261, 271, 316n27

Da Cunha, Euclides, 334n62
Da Matta, Roberto, 319n12, 337n12
Delegado, 68, 102, 167, 169, 179, 219, 247f, 279, 281, 284
Deportation, 129, 185–86, 209, 267
Desertion from army, 177–78
Detention without charge, 252–55, 284. *See also* Correctional punishment
Disciplinary punishment, *see* Correctional punishment
Discipline in military police, 91, 139, 145, 149, 151f, 174–75, 182, 233, 235, 242–45 *passim*, 279, 281. *See also* Military, corporate solidarity of
District judge, 50, 102ff, 167, 247f
Draft, *see* Conscription
Drunkenness: among police, 92, 95, 140, 151, 174, 237, 244; as offense, 127, 161, 168–69, 178, 186, 197, 237f, 243; as social problem, 218, 246, 257
Duty officers, 169, 171
Dynamic of history, 13–15, 16–17

Elections, 158–62, 166
Entrudo, 148f, 154, 179, 322n59. *See also* Carnival
Equality before the law, 43, 48, 90, 108, 286. *See also* Law enforcement
Escape, *see* Slave offenses
Estalagem housing, 23
Extortion, 243. *See also* corruption

Feijó, Diogo Antônio, 50f, 70–81 *passim*, 85–95 *passim*, 105, 115ff, 120ff, 138, 142, 150, 154, 156, 283, 290
Fernando de Noronha prison, 267, 269
Ferraz, João Batista Sampaio, 269, 271
Fines as punishment, 47, 59
Florianópolis, 335n2
Fonseca, Deodoro da, 269
Forces of history, 13–15, 16–17
Foreigners, 48–49, 128f, 185–86, 187–90, 209, 213, 255, 267, 275,

282; in military police, 173, 325n16, 332n48. *See also* Immigrants
Foreign influences, 5, 50, 278–80
Former slaves, *see* Freedmen
Forro, *see* Freedmen
Foucault, Michel, 4, 11–15 *passim*, 45, 282, 289, 309n25, 319n12, 337n14
Fountains, public, 33, 110, 146–47, 322n55
França, Manoel José de Souza, 65, 76, 79
"Free" Africans, 117–20, 201, 215, 228, 320n13
Freedmen, 39, 41, 43, 69, 81, 197
Free poor, 7–8, 17, 62, 93, 106, 134, 236, 273, 284; increase after mid-century, 24, 228, 272, 274f, 282; as focus of police activity, 44–45, 48, 82, 131–32, 161, 164, 179, 276, 291
Freyre, Gilberto, 7, 337n12
Frias, Miguel de, 97, 147

Galés punishment, 59, 251–52, 332n44
Gambling, 47f, 129f, 186, 198, 240f
Graciano, capoeira, 120–22
Grafitti, 137
Gramsci, Antonio, 290, 306n3, 337n15
Great Britain, 128, 186, 326n36
Guarda Real de Polícia, 33–47 *passim*, 51, 53, 62, 65, 77, 91, 94, 111, 135, 138, 156, 164, 183, 224, 280, 312n19; riot and dissolution, 71–75, 79, 87f, 278, 322n61
Guarda Urbana, *see* Urban guard
Guayamus, 267
Gypsies, 129–30

Habeas corpus, 101
Haddock Lobo, 220–21, 328n66
Hanging, *see* Capital punishment
Hobsbawm, Eric, 310n30
Homicide, *see* Murder
House of Correction, 55, 117, 132ff, 176, 192, 203f, 215, 225, 251–52, 332n44
House of Detention, 204, 213, 231, 239, 250, 252–54, 258

Illegal assembly, 67
Immigrants, 8, 26–27, 228, 253, 255, 284. *See also* Foreigners

Independence of Brazil, 28, 30–31, 46, 62 f, 65, 273, 285
Inquisition, 29
Inspetor de quarteirão, see Ward inspector
Insults, 80 f, 180, 199, 210, 241, 243
Intendancy of police, 27, 31–32, 42, 48, 50 f, 58, 62–68 passim, 75 f, 90, 102 f, 111, 164, 168, 252, 278
Investigation as reason for arrest, 213
Isabel, Princess, 269

João VI, 32, 43 f, 55, 95
Jornal do Comércio (newspaper), 238, 268
Judicial function of police, 14, 28, 32, 38–39, 50, 111, 165, 168, 192, 203, 229, 246–47, 252, 271, 281, 283 f, 324 n5
Judicial procedure, 29, 39, 43–44, 57, 168, 246–48. See also Procedural code
Juiz de direito, see District judge
Juiz do crime, see Criminal judge
Jury trials, 101, 192, 326 n38
Justice of the peace, 5, 46, 49–51, 63–69 passim, 73–84 passim, 90, 95, 101–16 passim, 122, 125, 134, 137, 141, 148 f, 153–67 passim, 231, 239, 278, 281, 284, 324 n3

Kettle makers' revolt, 112–16

Labor, see Public works labor
Lagoa district, 125–26
Law enforcement, selective, 8–9, 108, 136, 143, 264. See also Equality before the law
Law schools, 104
Leão, Hónorio Hermeto Carneiro, 123
Libambos, 205
Liberalism, 4, 6, 31, 43, 45, 49, 51, 58, 85, 91, 93, 101, 106, 115 f, 122, 133, 142, 145, 150, 167 f, 244, 246, 251, 270–78 passim, 283, 286, 290
Lima e Silva, Carlos Miguel, 108, 264, 318 n1
Lima e Silva, José Francisco, 72, 74, 97, 104, 108
Lima e Silva, José Joaquim de, 71 f
Lima e Silva, Luis Alves de, 74, 87, 95–

98, 103, 105, 117, 130, 135 f, 140 ff, 146–52 passim, 160, 163, 181 f, 209, 240, 245, 281, 290, 316 n17, 317 n53
Lima e Silva, Manuel da Fonseca, 72, 96
Limão de cheiro, 148
Lobo, Roberto Jorge Haddock, 220–21, 328 n66
Lomonaco, Alfonso, 241, 267
Luccock, John, 33, 36, 38, 53

Malta, 223–24, 228, 266 f, 329 n68
Manueline Code, 29
Matos, Tito Augusto Pereira de, 265
Marx, Karl, on criminality, 309 n26
Meirinho, 29, 109
Melo, Belarmino Peregrino da Gama e, 263–64
Militarization of police, rationale for, 36–37, 45, 91, 94, 142, 175, 179, 182–83, 233, 235–36, 242–45, 279–81
Military, corporate solidarity of, 66, 94, 98, 140–52 passim, 182
Military police, 88–95, 98–100, 107, 111, 123, 127, 134–37, 144–60 passim, 173–81 passim, 187–88, 209, 219, 225 f, 231, 237–46 passim, 260–73 passim, 280–81; barracks locations, 21 f, 135, 221, 312 n18; size of force, 135, 157, 173, 176, 232 f, 239, 245, 269
Militia, 30, 36, 51, 83, 85, 311 n5
Mina ethnic group, 120, 217, 222–23
Modernization, 4, 6, 285–91 passim, 306 n6
Moraes, José Manuel de, 72
Morality as distinct from legality, 10–11, 308 n21
Municipal guard, 68–95 passim, 156 f
Murder, 108, 192, 216, 225, 227, 256, 259, 262–65

Nabuco de Araújo, José Thomaz, 246
Nagoas, 267
National guard, 5, 69, 82–85, 153–54, 162, 170, 239, 268, 330 n6; as police, 85–89 passim, 95, 107, 112–13, 125, 127, 135, 144, 154, 157, 177, 194, 232, 271, 278 f; conflict with military police, 98–100, 141, 148–54, 159–

60; conflict with justices of the peace,
123f, 126
Neutral reasons for arrest, 201
Nonjudicial punishment, *see* Correctional punishment
Nonslave poor, *see* Free poor

Offense types, 9, 196–201
Officer-soldier battalion, 73, 87, 95f
Oliveira, Clemente José, 108, 264
Ordenanças, 30, 83, 85, 311n5

Palace square, 21, 35, 260
Palmatória, 113, 205, 215, 230
Pantoja, Gustavo Aguilar, 126
Paraguayan war, 95, 158, 229, 231f,
251, 258
Passéio Público, 21, 135, 142, 244
Passports, 49, 314n40
Patronage, 30, 164, 247, 272, 275–76,
280, 285, 287, 289, 337n16
Pedestres, 110, 124ff, 158, 169–73 *passim*, 186, 192, 194, 209, 220, 232,
244, 279
Pedro I, 38, 43, 49, 55, 58, 63, 92, 95,
106, 290, 313n31; abdication, 30,
65–67, 72, 77, 93, 97, 105, 147, 150,
160, 260, 270
Pedro II, 104, 176, 260
Penal code of 1890, 8, 58, 269
Pennsylvania system, 252
Permanentes, *see* Military police
Person, crimes against, 40, 61, 79, 192,
199–200, 213–14, 226, 255, 259,
271, 276
Philipine Code, 29
Police function of judges, 50, 101, 111,
165
Police institutions, 5, 29–30, 134, 164,
229, 281–84, 311n9; in Europe and
U.S., 4–5, 28, 233, 235, 317n52. *See
also* Civil Police; Guarda Real de Polícia; Intendancy of police; Military
police; Municipal guard; National
guard; Secret police; Social origin of
police; Urban guard
Political violence, 65–66, 71–75, 86–
87, 96–97, 108, 159–62, 261
Pombaline reforms, 34
Portuguese court, 1808 transfer to Rio

de Janeiro, 27, 30, 33, 65, 278
Presiganga, 86
Prisons, 22, 54–57, 86, 204, 251–54,
289, 314n51. *See also* Aljube jail;
Calabouço; House of Correction;
House of Detention
Procedural code, 58, 90, 100–102, 246,
318n59
Property, crimes against, 40, 61, 79,
127, 185, 200–201, 213–14, 227,
255, 259, 271, 276
Prostitution, 47, 60, 140, 186, 210,
240f
Protest crime, 309n22
Publicaos, 128
Public order offenses, 9, 40, 42, 61,
67f, 70, 79, 128, 197–99, 201, 203f,
208f, 210–11, 213–14, 229, 234,
249, 255, 259, 271, 276, 332n43,
333n52
Public transportation, 24, 260–61,
327n41
Public works labor as punishment, 40–
42, 59, 130, 132–33, 205, 211, 225
Punishments, 29, 43–44, 58–60, 251–
52, 315n55. *See also* Correctional
punishment; Detention; Fines; Galés;
Prisons; Public works labor; Whipping

Quadrilheiro, 29
Queiroz, Eusébio de, 103–5, 109, 116,
119, 123–42 *passim*, 153, 163–73
passim, 183, 209, 222, 226, 266, 290,
318n61
Quilombos, 35, 49, 52, 109, 137,
322n43

Rabelo, José Maria, 34
Race as arrest criterion, 38, 42, 47–48,
81, 91, 136, 138, 143, 147, 180
Racial composition of police, 173–74,
325n17
Rape, 60
Rebellion, *see* Riot; Slave revolts
Recife, 335n78, 335n2
Reform: of 3 Dec. 1841, 102, 108f,
164–68, 278, 284; of Sept. 1871,
246–48, 252, 271, 284
Reforma (newspaper), 238
Regency government, 66f, 70

Regional revolts, 7, 95, 149
Religion, Afro-Brazilian, 222–23
Repression and resistance, 80, 91, 119,
    122, 186, 207, 214, 228, 238f, 265,
    280; as dialectical process, 1–7 pas-
    sim, 15–17, 62, 82, 241, 276–79,
    289–90
Repression as police mandate, 45, 48,
    51, 64f, 70, 79, 105f, 114, 121, 142,
    149, 154, 161f, 164, 168, 179, 183,
    186, 231, 234, 237f, 249, 266, 270f,
    274f, 282–91 passim
Republic, proclamation of, 166, 229,
    245, 249, 285
Republicanism, 75, 86, 97, 105, 108,
    269, 278, 285
Resistance, 11, 16–17, 215–20 passim,
    229, 257, 262, 270, 277, 284
Rewards for arrests, 47, 53, 132–33,
    171–72, 241
Rio Branco, Viscount, 291
Rio de Janeiro, 17–23; economic func-
    tions of, 12, 23, 61, 94, 128, 163;
    suburban development, 23–24, 229,
    232, 260, 266, 272; judicial districts,
    24, 32, 102, 111, 170f, 233, 325n10;
    population of, 24–27, 125, 169, 171,
    253–54, 321n26; institutional
    growth of, 61, 163, 176, 209
Riot, 71–73, 137–38, 229, 259–62,
    264–65
Rocio Pequeno Square, 137, 310n38,
    321n43
Rocio Square, see Constitution Square

Saco do Alferes, 123
Sailors as public order problem, 21, 39,
    79, 128, 243, 282
St. Domingue slave revolt, 30
Salaries of police, 47, 89, 110, 133, 144,
    155, 169–70, 173, 248–49, 312n18,
    314n38, 317n46
Samba, 321n28
Santa Barbara island, 56, 131
Santa Casa de Misericórdia, 20, 139
São Bento Monestary, 71
São Paulo, 336n2
Sash of office, 68, 180, 189, 332n39
Secret police, 171–73, 240–41, 260f,
    265, 331n24

"Shrimp dinners," 35, 44, 91, 283
Slave offenses, 39–40, 52, 59, 197, 208,
    282; in the United States, 42–43, 54,
    313n29
Slave revolts, 59, 112–16, 121, 218–19,
    223, 320n17, 329n67
Slavery, 7–8, 17, 270, 287; abolition of,
    8, 229f, 254–55, 266, 269f, 275,
    282, 284ff, 289; coercive basis of, 62,
    114, 122, 138, 145, 225, 287
Slaves: in population of Rio, 26–27, 93,
    164, 207, 228, 231, 254, 272; as focus
    of police activity, 42, 45, 62, 77, 79,
    81, 161, 164, 175, 179f, 184–85,
    245, 254, 270, 276, 282, 291; hu-
    mane treatment of, 115–22 passim,
    208, 319n11; in military police, 173–
    74; acting as police, 220–21
Slave trade, transatlantic, 9, 26, 104,
    320n13
Social control as interpretive theme,
    310n31
Social origin of police, 7, 36, 73, 80,
    93f, 98f, 109, 123, 126, 144, 145–
    46, 151, 163, 169–70, 173–74, 235–
    36, 241, 244, 248, 279
Social space, 17, 36, 224, 228, 271,
    309n27
Social war, ix, 3, 12, 37, 69, 99, 143,
    193, 262, 278, 291
Society for the Defense of Freedom
    and National Independence, 160–61
Southampton incident, 186–91, 213,
    326n36
State: formation of, 1–2, 6, 272–73;
    institutions, 4, 15–16, 114, 156,
    167f, 270–77 passim, 288–89; au-
    thority, 116, 143–44, 157, 224, 271,
    281
Street lighting, 22, 33
Subdelegado, 167, 169ff, 178ff, 188,
    217, 225f, 232f, 247f, 279–84 pas-
    sim, 332n39
Suicide, 217f
Sunday arrests, 137, 195

Táscas, 257. See also Publicaos
Tavares Bastos, Aureliano Cândido,
    167, 251, 290
Taverns, 257. See also Botequim

Tenement housing, 23 f, 266
Terror as police technique, 12, 37, 44, 75, 121, 186, 282
Theft, see Property, crimes against
Tijuca, labor on public works, 40–41
Torture in judicial procedure, 29, 33, 60
Traffic violations, 199
Travelers' accounts of Rio de Janeiro, 23, 36, 176, 241, 264–65, 267 f
Trolleys, see Public transportation
Trovão, José Lopes, 260–61

Undercover police, 129 f, 181–82, 240. See also Secret police
Urban guard, 158, 231–46 passim, 251, 261, 265, 271, 279
Urbanos proposal, 154–58, 278

Vagrancy, 35, 45, 48, 77, 80, 123, 130–37 passim, 142, 153, 161, 171, 185, 210–11, 213, 226, 238, 257
Vasconcelos, Bernardo Pereira de, 50 f, 150, 167
Veiga, Evaristo da, 76, 150
Viana, Paulo Fernandes, 32–34, 37, 44 f, 58, 64, 109, 133, 156, 313 n31, 318 n53
Vidigal, Miguel Nunes, 35–38, 44 f, 58,

62, 75, 91, 183, 209, 224 f, 282 f, 312 n19
Vintém riots, 259–61
Violence, see Brutality
Voting eligibility, 69, 73, 83

Wages, 170. See also Salaries of police
Walsh, Robert, 36
Ward inspector, 51, 101–2, 107, 110–11, 125 ff, 137, 140–41, 156, 167, 171, 177–86 passim, 232, 279, 281, 330 n7
Waterfront as focus of police vigilance, 21, 74, 128, 175, 238
Weapons possession, 42–49 passim, 61, 68, 77, 79 f, 90, 99, 120, 136, 155, 192 f, 197, 219
Weber, Max, 11–12, 17, 289, 309 n25, 319 n12, 337 n15
Whipping: as correctional tool, 9, 35–49 passim, 54 f, 61, 67, 120, 122, 133, 218, 220, 225, 276; as legal punishment, 10, 29, 59–60, 192, 203; limitations on, 115, 122, 205, 207–8, 214, 230, 282 f, 286
Whistling as offense, 40, 47
Women, 54, 60, 195, 202, 210

Zumbi, 322 n43

Library of Congress Cataloging-in-Publication Data

Holloway, Thomas H., 1944–
    Policing Rio de Janeiro : repression and resistance in a
19th-century city / Thomas H. Holloway.
        p.   cm.
Includes bibliographical references and index.
ISBN 0-8047-2056-8
1. Police—Brazil—Rio de Janeiro—History—19th century.
I. Title.
HV8185.R5H65   1993
363.2'0981'53—dc20
92-45685   CIP